VAN WYCK BROOKS
A WRITER'S
LIFE

VAN WYCK BROOKS
A WRITER'S
LIFE

RAYMOND NELSON

E. P. Dutton   New York

Grateful acknowledgment is made to the following for permission to quote from copyrighted material:

Farrar, Straus & Giroux, Inc., for a passage from *Classics and Commercials* by Edmund Wilson, copyright 1950;

Holt, Rinehart and Winston, Inc., for "The Seven Arts" by Robert Frost, from *The Letters of Robert Frost to Louis Untermeyer,* copyright 1963;

Little, Brown and Company for passages from *Letters of Sherwood Anderson,* selected and edited with an introduction and notes by Howard Mumford Jones in association with Walter B. Rideout, copyright 1953.

Published in the United States by
Elsevier-Dutton Publishing Co., Inc.,
2 Park Avenue, New York, N.Y. 10016

Library of Congress Cataloging in Publication Data

Nelson, Raymond
Van Wyck Brooks: a writer's life.

Bibliography: p. 319
Includes index.
1. Brooks, Van Wyck, 1886–1963. 2. Authors,
American—20th century—Biography. 3. Critics—
United States—Biography. I. Title.
PS3503.R7297Z78 1981   818′.5209 [B]   81-2485
AACR2

ISBN: 0-525-03054-9
Published simultaneously in Canada by
Clarke, Irwin & Company
Limited, Toronto and Vancouver

Designed by Nicola Mazzella

10 9 8 7 6 5 4 3 2 1
First Edition

CONTENTS

CONTENTS

Eight pages of photographs follow p. 172.

PREFACE AND ACKNOWLEDGMENTS

I first went to Bridgewater, Connecticut, in the summer of 1970 when I was just beginning my study of Van Wyck Brooks, and I was alert for any hint about the nature of a life I must learn to know intimately. Bridgewater is not a particularly old New England village, but it is traditionally decorous and quiet, trimly laid out and well attended. The country roads that twist through town lead nowhere, it seems, that hordes of motorists are inclined to go, and especially in the absence of automobile noise, the pace and atmosphere of Bridgewater seem leisurely, even old-fashioned. With its imperturbable streets and pastoral vista, the place might belong to that lost America that Brooks had uncovered and restored in his series of literary histories.

The massive Brooks home at the village's center seemed old-fashioned too. Its defiant size and its design, which conceded little to efficiency, bore the marks of another era, and as I pulled the car up to the curb, I half expected to catch a glimpse of a servant girl in cap and apron emerging from the back of the house to shake a tablecloth or pour out the dishwater. Inside, the dwelling was comfortable and airy, but ponderous. The dark, heavy woodwork, the carved furniture, the huge family portraits: all existed, somehow, in a time that seemed gracious enough, but not entirely familiar.

Gladys Brooks, Van Wyck's widow, an old but remarkably vigorous woman, welcomed me, fed me, and gave me a chance to look around. Perhaps I was taught most on that first visit by the simple opportunity to move about the house, touching books and the polished wood of the bannisters, adjusting my long legs to the space of the parlor, feeling the ancestral presences on the walls of the dining room. We know the world in the palms of our hands before we know it by our intricacies of thought.

After lunch Mrs. Brooks led me on a tour of her perennial village. We visited the corner of the library Bridgewater has dedicated to its notable citizen, where Jo Davidson's bust of his great friend forever stares at vistas far beyond the walls, then drove out to the village cemetery to see his grave, which lies in the curling grass at the foot of a gentle slope. His stone is small, austere, undecorated save for a stylized symbol of an apple tree. Later, when I understood better Brooks's organic metaphor, I would recognize how appropriate that symbolism is.

Such observations were random and unfocused then. I had not yet the knowledge to direct my curiosity, lacked the sense of the man to which my impressions might be related. All I had was my sense of old-fashionedness. In his person, work, and reputation, Brooks seemed to belong to the nineteenth century he had marked out as his special province. To say so, of course, identifies only a personal and professional orientation; it evokes both the limitation and the power of Brooks's stance. But in another, more unsettling, sense, Brooks had come to seem old-fashioned because his work had gone out of fashion. Once he had claimed a major reputation; now his name was often only dimly remembered.

Many professional literary people today acknowledge Brooks's importance, if at all, chiefly in regard to his hortatory and analytic work in the service of the younger generation of 1915. Admiration for that youthful Brooks, the leader of a famous intellectual rebellion, is almost reflexively expressed, and unfortunately it is often expressed as part of a formulation designed to dismiss the later Brooks, the author of the five-volume series of histories of the writer in America that he entitled *Makers and Finders*. Brooks himself thought that these histories were the work of his maturity, to which the early material was merely preliminary, and he staked his reputation upon their priority. Probably the majority of the academicians, critics, and general readers of thirty and forty years ago found his claim persuasive. Here, people thought, was original scholarship that read as gracefully as fiction. Here was a heroic raid upon the forgotten and misvalued that at last gave density and perspective to our literary traditions.

Today the authority Brooks established in the first volumes of *Makers and Finders* has dissipated. His position is not so much resisted, attacked, or modified as it is simply ignored. Particularly in the academy, a generation of literary professionals has come of age either not knowing Brooks's achievement or knowing it only as a sort of curious anachronism. With its range and sweep *Makers and Finders* has seemed peripheral, even hostile, to the uses of the intense, specialized literary scholarship of recent years. Academic inquiry is more pluralistic than is generally supposed, but for some three decades it has tended to favor methodologies that emphasize the scrutiny and analysis of individual texts. That emphasis developed in reaction to the laxness of impressionistic and moralistic criticisms, and it has proved an invigorating corrective, but since it slights the communal functions of art it risks a certain unhealthiness as well. I would even suggest that our literary discipline becomes unhealthy to the degree that it has no place for the synthesizing work of a Van Wyck Brooks.

When Brooks died in 1963 a widely circulated obituary notice asserted that he, Edmund Wilson, and Edgar Allan Poe (alternately, T. S. Eliot) were the three great critics the United States had produced. The hierarchical system of ranking would have satisfied no critical standards then, and it need be taken as nothing more than funeral rhetoric now, but it does remind us of the general esteem in which Brooks once was held. Edmund Wilson several times took upon himself the correction of those who were "unable to understand [Brooks's] importance to American culture, his heroism in pulling himself together and carrying out his great achievement of reading the whole of American literature and giving a new description of it."

If we are to understand the life of Van Wyck Brooks we must recapture some of the immediacy of another generation's sense of his importance to American letters, particularly in regard to the monumental *Makers and Finders*. It is not that the five volumes of the history define Brooks's peculiar excellence so much as that the logic of his career leads toward them, and that during their composition the issues by which his life must be judged became obscured. This twenty years' controversial work, then, represents the great challenge to our feeling for his achievement. *Makers and Finders* is unique among American scholarly works for its range and hospitality. No other author has attempted anything remotely like the project by which Brooks read every work by every nineteenth-century American writer of even the slightest merit, then represented each writer and his or her accomplishment in a complex, proportionate narrative. More important, *Makers and Finders* is a major critical and historical work in the visionary American literary tradition that springs from Emerson and Whitman. In it Brooks reaffirmed the communal and humanitarian values of literature for an age that was more concerned with the aesthetic and individualistic.

My own work has been a privilege. This business of writing biography is both agreeable and deeply satisfying. Year in and year out, day and night, in the present as in the past, I have kept excellent company. Van Wyck Brooks has become best known to me, as I would present him to you, as, first and foremost, an American writer. He would have asked, I believe, no more kingly title than that. To be a writer, he felt, exhausted the possibilities of personal satisfaction, and beyond politics or residence he was passionately American, shaped and wounded by America. For most of his life he remained extraordinarily responsive to his times, as his times were responsive to his leadership, and his passage thus records much of the character, enablements, and turmoil of American culture during his years. I would argue further that he was above all a good man, a man to be trusted, as well as a remarkably talented man, and that it is both the privilege and the responsibility of his biographer to trust him. I have tried as best I can to get into Brooks's mind and to learn the power of his argument, to take up his quarrel in his many cultural battles, so long as I could keep myself on the right side of honesty.

Although a good deal has been written about Brooks, most of it has been partisan. Beyond a body of journalistic and critical commentary, which itself constitutes part of the record of his public life, his own three volumes of memoirs, Gladys Brooks's memoir of her life with him, and extensive selections from his correspondence with Lewis Mumford, the published sources for Brooks's life consist almost exclusively of a few biographical or critical studies, which are themselves specialized and more or less pointed to controversy. My biography is based chiefly on manuscripts, correspondence, interviews, and other unpublished sources. The great bulk of the documents upon which I have relied is housed with the Van Wyck Brooks Papers in the Charles Patterson Van Pelt Library of the University of Pennsylvania, but I have drawn upon many other institutions, and I have profited as well by the generosity of many private individuals, who gave me personal information, access to correspondence, and, often, helpful suggestions. Such sources are frequently identified in the text. In addition, a full annotation will be placed on deposit at the libraries of the University of Virginia and the University of Pennsylvania, and the public library of Bridgewater, Connecticut. It seemed inappropriate and impractical to include a lengthy scholarly apparatus, which would be without substantive information, in a book aimed at a general audience, the judicious "common readers" of Brooks's own aspiration.

I would be ungrateful if I failed to make particular acknowledgment here to the University of Virginia and the National Endowment for the Humanities for grants of time and money, and to some of the people who have worked to my benefit. J. C. Levenson helped me to get started on this project, and David Levin, with his characteristically scrupulous good will, helped me see it through. Robert E. Spiller and James R. Vitelli, both important scholars of Brooks and his times, gave me encouragement and invaluable assistance. Neda Westlake, the Rare Books Librarian of the University of Pennsylvania Library, has been wonderfully cooperative in my use of the Brooks papers. Malcolm Cowley, Lewis Mumford, and the late John Hall Wheelock granted me interviews, answered my letters, and generally made me aware of the peculiar goodness of the literary life. I have found my education much deepened by their demeanor and instruction. I wish to thank Gladys Brooks, Van Wyck's widow; Dorothy G. Whyte, his stepsister; and Marion Wescott, his friend, for generous gifts of time and attention, and I owe special thanks to Oliver Kenyon Brooks, his son, whose memory, patience, and remarkable amiability have left me with an unusually agreeable indebtedness.

I wish to thank the following individuals and libraries for permission to quote from unpublished materials: Daniel Aaron, for the correspondence of Newton Arvin; University of Arkansas Library, Special Collections, the John Gould Fletcher Papers; Oliver Kenyon Brooks, for manuscripts and correspondence of Van Wyck Brooks and Eleanor Stimson Brooks; Chien-fei Chiang, for manuscript material by Chiang Yee; University of Chicago Archives; Columbia University Library; Malcolm Cowley; Franklin Folsom; Forbes Library of Northampton, Massachusetts; Jean K. Frank, for correspondence of Waldo Frank; Horace Gregory; Harvard University, Houghton Library;

Catherine N. Lambert, for correspondence of Charles Lambert; Lewis Mumford; Newberry Library, Chicago; New York Public Library, Astor, Lenox, and Tilden Foundations, the Joel Spingarn Papers; the University of Pennsylvania, the Charles Patterson Van Pelt Library; Princeton University Library, the Frank Jewett Mather Collection; Smith College, the William Allan Neilson Library; Stanford University Archives, the David Starr Jordan Papers; Edward C. P. Thomas, for correspondence of Thomas Thomas; University of Virginia Library, the Van Wyck Brooks Collection (#6973); Phyllis de Kay Wheelock, for correspondence of John Hall Wheelock; Yale University, Collection of American Literature, Beinecke Rare Book and Manuscript Library; Yale University Library, the Walter Lippmann Papers; Michael and Anne Yeats, for correspondence of John Butler Yeats.

PART I

THE FOREGROUND
1886–1914

When we were in college together you remember we often swore that we were great men and shook hands on it and promised to let nothing turn us from our course. You are keeping your part. . . .

—JOHN HALL WHEELOCK TO VAN WYCK BROOKS,
June 6, 1908

I

LOOMINGS

Van Wyck Brooks was born on the afternoon of February 16, 1886, in his grandfather's house in Plainfield, New Jersey. He was the second son of Charles Edward and Sallie Bailey Brooks. If he could somehow have foreseen the effects of his early life upon him he might have wished to come into the world differently, but, even so, he could scarcely have chosen a more comfortable time and place for birth. Moneyed Plainfield society in the final decades of the nineteenth century was as complete an incarnation of the Gilded Age, that ostentatious gentility that flourished in the post–Civil War United States, as one was likely to find. His own parents had been married, in the words of the local *Constitutionalist,* before "one of the most brilliant assemblages ever seen in Plainfield, including the best of our higher society and many representatives of New York's most select families." "The subsequent reception," as the account continued, "was a display of representative wealth and tone."

The mature Brooks, both idealist and socialist, would have been offended by this presumptuous description, just as he came to be almost biologically offended by Plainfield itself. By the time he had reached adolescence he loathed his birthplace, and Plainfield retained permanently the power to depress him even beyond tears. Long after he had left his "unloved state of New Jersey" to its own concerns, a brief return visit dramatically interrupted his gradual recovery from a nervous breakdown, and even in his happy old age he could scarcely endure the few moments of driving necessary to show his wife the house in which he was born.

Located some twenty-eight miles southwest of New York City, Plainfield was, in Brooks's own phrase, "a Wall Street suburb." The Brookses inhabited a world in which one's neighbors were expected at least to be wealthy. By Van Wyck's count, some fifty millionaires made their homes in Plainfield during his boyhood, and families who, like the Brookses, could be considered only well-to-do were secretly defensive, as if they exhibited a moral weakness. Plainfield's bankers, brokers, and "professional capitalists" lived lives of quiet, substantial elegance and were unobtrusive, Van Wyck remembered, almost to the point of mousiness. "Financial buccaneers," he called them, choosing to deemphasize his own memory of the "solid men of money," and he described the rigorous process by which they led "double lives," bringing home with them none of the calculated ruthlessness, none of the acquisitive self-reliance, with which they battled for plunder on Wall Street. They were simply neighbors, well-mannered men who might own a delightful cherry orchard or otherwise benefit small boys. Only the shaded rooms where their wives endured "nervous prostrations"—as a kind of quietly desperate protest, Van Wyck thought—hinted at the terrible moral tensions involved in the alternating civilization and barbarity of speculative capitalism in the 1880s. At best ethically dubious, these men flirted often with criminality and sometimes succumbed to it. More than one neighbor suddenly disappeared, presumably into jail, and more than one fortune was conspicuously lost when its sustaining network of machinations collapsed. But it was only later that Van Wyck recognized the savagery of the war his neighbors fought at their offices in Manhattan, and for the most part even the scandals of patrician Plainfield were reserved and apparently innocuous. Brooks was surely right to assume that "people always think their own towns are dull" when he later tried to make peace with his boyhood, but Plainfield, with its carefully guarded serenity, must have been duller tham most.

Because it was so thoroughly fitted to the needs of its resident millionaires, Plainfield might be considered a symbol of one definitive development in late nineteenth-century society. Excepting such spectacular excesses of the period as the palatial "cottages" erected at

4

fashionable watering places, the gilding of the Gilded Age was no-where thicker nor its hue purer than in just such wealthy suburbs. In Grover Cleveland's America the millionaire was almost officially the model for mankind, the embodiment of moral energy, resourcefulness, masculinity. Bloated by preferential laws, individual fortunes were a favorite public display, and the industrial capitalism that spawned them seemed destined to expand infinitely, as a practical reflection of natural, even cosmic, purpose. Popular entertainments titillated audiences with the vicarious experience of success and reinforced the common assumption that financial gain and moral rectitude were forever wedded. The lordly figure of the captain of industry, a composite of puritan, pioneer, soldier, and trader, stood as the national image, but he stood, at least in cartoons from the fledgling radical press, upon desperate masses of honest workingpeople.

Although the economy was its visible conquest, the capitalist patriarchy dominated the moral and cultural structure of the nation as well. The personal life to which all classes aspired was characterized by the complex of attitudes we now stereotypically associate with Victorianism: patrician decorum, self-righteousness, sexual prudery, and ostentatious luxury. Refinements were left to the ladies, who devoured magazines and novels, attended musicales, and organized theaters—all of which their crudely practical husbands presumably tolerated in amused silence. To be sure, men devoted some of their new wealth to extensive private collections of art or to architecturally ambitious dwellings, but far more money was lavished on a shamelessly conspicuous consumption. Perhaps the ultimate cultural symbol of the Gilded Age was the yacht—the lavish steamship built by the multimillionaire for his personal recreation, and the magnificent racing cutter designed to defend the America's Cup against British and Canadian sportsmen. These aesthetically admirable vessels expressed at once the wealth, technological capacity, and egotistic assertiveness of American capitalism, and the yacht harbor was the familiar setting for the summer recreations of the well-to-do. Van Wyck's first professional pay—two dollars from *St. Nicholas Magazine* in 1897— was earned for a description of some impressive yacht illuminations at Newport, and images of ships and sailing recur definitively throughout his work whenever he describes his inner life.

"This happy era for the capitalist," as Samuel Eliot Morison calls it, must indeed have been an innocent idyll for its favored children, overgrown boys with the means to indulge to their heart's content their daydreams of trains, castles, and sailing ships. To aggressive, highly vocal masters of economic power such gaudy playthings seemed merely the visible reward for duty well performed, and Herbert Spencer's theory that history had progressed toward a muscular civilization dominated by its fittest men convinced them that they must stifle challenges to plutocratic growth. More than financial wizards, such men were genuine idealists, working with fierce moral energy to establish their millennium. But despite the strength of its institutions and the stabilities of Anglo-Saxon virtue, their Gilded Age was also an age of hysterically repressed anxiety, which governed them far more tyrannically than their teleological Social Darwinism could. As it earnestly rigidified its position, the patrician culture of the 1880s and 1890s set in motion the forces that would erode it. Beneath the placid surface of these confident years ran turbulent undertows of change, eddies of violence and fear that confirmed the hints of the Plainfield wives in their darkened rooms about the "double life" and its dangers.

The changes of personal orientation inherent in these processes, however—the self-analyses and breast-beatings that would characterize the next generation—seemed infinitely far from Plainfield in 1886. The structure of that suburban world stood fixed and sure, "permanently supported," Van Wyck writes in his autobiography, "by cast-iron customs, by a ritual of living that was immemorial, or assumed to be, and that extended into every corner of existence." Reinforced by an authority as absolute as it was anonymous, that tyranny of habit sometimes made life overly predictable, but it also gathered the haphazard activities of a day into a single leisurely order, "bespeaking not only security but endless time for everything, long hours for reading and dreaming of other sorts of worlds." It was like the ending of some supreme middle-class fiction, this child's garden of Plainfield, and Van Wyck never forgot the youthful conviction that they were an ultimate reality, those timeless girls "in white dimity and sashes, an endless succession of Alices in Wonderland, playing croquet on the lawn, all in the golden afternoon."

Van Wyck's mother had named him for his sixth great-grandfather, Theodorus Van Wyck of Fishkill, a prosperous surgeon and farmer of the early eighteenth century. Recording the generations of Van Wyck ancestors in her son's baby book, she could trace her maternal lineage through this family at least as far back as 1500. The

American history of the Van Wycks began in 1659, when Cornelius Barente of that name settled near Flatbush and established a sprawling, fruitful family. For many generations his offspring prospered in the areas surrounding Manhattan, to be honored in their communities as farmers and professional men. The story of their lands and lives reads like one of Washington Irving's dreams of the fat Dutch past, and they may be the very Van Wycks Irving had in mind in his *Knickerbocker History of New York,* when he included that family among "the sturdy chivalry of the Hudson" who "came waddling on" into a catalog of heroes. Irving was still a presence when Van Wyck was a boy. The names of the old Dutch families in Plainfield evoked the charm and romance of his Knickerbocker tales, and Van Wyck discovered that his grandmother had met the old writer when she was a girl, a literary coincidence of the sort that would fascinate him in later years.

He knew a great deal about his maternal ancestors, for his mother filled scrapbooks with genealogical material. The families that figure most prominently in his ancestral chronicles were the Platts and the Baileys, who had settled in the Adirondacks in the eighteenth century, between them giving the Plattsburg area its name and, for generations, its politicians, clergymen, professional people, merchants, and heroes. A history of the Platt and Bailey families, serialized in the *Plattsburg Sentinel* in the 1890s, memorialized their characters and deeds. Van Wyck felt particularly close to his Plattsburg relatives; he spent many boyhood summers with them, absorbing the family lore and poking among their attics for heirlooms. They thus became for him tangible extensions of history, and visits to their peaceful Adirondack homes made the past a personal possession. Both Baileys and Platts treasured anecdotes of family heroism during the American Revolution, and Van Wyck remembered having seen at the age of five his great-grandfather, Nathaniel Platt, who had witnessed the Battle of Plattsburg during the War of 1812. When years afterward Van Wyck thought about those summers again, he felt that Plattsburg had returned him to the old agrarian America, truer to its own promise than the mercantile nation that had succeeded it. He sensed in Plattsburg a type of the upstate pioneer town, the response of civilized men to wilderness of which James Fenimore Cooper's Templeton was the model and an equally real incarnation.

The Platts were the landed family, rooted to their earth; the Baileys with whom their history is inseparably interwoven were more inclined to public service and the marketplace. Van Wyck and his brother could have spent many a rainy afternoon, as their mother probably had, brooding over the collection of yellowing obituary notices that told the story of the eminent Baileys. They had been estimable men—soldiers, lawyers, judges, even a United States senator—who established community standards for success and propriety. Most celebrated of all was Admiral Theodorus Bailey, dead only nine years before Van Wyck was born. A hero of the Mexican War, decorated for his part in the Pacific campaign that led to the acquisition of California, he had also served the Union Navy with distinction during the Civil War, when, accompanied only by a junior officer, he had demanded and accepted the surrender of New Orleans. In an article for the *Century Magazine* in 1885, the novelist George Washington Cable, an eyewitness, described how Captain Bailey and his lieutenant walked abreast "unguarded and alone, looking not to right or left, never flinching, while the mob screamed in their ears, shook cocked pistols in their faces, cursed and crowded and gnashed upon them. So through the gates of death those two men walked to the City Hall to demand the town's surrender." "It was," Cable concluded, "one of the bravest deeds I ever saw done." One read proudly about one's ancestors in books, but the history they incarnated was not to be found in print alone. Conscious of their traditions and determined to preserve their integrity, the Platt and Bailey families were physically, as well as genealogically, proximate. They were living bridges to those tangible realities of the past that, losing their substance, become abstractions— history or myth—and they awarded a profound experience of America to the imagination that could follow them backward into time and space.

About his paternal forebears Van Wyck knew far less. His Brooks grandparents were long dead, and his father, chronically ill, no longer had the energy to maintain ties with his past. Of Mitchell C. Brooks, his grandfather, Van Wyck knew only that he was an "entirely honest" Wall Street cotton merchant, whose fortunes rose with the years until, following the depletion of the cotton market after the Civil War, they suddenly collapsed altogether—the first of a disquieting series of economic failures that troubled three generations of Brooks men. His paternal grandmother counted patriots of the American Revolution and a revolutionary Irish fugitive among her forebears, but Van Wyck seems to have contemplated his father's family with little of the fascination he brought to the richly documented chronicles of the Van Wycks, Platts, and Baileys; and the Brooks generations claim only a few sentences in his autobiography. Whatever his preferences among ancestors, both paternal and maternal lines must have impressed him with a single lesson. Such families provided sternly patrician models of enterprise and honor and, for a dutiful boy, an unambiguous definition of what a man should be.

Neither these reassuring traditions of family prerogative nor the pacifying tone of Plainfield life itself were ever deliberately put into perspective by Charles or Sallie Brooks. They were not bad parents. On the contrary, they were genuinely loving, and perhaps too indulgent. But neither parent did anything to stimulate intellectual curiosity; neither allowed for the possibility of moral confusion; neither was capable of preparing their sons for the world to come. They were Episcopalians and Republicans because they had been so from the beginning and because everyone who counted was, and they were solidly respectable people because they could scarcely have been anything else. The invisible "theys" and "best authorities" who still torment inquisitive boys swore to the rectitude of their customs and prohibitions. Morally lazy perhaps, the Brookses were nevertheless comfortable and graceful, and they adhered staunchly to the discipline appropriate to their station. Van Wyck noted his father's conscientiousness in giving up his holiday afternoons to ward patients. More amusedly, he remembered that his mother was conscientious too. She took her children on "nature walks" and read *Pilgrim's Progress* to them, even though "being conscientious" clearly bored her.

Charles Edward Brooks had been born in his father's home on Macdougal Street sometime around 1845. Raised in the prosperous security of a New York not yet the crudely dynamic city it became after the Civil War, he was graduated from the City College of New York in 1870 and spent ten years in Europe as a junior partner in a mining firm. We know Charles Edward almost entirely through his son's accounts of him, and possibly Van Wyck's own predilections colored his glowing descriptions of his father's happiness in Europe, where the older man had developed his social personality and to which he returned, it seems, whenever his spirit was sore. Unlike Van Wyck's, his Europe was little more than a magnificent refreshment, but he did love the stately life abroad, particularly in contrast to the wild mining towns in the western United States where he had also represented his corporation, and he inspired in both of his sons a deep affection for all things European.

By 1882 Charles Brooks had returned permanently from his foreign post, and in June of that year he married the pretty, lively, socially prominent Sallie Bailey Ames of Plainfield. He himself moved to that city, first to his own modest home and then to his father-in-law's more imposing house on Crescent Avenue, where his first son, Charles Ames Brooks, was born in the spring of 1883. The shift of residence goes unremarked in surviving family papers, but it might well have followed an already disturbing slump in business. Charles Edward continued to depart regularly for his office in Manhattan's financial district, but his devotion to the routine of success could not long disguise the deterioration of his investments. He had been infected with the Plainfield disease, and he was now working more successfully at his own "double life" than he was at making his fortune. In 1898 he reluctantly abandoned his embarrassing fiction and accepted a post as a minor executive in the Nassau Street firm of Harvey Fisk and Sons. Life continued to demand and fulfill its familiar patterns in the yellow house on Crescent Avenue, but the Brookses were now considered relatively poor by both their neighbors and themselves. That their poverty was indeed relative is easily demonstrated by the standard of living they continued to maintain, but their changed status seems to have left Sallie Brooks badly frightened.

Charles Brooks was a semi-invalid by the time his sons knew him, a retiring man who was characteristically absent, both physically from family excursions and morally from the place of authority in his household. Before he was well into middle age he was forced to attend zealously to his health, and photographs from the 1880s show that he was handsome but markedly slender and frail, with a distinct listlessness to his bearing. Despite the huge mustache he cultivated in deference to the aggressive masculinity of the period, his face, with its delicate features and pale color, seems introspective, and his attention is usually fixed at some point beyond the space of the camera. Van Wyck portrayed him less as a person than as a presence: an endless source of proverbs and a keeper of elaborate rituals—of grooming, smoking, dining—by which he ordered and mellowed his world. Receptive as if by instinct to the amenities of his complicated domestic machinery, he lived in it without wondering about either its workings or its legitimacy. Van Wyck later asked himself in a journal if his father had ever

10

entered the kitchen of his enormous home, and then noted by way of an answer: "I cannot conceive of anything that could have taken him there. Dinner was just something that appeared on dishes."

It was the vivacious, socially ambitious Sallie Brooks who dominated the Brooks household and left the stronger mark upon her sons. She was a beautiful woman—so beautiful that Arthur Ryder, the Orientalist who knew the Brookses in Italy in 1899, subsequently confessed to Van Wyck that he had not "distinguished her very clearly from the other Madonnas." Her cheekbones were prominent, her eyes mysterious, and in some of her photographs she appears mischievously Eastern, out of place in the drab costume of respectable America. The bulky scrapbooks with which she whiled away her leisure hours reveal an alert, playful, nicely "finished" young lady, trained to be proud of her family, decorative, entertaining, and socially graceful. Hers was the great era of the American girl, that fabulous creature whose sensibilities determined the language of novels, the priorities of social ritual, even the amount of sunlight permitted to fall upon a fashionable gathering, and Sallie Brooks flourished in it. Almost as defiantly impractical as the yachts that sailed majestically across the horizon of her summer days, she cultivated none of the domestic virtues—servant girls would see to those—nor did she distinguish sharply between her obligations to her family and those to the larger community in which she moved. A "go-getter," as one of her contemporaries remembers her, she indefatigably organized and attended dinners, teas, musicales, balls, theaters; and she was a powerful creative force among the Plainfield elite. Her living memorial is the Monday Afternoon Club, still active some ninety-five years after she founded it. Its membership limited to one hundred women "of the highest standing in the city," her group honored the usual idealistic commitment to community and in general justified itself by the philanthropic impulse of the moneyed classes. But its appeal to the ladies of Plainfield is probably better suggested by the New York society editor who in the late 1880s paid tribute to Mrs. Brooks's leadership and noted that her organization "bears the reputation of furnishing more real enjoyment than any other club in town."

That Sallie Brooks cherished her sons there can be no doubt, and as children they surely received plenty of the affection that spilled carelessly from her. But although warmly spontaneous, she was also shallow: vain and possessive, a little selfish, a trifle thoughtless. Despite her talents, her natural taste "was all for the frivolous and gay," and nowhere in her complicated but indulgent code would she find reason to refine it. If as a woman she personified all the beauty and vigor of her station, as a mother she also uncritically committed her children to many of its limitations. With her conservative belief, in Van Wyck's words, that "she had to support the official views," she nervously denied those around her the right to question "the laws on which our little world seemed to be built," and there is no indication among the papers she left to her son that she paused to take stock of herself. She could sometimes be teased into retreating in laughter before a boy's awkward heterodoxies, but she could never concede virtue to the audacities of the inquisitive mind. It is scarcely shocking that a genetic Republican and a Daughter of the American Revolution would be distressed by Van Wyck's tendency to socialism, which early rose to the enticements of Ruskin, but even before her children were old enough to think seriously about fundamental values Sallie Brooks had insinuated in them a complete system of almost unconscious assumptions about the nature of man and society. That none of these assumptions could be qualified without confusing all reality never occurred to her, who had never experienced significant change and could not guess how crippling her dogmatism might be. The normal growth of a boy toward intellectual and imaginative rebellion must have seemed to her personally disloyal, and Van Wyck felt, doubtless with cause, that his mother had neither understood nor sympathized with him after his mind began to mature.

Van Wyck never explicitly blamed his mother for the anxiety that beset him throughout his life, but he harshly criticized other American mothers in some of his psychologically oriented early books, and in private correspondence he complained about his mother's disapproval of his vocation. By the time he was eighteen he had conceived a theory of love in which the maternal was of a decidedly inferior type, an animal instinct merely.

Charles Ames Brooks was not too old to be a companion to his younger brother, and the two boys shared interests, kept competitive records of their adventures, and supported one another through such childish ordeals as dancing class, juvenile theatricals, and the tasteless pageants that adorned every important holiday. Nothing in their boyhood diaries suggests that the children were less than deeply loving comrades. But though he otherwise describes his family structure carefully, even to relatives several times removed, Van Wyck never characterizes Ames in his autobiography, and he sustained even among his closest friends a determined silence about the brother who lived and died in privacy. Appearing only incidentally in Van Wyck's journals and letters after the first years, Ames was apparently his mother's favorite, and he seems to have sided with her against Van Wyck in the realignment of family sympathies that followed the death of Charles Edward Brooks in 1906. These quarrels and alliances, of course, did not entirely displace family affection, but Ames and his mother resolutely set themselves against Van Wyck's attraction to the aesthetic bohemianism which was in vogue at the turn of the century, and they mocked his literary ambitions until he gradually came to consider himself something of an Ishmael in Plainfield. The dutiful son, Ames obliged New Jersey by taking his degree at Princeton, then studied law for a year at Harvard and went to work for a prominent Wall Street firm. At his mother's insistence—for Sallie's possessiveness became increasingly desperate as she aged, and she persuaded him to abandon at least two engagements—he remained a bachelor, staying in Plainfield to care for her long after she had made a comfortable second marriage. While he was reluctantly submitting himself to the demands of filial piety, his younger brother rushed through college and fled.

Van Wyck always felt that Ames was at heart a romantic, a frustrated artist crippled by the environment that he himself had escaped. In 1920 he wrote to his wife from Plainfield, complaining about the depression that always weighed upon him during visits to his birthplace and sympathizing with his brother: "His life is so empty and repressed—all his savageness comes from that." From the evidence of *Mauna Roa and Other Poems,* the book that Ames published in 1922, Van Wyck may well have been right about the creative spirit trapped in the prisons of Wall Street and Plainfield. It is a collection of unmistakably amateur verse, badly marred by poetical clichés and fuzziness of sentiment, but it is alive as amateur verse rarely is, and it shows an awakening talent that might well have been refined. Ames versifies conventionally but skillfully, is occasionally surprisingly delicate, and has control of a limited stock of almost hallucinatory metaphors. His poems show at least as much promise as those his brother published while in college. Viewed with more sympathy, perhaps, than the judicious critic should permit himself, they might be considered a badly sustained assault on the lofty style and visionary themes of Hart Crane.

The scholarship in which Ames also resembled Van Wyck was

equally promising, and equally uncultivated. As an older man he was an enthusiastic student of military history, but his first love was the ancient world, and he would recite Greek poetry at the insistence of the stepsister who delighted in the exotic sounds. Once he had aspired to a professorship of classics, before his father's last illnesses persuaded his mother to direct him to the more profitable study of law, and then home to support her. Sallie Brooks had cultivated an unrealistic apprehension of financial ruin, breeding a sense of sustained crisis for both herself and her son which kept him effectively within her grasp. His efforts to break himself loose, if such they were—to France with the ambulance corps during World War I, to the far West, to Europe repeatedly—all eventually failed him. In effect, he never left Plainfield.

Perhaps speculation about personal mysteries is futile, but Ames Brooks seems to have been a perpetually displaced person who never admitted to himself the possibility of grasping life firmly. He was a sickly man, never seriously handicapped but always plagued by minor ailments, and, although gregarious and popular, he seemed profoundly unhappy. Oliver Kenyon Brooks, Van Wyck's second son, remembers his Uncle Ames as the quiet man who spent weeks on the third floor, leaving behind him a room that to all appearances had never been occupied. That hint of a damaged life force in his nephew's casual recollection of boyhood impressions is reinforced by the themes and imagery of *Mauna Roa,* a book almost compulsively about a flight from life, in which death becomes an enchanted island, a place of sleep and sensual warmth where the "nameless beauty for which dreamers pine" exists in a sort of disembodied sentience. In an imagery startlingly similar to the nautical metaphor by which Van Wyck characteristically defined his own spiritual pilgrimage, the title poem celebrates a voyage through menacing seas to an island world of "far-flung mists of gold, / As though all life were stilled into a swoon, / Become a legend, and forever old."

However one interprets such indirect evidence, it does seem fair to insist that Ames Brooks was a victim of Plainfield and its ethos, a man confused by the conflict between his idealism and the demands of his society. Like many Americans he lost heavily in the stock-market crash, a collapse of a fundamental certainty that was exaggerated, perhaps, by a need to alleviate his mother's compulsive fear of poverty. One foggy winter morning in 1931 he left the house with word that he could not get to his law office that day but had other business in Manhattan. Between home and the Plainfield depot he either changed his mind or became confused, and he purchased instead a ticket to Allentown, Pennsylvania. After passing a moment with the ticket agent and walking about the platform in the damp cold, Ames suddenly caught the eye of an American Express clerk, who glanced up from his work and saw that the distinguished man he had noticed earlier had stepped onto the tracks in front of the *Philadelphia Flier,* which roared through the station at seventy miles an hour, smashing his body beyond recognition. With grim but provocative irony, Ames's suicide came just as his younger brother was finally pulling himself out of the morass of self-destructiveness in which he had been caught for several years.

Are these parallels coincidental? Or is there meaning to be found in the story of the brother who stayed at home and did his duty, but compromised with capitalism, and the story of the brother who ran away from home and danger, but lost his sense of belonging? Does this fraternal pattern, already established by 1907, lurk behind the bitterly intense parables that Van Wyck later worked into his studies of Mark Twain and Henry James? Like many of the remarkable analogues that crop up throughout Van Wyck's life, that parallelism is perhaps better suggested than asserted, but it cannot easily be dismissed. Without Ames's elusive story, Van Wyck's story is not complete, for Van Wyck saw in his older brother a part of himself that he both acknowledged and feared, and a fate he had thwarted only by flight and luck. Ames is the supreme witness to the perils Van Wyck sensed beneath the unruffled surface of family life in Plainfield. We have made a truism of our observation that nineteenth-century repressions bred a vicious psychic and social destructiveness in twentieth-century American life. Here is one example.

These profoundly unhappy developments, however, were far in the future, not conceivable when Van Wyck was a boy. Growing up in Plainfield was a relatively uncomplicated process, largely a matter of internalizing ritual in an atmosphere from which overt conflict had been all but banished. Following Ames through the excellent Plainfield public school system, Van Wyck won the awards that his family serenely expected, lent his voice to shouts of community enthusiasm, played his part in the juvenile social circles that imitated on a reduced scale the ambitious gatherings of adults, and in general behaved as a well-mannered boy of the period should.

Among his favorite playmates were Maxwell Perkins, a year older than himself, and Eleanor Stimson, also older, whose family often vacationed with the Brookses and was generally allied with them in the enterprises of Plainfield society. Despite the two years' difference in their ages, Eleanor and Van Wyck became remarkably attached to each other.

The Plainfield Van Wyck knew was not unredeemedly respectable, and like all imaginative children he soon discovered the particular wonders of his world. There were, for instance, a number of "queer" people: a maiden lady who cultivated an orange tree through her parlor floor; the mysteriously tragic widow Cecilia de Medina; and anachronisms like Miss Tweedy, who lived in the grand manner of a vanished age. Plainfield had literary associations as well: Julian Hawthorne had lived there, as had the daughter of Julia Ward Howe, the poet E. C. Stedman, and the abandoned family of Bret Harte, but the literary atmosphere of the place did not emanate from them alone. The townspeople of those days consciously modeled themselves on characters from Thackeray or Jane Austen—or so Van Wyck guessed later, when he tried to explain such rococo behavior as that of the local worthy who, in the best manner of Thackeray's Colonel Newcome, rebuked the austere mother of Max Perkins for licking a postage stamp in public. Romantic portraits and landscapes were displayed in the Job Male Public Library and Art Museum, and if the collection of paintings was small and rather smugly pleased with itself, it did stimulate a feeling for the arts. A taste for Old Masters was required of fashionable people, and Van Wyck and Ames were children of their age when, both of them still in elementary school, they invited their neighbors to their Union Art Gallery. Because they printed tickets but no catalog, we can only guess about the quality of their exhibition, but notice that their "philistine" culture (as Van Wyck was soon to think of it) impelled them toward an appreciation of art even in their childish play. Such cultural advantages and eccentricities were as much a part of Plainfield as its neurotic repressions, and when sixty years later he came to write his memoirs, Van Wyck remembered these things with an affection that may have surprised him.

Such were the joys of Plainfield, but for the boys the chief among them was probably the summer vacation, an elaborate ritual of relaxation which was itself one of the extravagant spectacles of the era. Sallie Brooks and her sons became nomadic during the summer and transported themselves to cooler weather and the palatial resort-hotels of the Gilded Age in what must have seemed an Oriental caravan of luggage and equipment. The Brookses regularly spent part of their vacation at the seashore: at Grand Isle, Beach Haven, or the exclusive Fishers Island. At other times the family traveled to the Adirondacks, to visit Plattsburg and the luxurious lake retreats, or to wilderness "camps," where Van Wyck and Ames could enjoy the strenuous life of the privileged out-of-doors, all the while dutifully reporting their adventures and acquisitions in bountiful letters to Charles Edward at his offices in New York. At one of these sophisticatedly rustic hotels in 1898 Van Wyck met his "first writer," a retiring Shakespearean scholar who was probably surprised when the boy asked for his autograph. More wonderful still, Van Wyck discovered at the same dining-room table his first Parsi, an exotic man who before touching his food "took from his pocket a phial of red pepper and covered his whole plate with a layer of it." That awesome culinary practice was one way of worshiping the god of fire, or so the Indian merchant answered a curious child, and the memory smoldered in Van Wyck's imagination until more than half a century later when, writing about Blaikie Murdoch, he called it forth to add spice to an already pungent sentence.

With its trustworthy promises of worldly success and its deep stability, the disciplined but gracious order of Plainfield life seemed hardly likely to produce rebels, but Van Wyck, who never lost his taste for its grandness of manner, quickly developed a fierce animus against the fundamental values of his town. In a diary he kept during his high-school days he complained that he "couldn't be a philosopher in Plainfield," and although he immediately recognized what the confession implied—"just another way of saying that I couldn't be a philosopher at all . . . for 'The mind is its own place' "—he went on to list some of the social pressures inhibiting his spirit: "But how can a person live in abstractions, as Heaven knows I'd like to do, when he has to manage a school-paper, edit football notes and live in such a town as this [?]" The language of his complaint is boyish, but the principle behind it is mature. Even at seventeen Van Wyck had recognized the importance of place to the creative personality, and he had sensed the complex problem created by the necessity for harmony, and the fact of discord, between the gifted individual and the demands of his society.

The paradoxical process by which the Plainfields of America both fortified and undermined their patrician way of life by adhering to European cultural authority is one of the principles of change informing those last years of the Gilded Age. Then, when native manners and native art seemed vulgar, it was fashionable to cultivate European ways, either by polite education at home or, better still, by sending young people abroad to acquire the taste and formality of the Old World. Admirably tailored though this procedure was to the continuity of traditional values, it inadvertently spun off a generation of young intellectuals who sensed an organic cultural life beneath the superficialities of social piety and returned to attack America in terms of the intuitions about culture they had gathered in Europe. Van Wyck early learned to conceive of the Continent as a sort of garden of delights for strolling Americans, but the very intensity of his juvenile innocence committed him emotionally to a high European culture which was far beyond the polite taste of his parents, who regarded the Old Masters as an afternoon's entertainment and not as an invitation to life. For years Europe was Van Wyck's study and his ultimate goal, and in essays for his high-school newspaper he was already using it to shame his own culture for its failure to catalyze native personalities.

He first visited Europe in 1898–1899 for a year of travel which, with its discoveries and its permanent influence, was surely the most important year of his early life. The Brookses had already completed their annual round of vacations for 1898, and why they chose to pack up that autumn for a staggeringly expensive tour of the Continent is something of a mystery. Ames refers in his scrapbook record of the trip to the suddenness of his parents' decision. Although there is no hard evidence either way, Charles Edward Brooks may have felt that his family needed the soothing atmosphere of Europe to soften the shock of the economic demotion he accepted that year. Whatever their motivation, the Brookses were veteran travelers, and they quickly transferred much of their domestic apparatus to trunks, departing from New York for Antwerp aboard the Red Star Line's *Friesland* on October 5, 1898. Once ashore, they traveled through Belgium and Holland to Germany, settling in Dresden for the winter of 1898–99, briefly visited Austria on their way to Italy, where they spent most of the spring, proceeded to the Swiss Alps, Paris, and finally completed their journey in London, after devoting the summer of 1899 to a tour of the British Isles. In September they sailed from England for New York aboard the *Cymric* of the White Star Line.

Charles Edward Brooks crossed to Antwerp and toured the Low Countries with his family but soon returned to New York to take up his duties with Harvey Fisk and Sons, leaving his entirely competent wife in charge of the family expedition. She led her sons on an efficiently scheduled but only casually directed tour of European culture, following the trail blazed by a much-consulted set of Baedekers. Although sympathetic to the edifying atmosphere of the great cathedrals and capable of passing a happy afternoon at an art museum, she was more attracted to fashionable shops and the social life available at the tourist hotels, always the best to be had, in which they stayed. She was profoundly conscious of her station, and in her son's diaries one catches glimpses of her sweeping grandly out of a carelessly managed *pension,* or procuring the most comfortable transportation to the local curiosities. Under her generous hand, Ames and Van Wyck had leisure to recognize and pursue their own interests, to wander for hours among the pictures in the gallery or sit in a monastery garden in the sun and stare at the Mediterranean. They were permitted to join every tour and organized activity that caught their eye, and although their experience was thus limited to the official Europe of the guidebooks, their exposure to that was remarkably full. The sheer amount and variety of their sightseeing probably introduced them, whose curiosity was still indiscriminately excited, more fruitfully to European life than any more theoretically efficient method could.

Van Wyck kept a boyishly enthusiastic record of his Europe in eight small composition notebooks. Complete with often respectable drawings by way of illustration, it was his first self-conscious attempt to be an author, and he dutifully imitated the august style of the popular handbooks that led him from masterpiece to masterpiece. He would find better models before long. Although he occasionally paused to mention his disappointment about the Blue Grotto, the deficiencies of English ice cream sodas, and a patriotically Protestant disgust with Roman Catholic "mummery," he greatly favored his more didactic descriptions of official displays, and the Europe that lived outside of its cathedrals and museums is usually left unremarked. For long stretches of particularly the Italian and German notebooks, one could almost believe that the Brooks family did not eat, sleep, address postcards, or wander aimlessly about the streets wondering where to buy their souvenirs, but that they spent their every moment looking for and at Old Masters.

The procession from one hotel to the next, with its attendant formalities and pretensions, may seem to us now wastefully superficial, but it afforded a sensitive boy a superb introduction to cultural tradition. Van Wyck grasped it eagerly. Exposed for the first time to the high enchantments of art, he responded with an intensity that he later described as a sort of religious conversion. "It was in Dresden," he realized later, "that my mind first came to life." Sallie Brooks and the boys (Charles Edward had already departed) arrived in the Saxon capital in November 1898, there to set up housekeeping until the following March. Van Wyck and Ames went to a local teacher to acquire German and continued their regular schoolwork at home, under the direction of an unparticularized "Miss Lewis"—whom twenty-five years later Van Wyck discovered teaching English at Smith College—who seemed to have acted as a chaperone as well as an instructress. There was an active social life for Americans with business abroad, but for Van Wyck, Dresden was essentially the Zwinger gallery which, according to his diaries, he visited almost daily; the opera (he attended twenty-five performances during that winter season); and his discovery of *Memoirs of the Early Italian Painters* by Anna Jameson, the book to which he attributed his awakening to "the religion of the history of art."

Under the spell of Mrs. Jameson, that Dresden, in the final year of the century, was typical of Van Wyck's youthful Europe. Here was an artistic surrounding, an endless storehouse of paintings, and it is precisely that feeling of the rich abundance of art, that sense of easy access to the life of the spirit, that Van Wyck would miss once he had returned to Plainfield. But he was awakened to more than art during his European year: he found his vocation as well. Mrs. Jameson started him on a course of reading that formed his ambition, quickly recognized and never qualified, to be a writer. Although he neglected it almost entirely in his journals, he read voraciously during his travels, and like many contemporaneous tourists he used such works of literary merit as *Pickwick Papers* and *The Marble Faun* as guidebooks to the streets and museums he visited. The art of writing thus became inseparably associated with the painting and topography of Europe even then. He quickly discovered that the writer who fascinated him most was John Ruskin, a name that begins to crop up with increasing frequency in the diaries after the Brookses reached Italy. Van Wyck read him then, probably in *The Stones of Venice* and *Mornings in Florence,* for his glimpses of a romantic past and his magnificent descriptions of Italian art, but this lofty Victorian thinker was also one of the important early critics of the society spawned by the industrial revolution, and he gripped Van Wyck's imagination more profoundly with the passing of time. Thumbing through Ruskin's difficult pages in 1899, the boy could scarcely know that he was being introduced to a theory of economics and a vision of critical responsibility, even as the sensuous prose evoked the Gothic past. In *The Stones of Venice* Ruskin attacked Victorian England and presented a model of the good society to come by such unlikely methods as the analysis of Gothic statuary art, and that lesson in the prophetic mission and creative power of the critic soon became the standard Van Wyck set for himself. Ruskin, he wrote, was "the favourite writer of my whole adolescence."

Another writer confirmed in the flesh the hints Van Wyck had caught from Ruskin about the glories of the intellectual life. Arthur Ryder would later be known for his translations of Sanskrit literature, but he was just twenty-two years old, still a graduate student, when the Brookses met him in Venice that March. Van Wyck quickly struck up with him the first of the intense, avuncular relationships through which he drew strength from older men during his adolescence and young manhood. Ryder became a teacher, model, and companion to a boy whose world had been almost wholly regulated by women. An academic colleague later memorialized him as a man of letters rather than a scholar, and he both preached and pursued the religion of art with a single-mindedness that offended many less fiercely dedicated people. Probably he spent those spare afternoons and rainy days with Van Wyck, touring the museums and antiquities of Venice, Florence, and Rome, largely for the sake of Sallie Brooks's gratitude, but he was the sort of man whom children usually find boring, and he may have been pleased and flattered to have an earnest boy hanging on his words.

Although Van Wyck eventually decided that Ryder had subordinated his humanity to the demands of intellect, he always remembered his early friend with both affection and admiration. Ryder seemed almost biologically incapable of compromising the demands of the life of the mind. He was one of Van Wyck's types of the sage, the ascetic disciple who renounces the world to savor truth, and if it was a type Van Wyck could not temperamentally imitate, it was also the type to which he was most compellingly drawn.

To suggest, however, that a thirteen-year-old boy lived only in such rarefied atmospheres would insult human nature. Probably feeling that Ames and Van Wyck were becoming unhealthily fond of the musty air in museums, their mother saw to it that they had plenty of sightseeing, boating, and simple trudging about, particularly after they reached Switzerland and the British Isles. Along the way, Van Wyck was introduced to other qualities of European life. He caught (in Paris, of course) a glimpse of the wicked sophistication of the Continent, made his first sustained contact with the culture and ritual of Roman Catholicism, and was alerted to the realities of nationality when he and Ames were one day stoned by German children on a Dresden street. But these were incidental experiences, significant only in mature retrospect, and what came home to Plainfield in 1899 was the new idealism Van Wyck had developed in Europe, a feeling that the artistic and the spiritual life were one and the same, and his first perceptions about the redeeming value of a living cultural past. Europe remained for many years to come his dream of the primordial land of plenty, and after the excitement of homecoming subsided Plainfield seemed hopelessly bland.

He energetically attempted to recapture Europe. During his high-school years he haunted the Metropolitan Museum in New York and began to slip into Catholic churches, where the color, odor, and familiar liturgy seemed to transport him sensually to Italy again. Although it was reinforced by Ruskin and other historians of Christian art, this still purely aesthetic inclination to Roman Catholicism may have troubled his Protestant conscience, for he contented himself temporarily by developing a taste for local preaching and the pageantry of high-church Anglicanism. He also read eagerly the stately prose of John Henry Newman, spinning daydreams around the figure of that romantic churchman, whose grand style badly infected his own adolescent efforts to express his new enthusiasm for theology and liturgical ritual. The career of the Anglican divine who followed his spirit to the College of Cardinals in Rome fascinated the youthful imagination to which Catholicism was coming to seem the exhilarating but fearful inevitability of religious logic, and Van Wyck made Newman his symbol of the priest: a romanticized vision of asceticism, mysterious ritual splendor, and what he called "mediaevalism," all lumped together and confusedly associated with the grandeur of art and his nostalgia for the European past. His journal entry for November 10, 1903, an account of a visit to Ames at Princeton, illustrates his dedication to that sentimental imagery: "Father Huntingdon preached in the college chapel, and reminded me strangely of Cardinal Newman. He has the same ascetic, monastic face which all High Churchmen seem to possess, and with his black, monkish robes and heavy breast-cross he was very mediaeval in appearance. As he stood out there in the middle of the chapel, leaning over the desk, with his strong, earnest words ringing through the chapel, he held the audience spellbound, and breathless, just as Newman used to do at Oxford so many years ago."

But while Van Wyck indulged his emotions with a mistily romantic orthodoxy, he was exercising his intellect to heterodoxy—a typical dissociation of mind and feeling that would later lead him from his course in troubled waters. During these formative years he developed a belief in social and spiritual evolution, probably less through his reading of John Fiske, the American popularizer of evolutionary theory, than through his excited study of Herbert Spencer, the master himself. He grasped only the rudiments then, a theory far removed from the deeply meditated idea of evolution that underlay the work of his maturity, but the principle of inevitable progress stirred his deepest imagination, and he was soon turning it to the explanation of all things. Using evolution as the logical structure of existence that would reconcile biblical authority, Platonic idealism, and a belief in transcendental love, he concocted an elaborate "religion," plotting carefully each step of the soul's progress toward deity. Ostensibly a justification to accept Christ, his youthful metaphysic disparaged the institutional church and was fundamentally atheistic in its premises. Evolution, he thought, worked through reincarnation (a reflection of the unspecified Oriental philosophies which also interested him at this time). Each soul born into the world floundered through incarnations until it discovered, through the "finite medium" of human passion, the one mate for which it had been created, and the harmony of man and woman established by love became a single consciousness. Each dual soul then gradually rose through a series of morally progressive planes until it reached, as all souls did reach, the ultimate plane, the "Christ-plane," an "all-annihilating comprehensiveness of the one infinite quality [e.g., love]." In Van Wyck's system Christ was simply the fulfillment of human potential, and evolution made all earthly things ultimately good.

That Van Wyck at seventeen could logically synthesize this hodgepodge of systems is proof enough of the power of his developing mind. Despite its naïve optimism and occasionally silly logic, his "religion" is complete in itself, and many mature thinkers have lived and died according to beliefs no more probable than these. But like the endless theological debates to which he subjected his friends, it was only a seriously played game. After filling eight manuscript pages with his well-prepared theological essay, he confessed: "All this I believe, but do not feel." Instead, he felt that he belonged emotionally to the traditional church, with its incense, quiet shadows, and the sacramental movements by which its officers partook of timeless mysteries. These intellectually treacherous things called him home to an idealized past, when art and life were gloriously one. It was harmless enough at the time, and this particular conflict was soon forgotten, but he had worked himself into an impasse.

Of course the precious intellectualism of what he was later to call his "hyperaesthetic youth" found more outlets than theology. If his juvenile notebooks are frequently limited to a fashionably world-weary tone, they are notable for their range of subjects and for the determination with which an apprentice writer trained himself in the use of many forms. Ruskin had impressed upon him the priority of criticism, and Van Wyck's first essay toward his new vocation analyzed in boyishly derivative prose, but with considerable erudition for a fourteen-year-old, the use of perspective by the early Renaissance painter Paolo Uccello. He also produced essays, critical and familiar, both for his secret notebooks and for the Plainfield High School *Oracle,* which he edited his senior year. For Eleanor Stimson, the childhood companion to whom at sixteen he already felt engaged, he composed alternately passionate and philosophical letters, and took the habit of copying them into his own journals. He wrote a didactic poem called "Parsifal" and worked earnestly on a verse-drama based on Byron's *Manfred.* Some rare inspiration even called forth a story. Under the particular influence of FitzGerald's *Rubaiyat,* he versified energetically, usually in philosophical odes or sonnets to Eleanor. None of this poetry was good, but it was lofty, and Van Wyck, seriously a writer and eager for criticism, sent it off for professional comment—receiving a less than enthusiastic reply from Professor Edward Howard Griggs that may still have persuaded him to push on. Griggs thought that Van Wyck's poems lacked passion and intensity but acknowledged that they were dignified and earnest. During these high-school days Van Wyck also began his lifelong practice of keeping lists of books read and to read, part of a vigorous program of self-education from which he emerged one of the most gracefully learned men of his time.

These, then, were the childhood years of Van Wyck Brooks. Spent within the walled gardens of Plainfield, shaped by a family acutely responsive to the pressures of their time, they were deceptively idyllic years, and they left an indelible mark on their precocious stepchild. By the time Van Wyck had entered his final term in high school he had already discovered his calling and fallen in love with the girl who would be his wife, had already adapted to his environment the personality he would wear for the rest of his days. However much he had consciously rejected Plainfield, the city he described in 1903 as a simple failure of taste, he had made its assumptions, its manners, its gentility, and its satisfaction in solid comfort part of himself, creating a submerged loyalty often in conflict with the idealism that also became irrevocably part of his personality during his contradictory boyhood. If he had rebelled, at least intellectually, against the mean smugness of bourgeois culture, he retained in himself many bourgeois attitudes. If he had grown to consider wealth despicable and business "the one profession which is wholly sordid," he temperamentally needed money and always acted as though it were plentifully at hand. If he thought the genteel innocence of Plainfield silly, he internalized many of its prohibitions so deeply that he reflexively obeyed them as natural law. If he had fervently accepted the patrician belief in the cultural superiority of Europe, he had made that belief a weapon and was already attacking the society that bred it. In other words, Van Wyck had responded to Plainfield by raising his own "double life," and the tensions thus created would haunt him throughout his maturity.

"Loomings," Melville might have called the story of such years. But for the moment the storm clouds were all beyond the horizon and the depths tranquil, still keeping their grim secret. On the eve of his departure for Harvard, Van Wyck Brooks was a superbly educated, impeccably mannered young man, handsome and slim, already beset by the shyness he would never lose but alive with fierce idealism and lofty ambitions. By any law he had known he could scarcely be better prepared for triumph.

II

HARVARD

Van Wyck had selected his college with some care. Already "museum bred," as he told John Hall Wheelock, no longer beset by the tentative inclination to several ways of life that tantalizes most adolescents, he was fully prepared to serve the rigorous apprenticeship demanded by a literary vocation, and interested in the best possible access to it. Probably his parents took note of such practical matters as prestige and future opportunity when they applauded his choice of schools, but Van Wyck acted firmly upon his determination to write and his conviction that Harvard was the best training ground for writers. He brought with him to school an ultramundane ardor for the cultural plenty he had long anticipated. "Perhaps, next winter in Cambridge will come nearer being satisfactory," he consoled himself in his Plainfield of 1903, "for there I shall study Philosophy and English, and can have an art gallery, and a theatre, and lectures and music, and above all, perhaps *with* all, Eleanor." Even that last desire was more idealistic than it seems. At this stage in their romance, Eleanor Stimson, already in school at Wellesley, was to Van Wyck "the incarnation of all good . . . a very near image of the Christ."

His first evening at Harvard he was overpowered by a water glass full of whiskey and had to be escorted home by a more temperate sophomore—"who later," as he reminisced, "became a famous Unitarian divine." Wiser his second night, he settled for beer at a *Harvard*

26

Monthly "punch." As college men traditionally have, Harvard students drank uproariously in 1904, and Van Wyck respected the special proprieties of his new life enough to succumb gracefully to its treasured vices. After his first experiments, however, his native reserve asserted itself, and he made sure to cultivate also a mature self-control. Diffident when expected to perform in unfamiliar situations, he nevertheless had a deeply ingrained code of behavior, and he could act decisively in any matter of social ritual for which he was prepared. Everyone noticed the shyness of the quiet, delicately built boy with the astounding knowledge of writing and painting; not everyone recognized the self-confident firmness of purpose beneath his retiring personality. In *A Casual Past,* which includes one of the best accounts of early-twentieth-century Harvard, Francis Biddle remembered that Van Wyck "seemed shy and young and fresh, as if everything in this strange world of Harvard outside of letters was a startling phenomenon." But like his brother George, Biddle came to know Van Wyck well during his college days, and he added that "in the smaller world which was almost already his—he was determined to conquer it—the figures and the essences were dear and intimate."

John Hall Wheelock had similar memories. He struck up a cherished, lifelong friendship over the "punch" the *Monthly* served that night in September 1904. Himself shy, he came away from that first meeting with an impression "of extreme sensitivity, of something fastidious, even exquisite, holding severely in check an extraordinary vehemence of thought and feeling." As he grew closer to Van Wyck, he also came to respect a certain man-of-the-worldliness in his friend, a sophistication about the little proprieties of manhood to which he gladly subordinated his own less experienced social conscience—or so he self-effacingly described Van Wyck's mentorship during their undergraduate days. One of the adolescent adventures he best remembered is illustrative:

> We'd been in the habit, when the weather got warmer, of going out into the Common in Boston and walking there in the evenings, and sometimes we would have dinner before that at some cheap little place in Boston.
> One day Van Wyck said, "Let's go to the Parker House. Have you got enough money?" And I said, "Well, I don't know. How much would it cost?" Well, he knew how much it would cost,

and we went there, and Van Wyck ordered a bottle of Burgundy.... After Van Wyck had filled up our glasses and we had drunk them, he started to fill them up again. I put my hand over my glass and Van Wyck drew back in astonishment and said, "What's the trouble?"

I said, "I never take more than a glass of wine."

He said, "Now, there's something you'll have to learn. Whether you take one glass or two glasses or three glasses is all very unimportant. There's only one thing that's important—that is being a good fellow. Now, you've got to learn to be a good fellow. If *I* take a glass of wine, *you* take a glass of wine."

I said, "Is that how it's done?"

"*Yes!* ... It won't bother you. You'll like it." So we finished the bottle.

This was in the spring, and we went on to a pop concert given in Symphony Hall.... As soon as we got to a table—I knew nothing about drinks—Van Wyck spoke to the waiter and ordered two gin fizzes. This curious pink liquid was put into the glasses, and we sat down. I was drinking very slowly, and Van Wyck said, "Finish your drink," and I did.

Then there was an intermission; we walked around and I said to Van Wyck, "What makes my knees feel so funny?" And I began to laugh. And he said, "Shut up! You're drunk!"

This was my first experience with the pleasures of alcohol. I found it very pleasant indeed, and we repeated this as often as we could afford it. I found Van Wyck very sophisticated about things of that sort.

A tempered indulgence in these masculine recreations was probably healthful for Van Wyck, whose taste inclined too much toward the precious, but he did not devote his first days at Harvard entirely to drinking and carousing. He sought out the intellectual challenges to which he had looked forward and dutifully endured registrations and initiations. He wrote home with boyish enthusiasm, and with a newly sophisticated economy of expression he invited Eleanor Stimson to dinner at the Wellesley Inn, explaining that "that is perfectly proper[,] unlike Fall River Boats." His first letter to his mother described such preliminary academic achievements as exemption from the freshman course in English composition and reported a well-balanced program of humanistic study that would be enough, he anticipated, to get him through college in three years without overworking. Under Harvard's elective system superior students could easily earn a degree in less than the traditional time, but the practice was not customary, and Van Wyck may have planned on three years from the outset because the family finances could not comfortably sustain four.

Money was always a problem. Forced to borrow small amounts from time to time, he demanded of his friends the same careless generosity with which he would have liked to conduct his own affairs. "When I ask for money," he lectured Jack Wheelock one day, "don't ever take out that little purse of yours and pick out a dollar bill or two dollar bills. . . . Keep your money in a bureau drawer and when anyone asks you for money—money is a mere convenience and not of the slightest importance—put your hand in and take a handful of it." Wheelock later wondered aloud whether Van Wyck might not have inclined more to counting if it were his money being handed out, but he quickly decided that his friend would not have hesitated a moment to give away even his last few dollars. "It was his code," he said.

For young men without ample means Harvard in 1904–1907 was often chilly. Too much of the university had divided into pockets of mutually exclusive social activity and become snobbish. Later Van Wyck added together the special strains of intellectual "snobbery"— Anglo-Catholicism, the cults of Dante and Donne, French Symbolism, the hostility of George Santayana and Irving Babbitt to America and the idea of progress, Sanskrit studies, even "a semi-serious cult of royalism"—and he came up with T. S. Eliot, whom he called the quintessence of the Harvard he knew. That symbolism described accurately one sheltered corner of Harvard's formal gardens, but it scarcely represents the climate of the entire place. The genuinely obnoxious snobbishness was represented not by Eliot but by the wealthy young animal who endlessly drank and played, avoided all but the most congenial courses, and graduated to an executive position in his father's business —remarking in subsequent alumni reports that he had been playing considerable golf. Such men were welcome in the clubs. Less wealthy students often were not. Neither were those outsiders who had come to Harvard from far parts of the land or had failed to attend the right preparatory schools. Francis Biddle described what he called Harvard's attitude of laissez-faire toward less privileged students. Those without

29

clubs were in effect denied access to social contacts, even to a decent academic advisory system, and left to shift for themselves as best they could.

The bolted doors and private gardens of Harvard in 1904 could not have seemed hospitable to a relatively impecunious young man from a public high school in New Jersey, but, strangely enough, the club system gave Van Wyck little trouble. He was fortunate that Max Perkins had entered Harvard a year before him. Going out of his way to exploit the acquaintanceships he had developed at his fashionable New England preparatory school, Perkins made sure to introduce Van Wyck to all the "right people." Probably Van Wyck's easy elections to the Stylus at the end of his freshman year and the Signet at the beginning of his second were largely tributes to his own accomplishments—both were fundamentally literary clubs—but it was doubtless Perkins who got him into his "final" club, the Fox. Van Wyck made Stylus headquarters the center of his college life and was enthusiastic about membership in the Signet, "absolutely the nicest thing in college to belong to," as he wrote his mother, but he lacked sympathy for the roughnecks in his final club, and his purely social triumph there had little effect upon him. By January 1906 he was writing Eleanor: "All this 'man-of-the-world' business is a mere bluff, but it is playing with fire. Clubs & poetry are at the opposite poles, and when you try to reconcile them, at best you strike an equator, neither one thing nor the other."

In addition to Max Perkins, whose literary ambition had not yet settled on the editing for which he would be famous, and Jack Wheelock, already at work on his durable poetry, Van Wyck counted among his closest friends Ned (Edward Brewster) Sheldon, a romantically handsome young man with an infectious charm and a passion for French drama. Before his undergraduate work was finished, Sheldon had written the first of his Broadway hits, *Salvation Nell* (produced 1908), and in effect he stepped from his commencement platform into a leading position in the American theater. Until a crippling disease ended his career unhappily soon, he enjoyed a storybook success with his romantic but realistically delineated melodramas, among them *Romance* (1913), one of the most popular plays ever written in the United States. Brooks, Perkins, Sheldon, and Wheelock were inseparable companions at Harvard, stimulating one another intellectually, relaxing together socially, and they would remain deeply intimate as long as they lived.

Other members of the Harvard class of 1908 also had notable careers before them: Samuel Eliot Morison as a historian, Lee Simonson as a stage designer, George Biddle in graphics and painting, and Charles Seeger as a musicologist. Van Wyck was friendly with all of these men, then and later. He may also have made the acquaintance of two other famous classmates: Alain Locke, whose anthology *The New Negro* would become the manifesto of the "Harlem Renaissance" of the 1920s, and Joseph Pulitzer, the son of the great publisher, preparing for his own distinguished journalistic work. Walter Lippmann (1910) was at Harvard during Van Wyck's time, as were the poet Alan Seeger (1910), Francis Biddle (1909), the future biographer Hermann Hagedorn (1907), and John Reed (1910). T. S. Eliot (1910) entered Harvard during Van Wyck's last year, and while he was decidedly not a friend, in college or at any other time, he later became important to Van Wyck as a sort of demonic anti-self.

Rich in the traditions and lore of heroic bookishness, academic Cambridge was well calculated to confirm the intuition Van Wyck had caught in Europe, that writing was all that mattered of life. William James, Josiah Royce, George Santayana, Bliss Perry, Barrett Wendell, Irving Babbitt, and George Lyman Kittredge were all on the Harvard faculty, and all were, or were about to become, well-known authors. Two much-admired teachers of writing, Charles Townsend Copeland ("Copey") and Dean LeBaron Russell Briggs, turned out from their crowded classrooms students whose fame often outstripped their own, and influenced thus three generations of American letters. George Pierce Baker opened his famous "47 Workshop" of dramatic writing in 1905 and for the next thirty years exerted a similar influence on the American theater. Among the first students to enroll in his course were Van Wyck Brooks and Edward Sheldon.

Literature, however, was more than simply a profession, more even than a way of life. It was a discovery of truth, and one judged a literary text, finally, less by its technical than by its moral mastery. In Irving Babbitt's classroom, for example, the study of literature was a study of the nature of man and history, and of what had gone wrong with both. A fervid antiromanticist, Babbitt was relatively indifferent to intrinsic merit in works of art. He esteemed them rather to the degree that they displayed certain classical principles of what he called "Humanism." Given such invigorating examples, students brought to literary debate an ideological zeal that contributed much to the markedly cultist mentality of their Harvard milieu. The cults of John Donne and of Dante, whose devotees met in the home of Charles Eliot Norton, were venerable New England traditions, but a fashionable cult of Walter Pater also flourished among the intellectual epicures. A rival cult of Rudyard Kipling attracted the loyalties of literary red-bloods. Even Bernard Berenson, the art historian and collector, had a cultist following, part of a rage for Italian painting and the misty past.

There was no cult of Herman Melville, however. Neither was there a cult of Thoreau, of Mark Twain, of Emily Dickinson, nor any of Walt Whitman. There was not even a Harvard cult of Ralph Waldo Emerson. Some of those names were practically unknown in Cambridge in 1904. Just as Van Wyck confirmed his sense of vocation in Harvard's bookish climate, so he strengthened his juvenile assumption that writing was a sacramental activity essentially foreign to acquisitive America. Undergraduate literary taste by and large ran to French Symbolism and the slightly overripe aestheticism imported from England. Oscar Wilde was popular then, as were Swinburne, Maeterlinck, and the early William Butler Yeats, whose poems were to be found written out from memory in many an undergraduate notebook. Van Wyck summed up that milieu when he attempted to satirize it in an unpublished freshman essay: "Walter Pater *is* in every college bookcase. De Quincey *may be* on the bottom shelf. Maurice Hewlett on Italy is the reigning authority, but Goethe or Heine be damned! Every college-man of culture is a life-member with Mr. Elbert Hubbard. . . . we see the rooms of these intellectual devotees and patrons of the fine arts plastered with Mona Lisas and Vierges au Rochers; . . . We are sure to find certain wall-schemes with a single Rembrandt and a couple of aesthetic candles (going, if possible, all day)."

Some authorities conceded that there had been a minor American tradition, but they insisted that it was dead. Van Wyck remembered Barrett Wendell, a historian of American literature, asserting that native authors had been "of little lasting potence." "All Americans are born Philistines," Van Wyck dutifully noted in one of his workbooks, "and whatever they may acquire that is anti-Philistine comes from contact with Europe." Fashionable students, of course, adopted the European tone even more enthusiastically than did the classicists and

Anglophiles on the faculty. Van Wyck and Francis Biddle both glee-fully memorialized Harold Bell, who had the color of a Pre-Raphaelite painting and the taste for elegance of a Renaissance pope. They also remembered Pierre de Chaignon La Rose, "a fat, sophisticated dilet-tante, who did less each year, yet wrote an occasional piece for the *Atlantic Monthly,* sent in anonymously to see if they would still accept him on his merits, or designed a bookplate for a friend, or did a little work on his book on ecclesiastic heraldry that he might some day pub-lish." His real name may have been Peter Ross, and the description is Biddle's. These interesting characters typified the fastidious version of medievalism that then went hand-in-hand with a melancholy fascina-tion for Anglican and Roman Catholicism. Like many of his fellow un-dergraduates, Van Wyck seriously considered converting to the Roman religion, and John Hall Wheelock remembered that his friend often requested his company for visits to the Catholic churches in Bos-ton. Van Wyck might well have acted upon his impulse if Eleanor Stimson had not set all her Protestant influence against it. As much as Van Wyck assaulted her with arguments about the relativism of theo-logical points of view and the ritual significance of the Mass, she per-sisted in asserting both fear and scorn for what she considered the cor-rupt religion of cowardly men.

In their sublime surrender to the *fin de siècle,* Pierre La Rose and Harold Bell epitomized also the mannered hedonism of an "aristo-cratic" social code that encouraged the cultivation of exquisite—or ec-centric—tastes. Van Wyck Brooks was probably not the only Harvard freshman who breakfasted on maraschino cherries and new cider, or affected other approved forms of heroical self-indulgence. During their junior year Ned Sheldon wrote to Van Wyck: "I am rather dizzy with labor, and drink nothing but coffee and whiskey all day long with a copy of Cowper in one hand, a Wycherly in the other." He seemed un-aware of how remarkable his dexterity was. Dandyism flourished—Van Wyck became particularly expert in the necktie—and Harvard gentlemen enjoyed intellectual speculations about the responsibilities and privileges of good breeding.

Harvard sophisticates thus announced that they were familiar with all that mattered of the world, but beneath their presumptuous boredom lay a naïveté about certain matters of the flesh that is almost as shocking as it is quaint. The sexual prudishness of their era is now proverbial, and although some Harvard men indulged in the careless whoring to which they felt entitled by station, they respected scrupulously their distinction between the professional ladies to whom they admitted no courtesy and the "respectable women" whose purity would be blasphemed by even the appearance of contact with the world. Van Wyck himself was no sexual rebel. He avoided the fleshpots of Boston, idealized women, and was mildly shocked, even at that late date, by Henry James's *Daisy Miller.* To Eleanor he delivered a priggish epistolary sermon on the distinction between passion and love, insisting: "You have brought up the most horrible & terrible subject in speaking of Carmen, and the world is a terribly, horribly queer place." Slightly older than her lover, far more cosmopolitan, Eleanor gently mocked Van Wyck's niceties in her reply, but could not keep him from returning solemnly to them the first chance he got. Suppose, he suggested, some girl of twenty-two "is merely seen in the streets a good deal, as so many girls are—she becomes, I don't know—a *little* common[,] a little obvious, a little to be taken for granted," and he went on to recommend a cultivated shyness and rigid propriety.

The genteel European influence dominated Harvard life in 1904, but there were other, less obvious, influences abroad in Cambridge, and other Harvards to nourish the imagination that could discover them. The very traditionalism of academic instruction helped save Van Wyck from extremes of literary and social modishness, as did his self-imposed program of reading Ruskin and other earlier writers, and he managed to avoid being trapped in the aestheticism to which he was dangerously susceptible without falling into the antithetical worship of Kipling, who was wildly popular in the United States at that time. Among teachers of writing he preferred the belletristic Dean Briggs to the more popular Copey, who delighted in the unobtrusive skill and sharp detail of the reportorial style, but his own undergraduate literary career was spent in the service of the *Harvard Advocate,* with its social interests, rather than the aesthetic *Monthly.* For his initiation to the *Advocate* he read a metaphysical Gothic tale, unmistakably in the style of Poe's "Fall of the House of Usher," and in a notebook version he commented parenthetically that his poem "Misconceptions" was written in "Walt Whitman's manner, for the moment mine and vitally sincere." Retitled "No Longer I Exalted" when it appeared in print, the poem does credit to neither Whitman nor Brooks, but it does suggest a healthy openness to diverse influences. Of American poets available at the turn of the century, the energetic, impolite Whitman would seem least likely to interest Harvard men of taste. That both Van Wyck and his friend Wheelock were "intoxicated" by *Leaves of Grass* when they were in college says much for their independence of mind.

The most important American influences alive at Harvard then were more elusive. Almost without name or honor, a subtle presence that easily went unnoticed, the cultural traditions of New England lingered on in an institutional belief in self-reliance, some old buildings, a few dying people. Miss Alice Longfellow, the poet's daughter, and "Waddy" Longfellow, his cousin, were familiar local figures, as was Charles Eliot Norton, the friend of Emerson and Lowell who, despite his Anglophilia, thus formed one of the rare, fragile links to the great Cambridge past. The old abolitionist Thomas Wentworth Higginson was another. A distinguished soldier, a notable biographer, historian, and editor, as well as the discoverer of Emily Dickinson, Higginson still delivered an occasional lecture to Harvard students. In nearby Concord, to which he made several excursions, Van Wyck could catch a glimpse of Miss Emerson, Ralph Waldo's daughter, sitting at the window of the Emerson home, or walk out to Walden Pond, feeling irreverent when he broke the silence of the country roads once tramped by Henry Thoreau. His notebook accounts of these pilgrimages are sophomorically condescending toward Concord's cultural remains: he sneered at the Lexington Monument, ridiculed the lack of modern conveniences at the lodgings he purchased, and thought that "the displaying of dates & the flaunting of wholesale history is much like talking of your ancestors—very American and very cheap." But he felt driven to arrogant sarcasm by the painful contrast of decadent present to heroic past. Concord had manufactured, he thought, the commercially profitable history represented by shoddy souvenir busts of Emerson, while letting many of its true literary monuments decay. An ambitious urchin tried to sell him a tour of the "principal graves"—Thoreau, Emerson, Alcott—in the Sleepy Hollow Cemetery, and he was depressed by the neglect of the legendary dwelling where both Emerson and Hawthorne had written famous books. The "Old Manse" was boarded up, lonely and unkempt, "a haunted house—the grasses grown wild, the wood rotting."

The image of bleak physical ruin that he took away from Concord might stand as well for the reputations of New England's classic writers in the first years of the twentieth century, and Van Wyck often returned to it when he described later the homelessness of American artists at home. But while the names of Emerson and Thoreau had no currency during Van Wyck's college days, they may remind us of the New England respect for tough individualism that informed Harvard life long after the individuals themselves had gone out of fashion. Van Wyck later thought that the great virtue of Harvard was to nourish the "inner-directed" mind, to cherish self-reliance beyond all other values, and he learned in its invigorating atmosphere a new confidence in his ability to play the self-sufficient man of letters. His student years were among the last in the presidency of Charles William Eliot, the innovative educator who had developed the controversial elective system. President Eliot believed in the maturity, dedication, and good sense of Harvard men. During his tenure a student needed only to attend classes regularly and complete a certain number of courses to earn his degree. Except for English A, from which Van Wyck easily won exemption, there were no required studies. For the rare man who understood his intellectual needs precisely, the elective system was surely a superb approach to study, at once enlightening and ennobling, a tribute to the scholar who created it. For men with less self-discipline it too often lacked starch.

Later in life Van Wyck freely admitted that he had taken more advantage of the permissiveness of the elective system than a wise man should. He used Harvard to confirm his already strong sense of personal identity and vocation rather than to investigate new possibilities, and he avoided professors who might distract him, or about whom he lacked curiosity. Of all possible benefits Van Wyck might have found at college, he needed most the influence of a strong man, someone to inflame his imagination and give him direction. The man was available. We can only speculate now about how a sustained exposure to William James might have helped Van Wyck solve the emotional and intellectual problems of his maturity, but "this enemy of all despair, of authority, dogma, fatalism, inhumanity, stagnation," as Van Wyck would celebrate the great psychologist, at least *could* have provided him with the ideological basis for a life's work that he subsequently acquired only through suffering. "To think that I was such a puppy as to go through Harvard College without once seeing or hearing William James," Van Wyck rebuked himself later.

Probably his evasion of James was simply a matter of indifference, but Van Wyck did entertain strong feelings about other professors. Even after fifty years he could not entirely forgive Copey for calling him "wilful and stubborn"—although Copey was probably right—and we find him complaining in his college notebooks that "Mr. Copeland does not know *me:* therefore Q.E.D. he does not know my style. If I said something in a way quite characteristic of myself he would step on my toe and lop it off." He had a similar, if less traumatic, problem with Dean Briggs about what he called "certain tricks of language which actually are as dear to me, and for which I really feel as profound an affection as I do for some of the more obvious characteristics of my friends," but he remembered Briggs warmly as a good teacher and a good man. About George Santayana he developed mixed feelings. He read *The Sense of Beauty* with enthusiastic sympathy and enrolled in Santayana's celebrated courses, among which "Three Philosophical Poets," a study of Lucretius, Dante, and Goethe, had become a Harvard legend. Charmed by the Spanish philosopher's style, attracted to his ironic assaults on the American Philistia, his Old World personality and grand intellectual sweep, Van Wyck came so strongly under Santayana's influence that it probably continued to inform much of his hostility to American culture for the next twenty years. But despite the great impact upon him, Van Wyck somehow escaped discipleship. Perhaps his reservations began with Santayana's cynical "Toryism," which would surely have discouraged the young admirer who was already thinking of himself as a socialist; probably he was bothered as well by the personal coldness—Van Wyck called it "feline aestheticism"—that even Santayana's defenders find in the man. Whatever the reason, the slight distance Van Wyck maintained while at Harvard grew with the years, and he would finally lump Santayana with the enemy, among the life-deniers, describing his old teacher somewhat uncharitably as a morbid snob who thought he was special because of the accident by which he had been "hatched from a Spanish duck's egg in a Yankee barn-fowl's nest."

Such irritations were as nothing compared to the fundamental antagonism Van Wyck conceived to the personality and ideas of Irving Babbitt. He took Comparative Literature 22, a full year's course in the history and philosophy of criticism, from Babbitt, but he found himself entirely out of sympathy with his teacher's dogmatic classicism, reactionary politics, and "curiously inhuman brand of humanism." More immediately important, Van Wyck objected violently to Babbitt as a man. He described him in the autobiography as a sort of literary thug and mocked his bearish "grunts, blowings, and gurgitations." The ponderous physical presence itself was only a superficial annoyance—or so Van Wyck claimed in a letter of 1939 to Frank Jewett Mather, the art critic who was one of Babbitt's staunch defenders. "It isn't the crudities that I chiefly remember," Van Wyck wrote. "It is the lack of the fundamental grace of soul which I found in Mr. [John Butler] Yeats,— who was so much more my teacher than Harvard was. . . . My gorge always rises against any human being who depreciates the *humanitarian* feeling that seems to me of the essence of our tradition. . . . If Babbitt had really meant the 'Superior man,' and if he had talked Confucius as one who knew him, what a great light would have broken over my youth."

Although Van Wyck was persuaded that Babbitt's disabilities of character denied him greatness, he did not leave the matter there. He puzzled over his letter to Mather, wondering if he must not have been blind to some redeeming grace in Babbitt. Perhaps he considered also the personal kindness with which Babbitt had tried to help him in his first years away from school. He went back through the notes he had taken from Babbitt's lectures, remembering an often noble austerity of method, commenting on important critical insights, and finally admitting to himself, as he would publicly admit in his autobiography, that although he could not like the man he must respect him, and that among Harvard professors he had probably learned most from Babbitt. Certainly he owed his discovery of Sainte-Beuve and the other French critics upon whom he was soon to model himself to the stimulation of Babbitt's classroom. Allowing for their radically different conceptions of man and society, Babbitt and Brooks agreed remarkably about both the fundamental human significance of art and the type of norms by which it must be judged. Above all, Van Wyck would have learned in Babbitt's classroom that the criticism of literature was a rigorously ethical discipline, concerned less with taste than with the defense and perpetuation of truth. To Babbitt, to Brooks, the misvaluation of a literary text was an implicit crime against life. Their critic was a moral arbiter, the creator of worlds past and to come.

The distressing narrowness which Van Wyck felt in Babbitt's presence, then, proved rich in implicit provocation after he was far enough from his college days to distinguish functional intellectual influences from his somewhat confused emotional reaction to an entire three years. The same conflict of apparent single-mindedness and potential variety might be used to describe his exposure to Harvard College in general. Despite the school's ideological rootlessness and the special nature of the privileged society it sheltered, it was well adapted to the taste of the rootless, specialized young man from Plainfield, who gladly accepted its privileges and responded, not always consciously, to its stimulation. As a freshman Van Wyck discovered it excitedly. He quickly succumbed to the romance of scholarship and wrote an enthusiastic essay, "Of Beginning Horace," happy that he was the carrier of a venerable tradition when he approached for the first time the classic poet to whom all generations had come in their turn. He worked industriously at assigned exercises, took dutifully full notes on lectures, and compiled an adequate if undistinguished academic record, completing his requirements within three years and earning honors in English and election his final term to Phi Beta Kappa.

Although he could relax his sophistication enough to enjoy the animal outlets of a healthy boy—John Hall Wheelock recalled sitting by amazed as Van Wyck and Max Perkins settled their differences by rolling around on the floor, clawing and hitting at one another—he quickly found that the role of the dandified bohemian suited him best. His lodgings were melodramatically literary. First on Charles Street, then at the Stylus building on Winthrop Street where he shared quarters with Max Perkins, he kept his room in romantic disarray and the walls adorned with death masks of Keats, Thackeray, Pascal, and Canova. Such surroundings expressed the vision of careless literary aristocracy which had become part of his deepest sense of personal identity, informing even his courtship of Eleanor. He wooed her with philosophical treatises, social essays, book reviews, or long quotations from whatever reading interested him at the moment. Part of his loftily intellectual tone was Eleanor's fault—she discouraged passionate words by deploring "a certain subject" and was herself of an enthusiastically literary turn of mind—but more of it grew out of Van Wyck's innermost conviction that for him literature and love were not distinguishable functions of personality but basically a single expression, in a variety of terms, of his fundamental life.

There was no pose in Van Wyck's commitment to discover a social expression for his spiritual self. For a shy man, in fact, it must have been a painful discipline. But to adopt the role available to him at Harvard required strain, artificiality, and some verbal substitutions for natural behavior. The selfish aestheticism that characterized most accessible literary culture during his college days could scarcely have

settled comfortably with the lesson Van Wyck had learned from Ruskin about the social mission of the critic, and the two definitions of artistic identity conflicted dynamically within the headstrong young man
who had dedicated himself to acting out his ideas. While he was involved in the challenges and triumphs of college life, however, Van
Wyck discovered that the spiritual authority of Ruskin was momentarily overshadowed by the unique practical advantage offered by
Harvard's aestheticism: it was a specific way to *be* a writer, a curricu-
lum of life that solved many of the problems faced by young men at
the beginning of a literary career. It set forth an attractive point of
view, introduced apprentices to the decorum of the literary life, provided outlets for publication, and above all made available an abundance of immediate rewards. In fact, unless he could indulge his vague
fancy about "living in an attic and wearing a green coat," because Ad-
dison and De Quincey had, Van Wyck had encountered no way to be-
have like a writer except in the model for the creative life developed at
Harvard. In that closed society the Ruskinian vision which still dominated his spirit had neither a practical vehicle for expression nor any
ready audience, but it remained the standard to which he intuitively
shifted whenever he judged himself or his work, and thus created another submerged tension in an increasingly complicated life.

So long as Van Wyck was emotionally free to follow his enthusiasms wherever they led him he could ignore such potentially troublesome contradictions. They bothered him only enough to inspire an occasional nagging uneasiness and keep him from submitting altogether
to the prevailing aestheticism. He muted them satisfactorily by showing more interest than most of his peers in the social aspects of art. But
if unacknowledged, the problem remained dynamic, and Van Wyck
solved part of it, at least temporarily, by a shift of emphasis which he
announced to Eleanor in a letter of September 10, 1905. "There are
some sorts of personal poetry," he wrote,

> which I think it best to give up writing altogether. I have been
> morbid & mawkish[.] I have played with sentiment & uttered it
> too freely I'm afraid—& much of this state of mind has been fos-
> tered by ideas & ambitions that have been in a sense unmanly. . . .
> The result is that I have been in a perfect fever to do something
> great for other people:—desire for fame may really be at the bot-
> tom of it, but I don't know & I don't think about it. I have devel-

oped a sudden thirst for institutions, for races rather than individuals, for the people rather than the classes, almost for economics—& along with this prose as appealing to me almost more than poetry—I don't know but that to write Socialist pamphlets is the most precious desire I have. But in them would be thoughts on art, and really aiming at a general system of culture.

Van Wyck did not trace out for Eleanor the process by which he arrived at these conclusions, but they probably came suddenly into focus during the summer he spent in Italy after his freshman year. He was a slightly more experienced, certainly a more sophisticated traveler when he departed for southern Italy with Ames and his parents in June 1905, and he cultivated a supercilious attitude toward all shipboard life except the steerage, whose colorful passengers stirred in him a lively, if patronizing, aesthetic interest. Once in Italy he went about usually on his own, for Ames could no longer provide him with companionship. He went to Mass whenever he could, and he studied the life of the people. Perhaps part of the unmanliness he reported to Eleanor impressed itself upon him when he found a Neapolitan slum quaintly picturesque. "What a pity it is," he wrote in the journal he kept that summer, "that a Hell for Humanity is so often a Paradise for artists! They are so *beautifully* miserable. The beggars covered in patches, the children wholly naked, all, diseased, weary, misshapen— what far better pictures they make than Bank Presidents or American grocers!" On the other hand, he looked for expressions of history, cultural tradition, and national integrity in the faces of the people he encountered on the streets, elaborating on such interests in his remark that "anybody understands what personal touch means with the great characters of history, for it is such that brings our culture home to us and makes it really vital." While he did not neglect his museum-going, or forget to wax romantic among medieval ruins, his second visit to Europe was generally less an art feast than his first, and more the discovery of an entire past, which he perceived in sensual, historical, and cultural terms, and to which art was a primary means, but not the end itself.

Although he remembered in his autobiography a "beatific summer" which fired his imagination to things Italian for years to come, Van Wyck used much of the space in his journals to complain about boredom. His father had been progressively weakened by a number of painful diseases and became alarmingly ill in Sorrento, where the family interrupted its itinerary to nurse him back to health enough for the return voyage to the United States. Deprived of his tour of Italian museums and thrown back on his own devices, Van Wyck ventured an occasional expedition to attractions close to Sorrento, but he quickly exhausted his rather specialized interests and spent most of his summer days obdurately lounging around his hotel.

His enforced idleness in Sorrento yielded unexpected benefits. On one of the diversionary trips he made to Capri, he met a young Englishman named G. E. Marshall and struck up one of the rewarding friendships of his life. This peripatetic scholar and teacher happened into Van Wyck's way at precisely the right time to influence his development more intimately than a more famous or talented figure could. He was the bohemian *par excellence,* living the casual, wandering life that Van Wyck always considered natural to artists and supporting himself by working from time to time as a tutor for English or Italian families. Spilling over with good talk as he and Van Wyck walked energetically through the Italian countryside, he was infatuated with the life of the mind, and, himself a Catholic, he gave his companion special insights into the religious and social culture of Italy. Marshall was perhaps too disinclined to hard work ever to become the ascetic pilgrim of Van Wyck's fancy, but he seemed to incarnate all the freedom and unconventional wisdom of the spiritual nomadry which the impressionable younger man admired.

Except for the indirect record Van Wyck later insinuated into a book, nothing remains of the conversations the two young intellectuals shared during their brief Italian summer, but they continued to write for at least five years after they last saw each other, and some of Marshall's correspondence survives. He sent Van Wyck breezily masculine, almost flippant letters, cynical but affectionate, offering pungent advice to a younger man, but treating him always *as* a man and an equal. Probably his long, pornographic translations of Catullus' priapic poems and his ironic gossip about the adulteries of aristocratic Italy introduced Van Wyck to a sort of worldly wisdom he sadly needed, but Marshall's letters also analyzed ideas, attitudes, social organizations by reference to national history and character. His own orthodoxy was somewhat in need of patching, and he set himself against Van Wyck's inclination to Roman Catholicism, pointing to the debasements of papal politics and the moral decay which he claimed underlay the dig-

42

nity and religious ritualism of the Italian nobility. Van Wyck's heritage was Protestant, he argued, and men grew in character as they heeded the genius of their native place: "I know all Americans have a strange passion for demonstrating that America and everything American are far and away ahead of the rest of the world, but when you want to rival Catullus in dirtiness & the Italian aristocracy in immorality I can but say 'How are the mighty fallen' & remind you of your splendid (& natural!) ancestors the Pilgrim Fathers who if they had broken away from the Catholic faith of their ancestors & had adopted a narrow, one-sided & illogical travesty of Christianity were anyhow sincere & rigidly moral."

Marshall confirmed Van Wyck in his taste for intellectual vagabondage, bore witness to his scornful dismissal of all that was efficient and orderly in modern life, and introduced him to the special advantages of appraising culture by reference to racial or national identity. At the same time, he was cynically contemptuous of the United States and its pretensions to respectability. American nationality, he thought, lacked experience, depth, and soul—a verdict to which his companion only too readily agreed—and he left Van Wyck more than ever persuaded that racial wisdom belonged exclusively to the lands across the water, that it became accessible to Americans only after they had purged themselves of homeliness. Van Wyck determined to apply himself to a bitterly negative criticism of the American cultural scene, as the only way of redeeming it, and after his summer in Italy he fell more and more naturally into a tone of prophetic admonishment.

Perhaps Marshall served Van Wyck best, however, simply by telling dirty stories about the Italian nobility. Not only did these scandalous anecdotes reawaken Van Wyck's sense of the economic injustice and debilitating personal effect of the old class structures; they disabused him of much of the adolescent romanticism with which he had viewed the picturesque displays of aristocratic life, and they taught him that excessive refinement might simply represent a compensation for moral inertia. To that insight we can probably attribute Van Wyck's discovery of at least part of the "unmanliness" in his own tastefully romantic verses, but, whatever his reason for abandoning personal expression for collectivism, he stood by the sudden decision he had announced to Eleanor and after that autumn he gave up poetry altogether. Upon returning to Harvard, he collected some of the work he liked best, talked John Hall Wheelock into sharing expenses, and had printed in collaboration with him a small anonymous pamphlet called *Verses by Two Undergraduates*. As Wheelock recalled it, he and Van Wyck were more concerned with inscribing copies for presentation to their ladies than with distributing the few that Wheelock took with him to Manhattan during Christmas vacation, and they regarded their first venture into authorship more as a gesture than an assault upon the literary world. For Wheelock *Verses by Two Undergraduates* was the promising beginning of a poet's career; for Brooks it completed and recorded one active period in a rapidly developing consciousness.

Van Wyck contributed ten poems to *Verses*—he appeared on the right-hand pages, Wheelock on the left—and although most of them are at best slight, it would do him an injustice to dismiss them altogether. Certainly there is promise in "Cui Fata Parent," for instance, with its heroical imagery and its crisp movement toward the statement about the heroical life in the final stanza:

> What though a thousand sages
>   Thundered beneath the slough,
> The Mongol of the Ages
>   Is the Mongol of the Now.
> Not omenless the finger
>   That points across the sea
> Where the angry storm-dogs linger
>   In the leash of destiny!
>
> And knowing the requital—
>   It is written in The Book
> How he digged and hid his title
>   For the toil he would not brook—
> And knowing the requital,
>   Is it not worth thy breath
> To rescue what is vital
>   From the quicksand that is death?
>
> Older than all thy brothers,
>   Mightier born than they,
> Thou, Teacher of the others,
>   and sleeping life away!
> The Master comes; no longer

Thy birthright disavow,
For Jacob still is stronger
  And night is closing now.

From Behemoth no bellow
  Moves from the sluggish mire,
(God save us from the yellow
  When yellow turns to fire!)
The lamps of Death are burning,
  The watchers are at hand,
And there is no returning
  For whom the Fates demand.

The publication of *Verses by Two Undergraduates* might be considered Van Wyck's public exposure and purgation of one emotional identity he had learned to distrust. It is at least suggestive that he never again displayed any interest in the art of poetry, and he eventually gave up reading contemporary verse. But even if we do see *Verses* as a sacrifice to a developing identity, it could propitiate only one of the many forces that were silently challenging Van Wyck's mastery of himself. Invigorated by the reckless integrity with which he honored even his contradictory impulses, the radical "doubleness" he had brought from Plainfield extended itself into the new developments in his life. Not only was he now torn between his sense of duty to America and his passion for Europe, between an emotional hunger for a deeply "racial" self and a disdainful rejection of the native past; he was also drifting toward a dangerous conflict of loyalties in his increasingly serious devotion to Eleanor Stimson. They would not announce it until Van Wyck left college, but the lovers had already decided that they were engaged, and Van Wyck had thus committed himself to the steady life and financial responsibility of the married man. Much as he warmly desired domesticity, however, he was attracted also to the wandering existence of Arthur Ryder and G. E. Marshall, and, envying their bohemian refusal to entertain the little worries about efficiency and security, he considered theirs the nobler way. Eleanor was a young lady of remarkably liberal opinions, who shared many of Van Wyck's intellectual enthusiasms, but his sense of responsibility to her and her comfortably moneyed way of life engendered a typical paradox. If he was to support her as she deserved he must make a great success as a writer, but writers, as Van Wyck was convinced, could thrive spiritually only by abjuring success.

As long as he was in college he was free to indulge his assumption that he could eventually reconcile his two models for life and thus solve all of his problems at once. But the dissociation of energies, the disharmony of emotion and intellect that he banished from consciousness in his daytime world, may still have retained the power to trouble his sleep—or so we may speculate from the evidence of a dream he described to Eleanor in a letter of January 1906. It is one of the rare glimpses Van Wyck allowed into his secret self during these years:

> I am going to tell you a *wild dream* I had last night, the first I have had in a month: I thought we had each loved the other ever so much, but that my nature had split up into so many motives & furrows, which ran along quite independently that I had become incapable of any action or feeling which was absolutely whole-souled. Thus if one desire or feeling ran along one furrow, its opposite might run along the next. With this complexity you became confused & disgusted. Meanwhile a man came in whose mind was entirely trained in one channel: whose motives were consistent, and whose whole life was simple & obvious. To my mind all his actions were puerile, because where he saw them from one point only, I (though incapable of performing them) weighed them from a hundred. Of everything that he did I would say: "How *simple:* but I would disdain to do anything so obvious." I was unable to perform the great complicated actions: the simple ones I despised; and consequently did nothing[.] There was a certain nobility in his simple actions: and you fell in love with him. Now see what the case was: nobility of heart is what one loves. I judged wholly of a man from his mind. My own mind, inconsistent & complicated, had destroyed my soul: so that to me the other man seemed ignoble. Thus feeling my own superiority of intellect, I was hurt again to think you cared more for him than for me, feeling as I did that I could prove him my inferior. It was wounded pride, among other disappointments. In this interesting state of affairs, I went off after him with a pistol (I only loved you now in a fierce mad way), and was just ending up by blowing out my own brains, when I woke up. . . .

The interpretation of dreams, especially dreams taken out of psychological context and ordered by a literary consciousness, is a tricky business at best. Van Wyck blamed this one on four pieces of gingerbread, and since it expressed a frustration intellectuals commonly experience with the problem of action, the condition Van Wyck a few years later called the "malady of the ideal," we might be misled if we read it too eagerly for pathological data. All such qualifications admitted, we should note strong overtones of repressed sexuality in the imagery of the pistol, an explosive phallicism that might well be expected of a young man whose only sexual outlets had been those carefully restrained letters to Eleanor about the wickedness of the flesh. Given the purity demanded of respectable young people then, it is only natural that Van Wyck's ideological confusions would be intensified by the eruption of forbidden impulses within him.

Van Wyck had other troubles in 1906. After years of illness, Charles Edward Brooks died in August. Documentary evidence relating to Van Wyck's personal life during that year is, except for a few letters in January, entirely missing. His letters to Eleanor (106 of them, to judge by her habit of numbering each envelope) are gone from the substantial correspondence that survives, and if he continued to make his usual journal entries, they too have been lost. Lacking those documents, we can only speculate about the shock and pain of his father's death. Van Wyck had never truly known Charles Edward Brooks, who had not been fully able to play the masculine role in his household, but father and son were warmly affectionate toward each other, and Van Wyck remembered his father with more kindness than he entertained for any other member of his family. Van Wyck faced a sadly changed world as he prepared for his return to Harvard in September.

All we have from that idle, unhappy summer in Plainfield is a series of "Imaginary Letters," an experiment in literary form that reflects Van Wyck's inability to reconcile divergent sensibilities in a calm center of self. With typical earnestness, he projected onto his fictional correspondents fragmentary aspects of his own character, and a simple listing of his titles reveals much about the various impulses that from time to time occupied his consciousness. Some of his letters were: "From a Victim of the Literary Temperament to an Artist," "From a Young Irish Poet to a Gentleman of Fashion," "From an Artist in Italy to a Philosopher," "From a Dilettante to a Student of Art," "From an Old Writer to a Young Writer," "From a Purist to a Journalist,"

"From a Popular Novelist to a Historian." Each brief essay attempted to expose and understand the basis for the contradictory points of view suggested by its title, and to establish a relative standard by which diverse stances could be justified.

Few of these epistolary essays are developed beyond their basic contrast of ideas; most are slight. But in the longest and most significant, "From a Critic to a Poet," Van Wyck advances his first truly sophisticated defense of his vocation. The poet and the scientist, he argued, personify opposites of human possibility: "Poetry makes men human, and to be human is to be primitive. Science, on the other hand, furthering the evolution of ideas, tends to make men mechanical. Each fulfills its place, balancing the other. Ideas progress, but humanity does not progress, for humanity is elemental." Entirely self-fulfilling in their pure forms, however, neither poetry nor science can have any practical existence in themselves. To contribute their potentially redeeming function to a truly humane society they need the mediation of the critic, "who yokes them together, restraining their centrifugal energy, to the common purpose."

"Let me," Van Wyck continued, "make the distinction more clear between the poet, the scientist, and the critic. Where the scientist *advances* ideas, the critic finds in the poet the material by which to *adjust* the ideas. They must be learned by the critic and the lesson exists in the poet. Theories are never vital until they are mixed with humanity. And it is for the critic to mix the theory of the scientist with the humanity of the poet." This accomplished, of course, potential spiritual power was made real, and the critic had played his unique part in the progress of human history toward a collective magnanimity of life. By thus keeping his contract with destiny, he could also earn for himself an incalculable personal benefit. Van Wyck concluded his essay with the confident assertion that "between you both [poet and scientist], the opportunity is given me of the sanest life, the most philosophical, the most secure, the most balanced. For with my standpoint of comparison, with my powers and duties of proportion, I see things without bias as they are."

During his final year of study his conversion to functional writing led him to experiment with journalism, itself a form of romance much favored at Harvard then and symbolized a few years later by the spectacular career of John Reed. Van Wyck was inspired, as Americans in general were, by the war correspondent Richard Harding Davis, whose romantic adventures and melodramatic writings had created a new type of hero, and he was particularly influenced by Frederick Moore, a correspondent for a London newspaper who had returned to Harvard for a year of postgraduate study. Opportunistically, he saw in journalism a chance to live the vagabond writer's life for which his bohemian soul yearned without abandoning the prospects for respectable success that would bring him Eleanor. Moore assured him that he would have little trouble finding remunerative journalistic work in England, and, armed with a letter from Irving Babbitt, Van Wyck impatiently betook himself to New York during his Christmas vacation, determined to lose no time in learning the approaches to his new trade and establishing his name among literary editors. He talked to the essayist Paul Elmer More, editor of the *Evening Post* and *The Nation,* who encouraged him by giving him a book for review but could predict no certain success in a highly competitive profession, and to William Dean Howells, "such a funny little round-shouldered *bunch* of a man," as Van Wyck described him to Eleanor, wonderfully sympathetic to the innocent ambitiousness of his young inquisitor, but capable of advising him simply that one could expect to make his way only with time and hard work. With a full semester at Harvard yet before him, Van Wyck accepted as a lark his disappointment in New York, and so he reported it to Eleanor when he returned to Cambridge, assuring her at the same time that he remained optimistic about his ability to earn a good living at newspaper work, at home or abroad.

Van Wyck's sudden emotional need to be immediately at some sort of worldly employment indicates the growing impatience with which he endured his last months at Harvard. The irksome assumptions about intellectual dependence built into the student's role came to seem to him more than ever arbitrary, and in his notebooks he defiantly claimed title to the rights and duties of a writer, beyond all the petty laws that governed the classroom. Testing for himself the central ambiguity of his new identity, the apparently deceptive self-consciousness that distinguished the public writer from the private man, he brooded about the eccentricities of "the literary temperament" and wrestled with the problem of sincerity in art. He thought that the writer must be responsible to the possibilities of imagination rather than the practical demands of day-to-day life, and thus was often obliged to assume an identity richer in some respects than the mundane self his literal-minded acquaintances would recognize. The practice was creative and benevolent, deceitful only to the philistine. "For my part, I have never posed: but I have always attitudinized," Van Wyck argued, and he went on to explain: "the poseur is playing to the galleries of today; the attitudinizer, of tomorrow." Looking around for further justifications for his literary privilege, he compared personalities with earlier writers and poked industriously through his own characteristics for signs of genius.

While Van Wyck's youthful "attitudinizing" sometimes pains a sympathetic reader, his egotistical introspection was a natural expression of growth, a way of establishing by an arrogant manner new standards he must force himself to meet. Harvard had prepared him well to outgrow his undergraduate role, and he was bearing witness to the excellence of his education when he aggressively discarded its restrictions, declaring: *The University is the very worst place possible for a man with literary ideals.* Of course he knew where the *best* place was—every literary person knew that—and as spring came to Cambridge in 1907, bringing with it warm days, aroused hopes, and the final ordeals of college life, he restlessly prepared to go there.

III

OTHER SORTS OF WORLDS: 1907–1911

He must have seemed out of place in the steerage, the dapper, quiet young man, with his black hair and boyishly handsome features, who walked thoughtfully about the deck or sat on a coil of rope, reading *Tom Jones*. It was July 1907, and Van Wyck was off to England to make his fortune. By all the laws of his artistic conscience he could have taken no other accommodations, and in his affection for the mean surroundings of the poor and disenfranchised he was, once again, typical. With its mélange of costumes and tongues, its unembarrassed noises and smells, the steerage was the setting for one of the sentimental daydreams of his generation. The preceding summer Jack Wheelock had written enthusiastic letters to Van Wyck from on board the *Deutschland,* describing how he nightly risked a fine of one hundred dollars to slip into the bow of the ship, fascinated by the sense of natural community there, happy to sit on deck in the quiet evening air among the murmur of foreign voices. Ned Sheldon had "steerage dreams" also, and he wrote Van Wyck a few days before his friend departed from New York to envy him his adventure and tell him about a young millionaire with socialistic ideals who "married a very chic debutante & took her to Europe *on the honeymoon* third class!"

When he arrived in Liverpool at the beginning of August, Van Wyck was forced to admit to Eleanor, who was then living in Paris with her mother and brother, that his voyage had turned out to be disappointingly uneventful, with only bland food and lack of privacy to serve for hardship. Still, he was in England—even Liverpool seemed charming—and he quickly made his way to London's Soho district, where he could feel "at home among the anarchists." After trying out a succession of bleak, uninhabitable lodgings, he settled into a room over Roche's, a French restaurant with a bohemian clientele. Although he wrote glowing letters to Eleanor about a comfortable life in spacious quarters, with soft beds and ample meals, insisting that "my only trouble is one of conscience that I am, perhaps, living *too well*," he suffered genuine physical privations during his stay in London, sleeping for many nights on bare floors and often going without food. It was a difficult eighteen months, but material hardships seem to have bothered him not at all. As John Hall Wheelock put it, Van Wyck was in love with "my lady Poverty," and, invoking his heroic ideal, he would probably have felt cheated if Soho had treated him gently. "For a while he rented an old abandoned studio that did not have a stick of furniture in it," Van Wyck remembered later, describing himself in the third person. "There was nothing but a model's stand, which he used for a bed, and a moth-eaten bearskin that served him as a blanket. He lived for one whole summer on buns and tea, and once he was so hungry that he fainted. But he said he had as much fun as an arctic explorer."

While he was passing his first hard days in this new life of artistic poverty, Van Wyck kept busy by visiting the offices of editors and literary agents, introducing himself with a handful of letters from Frederick Moore. Moore's name proved to be a wonderful Open Sesame in London. He was a free-lance correspondent in the style of Richard Harding Davis, destined to achieve his romantic image a couple of years later when he was seriously wounded during a civil disturbance in Constantinople. Also the author of well-received books on international affairs, Moore was warmly admired among influential literary people, and the respect his name commanded seemed to Van Wyck to augur well for his own success. During Van Wyck's first weeks in England Moore was on assignment in Morocco, covering the Casablanca massacres for several press services, but he soon returned to take his protégé in hand, and during those months he could from time to time spend in London, he acted as a sort of older brother, influencing Van Wyck's personal as much as his professional life. More important, at least for the moment, he generously attempted to link Van Wyck's career to his own, and inspired by the success that had come to him almost too easily, he projected a future so gloriously prosperous that Van Wyck was moved to write to Eleanor: "By the chance of Moore's introductions I have stumbled into a kind of El Dorado."

Moore's influence did help Van Wyck find editors to read his manuscripts and got him many courteous interviews, a few free lunches, and even some work, but the professional triumphs he recklessly encouraged Van Wyck to anticipate never materialized. During those first optimistic weeks, however, everything seemed to fall into place according to some benevolent master plan. On the strength of Moore's recommendation Van Wyck obtained a position with the reputable and affluent literary agency of Curtis Brown at the salary of a pound a week—a pittance that would be substantially increased, Moore told him, once he had learned the trade. Immediately he began multiplying his salary by his prospects in the exuberant letters he composed for Eleanor, assuring her that one pound now meant five within six months and something close to wealth within a year—all of which added up to marriage. Building security upon the salary he was about to get became an optimistic habit of Van Wyck's, and it would dominate his correspondence with his fiancée for several frustrating years to come.

The work to which he was assigned at Curtis Brown's could be taken as evidence of a brilliant future only with considerable irony. It was drudgery, and although he put on a brave face for Eleanor, Van Wyck resented it. Most of his working day was spent transforming, or "vulgarizing" as he thought, discursive articles from European journals into brisk prose for release to the American press. At other times he wrote on American topics—Harvard, Tammany Hall, Theodore Roosevelt—for British newspapers and magazines, and he sensed that he had attained some ultimate triumph of professionalism over taste when he was assigned, and completed, an article on William Jennings Bryan. His infrequent opportunities to report English news in local publications must have comforted him even less. He did an article on some "absurd little dogs" that were used to collect charitable contributions in London railway stations, and apparently made such a mark with it that he earned the chance to follow up with a color story about the "fascination" of the stations themselves. With Moore's blessing he also wrote a more congenial series of articles on famous correspondents and was permitted a few interviews with literary figures. Van

53

Wyck seemed to enjoy the idea of behaving like a reporter, and he kept alert to the possibilities of advancement in his new profession. "In journalism," one of his instructional notes reads, "centralize your successes, scatter your failures. Here is the secret of reputation." And he jotted down, although he knew he could not follow, some worldly advice to make a name by creating a scandal. But however he prodded himself to duty, his journalistic efforts lacked conviction, and it was not long before he gave up thinking of them as anything more than a distasteful way of buying time for his own work.

He sent around to any editor who would read them ambitious critical essays on Hazlitt and other English writers, and refused to be discouraged when they were not accepted. As part of his daily routine he visited the British Museum to gather material for a study of the critic Vernon Lee, a project which occupied him for several years and boiled down to a single article. He made bountiful plans for future books. There was to be, among others, a book about the American humorists, one about the English sentimentalists, two or three about art and its critics, a series of metaphysical "letters from the sea," a satirical diary to slay the American philistine, and a collection of character studies of various representatives of the American temperament. He put considerable work into "A Book of Limitations," a collection of Addisonian essays "about my own foibles" in which he attempted to master the English familiar style, presenting himself as the traditionally shy and myopic but sensitive soul who unwittingly ridicules social norms by his bumbling efforts to meet them. Most of his sketches are dull. A series of attempts to *be* English by adopting an English manner, they lacked the firm point of view that might have established a strong literary personality. They are of interest now only as an illustration of the affected Anglophilia that led the older Van Wyck to write on the title page of one of his London notebooks: *"What* an ass I was at the age of 22!"

Van Wyck seems to have made no attempt to place any of the essays from "A Book of Limitations," and he left the manuscript unfinished. By the end of 1907 he was eagerly at work on a book about America, struggling to define his personal relationship to his national heritage even as he analyzed the causes of his country's deficient culture. His ambitious study gradually evolved through a sequence of increasingly appropriate forms. The first version (apparently now lost) was epistolary, perhaps an extension of the "Imaginary Letters" of 1906, but in February 1908 Van Wyck submitted to Reginald Smith, a

London publisher, a manuscript tentatively entitled "What Is America?" which by that time had become a straightforward analytical essay. Writing with more ingenuousness than he had previously displayed, he opened this revised version with an acknowledgment of the personal need that had determined his subject: "I have aimed at this [to discover the 'spiritual average' of America] primarily for the purpose of answering if possible that question, most disquieting to myself— Why is it that as an American, feeling as I do about my own country and about the necessity of cultivating one's own national instincts, I am at present abroad?"

In a coldly abstracted discussion which often ignored critical problems of definition and evidence, Van Wyck answered his question by analyzing American life as a triumph of practical intellect over "instinct," the racial inheritance which nourishes the artist. He argued that Americans had been forced for centuries to rely solely upon intelligence to solve the innumerable problems of building a society in a new world. Shaping an entire way of life to that single need, they had gradually come to mistake "getting a living" for living itself. The blame, he thought, must be laid to the Puritans, those earnest people whose pioneering labors encouraged them to endow sober, unrelaxed industriousness with moral authority, at the same time equating man's instinctive happiness in sensuous things with sin. They had established a cultural habit in America, a proclivity to imitate their unimaginative virtues and to go on solving the kind of practical economic problems they had faced long after their theology had been discarded and their problems were no longer urgent. A victim of this cruelly utilitarian birthright, the American artist found himself obliged to express America when his milieu was in Europe, and he became the "strange, vain, fantastical creature of No Man's Land," best represented by James McNeill Whistler.

Van Wyck prefaced his dispassionate cultural analysis with a curious biographical account of "Charles Graeling," a character whose eventful life was often based on details from his own but whose personality, as he told Eleanor, was borrowed from G. E. Marshall. It is a fantasy of triumph or even escape to which Van Wyck dedicates his ethereal hero, the sensitive young genius, born in an America hostile to both his youth and his idealism, who settles in Italy to discover in youthful idealism the highest morality of man. The study of his life and untimely death was, of course, to be the personal example of the general problem discussed abstractly in the essay, but his "memorials" are never directly related to the analytic text.

Smith was kind, even flattering, but Van Wyck had anticipated his letter of rejection, in fact welcomed it, since he now had a chance to rework what he had already recognized as a premature effort. Eleanor had gone through the manuscript with an editorial pen, praising it enthusiastically but carefully noting its lapses of style and logic, and objecting in particular to its structural looseness. Van Wyck had had second thoughts himself. Again, Frederick Moore came to his assistance, finding him a comfortable room in the Friars, an ancient farmhouse, once part of a monastery, in West Chiltington, Sussex, some forty miles south of London. For four months Van Wyck subsisted on a diet of mutton and rewrote *The Wine of the Puritans,* the little book brought out in London by Sisley's in the fall of 1908. The author assumed half the cost of publication.

During his four months in Sussex, Van Wyck's manuscript quietly blossomed into a work of art. There is no explaining adequately how it happened: it was simply the old, mysterious, always surprising act of creativity that transformed a sprawling thing into form and awarded its reader, instead of dry theorizing about life, the shared experience of two idealistic young men on a sunny hillside in Italy, earnestly talking about America as they gaze at a placid Neapolitan bay. Whatever its deficiencies, *The Wine of the Puritans* possesses the unique excitement of any book in which a struggling writer, for the first time and permanently, crosses over. It marks Van Wyck's literary coming-of-age.

It was under the influence of G. Lowes Dickinson's *A Modern Symposium,* Van Wyck remarked later, that he had abandoned the parallel structure of "What Is America?" and recast his essay into a dialogue between an unnamed narrator and "Graeling," whose biography was dropped altogether. He was probably imitating nature as well by recalling the conversations he had held with G. E. Marshall in Italy. He also abandoned the personal confession which had led to his argument in the earlier version and threw both of his characters immediately into the problem of America, dramatizing his subject, justifying it by the fact of their situation and the earnestness of their debate. Much of his basic analysis survived substantially unchanged, but his discussion this time was better balanced, less an outright attack than a consideration of a genuinely complex problem. Such representative men as the American vernacular humorists and P. T. Barnum added a much needed specificity to the basic analytic thrust, as did the Italian setting, itself the definition of a milieu, and the adoption of the metaphor that gave the book its title.

" 'You put the old wine into new bottles,' I [the narrator] suggested, 'and when the explosion results, one may say, the aroma passes into the air and the wine spills on the floor. The aroma, or the ideal, turns into transcendentalism, and the wine, or the real, becomes commercialism. In any case, one doesn't preserve a great deal of well-tempered, genial wine.' " The image illustrates the new dimension Van Wyck had added to his critique of Puritanism, anticipating his famous polarization of American character into "highbrow and lowbrow" in *America's Coming-of-Age*. Without slackening the pace of his attack on the American worship of practical intellect, which had anachronistically survived the "stern economic need" of the Puritans, he admitted that those remarkable people had bred a native idealism as well, but an idealism totally divorced from the life around it.

This appalling philosophical climate, hostile to significant evolutionary development as well as to art, was due, the conversationalists agreed, to the peculiar historical accident that had deprived the American "race" of the inherited patterns of traditional behavior, so long established that they were almost instinctual, which were the prerequisite for art and spirituality. Americans were left instead with a deep nostalgia for Europe, especially England. But they had settled too far from their old home to return emotionally there. European culture, moreover, was dying. Looking, then, toward a utopian as well as an aesthetic goal, the American artist faced the problem of creating a native tradition from which future generations could draw strength. "We have reached a point," the narrator says, "where we must sacrifice ourselves." American artists must absorb American ideas and American life, no matter how distasteful, as a way of discovering the elements of a great art. "I think the day will come," the study concludes, "when the names of Denver and Sioux City will have a traditional and antique dignity like Damascus and Perugia—and when it will not seem to us grotesque that they have."

Despite its occasional lapses of taste and incongruously affected style—one almost hears the phony English accent—*The Wine of the Puritans* was the brilliant beginning of a life's work. With impatient audacity, Van Wyck had uncovered powerful themes that would preoccupy an exceptionally talented generation of American artists and

57

intellectuals: expatriation, the rediscovery of the American past, the possibililty of utopian revolution through the creation of native culture. In the Puritans and their curiously inorganic relationship to the New World, he had found an explanation for the deficiencies of American civilization that for a quarter of a century would satisfy his introspective contemporaries, and that satisfies still, once we remember that the Puritanism Brooks flayed is better understood as a metaphor for an American trait than as an objective analysis of history.

For all of its staunchly American ideology, *The Wine of the Puritans* might almost serve as another illustration of the American dissociation of emotion and intellect that it deplores. Although his characters readily acknowledge their citizenship, their common point of view is that of the outsider, who tries to solve with his head the problem he cannot feel in his guts, and their determination to make themselves emotionally and spiritually American demands a spectacular triumph of will over "instinct." Neither Graeling nor the narrator has much chance in this life of "absorbing" Sioux City. The discrepancy of impulses results from the intense Anglicization to which Van Wyck directed himself while in London. Although John Hall Wheelock shrewdly noted the influence of Emerson on *The Wine of the Puritans*, the book more forcefully reveals Van Wyck's emotional need to be an English stylist.

He dedicated more than prose style to his efforts to approximate English citizenship. Before he was a day off the boat he had convinced himself that he had reached the land of elegance, and he devoted many of the entries in his English journal to the definition of the gentleman, that naturally cosmopolitan aristocrat, known by his response to the nuances of social intercourse and "a certain indefinable negligence in the arrangement of a cravat." (Van Wyck clung stubbornly to his fixation on neckwear, and Eleanor was forced to tell him that one of his recherché allusions to ties was out of place in "What Is America?") Convinced that he must attain the man-of-the-worldliness of the writers he admired then, he ignored his own advice to American expatriates and deliberately tried to assume personally the body of English tradition: to enjoy English food, be alert to the fine distinctions of English manners, and respect the morality of the English caste system. For a while he managed to persuade himself that he retained no American literary responses whatsoever. "If I were to name the authors whom I chiefly love and understand and who have chiefly influenced me," he wrote in a notebook, "I should find the greatest number in a language I cannot read!" He went on to list at length his favorite writers from classical antiquity, from Italy and Germany, and predominantly from France and England, concluding: "In American—nothing: only the personality of Margaret Fuller has touched me. There is a portrait of my mind!"

During the Christmas season of 1907 Van Wyck crossed to Paris for a long-awaited visit to the Stimsons, staying two weeks in the makeshift studio of Karol Ferencz-Winzer, an Anglo-Polish painter he had met at the British Museum. Back in London he took genuine pleasure in mingling for hours with people on the streets and in the coffeehouses, attended both political and artistic lectures, went to concerts when he could afford them, and, of course, saved time for pleasant afternoons among the pictures in the galleries. Although a stranger in a foreign city, he did not lack for companionship. Besides Frederick Moore there was J. L. C. Booth, Moore's friend and an artist for *Punch,* "Tommy" Thomas, with whom Van Wyck roomed for several months, and Joe Breck, like Thomas a friend from Harvard now in Europe to make a career as an art historian. Other Harvard acquaintances passed through London from time to time. Even Irving Babbitt showed up one day in the British Museum, and the literary curmudgeon and his precocious student walked quietly together around Russell Square. Van Wyck left no record of their conversation.

The friend he remembered most warmly from his London days was Stanley Edwards (the "Uncle Nick" of the autobiography), another of the avuncular counselors he continued to adopt until his marriage to Eleanor. Edwards must have been about sixty when Van Wyck first met him, a confirmed bachelor, bohemian, and rationalist, who modeled his mild idiosyncrasies on Sir Roger De Coverley and haunted secondhand bookstalls in search of rare editions. Van Wyck saw this invigorating old gentleman at least once a day almost without fail, for Edwards roomed above him at Roche's and had a stock of good stories. Although he had spent much of his life as a lawyer in New Zealand, he had once met Matthew Arnold, and he had been among the regulars at Roche's when Samuel Butler and Ernest Dowson, leading their rival factions, held sway there. With his eye for significant detail, his epigrammatic wit and crowded memory, he made excellent company, and Van Wyck loved the eccentric dignity with which he honored the bohemian way of life.

Edwards's sympathetic advice and unselfish affection created a sort of family atmosphere in London that was all to the benefit of his young companion, whose most intimate ties, to Eleanor and his natural family, had been seriously weakened by circumstance. It was a healthy, spontaneous relationship they shared, and it more than compensated for the somewhat unfortunate model that Edwards held up to an impressionable alien. For all of his virtues, Uncle Nick seems to have worked hard to enhance his visibility as a local character, and Van Wyck's Anglified mannerism could have done without encouragement. But this spirited old man did introduce the grateful young man to an enchanting London he could not have discovered for himself, teaching him how to eat adequately, dress respectably, and keep himself amused on almost no money at all. He understood the emotional need that made young intellectuals irresponsible, assuring Van Wyck that he had done right by running off to London, and he read his manuscripts with sympathy enough—so Van Wyck told Eleanor—to help him develop their inherent structure. Long after Van Wyck had left London Edwards maintained contact with a stream of witty, openly affectionate letters, cheering up the moody young writer, reminding him that he was always welcome "at home" in England, discouraging self-deception, and delivering stern neoparental rebukes.

Despite Uncle Nick's good offices, it was during Van Wyck's eighteen months in London that he first began to shift for no apparent reason out of his usual good spirits and swing back and forth between cycles of euphoria and severe depression. All of the cheerful, sometimes unrealistic confidence he reported to Eleanor would suddenly drop away, and he would find himself tortured by spasms of insecurity and self-loathing. This alarmingly simple fluctuation of moods hid the complexity of a number of emotional problems. He was lovesick, for one, sexually and emotionally in need of Eleanor, desperately afraid of losing her, and his notebooks are filled with passionate cries for the redeeming love that was being denied him. Money, of course, was another problem, the root of them all, he felt, and he worried about it with an anxiety disproportionate to his actual situation. Apparently he had made some nagging debts before leaving the United States, and during his stay in London he was once or twice forced to rely upon the generosity of his mother, who disapproved of his literary ambitions and did not part with money gracefully.

Van Wyck could not continue to live and work in London without some kind of stable income, and, of course, even relative prosperity could open the way to marriage. Persuading himself by sheer mental gymnastics that he was the master of his situation, he let himself in for a regular succession of economic frustrations which, with the passing of time, came increasingly to seem like signposts toward a bleak future. Each Monday, as it were, he counted up his prospects, optimistically concluding that he would be solvent within a year, only to be forced to admit by Saturday that he had been chasing phantoms—which left the whole process of cheering himself up to be faced again next week. In the summer of 1908 he noted with some astonishment that Frederick Moore, who had been recently married, owed him more than eight pounds, no trifling sum to a man accustomed to going hungry to bed. If one of the rising young captains of London journalism had trouble supporting a wife on his earnings, what hopes could be entertained for a Fleet Street hack?

Van Wyck was also tormented with doubts about his literary destiny. He was dried up, he told his notebooks, unable to produce, in a stupor. "Why do I write," he asked, "when I ought to be a bank-clerk?" Even the arrangements with Sisley for publication of *The Wine of the Puritans* stirred in him only "the sense of my mistakes and of my foolishness, of the amateurishness of the book, of its giving *me* away. . . ." Obsessed by daydreams of masterpieces, he convinced himself that to find his work less than great was to find it contemptible. He jealously compared his achievements to those of Joe Breck and Tommy Thomas, who had both published studies of European art since leaving Harvard, and he was forced to confess to himself that they had outstripped him. At college he had been an authority on painting, in the habit of counting the world of art as a personal domain, and he had gone on relying on his juvenile expertise to justify a professional assumption. He would never be an art critic now, he thought—all his idealistic ambitions had come to nothing. Sometimes, in desperately lonely moments, he believed that he had become a moral fraud. Hungry, depressed, at least once on the verge of giving up altogether, he kept on plugging away at his writing, lured by some fatalistic gambler's hope against hope for an inspirational miracle in each fresh notebook. Although he took little comfort from his perseverance against the odds and had no idea how much stubborn courage he was displaying, this was, as Malcolm Cowley later said, a "truly heroic period."

To cap his emotional problems during his London sojourn, Van Wyck went through the crisis of his long flirtation with Catholicism. Celebrating saints' days and attending Mass each Sunday, he let his emotions be soothed by the evocative ritual, "the apotheosis of the physical and spiritual life of human nature," and he returned compulsively to an idyllic vision of an old monastery he had seen at Camaldoli in Italy, an image of escape, peace, contemplation, described in a wistful tone that combined spiritual homesickness with self-pity. But he also, with traditional American intolerance, saw in Catholicism a kind of insanity, a loss of individual identity. "Every moment you are off your guard," he warned himself, "you are a Catholic." And he wrote to Eleanor that although Romanism was a moral cancer, it was so inextricably grown into the fiber of European culture that it had become a life-rhythm as well. He could discover no compromise with his impulses, believing, according to his youthful absolutism, that he could "abide only in Rome or Rationality," and he continued to be pulled between his desire for the calming assurances of orthodoxy and his fear of surrender to moral slavery. Once, he recognized with a start that the peace he was seeking was ultimately nothing less than the annihilation of consciousness. Van Wyck puzzled over such alternatives with remarkable self-honesty, but he found no dramatic resolution to his problems, and his religious sensibilities continued to exacerbate his emotional troubles.

During the summer of 1908 Van Wyck recorded two extraordinary psychic experiences which probably should be regarded as hallucinatory symptoms of mental distress. The first was confused, but revealing:

> I am thinking of a certain balcony in Wengen where it is already growing dark. There are some red poppies under it and a vine against the white wall, but not a sound. In a fancy of someone standing there dressed in white, I see myself, an obscure, indistinct figure hurrying in and out among yellow gaslamps and the stream of human beings. It is a moving picture without sound and without order.— —That is the only reality that I can form.

Here the extreme detachment of perception—into a nameless, faceless, sexless body—emphasizes Van Wyck's reduction of himself to a shadow in a world defined by light. The anonymity is significant, but

Van Wyck was surely associating the person in white with Eleanor Stimson, who that summer, as annually, vacationed with her family in Wengen, Switzerland. Much of the eerie tension of this psychic vignette comes from Van Wyck's idealization of her—as a white radiance, bordered by increasingly impure colors, indifferently viewing from on high the drab spectacle of humanity. The furtiveness suggested by the contrast of Eleanor's lofty purity to his own "obscure" movements through a half-light of dirty grays and yellows is probably a compensatory response to the intense sexual energy that informs the scene. The radical displacements of point of view absolve both figures of direct emotional responsibility, attesting to the stringency of the repression under which the imagery was shaped.

The other disembodiment Van Wyck noted followed about three weeks later and took a classic purity of form:

> Today I had a strange adventure. I saw myself from the outside like another person, perfectly, distinctly standing there. And then it seemed so odd when I said "But you're *myself*, the particular person my soul lives in!" And for the moment I could see no reason why I shouldn't be somebody else. Surely, said I, there's no reason why you should be locked up in that particular person. I'm sure you would never have chosen *him* to live in if you'd had your wits about you! Look at him. Here you are entirely free and you go and choose that very ordinary person when you have the chance of your life. Then I suppose I began to feel sorry for this figure standing there without a soul in his body and before I knew it I was inside of him again.

The split of the personality into detached percipience and object, soul and body, has been described with some frequency in religious and psychological literature, but it is nearly always associated with either advanced stages of mystical ecstasy or psychotic trauma and attended by an emotion, at once terror-stricken and exhilarated, that is strangely lacking here. Since Van Wyck was neither a mystical adept nor insane we should probably consider the possibility that the light-headedness of physical hunger had something to do with his apparition, even though this was not his period of greatest want. Whether its origins lie in the soul, mind, or body, however, Van Wyck's second dualistic vision expresses an even more alarming self-hatred than the first.

63

Perhaps such nerve-racking experiences played some part in his decision to leave England. I can only speculate about that possibility, since the ten months from September 1908 to July 1909 are another period in Van Wyck's life for which I can find little documentation. His letters to Eleanor from that time are missing, and his English journal breaks off in August 1908 to be resumed in New York in midsummer of the following year. In any case, he had plenty of other reasons to return to the United States. The first was surely that Eleanor herself was back, living with her family in Berkeley, where her brother studied at the University of California. His mother was calling him home as well, and by this time he was forced to agree that he had no chance of success in British journalism. He may have been influenced also by the possibility that the author of a book published in London would find important doors open in New York. It was probably with all of these things in mind that he took ship during the winter of 1908–1909. Once back in New York he settled down for another attempt to establish the financial security that had eluded him in England, but without which, he felt, he must resign himself to the various frustrations of bachelorhood. Almost immediately, he resumed his practice of sending Eleanor optimistic letters.

Through Max Perkins, then with *The New York Times,* Van Wyck found an opening in the publishing house of Doubleday and Page, where he divided his time between routine editorial responsibilities, such as getting President Taft's campaign speeches into publishable form, and journalistic drudgery with *The World's Work,* the newspaper edited by Walter Hines Page. He interviewed William Dean Howells again, more professionally this time, and Augustus Thomas, the playwright, but opportunities for even such peripheral literary activity were few and far between, and Van Wyck soon found most of his days intolerably dull. By August 1909 he was complaining to Eleanor about the stultifying effect of the office upon the artistic temperament, and one day that fall he quit.

He next took a job with Funk and Wagnall's, becoming part of the crowd of hacks who composed definitions for their *Standard Dictionary* at a nickel a word. John Hall Wheelock later joined Van Wyck on the dictionary and found that his friend was skillful at his duties, which consisted largely of rephrasing definitions from other dictionaries in order to avoid copyright violations. In a good week Van Wyck could earn between twenty and thirty dollars without compromising his lofty disdain for the work, which he cheerfully milked for optimum pay at minimum effort, but he was upset the day Wheelock was fired and he was kept on. He felt that his friend had failed as a drudge because he was a true genius and that his own adaptability must be a sign of intrinsic mediocrity. Except for a brief try at writing articles for *Collier's Encyclopedia,* however, he stayed with the dictionary until he left New York. It provided him with a steady, if finally insufficient income, a few interesting acquaintances, and a practical education in words and their organization. The monotonous work, he told himself, demanded less of his integrity than did the continual compromises of journalism. While thus engaged he managed also to enhance his literary credentials by arranging an American edition of *The Wine of the Puritans* with Mitchell Kennerley, an imaginative young publisher who was willing to print the work of unknown authors, but reluctant, as it turned out, to pay them. Van Wyck would stay with Kennerley for five uneasy years.

Work or no work, these were often happy days in New York. After a few moves Van Wyck found lodgings in a shabby but agreeable rooming house on West Twenty-third Street, and he cheerfully settled again into the bohemian poverty that would never lose its hold on his imagination. "I delighted in holes in my trousers and the bottoms of my shoes," he wrote in his autobiography, making himself the symbol of a generation—"wearing at the same time a flower in my buttonhole or dressing as far as I could in the opposite extreme. I felt I acquired a secret strength by reacting in this way against the popular pattern of the young business man. . . . I supposed that by so doing I somehow connected myself with the venerable cult of shabbiness, poverty and failure."

He may have self-consciously been connecting himself also with the venerable literary cult of foolish virtue when, much to Eleanor's alarm, he took in a waif, the wild Scots stray whose pseudonym in the autobiography is "Tom Mackenzie." Before coming to work on the dictionary, this golden-tongued seventeen-year-old adventurer had been a strike-breaker, killed a man, became addicted to laudanum, and won at least the heart of a much older Wellesley girl—or so he persuaded his host, who was delighted at the opportunity to redirect such romantic energy. Van Wyck was eager to believe that Mackenzie would "play square" once he understood the masculine code of loyalty, but he confessed to Eleanor that he could not help but wince whenever his young picaroon encountered the novel idea of moral choice. His patronage was innocent and sentimental, a vicarious participation in the romanticized criminal activity about which Mackenzie often bragged, and he could not have been greatly shocked when the wayward boy sailed without notice one day for England, pleading the urgency of a dying mother, and accompanied by a large camera from the Funk and Wagnall's office. Determined, as it were, to remain innocent, Van Wyck stoutly resisted Eleanor's suggestions that the unaccountable disappearance of his watch and some money might be more than coincidentally related to Mackenzie's abrupt departure, and he rebuked her also for her suspicions of a certain elderly chambermaid in his rooming house, insisting that he would rather lose a few things here and there than go about distrusting his neighbors.

Whether or not Mackenzie was indeed guilty, Van Wyck had certainly invited disloyalty. He would have contended that such impracticality was the special virtue of the romantic artist, the spiritual man's apparent folly in the midst of worldly things, and it is impossible to suppress completely the suspicion that he deliberately cultivated naïveté. Van Wyck thought he was being nonchalant and irresponsible during these lean years, but his bohemianism was only the social manifestation of the romantic ethic by which he trained himself to a morally rigorous life. As for Mackenzie: he turned out well.

Van Wyck's other New York companionships were less studied. He often saw Max Perkins and Ned Sheldon, who was in town preparing his second play, *The Nigger,* for its opening in late 1909, and soon Jack Wheelock returned from an adventurous two years in Europe. Sheldon was eager to be generous with his success, keeping his friends supplied with tickets to the theater and introductions to actresses, but Van Wyck seems to have been more amused than attracted by the glamour of Broadway, and he was happier among the writers and painters downtown. He soon became part of the now legendary group that gathered at Petitpas', a small rooming house on West Twenty-ninth Street, where three Breton sisters also maintained a popular, inexpensive restaurant. Van Wyck often dined there among a lively crowd that included R. L. Sneddon, the perpetually gloomy Scot who made a living as a humorist, and his countryman, Blaikie Murdoch. Eric Bell and Alan Seeger were also regulars at Petitpas', both of them talented, rebellious poets who were to die young—Bell in a sanatorium for the tubercular, Seeger during the Battle of the Somme. Walt Whitman's friend Horace Traubel also showed up from time to time, as did a number of other writers, but it was the assembly of painters that made Petitpas' one of the important American artistic centers in the period just before World War I. George Luks, Rockwell Kent, William Glackens, George Bellows, Charles and Maurice Prendergast, Robert Henri, and John Sloan: all came for companionship to the little restaurant, and all subscribed more or less warmly to the principles of the so-called Ashcan School of American painting, the movement away from academic propriety toward a naturalistic assessment of particularly urban life. With Sloan, whose sympathetic but unromanticized tenement rooftops, barrooms, and street scenes had already earned him a certain notoriety in official circles, Van Wyck developed a special affinity.

Such artists and intellectuals were among the advance guard of an American modernism that would come into its own after the famous Armory Show of 1913. Meanwhile, they gathered at Petitpas' to talk about art, money, the iniquities of official selection committees, and sometimes about the promises of socialism, for most of them were interested in radical politics. But probably they talked less than they listened, assembled, as they were, at the long table governed by a magnificent conversationalist, the white-bearded, hearty old Irishman, John Butler Yeats. For many years, he dominated the evening's ritual talk at Petitpas' with his witty reflections on the life of art and his apparently endless supply of anecdotes about the great figures of the Celtic revival, a flowering of national creativity which must have impressed many of his self-consciously American auditors with parallels to their own emerging program. Yeats's racy wisdom and talent for friendship made him indisputably the paterfamilias of the boardinghouse.

Yeats was a remarkably curious and adventurous old man, the wayward father of a good painter and a great poet. He was approaching seventy when he came to New York in 1908 for a two-week visit. Delighted by the energy and spectacle he discovered there, he stayed on until his death in 1922. The fiddles were tuning all over America, he said, and despite the urgings of his worried family he refused to return home and miss the fun. His readiness in old age to take up for his soul's sake the insecurities of a new life impressed Van Wyck—more so, perhaps, after he had followed newspaper accounts of the final days of Leo Tolstoy during the fall of 1910. Old and sick, Tolstoy had run away from home at the last to die in a railway station. Although his desperate flight was commonly attributed to terminal insanity, Van

Wyck believed that the old writer had simply abjured aristocratic surroundings to return to the wellspring of his art among the folk. As in
Tolstoy, then, he saw in Yeats a type of the creative pilgrim who was
perpetually renewing his voyage. It was a romantic response, but the
romance seems appropriate. Yeats must have seemed like old Odys-
seus, whom the years could not domesticate, hoisting sail again to
search for marvels in the West, or like some new incarnation of Fal-
staff, reliving the sweet excitement of his youth through an assembly of
American Prince Hals. Van Wyck loved him unreservedly.

Yeats's lifelong habit of examining minutely the basic supposi-
tions about human and social nature established his moral authority
among his young friends and helped awaken them to a sense of common purpose. For all of his life Van Wyck would think of Yeats as his
greatest teacher, a praise echoed by other members of the Petitpas'
group, notably John Sloan. What Yeats taught these men was not
craftsmanship, for he was himself, as he said, "trapped in an imperfect
technique." Rather he preached the respect for life and the imagination that made craftsmanship worthwhile. "Don't worry so much
about technique," he advised Van Wyck. "When life takes a deeper
hold on you, it will find for you its own technique. . . ."

Yeats argued that art was founded in the specifically rendered detail, stressing the priority of concreteness to abstraction, of description
to speculation. Furthermore, since he saw art essentially as creative
living (rather than the created product), his artist was ultimately
obliged to perfect his work only through the indirect, more difficult,
process of perfecting life. Personality was to him, as Richard Ellmann
quotes him in *Yeats: The Man and the Masks,* "a man brought into
unity by a mood, not a static unity, (that is character) but alive and
glowing like a star, all in harmony with himself. Conscience at peace
yet vigilant; spiritual and sensual desires at one; all of them in intense
movement." The purpose of art was "the birth, the growth, and ex-
pansion of everliving personalities," and the value of art "depends on
whether the artist's personality is fully engaged in it."

Such respect for the individual personality was not new to Van
Wyck. It cropped up in his literary notebooks almost from the moment
he began to keep them. In fact, it was a relatively common attitude
during the nineteenth century, and Van Wyck could have taken it,
directly or indirectly, from any number of his favorite writers—Emerson or Whitman, Carlyle or Ruskin, to name just a few. But Yeats

lived as an example of what had been only a concept. His own personality clarified the abstraction, made it tangibly the basic truth from which other truths inevitably followed. Yeats's personal influence is thus of far greater importance than might be suggested by the relative familiarity of his ideas. Unless we recognize the extent to which Brooks's understanding of that nineteenth-century concept of personality shaped the development of all of his intellectual life, we cannot fully appreciate his later growth as an artist and a critic.

Such was the pattern—the "method"—of Yeats's teaching: Van Wyck found many of his treasured attitudes confirmed in Yeats's personality. The older man cordially hated American materialism and the cult of efficiency, felt it was the duty of the creative artist to cultivate a fruitful idleness, and accepted poverty as an annoying (but not absolutely necessary) condition of artistic freedom. Even his gentlemanly attire and eighteenth-century mannerliness left their mark on Van Wyck. More immediately influential, perhaps: Yeats abhorred Puritanism. In the celebratory biographical sketch he published in *The Freeman* by way of an obituary, Brooks quoted his old teacher's description of the Puritan minister "sitting in company with the father of the family in a sort of horrid conspiracy to poison life at its sources." Again, Brooks's assault upon the Puritan heritage in America antedated his association with Yeats, but he had hitherto discussed Puritanism as an accident of history, and possibly Yeats's anger against the mentality that might have called Hamlet "Mr. Looking-Both-Ways" persuaded him to see in the Puritan a psychological type, an aberration of the human spirit, as he would more consistently in *America's Coming-of-Age* and *The Ordeal of Mark Twain*.

For his part, Yeats responded to a disciple's artless tributes with magnanimous warmth. He was forever demanding Van Wyck's company, and he gave freely of his time and energy for the sake of a friendship that seems to have contributed much to the sense of personal fulfillment he enjoyed during his final years. It was, of course, a special virtue of Van Wyck's own that he could win the respect and companionship of distinguished older men. Yeats painted two portraits of Van Wyck, using the pastels he had taken up since coming to New York, and working, as always, as much for the pleasure of his sitter's company as for the achievement of his art. He never could bring himself to paint for money. Both portraits were done in September 1909, and Van Wyck explained to Eleanor how Yeats had insisted

69

upon a second attempt at his likeness: "The portrait is finished," he wrote. "Max & I (& Mr. Yeats too) were carried away by it: but the next day the dear old man came to my office in the rain, downcast, and said he could not sleep for the melancholy of its failure. He had lost the moment's satisfaction and was in despair. So then he said he had got another canvas and I must sit again. I argued in vain that we must find a sitter more profitable. But he said, No, he knew my face now, and was determined to do it to his own satisfaction."

By 1909 Yeats had developed a compulsive habit of overpainting that spoiled many of his compositions; but he painted "for the noble pleasure of praising," as Van Wyck said, echoing Swinburne, and both portraits are attractive. Francis Biddle was describing the better-known full-faced picture, but his words could be applied to the profile as well, since both show "a dark handsome boy with a straight firm mouth, still looking at that other world from the real one within his heart and mind." Biddle's perceptive sentence is as much a tribute to the artist as his subject, and it suggests something of the power to bring out the best in each other that Yeats and Van Wyck found in their mutually sympathetic relationship.

Van Wyck was happy with his writing during 1909 and 1910. By a stroke of good luck, as he wrote Eleanor, Francis Hackett had agreed to give his material regular space in the literary section of the Chicago *Evening Post*. Van Wyck decided to call his column "Mortal Things," and he was grateful to Hackett for the chance to be exposed to a wide audience. With a little more luck, he thought, his work would catch on elsewhere, and the column might be syndicated. "Mortal Things" ran weekly through much of 1910 as a series of brief personal essays, giving its author his first opportunity to publish many of his long-contemplated observations on nature, art, and society. Written in the wistfully romantic style that haunts all of Van Wyck's work during this period, the series takes much of its character from the fiction of "Storrington," a youthful philosopher recently dead, whose notebooks the author of "Mortal Things" frequently quotes. This device, of course, is the fiction of Graeling (from "What Is America?") renewed. Van Wyck was also to use it in the articles "by Henry Wickford" he wrote for *The Freeman,* and years later it would reappear as the informing fiction of *The Opinions of Oliver Allston.*

Mechanical as it was, the device added to the metaphysical distance from worldly things that Van Wyck deliberately evoked, at least in the earlier work, and it idealized a critical voice that had passed beyond all temptations to compromise with authority. From another point of view, the retreat from direct responsibility might suggest a variant expression of the dreams and hallucinations Van Wyck had reported earlier about a fragmented identity, another instance of his fear that his worldly self could not do justice to the intuitions of the soul. These are, of course, only speculations, and the muted self-destructiveness, even the self-pity, implicit in his narrative fiction may be as well explained by Brooks's own remarks about his romantic allegiance to literary cults of unworldliness and failure. Whatever the case, Brooks was well pleased with his efforts for the *Evening Post,* and he took considerable satisfaction in seeing his essays in print from week to week.

Satisfaction was all he took from "Mortal Things." Hackett was unable to pay for the column, and it soon became obvious that Van Wyck's dreams of syndication were unrealistic. The collapse of these hopes was a serious frustration, since his financial situation had deteriorated further while he was in New York, and he had caught himself up in a self-perpetuating cycle of borrowing and repayment. He had only just staved off one lawsuit, he told Eleanor, and he was forced to avoid several other importunate creditors. He earned enough to marry on, he insisted, but somehow he lost control of money once it was in his hand. He simply could not shake these "nightmarish debts." She would have to manage the finances once they were married. Or would they be married? Van Wyck was no longer sure. Their long separation worried him: California seemed so distant and foreign. He could no longer rely on a fixed income from the dictionary and, what's more, the work was getting on his nerves. Apparently he showed signs of the same violent alternation of moods that had troubled him in London, for John Butler Yeats wrote to him in the autumn of 1911, describing the two Brookses he had known. One Brooks, Yeats said, was "care free, carried hither and thither by varying influences—the most impulsive man I ever knew—then there was Brooks, in misery, with gleams of mad hope. This was your last appearance."

Pressed and confused, Van Wyck took his usual solace in writing. By early 1910 he had begun the only work he was ever to publish in which he examined directly his immediate personal problems. In June of that year he tried out a preliminary version on Mitchell Kennerley, who complimented him on the pamphlet-length manuscript but thought—accurately, as it turned out—that it wouldn't sell fifty copies. Van Wyck revised his work extensively during the remaining months of 1910, and in December Eleanor was happy to hear that he had finished "the little book on yourself." He took the manuscript with him to California early in 1911, and (although the title page is dated 1910) he published at his own expense in San Francisco that March his second book, *The Soul: An Essay Towards a Point of View.* By dedicating it to *"lo mio maestro,"* John Butler Yeats, he acknowledged his debt to Yeats's concept of personality. Although he tried vainly to sell a few copies of his pamphlet and to find an English publisher for it, he was interested chiefly in putting himself on record and in eliciting criticism of his achievement in the relatively unfamiliar genre he had attempted. Arthur Ryder claimed he was unable to understand much of *The Soul,* and John Sloan thought it was beautifully written, although he couldn't make much sense of it. Perhaps Ryder and Sloan didn't read carefully enough. The lyrical structural logic, elliptical compression of thought, and sometimes enigmatic self-analysis of *The Soul* make it difficult, but, considering the elusiveness of the spiritual problem it represents, it is surprisingly free from unnecessary obscurities.

An unabashedly confessional reverie, *The Soul* takes as its subject the problem of consciousness itself. "How does the soul thus become walled about, local, definitely and awkwardly formed?" Brooks asks, troubled by the paradoxical condition in which men are inevitably born to disappointment. It is the law of our nature that "we desire all, all, all," that we yearn to discover by experience an absolute justification for our identity. Yet we are fated to relativism. Even perception exists only as a function of a point of view.

Society is responsible for our frustration, the melancholy voice suggests, echoing a traditional romantic attitude. Society insists that we "be something" and "do something," imposing littleness upon us and dirtying the soul with the fallibilities of the world. It was not always thus. In his last passionate tribute to Catholicism and the medieval past, Brooks posits a lost Europe, an organic community of heaven and earth where science and mysticism were one and men could be simultaneously true to both their practical and their ideal natures. Since that time, he suggests, the increasing compartmentalization of society has forced the idealist to choose between action and contemplation. From this historical vision he derives a discourse on poetry as a "parallel of the soul's history in the midst of life." Defining poetry in Emersonian terms as the radical language inspired by the primordial divinity, bearing power to restore men to their original relationship with the universe, he briefly describes a process of rigidification by which the poet learned of his opportunity to control others through words, became a social officer, and turned his abilities to rhetoric—"the poetry of the social man." In this hopeless condition the soul could aspire only to grasp the fleeting moment of true self-expression as firmly as human art can.

Little of this philosophy originated with Brooks. *The Soul* is rather his reinstitution of the fundamental premises of romanticism, and much of it reads like a brilliant but headstrong paraphrase of Emerson. It is not for its ideas, however, that it is valuable. Its truth lies in the evocation by sensuous images of a deep youthful mood, and in an almost hypnotic imitation of the meditative process by which youth discovers anew the ancient romantic vision of man and nature and art. For the first time, perhaps, Brooks's ambitiously romantic style, shot through with rich figures and portentous rhythms, takes wing, fitted as it is to a subject that is itself romance, and not the social criticism to which he had previously tried to bend it.

The Soul has not been read these sixty years. Only a few scattered copies survive, and the text has never been reprinted in its entirety. Brooks himself is largely responsible for this neglect. Once he had published his lyric reverie, he did his best to forget it, leaving it unmentioned in lists of his publications and suppressing it when he wrote the story of his life. Probably he felt that his book was self-indulgent and revealing, that he had blurted out too many of the secret emotions of immaturity. He should have known himself better. "Truly we cannot be less than tender, serious, and merciful"—this is the moral imperative of *The Soul*.

> To caress life with its little fragile offerings of light, to reject nothing but the fixed forms of half-truths, to learn without cynicism to see through everything as one sees through a crystal, to be in solution, in perpetual readiness, . . . never to think ourselves small because the universe is large, . . . to wait and hope and dream until the whole world has become vibrant with sense and the apparency of things has melted away and we see in everything a connection with everything else, meaning within meaning—surely this, or something like this, might be truth.

IV

TUNING THE FIDDLE:
1911–1914

The publication of *The Soul* must have been among the first matters Van Wyck took up after he arrived in California in February 1911. His trip across his native *terra incognita* had been long planned but many times delayed by distance, money, and his provincial notion that the West was an appendage to the civilization of the Atlantic seaboard. Van Wyck was still looking eastward for the good life, and he may half-consciously have conspired with Eleanor, who was vaguely suggesting that she might return soon to Plainfield, in persuading himself that he should remain in New York. The lovers had developed a private ritual, which kept courtship alive even as it protected them from the need to make decisions. From time to time Van Wyck would hint that he was about to pack up and come to California. Eleanor would promptly find reasons that he stay away. During the winter of 1910–1911, however, it became dramatically clear that if they persisted in their gamesmanship the ritual would itself become the decision. They were, in effect, working themselves free of the engagement to which they had tenaciously clung for several lonely years. The many obstacles to their marriage had suddenly coalesced, creating a single desperate situation, and Van Wyck had rushed westward to see the crisis through.

In 1911 Eleanor Kenyon Stimson was fresh and pretty, a full-faced young woman with a shy, thoughtful smile, but beneath the demure femininity she owed to her time and station lay self-reliance, intelligence, and an understanding of worldly realities that was far beyond the reach of her forever idealizing lover. She had traveled widely with her parents in both the United States and Europe, and the propriety of her upbringing had in many ways sheltered her less than Van Wyck's had him. For a well-bred young lady from Plainfield she had developed unusually forthright habits of freethinking. Without any sense of irony, she could point out to Van Wyck in 1907, "I *am* fundamentally a radical, as you are fundamentally a conservatist," and her politics were, in fact, consistently further leftward than his, even though her idea of domesticity remained sternly old-fashioned.

In some ways theirs was an improbable romance, a rare conjunction of earth and fire, but the feeling Van Wyck and Eleanor shared for each other was rooted deep. These handsome, talented young people had known each other, as Van Wyck later told S. K. Ratcliffe, from the time that they were of kindergarten age, and they had spent much of their childhood together. When they grew too mature to consider themselves playmates, they decided that they were in love, and they considered themselves engaged when Van Wyck was sixteen. By then, Eleanor was away at Wellesley, and for some nine years thereafter they had only a few scattered opportunities to keep company. Predictably, however, their long separations rather enhanced than discouraged their feelings. Eleanor was surely not exaggerating when she wrote to Van Wyck in 1910, "To me *marriage* has always meant you, *man* has always meant you." To Van Wyck, of course, Eleanor was all womankind, the focal point of his idealizing impulses.

But by the fall of 1910 the sheer duration of physical absence was beginning to take its toll. The lovers had scarcely seen each other in almost three years, and as memories dimmed, Eleanor's reservations about Van Wyck's financial incapacity, Catholicism, and general otherworldliness became increasingly serious. Such doubts were encouraged by her mother, whose husband, John Ward Stimson, a poet, painter, and teacher of note, had several years earlier gone his own way, leaving her to shift for herself and her children on a limited income. Mrs. Stimson was understandably reluctant to welcome another bohemian into the family, and while they lived on the Continent she did her best to interest Eleanor in the eminently suitable young men who were to be encountered at the balls and dinners that occupied the American social calendar. Under such pressures, from her family and from Van Wyck, whose demands for an immediate marriage were becoming increasingly importunate, Eleanor's confidence faltered. In September 1910 she sent Van Wyck a desperate letter, begging, in effect, that he release her from her obligation to him.

This moment of panic quickly passed. By early December Eleanor was cheerfully writing again about the possibility of a summer wedding. But later that month Ralph Wescott, an old acquaintance, appeared in Berkeley and began an intense, persuasive courtship. Eleanor had always enjoyed her mastery of the flirtations that enlivened an otherwise monotonous social routine, but she wasn't able to hold off Wescott, who had been her brother Frank's roommate at Yale and whose attentions were vigorously seconded by Mrs. Stimson. She thought she had betrayed her trust when she found herself attracted to this darkly handsome, good-natured young man who gave promise of becoming (as he did) a successful attorney. Van Wyck announced he was coming in March after she blurted out her predicament to him, and Eleanor, who was dangerously close to being engaged to both men at once, probably could not have long withstood a determined assault upon her emotions by either suitor. Mrs. Stimson urged just such an assault upon Wescott, but he seems to have sensed, and respected, Eleanor's confusion. He left California after a few weeks, perhaps at her request that he give her more time to think things over. Eleanor wrote in a similar vein to Van Wyck in late January, telling him that he absolutely must not come west, and that nothing could be decided until she returned to Plainfield.

One day that February Van Wyck called on Jack Wheelock in some agitation to tell him about the uncomfortable situation in California. Mrs. Stimson was pressing for a decision in favor of Wescott, and Eleanor was at her wit's end. Van Wyck, Wheelock remembered, had already decided what he must do. "I'm going to buy a new necktie," he said, "this one looks a little shabby. I'm going to borrow some money and I'm going to take the first train to California." He prevailed on Ned Sheldon for $2000, made the necessary addition to his wardrobe, and departed immediately on the long journey across the American hinterlands to the Pacific Coast—only to find, when he arrived in Berkeley, that the Stimsons had moved some ninety miles south to the seaside village of Carmel. For the moment outflanked, Van Wyck contented himself with tactful letters and an occasional afternoon's visit. Much of his enforced leisure in Berkeley was given to attempts to find a teaching position for the following autumn at the University of California. He counted heavily on the influence of Arthur Ryder and Irving Babbitt to make a way for him there.

Although his plans for a lightning campaign were at first discouraged by Mrs. Stimson, she soon weakened to the extent of forbidding only "urging" letters. Van Wyck was deferential but relentless. Eleanor, nervous, was thrown back upon trivial practical objections. She stalled, conjuring up worries about what Plainfield would think about his trip to California. Van Wyck persisted; Eleanor stammered and hedged. The decision so long postponed became almost impossible to make, and for all of Van Wyck's aggressive confidence the matter was apparently unsettled until the very last moment. I found among family correspondence from that time an undated, hurriedly penciled note from Eleanor addressed simply to "Mr. Brooks." "I *can't* let you go," it reads. "Come back and we'll get the license today and be married tomorrow." It must have been a difficult two months for everyone concerned, but despite the bridegroom's lack of work, of prospects for work, of money itself, Van Wyck married his Eleanor on April 26, 1911, in Carmel, California. For their honeymoon the newlyweds went camping—sleeping on the ground without tents, as John Butler Yeats put it—and while it was a far cry from the grand tour of Italy Van Wyck had long planned, we can guess that their wedding journey was a happy one.

With his marriage Van Wyck entered upon a period of quiet happiness. Setting up housekeeping with Eleanor, he discovered that his commitment to her and her values displaced much of his old, frightening attraction to Catholicism. Money still was and would be a problem, but now it was simply another difficulty, no longer the maddeningly elusive secret that would determine an entire future. And, of course, marriage relieved the sexual tensions which for years had exacerbated his other worries. The distressing fluctuations of mood and visionary eruptions which had haunted Van Wyck in London and New York seem to have disappeared altogether for at least the next seven years, and his intimate life with Eleanor passed, so far as I can tell, rewardingly and uneventfully. " 'Of all blessings, which ever fall to the lot of men,' " Van Wyck wrote to her many years later, quoting George Bancroft, " 'a virtuous and affectionate wife is the one most highly to be valued.' " "And," he went on in his own voice, "if you think I don't value you, you should have a good look into my palpitating innards. . . . For the more I read about other men and their wives, or lack of them, and the more I see them in reality, the more I am convinced that I drew the first prize on April 26th, 1911."

In the fall of 1911 Van Wyck began teaching at Stanford University, but only after he had endured a nerve-racking struggle to find a job. The post at Berkeley on which he had counted heavily seemed at first assured, but fell through almost at the last moment, when the university budget precluded his appointment. He was forced to look around hurriedly for openings among secondary schools in the San Francisco Bay area and at other Western universities. He even thought that a year in Missoula at the University of Montana would be tolerable, if only Eleanor could be with him. As it turned out, he was spared such improbable pioneering when he was appointed to an instructorship at the rapidly growing new university at Palo Alto on the San Francisco peninsula, where he would teach the usual courses in composition and surveys of English and American literature. His success at Stanford was due in part to the efforts of Dean Briggs, whose aid Van Wyck had enlisted even before leaving New York, but it was probably more the work of Mrs. Stimson, who was an old friend of Mrs. David Starr Jordan, the wife of Stanford's president.

Only one incident comes down from those years before World War I to give us a glimpse into the Brookses' domestic privacy. On a rainy night in February 1912 two young women from the university appeared at Van Wyck's door to call upon Eleanor, a courtesy customarily extended to the wives of new faculty members. Van Wyck answered the knock, mumbled, yes Mrs. Brooks was at home, but occupied at the moment, and invited them in. They sat, tried to make conversation, and waited for their pale, nervous young professor to go off and summon his wife. He sat and seemed not to listen. The atmosphere became strained. Young and perhaps a bit intimidated by Mr. Brooks's formal reserve, the girls did not know how to leave without appearing rude. Finally they were rescued by a woman, perhaps Mrs. Stimson, who whispered something to Van Wyck that sent him scurrying from the room. She told the visitors that Mrs. Brooks was not feeling well. It was not until the next morning that the mystery was explained, when the girls learned that the Brookses had a new son, a healthy baby who was welcomed into the family with the name of Charles Van Wyck.

Van Wyck prospered in other matters as well. Although it is perhaps surprising that the famous president of an important university would pay much attention to one of his obscure junior instructors, David Starr Jordan and Van Wyck soon were getting along remarkably well, and their friendship was clearly built upon more than the social influence of Mrs. Stimson. Jordan demonstrated his respect for the younger man later, when he prevailed upon him to act as his secretary during an important pacifist lecture tour through Britain in 1913, and by writing long personal letters after Van Wyck left Stanford, urging him to return to his work there. The letter of recommendation he sent in support of Van Wyck's application to Brown University in 1915 is revealing: "To me," Jordan assured W. H. P. Faunce, who had expressed reservations about the stability of creative types, "Mr. Van Wyck Brooks, is a very lovely as well as a monstrously clever man. He is small in stature, whittled to a point; has a charming disposition, writes excellent English, has a delightful wife, and looks upon life as a place of many adventures in an analytical sense. As to morals and habits, he is above reproach. . . . He is not eccentric, he is modest and wholesome looking, and maintains no strange notions, except that he has remarkably keen insight. I believe he is a genius. . . ."

For his part Van Wyck reciprocated Jordan's good will, describing the sometimes controversial president in his autobiography as a man who was essentially too good for his job. Their mutual regard must have been entertained under some difficulty, for Jordan was proud of his Puritan ancestry and remained hostile to alcohol, tobacco, coffee, dancing—frivolity in general—and dedicated to leading the Stanford community toward that same rigorous morality. When he told Faunce that Van Wyck was above reproach in morals and habits, he paid his anti-Puritanical young friend a rare compliment. Despite his narrow idea of morality and his blatantly racist theories of Anglo-Saxon destiny, Jordan was characteristically gentle in his dealings with others and inclined toward a much greater tolerance in practice than his beliefs might suggest. Most of all, Van Wyck admired the burly scholar for the "naivety" of his efforts to build a better world and because "he was by nature a dreamer"—qualities which were irrelevant to Jordan's theory of ethics but central to Van Wyck's own.

Van Wyck made other friends among the academicians at Stanford, most notably Hans Zinsser, the bacteriologist, who would later help him to survive his most difficult years, but he found more congenial the lively atmosphere of the small radical community which had formed on the fringes of the university. The metropolitan area around San Francisco was unusually rich in progressive and revolutionary activity and boasted already a tradition of sophisticated hospitality to radical dissent that would have had the militia on the streets in most parts of the United States. Stanford itself was at least as tolerant of political nonconformity as other major American universities. Although Jordan had acquiesced under financial pressure to Mrs. Stanford's demands that Professor Edward A. Ross be discharged because of his socialist beliefs, the president earnestly believed in the free dissemination of ideas and was more inclined to protect than discourage the expression of unpopular opinions. Consequently, a number of both native and foreign radicals had found places on the Stanford faculty.

Van Wyck himself seems to have been only vicariously involved in radical activity. As far as I can tell he remained uncommitted to any political organization until he joined the Socialist Party of New York in February 1916, and probably his radicalism at Stanford was limited to long evenings of talk and the development of his theories about the mutually reinforcing functions of utopian politics and literature. One of the men with whom he may have talked most enthusiastically was Max Lippitt (known then as Max Larkin), a cynical Russian émigré who taught economics at Stanford. Lippitt was a Social Democrat who had been forced to leave Russia after the uprisings of 1905, and he may have been the source of much of what Van Wyck knew and believed about practical socialism—or so the dedication to Lippitt of *The World of H. G. Wells* would suggest. Van Wyck would also have found good conversations going at the socialist local in Palo Alto, where he heard several of the famous revolutionaries of the day, including "Big Bill" Haywood, the legendary one-eyed roughneck who led the most famous battles of the Industrial Workers of the World (I.W.W.). Probably the best indication of Van Wyck's stance at that time is to be found in his own letter to an unsympathetic correspondent concerning the presidential elections of 1912. He could vote for neither Wilson nor Roosevelt, he said, because "there is little choice between the orthodox candidates nor will [there] be so long as philanthropy is the only thing demanded of capitalism and financial rearrangement remains the chief work of legislation. Also I do not believe in 'stemming' popular movements; which can only be stemmed by accepting in moderate form the very principles of the movement itself and hence acknowledging their legitimacy. Socialism is only incidentally a body of doctrine. You may destroy its intellectual basis but you cannot prevent the union of politics with sociology and with poetry." No doubt his vote was among the 900,000 that went to Eugene Debs that autumn.

Of all his radical friends in California, he seems to have enjoyed most Har Dayal, a fanatical Indian nationalist who taught philosophy at Stanford, but only to disguise his revolutionary activities in Berkeley and San Francisco. Although Dayal was genuinely committed to Indian independence, he embraced the asceticism of the revolutionary more for its own sake than as the means to an end, and it is not entirely ironic that he died almost immediately upon learning in 1938 that he was at last free to return home. Since he was already notorious for both his zeal and his ability when Van Wyck met him, the dangers Dayal paranoically felt lurking on all sides were often real dangers, but he practiced his elaborate mystifications and circumventions more for the fun of the game than as a method of self-protection. At least it is hard to believe that an Indian disguising himself as a certain "Israel Aaronson" would have fooled many people in Holland during World War I. For years he kept letters coming to Van Wyck from all over Europe, continually requesting speeches and other services to the cause and lecturing his moderate comrade on the responsibility of the intellectual. In 1915 he pleaded with Van Wyck to go to India as an ostensible correspondent or lecturer—apparently as part of his nationalist Ghadr conspiracy, which, in collaboration with German agents, was the most serious threat raised against British rule in Asia during World War I.

Van Wyck never took Dayal fully seriously, but he admired the Indian's dedication to the romance of revolution and was drawn to the personality of the man himself. In return Dayal made Van Wyck a rare exception to his rule of refusing friendship with men who did not accept his inflexible ideology. When Dayal's propagandistic and organizational activity in California became so flagrantly illegal that it could no longer be ignored he was discharged from Stanford, arrested shortly thereafter as an "undesirable alien," and faced with extradition to India—apparently in connection with a bombing in Delhi, among other charges. He was probably the "Indian friend" for whom Van Wyck tried to intercede in 1914, but by that time Dayal had already jumped bail and made his way to Geneva. After the war his nationalistic program mellowed dramatically as he turned to theories of reform and education, but Van Wyck always remembered Har Dayal best as the elegantly loquacious firebrand who introduced him to the world of the professional revolutionist, enlivening those generally quiet days when they were young together at Stanford.

Van Wyck soon discovered that teaching itself weighed heavily upon his time and energy. He believed that he was fully alive only when he was writing, and he was then at work on three books at once. Furthermore, Van Wyck was not the ideal instructor for a Western university in 1911. Shy as ever, he had the misfortune to prefer flowered waistcoats, inspiring hilarity among the young yahoos in his classroom, which seemed always to be hopelessly out of control. His students resented his uncompromising approach to his subject and the "Eastern" quality of his voice, and complained that they were unable to understand him. (Someone in London had once told Van Wyck that he spoke "American with a strong English accent.") "The behavior of the boys in his class was unspeakable," one of his former students remembered. "About ten minutes before dismissal, they shuffled their feet on the floor, making such a noise that in desperation, he would dismiss the class."

Faced with the hellish possibility of teaching generations of such students, Van Wyck responded eagerly when Alfred Zimmern, a socialistic English scholar, educator, and political theorist, arrived at Stanford with a letter of introduction from Eric Bell at Petitpas' and much enthusiastic talk about the possibilities of working in the new Worker's Educational Association, which he was organizing as part of a British governmental program. The socialism of Zimmern's proposal appealed to Van Wyck, as did the probability of finding a responsive audience among Englishmen, and he applied for, and received, a leave of absence from Stanford that took effect before the spring term of 1913. One wonders how Eleanor felt as Van Wyck happily prepared himself for his new voyage eastward. Clearly, marriage had yet to dull his impulsiveness. It is a tribute to both her toughness and her spirit of adventure that she was willing to make such a drastic move with a child less than two years old, for Van Wyck had agreed to leave the United States without any assurances that he would have his job once he got to England.

The Brookses probably started from California for the East Coast

in the early spring of 1913 and passed a month or two in Plainfield before departing for England that June. Once arrived, Van Wyck's first
move was to obtain comfortable lodgings for Eleanor on the Isle of
Wight, where she spent the summer with Charles, while he tried to secure his position with the W.E.A. and attended with Zimmern a summer conference of educators at New College in Oxford. Although he
described his week at the old university with some irony in his autobiography, his letters to Eleanor from that time are almost childlike in
their pleasure with the demure pace and venerable academic rituals of
Oxford life. For once his plans did not fall through. He was examined
as to his qualifications to teach the course on the Victorian essayists he
had proposed to the W.E.A. and was eventually offered a position at
South Norwood, a few miles outside of London. His contract was to
run from October 1913 to April 1914 and paid the less than princely,
but apparently adequate, salary of sixty pounds for the term.

Teaching in England, Van Wyck quickly decided, was both challenging and pleasant. His students were mature, eager to learn, invariably courteous—and by all indications he was infinitely more successful with them than he had been among the red-bloods at Stanford.
More important, his responsibility for only a single course permitted
him to work at his writing, while leaving ample time to resume the leisurely social life he had enjoyed in London earlier. Stanley Edwards
still had headquarters at Roche's, sallying forth to raid the bookstalls
or to stroll through the streets like Sir Roger De Coverley, openly
commenting upon the passersby, and Van Wyck promised Eleanor
that the old bohemian was to be one of their great friends, "not nearly
so distinguished as Mr. Yeats, but in a sense perhaps more human."
Van Wyck was soon also drawn to the group of predominantly leftist
intellectuals who gathered informally at the small Soho bookstore run
by Daniel J. Rider, an active socialist who was happier talking about
books than selling them, and who served the bohemian community
also as an editor and publisher.

The artists and writers Van Wyck encountered at Rider's shop
made up a nice cross section of London intellectual life. He met there
several aging aesthetes from the days of *The Yellow Book* and eccentric
personalities from all of intellectual Europe, as well as the renegade
American Frank Harris, the energetic young political theorist Walter
Lippmann, and Jo Davidson, the sculptor whose friendship was to be
one of the joys of his later years. Another American who later drew

close to Brooks, the poet John Gould Fletcher, was first encountered in a nearby restaurant. With Dan Rider himself Van Wyck quickly struck up a warm comradeship that seems to have been based originally on a common interest in Henri Amiel's *Journal.* Rider—so he remembered in a letter to Brooks of 1943—had grown accustomed to thinking of himself as the lonely devotee in England of the French critic, and he was delighted to run across a similar enthusiasm in the young American, who that summer was finishing up his discussion of Amiel for *The Malady of the Ideal,* the expressionistic critical study brought out by Arthur Fifield in the autumn.

In the introductory section of *The Malady of the Ideal* Brooks restated the familiar conflict of life and art that troubled him throughout his early years. Social order, a creation of intellect, was opposed to universal order, known by intuition—a disharmony of human life attended by a parallel opposition of form (rhetoric) and truth (poetry). The artist, he thought, must compromise between the two orders if he is to make intelligible to others his apprehension of universality and the individual personality created by it—that is, the act of translating truth into form must necessarily adulterate truth. The "malady" of the title arises from the incapacity of men obsessed with universal ideality to function in terms of the social and practical. Some rare souls, perhaps the most advanced human types, could not bring themselves to collaborate with the social institution of form, thus living on in weariness of spirit, frustrated and inarticulate in this world. Their peculiar "form" is the journal, "shaped" according to their alogical perceptions of a truth which is beyond art.

To this thesis Brooks brings the example of three French writers of the nineteenth century—Etienne De Sénancour, Maurice De Guérin, and Henri Amiel. Justifying his biographical approach with the observation that "it is only by the study of personality that we can understand the obstructions that exist in the world and the methods of removing them," he analyzes their particular "maladies" according to their nationalities and philosophies—especially their conflicts of science and religion, Catholicism and Protestantism. Each writer is somehow betrayed by his heritage, that common problem of men confronting fragmented traditions, which is best displayed, Brooks feels, by the French culture in which all expressions of the spirit, including religion itself, are conceived "almost solely as an adjunct to the social order."

Brooks pursued further such explanations for failure in *John Add-*

ington Symonds, which, published by Mitchell Kennerley in 1914, followed closely upon *The Malady of the Ideal.* This time he sought to explain spiritual tragedy by the scholarly use of biographical detail instead of the intuitive narrative empathy which characterized the lyrical earlier book. As Brooks conceived him, Symonds was potentially a more rewarding subject than the French writers, since he had made the compromise necessary to literature and continued to struggle with his problem of creativity as long as he lived. Two aspects of Symonds's career prefigure with startling accuracy developments in Van Wyck's own: the discovery of Walt Whitman, not as a true influence or model, or even as a figure completely understood, but as a principle of health; and his passing through what Brooks describes as a sort of Dark Night of the Soul, the period of insane despondency that precedes mystical conversion. In more familiar terms, Symonds suffered a nervous breakdown. The various pressures on him "had turned him from art to aesthetics. The speculative element of aesthetics had gradually pursued its course, draining the imagination, the nerves, the will until it had reached its logical climax and put the last question to life." This descent into the caverns of the self, Brooks argued, was the only possible "cure" for the malady of the ideal. It permitted Symonds to do substantial work, as Amiel, who had never risen to a similarly restorative crisis, could not.

Brooks made the connection between his psycho-aesthetic interests and his socialism most clearly in one of the theoretical pieces he published during this period—"The Twilight of the Arts," an essay almost shockingly modernistic in its invocation of what amounts to an anti-art. This excellent little study restates the problems of the artist already discussed, and it describes the purpose of social reform as a reconciliation of the world-economy with the universe-economy, a spiritual utopianism to be achieved in part by eliminating the middle class. In literary terms it is a matter of creating by the indirect process of institutional reform an audience responsive to the highest artistry, so that rhetoric, which is only *"political economy masking itself as the ideal,"* would be effectively abolished. Under those circumstances, art might finally become the unqualified expression of life, no longer a self-consciously distinct *kind* of activity. Art would, in a word, annihilate itself.

Van Wyck was finishing all of this work at the same time that he taught his course in the W.E.A., enjoyed hugely his return to English life, and became more deeply involved in socialism. He saw much of

85

Walter Lippmann, who invited him to become a regular contributor to an ambitious journal, *The New Republic,* that he and some friends were launching in New York, and to whom Van Wyck talked excitedly about a new book on America which was just beginning to catch hold of his imagination. "Lippmann makes a great impression on me," Van Wyck wrote to Eleanor on the Isle of Wight, "—very young & attractive—full of splendid ideas. You feel he is a really big man and bound to have some sort of remarkable future." He also met, perhaps through Lippmann, S. K. Ratcliffe, an English socialist with whom he maintained a long epistolary friendship, and he spent much of his free time attending the open debates on governmental policy that reflected something of the impression socialism had made on public life in Britain. Zimmern's success with the W.E.A., Van Wyck thought, was itself an example of the capacity of English institutions to be reformed according to the suggestions of their intellectuals. Nevertheless, although England was in this respect far ahead of America, he soon found himself out of sorts with the brand of socialism he found there. "Liberalism is doing most of the things—the tangible things—that socialism set out to do," he complained to Eleanor. "It is the most disconcerting thing imaginable to see socialism in *esse* & having precisely the opposite effect one dreams of."

As part of his personal contribution to the socialistic cause, he crossed to Brittany in the summer of 1914, taking lodgings in the village of St. Jean du Doigt long enough to finish *The World of H. G. Wells,* which Mitchell Kennerley published in 1915. Before World War I, Wells was regarded by young intellectuals everywhere as a major social prophet. Brooks's study used his speculative fictions as a point of departure for what was essentially a long monograph on the nature of socialism. Although it is perhaps the weakest of Van Wyck's early books, *The World of H. G. Wells* is a fortunate biographical document, since it represents his only attempt to map out the idea of social order which underlay his entire life's work.

Van Wyck's socialism was less a theory of political or economic structure than a metaphor for a complex of ethical beliefs about the nature of man, society, and history. It was neither orthodox nor complicated, and it owed little, if anything, to Marx or other nineteenth-century philosophers of communalism. In fact, he could scarcely have subscribed to any theory that defined socialism precisely, since he saw it essentially as the moral stance with which one responded to a constantly changing world, and as itself a part of the evolutionary process of social growth. That is, the meaning of socialism waited only at the end of the socialistic process; it could not be abstracted in some theoretically correct form by purifying or balancing the various expressions of contemporaneous socialistic thought.

To the degree that one can abstract Brooks's doctrine from what was basically an agreement with emotion, he believed that man was in essence good, capable of his own salvation, and that if the self-aggrandizement he had mistakenly built into his institutions were put under control, he would naturally live harmoniously with others. Once the economic institution, in particular, was subsumed by the state, abolishing extremes of both poverty and affluence, men would be freed from the necessity of devoting their best energies to the competition for money (that is, a "living") so that they could let their individual personalities develop. Such a program, if it can be called that, presumed no necessity for political revolution, and Van Wyck, often personally sympathetic to revolutionaries and their causes, himself never practiced or endorsed coercive action against the political structure. That would be wasteful behavior, he thought. The restructuring of political institutions, at least in nations with a working tradition of democracy, was extraneous to the real mission of socialists, who need only break down those barriers—primarily the apparatus of capitalism—that kept the process of evolutionary growth from taking its natural way with history. Over the years Van Wyck meditated upon these rudimentary ideas, extended them, elaborated upon them, mined them for their every implication, but he never systematized them fully, nor did he change them.

Despite his reservations about Wells's cruel manipulation of his characters, Brooks read his fiction with high seriousness, as the work of the prophet of the socialist millennium. Like socialism itself, Brooks suggested, Wells's vision could scarcely be true to the present but might very well be true to the future. Furthermore, in a somewhat startling final chapter, Brooks asserted that in H. G. Wells was to be found the essential spirit of America. The naked intellectualism of the English writer, his atraditional stance, his ability to build upon abstract ideas convincing models of worlds that might come: all seemed to Brooks typical of the character of his own country, where radical change was more to be anticipated than was a logical continuity of life. Like all of his discourse on socialism in *The World of H. G. Wells,* that last is precariously ingenious, far removed from his ostensible subject. Wells himself told Brooks many years later that his book had been "young and unwise." Brooks could not contradict him, and no one else has cared to try.

"I am a convinced socialist," Van Wyck wrote in 1915, "but I believe that the terms of socialism will have to be fundamentally and coherently restated before the word can regain the effectiveness which it possessed a generation ago. Let me add that though I believe in the humanitarian mission of socialism, my own angle of approach is not humanitarian but personal. I consider individualism the very worst enemy of personality. So long as people's minds are set on 'enterprise' and money-grabbing they will continue to have—as the typical business man of to-day has—a convenient, stereotyped, inexpressive, inexperiencing outlook on life."

As he worked on his book in the quiet seaside town of St. Jean du Doigt that summer of 1914, Brooks was planning to return for another year of teaching in the Worker's Educational Association. But the world changed in August. War unexpectedly broke out in Europe, and the Brookses were forced to make an anxious, difficult return trip, several times delayed by lack of transportation, through bureaucratic and military lines to England. Back in London, Van Wyck discovered that government funds for the W.E.A. had been diverted to mobilization, and he had no choice but to return to the United States. He came home now with a mission to rescue his culture to which he had been summoned by Walter Lippmann earlier that year. "And oh, the lack of irony, the lack of that flavor which turns knowledge into wisdom, that fearful unmitigated adolescence—slay it for us. Please do." And he had with him the manuscript, finally completed, of his new study of America. He knew he had written it well—Lippmann's comments would have convinced him of that—but he could not have guessed, as he sailed westward again, how instrumental it was to be in changing the America of artists and thinkers that he knew.

PART II

AN AMERICAN PROPHET
1915–1931

Be sure of this, Brooks. No matter how much you may seem to yourself to work in isolation, it is not true. Your voice always comes clear to me and will to some others. You have been the bearer of a lamp that has illuminated many a dark place for me.

—SHERWOOD ANDERSON TO VAN WYCK BROOKS,
December 1919

V

THE PRECIPITANT: NEW YORK, 1915

After a winter in Plainfield, Van Wyck decided to stay in New York rather than go back to his instructorship at Stanford. In spite of the uncomfortable prospect of living near his mother, since 1911 Mrs. Henry Hibbard, and Ames, who was well established in his Manhattan law firm, it could not have been a particularly agonizing decision. He had learned to be wary of the casual society and luxurious climate of California, where, he felt, a writer might too easily succumb to the murmur of waves and the spectacular beauty of the coastal wilderness. More important, literary New York was itself a more attractive place than the professionally closed, hierarchical city he had left five years earlier. Not only was Mr. Yeats still holding forth at Petitpas', but a large colony of artists and intellectuals was thriving farther downtown in Greenwich Village, and the entire island of Manhattan, or so it seemed, was coming alive with the ideas and movements of the twentieth century. Emboldened by his success in the Worker's Educational Association, Van Wyck applied for teaching appointments at least to Columbia and Brown universities and offered a course of fifteen lectures on world literature in the Bookseller's School B. W. Huebsch had organized through the Y.M.C.A. After a few months in a furnished room, while Eleanor boarded on Long Island, Van Wyck leased an apartment on West 118th Street, where the Brookses settled in, as it were, to grow up with an era.

In 1915 New York was still dominated culturally by the patriarchs of the Confident Years, but the city was about to become the intellectual center of a new radicalism as well. A self-consciously generational rebellion against Victorian morality, capitalism, the middle class, and bland realism in the arts had infected young people all over the country, making "Young America" a catchword and a battle cry, to rouse the sluggardly and shock the old. Although it spread with surprising rapidity, this genuinely national uprising had not broken out overnight. It found its spiritual ancestry in the native traditions of Walt Whitman, the naturalistic novelists, and the muckrakers, whose time was just winding down. But it was new, dramatically so, for its outright hostility to the older generation and its works, and it introduced to American life the idea of a cultural "underground."

The younger generation had already found significant voice a few years earlier, when, inspired in part by such older men as Theodore Dreiser and William Vaughn Moody, Midwestern regionalists had banded together in spirit to assert their democratic modernism. Young writers from throughout the central United States flocked to the newspapers and journals of Chicago and made that city, as H. L. Mencken thought, the literary capital of America. Whether or not one honors Mencken's typically institutional metaphor, Chicago was, just before World War I, the most self-consciously native of American cities and the center of a widespread intellectual insurgency. The unmistakably American idiom of the Chicago Renaissance remained for more than a decade synonymous with all that was new and best in national art, but by 1915 momentum had gradually shifted to New York City. Dreiser had moved to Manhattan early, as Ring Lardner and, for a while, Sherwood Anderson did later. Francis Hackett left the Chicago *Evening Post* to try his luck back east in 1911, and within two years the barometric Floyd Dell followed him, settling in Greenwich Village to become the social and sexual apologist for that exotic community. Margaret Anderson was to relocate her *Little Review* from Chicago to New York in 1917. The influx from Chicago typified a great migration of intellectuals from every region of the United States. Enthusiastic young people began to form small, intense artistic colonies wherever rents were cheapest. And so Van Wyck found the city in 1915—"fermenting," as he described it later, with new ideas and cheerful hopes for the future. The Great War which was already plunging Europe into moral gloom had not yet made its emotional shock felt in the United States, and the general mood among intellectuals was still reflected accurately by the optimistic progressivism Brooks had chronicled in *The World of H. G. Wells.*

In 1913 two great spectacles had brought to New York both the shocking modernity of the twentieth century and the newly militant alliance of art and politics. That February an international exhibition of postimpressionistic painting and sculpture opened at the armory of the 69th Cavalry Regiment, where crowds of alternately interested, puzzled, and outraged citizens gathered to stare at the work of their most advanced contemporaries. The Armory Show brought modern painting for the first time to a growing American audience. It encouraged young artists to be daring and made worth while the efforts of such patrons as George Quinn and such critics as Walter Pach. Mabel Dodge's essay on Gertrude Stein, a supplement to the display of visual artifacts, opened an important line of literary influence. A sort of cultural baptism by total immersion, the Armory Show remains probably the single most important artistic event of the American twentieth century.

Even more disturbing to that majority of Americans who wished to feel secure in the traditional order were the masses of workers from the silk mills of Paterson, New Jersey, who in June, angered by the dishonesty of the press, moved into Madison Square Garden to reenact the events of their cruelly long strike. The Paterson Pageant, as it came to be known, was organized on a heroic scale by John Reed, with help from Mabel Dodge, the writer Ernest Poole, and Dolly Sloan, among other members of the intellectual community downtown. Allied with the bohemians toward whom they usually expressed contempt, the leaders of the striking Industrial Workers of the World—Big Bill Haywood, Carlo Tresca, Arturo Giovannitti, and the diminutive but explosive "Rebel Girl," Elizabeth Gurley Flynn—were on hand to recreate their own roles in the strike and to lead the workers on a dramatic march through the streets to their huge auditorium. The men and women of Paterson sang their songs and enacted their history with a dignified naïveté that by all accounts touched even the idly curious and the mockers in the audience. A rare triumph of art *by* the proletariat, the pageant allowed cultural and economic radicals, at least for the moment, a chance to join their considerable forces in a mutually satisfactory method of approaching complementary goals.

The Armory Show soon went on the road, and the pageant of the Paterson silkworkers, whose strike was ultimately crushed, passed into history after a day, but these sensational rebellions were only the most dramatic expressions of a widespread activity that was changing the cultural institutions of New York. The artistic insurgence was sustained by an important group that gathered regularly at "291," the loft on Fifth Avenue where Alfred Stieglitz had studios and from which he issued his seminal quarterly, *Camera Work.* The Armory Show was in a sense the first culminative triumph of Stieglitz's pioneering work. At one time or another during his long career he influenced, or helped to establish, such American artists as Arthur Dove, Marsden Hartley, Charles Demuth, Gaston Lachaise, Max Weber, and John Marin, as well as a number of writers, among them William Carlos Williams, Waldo Frank, Hart Crane, Alfred Kreymborg, and Sherwood Anderson. Stieglitz in 1915 was already a weathered veteran of the cultural revolution, a power in European as in American intellectual life. More than any other person he made New York dynamically part of the international scene, even as he provided an unyielding center about which the various intellectual currents of the city swirled.

Stieglitz's influence was complemented by that of two important political journals which began publication in New York just before World War I. *The Masses* had first appeared in 1911 as a fiercely Marxist paper, locked in its own dogma and groping for an audience until Max Eastman took over the editorship in December 1912. Under Eastman and, later, Floyd Dell, who became an editor and the only paid employee in 1913, the magazine assumed a playfully feisty tone and spread its influence far beyond the doctrinaire left wing. Until it was suppressed by the government in 1917, it was distinguished for its satiric assaults on capitalism and the follies of the bourgeoisie, the excellence of its book reviewing, and especially its imaginative visual quality—the achievement of an editorial board that included George Bellows, John Sloan, Boardman Robinson, and the cartoonist Art Young. Literary contributors to *The Masses* were an equally distinguished lot, permitted eccentricities of ideology so long as their work was good, and the magazine published many of the better new writers of the day—including John Reed, Claude McKay, Ernest Poole, Sherwood Anderson, Carl Sandburg, and Upton Sinclair.

Politically more moderate, "socialistic in direction, but not in method," *The New Republic* started weekly publication in 1914. Herbert Croly, an influential liberal theorist, was general editor, while Walter Lippmann and Francis Hackett headed strong political and literary departments. On the advice of the historian Charles Beard, Croly also hired an acidulous young essayist named Randolph Bourne, fresh from Columbia and the *Atlantic Monthly,* guaranteed him a thousand dollars a year, and soon discovered that there was no real place for him on the magazine. Bourne was at his best writing about literature or politics, but Hackett and Lippmann held those subjects under a sort of territorial privilege, and he was usually restricted to articles about education. Despite his tendency to hover, as it were, just off of the paper's center, Bourne was clearly one of the chief reasons that *The New Republic* quickly became a leading journal for the young.

The Masses and *The New Republic* were among the foremost expressions of the action that was breaking out along what a subsequent generation of radicals might have called a cultural "front." In 1915 Thorstein Veblen was the economist for the young intelligentsia, as Sigmund Freud was its priest and Isadora Duncan, splendidly pagan, its dancer. Already famous for art and scandal, Miss Duncan had also become, as a representative of the new feminism, the unlikely moral ally of the anarchists Emma Goldman and Elizabeth Gurley Flynn. H. L. Mencken was launching his first attacks on the Puritan, the Professor, and the Boob from the pages of *The Smart Set,* and John Macy had opened the way to a rediscovery of native values with his pioneering study, *The Spirit of American Literature* (1913).

Greenwich Village itself was a pristine Bohemia, European in flavor and population, where rents were cheap and the local curiosities as yet undiscovered by the smart people uptown. This was Floyd Dell's Greenwich Village, now in its halcyon days, when Dadaists might picnic atop the Washington Square Arch, or Harry Kemp absentmindedly recognize aloud the nude body of a recent bedmate in a painting her husband was exhibiting at the Armory Show. Artists and thinkers could satisfy their dreams of the Left Bank in Greenwich Village— could live there a wildly uninhibited or a rigidly disciplined life, or, more often, simply a pleasant one, gathering, perhaps, for supper and talk at Polly's Restaurant on MacDougal Street, where the legendary Hippolyte Havel, the spiritual father of the New York waiter, addressed his customers as "bourgeois pigs." In the evenings, restless bohemians might drift over to 23 Fifth Avenue and the aristocratic brownstone house where Mable Dodge, with the encouragement and cooperation of Carl Van Vechten, Jo Davidson, and Lincoln Steffens, had instituted the most famous of American salons, a headquarters for raids upon the strongholds of the philistine, and an important development in a growing sense of intellectual community. Another fresh new spirit had been introduced to the Village in 1912 with the publication of Edna St. Vincent Millay's "Renascence." Beautiful, talented, and free, Miss Millay would come to embody many of the aspirations of the new age. Other New Yorkers were building culture in Provincetown on Cape Cod, where an enthusiastic group was developing an experimental theater that produced, among other new plays, the first efforts of a young misanthrope named Eugene O'Neill.

The names are stirring, but in 1915 the reputation of most of these people existed only in the future; few of them were known outside of their own circles. Except for the poets, who under the leadership of Ezra Pound were developing a loosely purposeful program for the reform of their craft, and those painters who rallied around Alfred Stieglitz, most young intellectuals were split up into relatively small groups, defensive and self-congratulatory. Allied only by a common hostility to everything they vaguely felt to be old and shabby, they lacked a clear idea of what their positive purpose might be, and they had little or no sense of the influence they could impose upon American culture. Their theoretical quarrels and narrow range of both contacts and interest were an expression of the nationwide disorganization that Floyd Dell described a few years later. "It was a generation," Dell wrote in 1920, "who throughout the long years of their youth felt themselves in solitary conflict with a hostile environment. There was a boy in Chicago, and a boy in Oshkosh, and a boy in Steubenville . . . —one here and there, and all very lonely and unhappy. They did not know of each other's existence—they only knew of themselves and the great ugly environment in which they were imprisoned. They were idealists, and lovers of beauty, and aspirants toward freedom; and it seemed to them that the whole world was in a gigantic conspiracy to thwart ideals and trample beauty underfoot and make life merely a kind of life imprisonment." Such young people had will and energy; they lacked leadership.

Partly because the young had not yet pooled their resources, but more because of the timeless nature of institutions, the old guard still held firm control of the chief outlets for publication and, with them, the possibility of earning a living as a writer. The important literary monthlies of the time, brandishing the authority they had acquired during the nineteenth century, were, in the words of Malcolm Cowley and Henry Seidel Canby, "the guardians of the tradition of ideality, which, with the fabric worn shabby, and more starch to conceal it, had become the genteel tradition." The *Century* was edited by the priggish Robert Underwood Johnson, who announced as his purpose to appeal to "women, religious people, and the West." Charles Dudley Warner was the literary editor of *Harper's,* a magazine still dominated ideologically by William Dean Howells, who continued to occupy its editorial "Easy Chair" until 1920. These were excellent men, who had long been personally hospitable to unknown writers, but they simply were unprepared to respond to an iconoclastic new generation. Ellery Sedgwick of the *Atlantic* had sympathy enough to recognize and befriend Randolph Bourne, but he also coached the fierce apostle of youth in what Paul Rosenfeld called "the gingerly *Atlantic Monthly* style, with its mincingness of persons perpetually afeard of stepping on eggs." Bourne was happy to break free of the venerable magazine when the chance came. Among New York's influential periodicals, only the liberal *Nation* set itself resolutely against the old gentility, but, so far as Brooks and his allies were concerned, that journal as well was in enemy hands. Until 1914 the literary editor was Paul Elmer More, after Irving Babbitt the chief exponent of the New Humanism. More was seconded by Stuart Sherman, Babbitt's pupil, who for several years took upon himself much of the rough-and-tumble infighting of the warfare the Humanists relentlessly waged against all comers. The other great monthlies, *Scribner's* and *The North American Review,* continued to appear for many years, but were effectually moribund, even in 1915. In general, the opportunities for publication open to the rebellious young remained largely in what were coming to be called "little magazines."

Much of same condition prevailed in book publishing. Houses that thirty years earlier had responded to a new fiction insisted upon applying their old standards to the puzzling manuscripts that were appearing in rapidly growing numbers. As owners refused to reassess the composition of their lists, the industry became stodgy and arrogant. After his attempts to find academic employment had fallen through, Van Wyck had taken a job in the editorial department of the Century Company, one of the most hidebound of the important houses, where William Dean Howells was a frequent visitor. Van Wyck remembered how "other kindly old men of letters, often wearing beards, dropped in, uniting the Century Company with the Century Club, where with one voice they denounced the new novelists and poets who were equally outlandish in their literary manners and their names."

Charles Scribner's Sons, a family house prominent since the 1840s, might illustrate the curious mixture of integrity and myopia that characterized American publishing in 1915. According to Charles A. Madison, Scribner's was probably the most distinguished firm in the country during the early years of the century, but it was also reactionary and authoritarian, "a citadel of smug complacency." Charles Scribner himself was a man of catholic interests and excellent taste—his huge lists included such masters as Henry James, John Galsworthy, George Washington Cable, Maxim Gorky, Edith Wharton, and George Santayana—but he was known for his Victorian prudishness and distaste for impolite realism, and he selected his lieutenants with an eye to ensuring respect for such attitudes throughout the firm. For many years his senior literary editor had been the capable William Crary Brownell, himself rigidly moralistic, who was ideologically close to the Humanism of Babbitt and More and quite as willing as Scribner to censor whatever offended his sense of propriety or tradition. In 1915, much to the distress of Max Perkins, just promoted to a junior editorship after four years in the advertising department, Brownell, acting upon principle, rejected Van Wyck Brooks's briskly written manuscript, "A Fable for Yankees," because it "swept these fellows [Longfellow, Whittier, Lowell] into the dust-bin of the past with a contemptuousness of gesture." Brownell "disliked the book very much," John Hall Wheelock remembered, "found it frivolous—I think partly because it does really pull the leg of a few people like William Crary Brownell. You would have thought for that reason he might have been scrupulous and taken it on, but he was very firm about it and the book was declined. . . ."

The situation at Scribner's was typical. Established publishers always remain a few years behind advanced writers, but here the natural lag was exaggerated by a moral commitment to a threatened standard, and the rejection of insolent manuscripts was often as much a matter of personal integrity as practical economics. The fight against censorship had not yet begun—most publishers agreed in their hearts with Anthony Comstock—and the young Horace Liveright and Alfred Knopf had not yet taken control of their innovative firms. Thus far, only

Mitchell Kennerley had successfully defied the general conservatism, publishing since 1905 such new and often controversial writers as Frank Harris, Vachel Lindsay, Edna St. Vincent Millay, Walter Lippmann, Max Eastman, and D. H. Lawrence, as well as Van Wyck Brooks. Kennerley had also been the first to fight Comstockery openly in the courts. Arrested in 1913 by Comstock himself for bringing out D. C. Goodman's *Hagar Revelly,* he refused to suppress the book, the usual recourse of harried publishers, and he established an important precedent by winning acquittal before a jury.

Often admired for his adventurous independence, Kennerley had acquired a bad reputation for his eccentric bookkeeping. He seems to have felt that he had more than obliged his stable of relatively unknown writers by making their work available, and his financial irregularities were probably more the result of carelessness or indifference than outright dishonesty. Walter Lippmann wrote to Brooks in 1916 that he did not "believe that there is any author on record who has not been badly treated by Kennerley." Lippmann proposed a joint action against their old publisher, and Van Wyck had himself already contemplated asking Ames to bring suit. Whether or not the prospect of such trouble deterred him, Kennerley all but abandoned publishing after 1915.

Thus unable to fall back on Kennerley after Scribner's had rejected him, Van Wyck took "A Fable for Yankees" to B. W. Huebsch, who was already developing a reputation for enlightened hospitality to books that more firmly established houses refused to consider. Huebsch maintained only a small list, distinguished chiefly by serious foreign writers and books on radical politics, but in 1915 he was about to come into his own as the American publisher of James Joyce and D. H. Lawrence, and he would bring an unusually impressive group of important writers with him when he moved over to the newly organized Viking Company in 1925. From the first, the relationship between Brooks and his new publisher was one of warm friendship, a meeting of equals rather than a business association. In the evening of his life Van Wyck would write with all his "admiration and affection" to the man he had continued to regard as "the one inspired publisher." Huebsch quickly recognized the quality of "A Fable for Yankees" but accepted it with the condition that the title be changed. It wasn't a fable, he told Brooks, and the equation of "American" with "Yankee" was not only anachronistic, it would restrict sales. Van Wyck complained to Eleanor about the emendation, fearing that Huebsch might demand additional revisions in the text, but he soon found a new title for his ambitious essay and apparently had little other trouble getting the book ready for the printer. Huebsch brought out *America's Coming-of-Age* in time for the Christmas market of 1915.

By common agreement an American classic, *America's Coming-of-Age* was Van Wyck's first major book, and it remains one of his most persuasive. It is the single work, many of his admirers contend, on which his reputation must eventually rest. Their judgment may be reductive, but this slender volume does assert, now as then, an extraordinary authority for the work of a man so young. In it Brooks summed up and fulfilled much of the developing power of his previous work, especially the theme of personal wholeness that runs almost compulsively from his precocious high-school essays through *John Addington Symonds* and *The World of H. G. Wells.* Here, the eternal hostilities—of truth and form, the universal and the social, intuitive idealism and materiality—by which he had defined the spiritual malady of youth are worked into a native metaphor, illuminating national as well as individual character, and growing almost of its own accord into a theory of history and social order. Quietly but unmistakably asserted, Van Wyck's confident new authority was a tribute to the integrity with which he had continued to develop his point of view.

For it was rather according to the point of view than the nature of the discourse itself that the study triumphed. Young America gleefully seized upon *America's Coming-of-Age* as a definitive statement of literal truth, but Brooks never suggested that his metaphor was either literal or exhaustive. Rather, he felt that he was examining and defending one attitude toward America, clearing through an overgrowth of cultural weeds and wildings a single path that might lead his contemporaries to a possibility of definition. He created, almost as a fiction, a firm point of view from which to indicate the way. "I am speaking myself as a thorough-going Yankee to other thorough-going Yankees," the author says, and if we know that claim to be misleading, it should remind us that he had exploited similarly fictive spokesmen in the past.

The characterization of the narrator becomes especially important whenever his voice drops into the first person, for it is by such apparently unrehearsed interjections of personality that Brooks tries to elicit an almost reflexive assumption of community from his "Yankee" audience. It is that "I" who wonders if young people these days are not

100

rather too eager to own a shoe factory—the same "I" who contends that immigrant philosophies cannot touch the center of American problems, or says,

> I confess to an old-time and so to speak aboriginal affection for this man [Jonathan Edwards], so gently solicitous to make up in his daily walk and conversation for the ferocious impulsions of that brain of his. He was even the most romantic of men, as I thought once, and I well remember that immense old musty book of his theology covered with mildew, with its desert of tiny print, which I carried out with me into the fields and read, in the intervals of birdnesting, under the hedgerows and along the borders of the wood: the sun fell for the first time on those clammy old pages and the pallid thoughts that lay in them, and the field-sparrows all about were twittering in a language which, to tell the truth, was no more unintelligible to me.

With its sharp contrast between the bright innocence of nature and the gloomy works of men, this is the voice of Hawthorne, pure and simple. Such echoes of the classic writers of New England—and there are others—are probably deliberate, calculated to evoke a sense of a common past. The tableau itself is almost certainly fictive, but need not be—its biographical accuracy is irrelevant. As a literary device it draws upon honored traditions of New England: precocious erudition, theological seriousness, the homely pastoral setting. It is a Yankee genre piece, as unmistakably stylized as scrimshaw.

Credentials presented, the narrator goes on slick as any lanky Connecticut peddler to acknowledge a similarly creative responsibility for his material itself—"Issues . . . do not spring spontaneously out of the mass. . . . they have almost to be created like works of art"—and he slyly discloses the ideological relativism he plunders for all it is worth. "It is a principle that shines impartially on the just and the unjust," he whispers aside, "that once you have a point of view all history will back you up." Thus releasing both his reader and himself from the futile dream of objectivity, he argues much of his case in the conditional mood, relying heavily upon such devices as the rhetorical question and the hypothetical example—"Let us figure to ourselves a typical American, who has grown up, as an American typically does grow up, in a sort of orgy of lofty examples, moralized poems, national anthems, and baccalaureate sermons; . . . —until he comes to feel in himself the hovering presence of all manner of fine potentialities, remote, vaporous, and evanescent as a rainbow. . . . Let us imagine that, having grown up in this way, he is sent to college. . . . Having arrived there will he be confronted with an Angry God, or any sort of direct theological dogma? By no means." James Vitelli, who was the first to identify the significance of most of these diversionary tactics, takes the "fable" of the original title quite seriously, a generic approach that may itself wring too much from a metaphor, but which is invaluable for its reminder that Brooks's essay must be read as a work of the creative imagination and not primarily as an intellectual discourse.

"It would be fatal," Van Wyck wrote to Eleanor just before the book was published, "if in any of the sketches of writers which I have given it were to be assumed that I have treated any but one aspect, the one most necessary to my argument. The nature of the book itself indicates that this is not intended to have the qualities of a history of literature, namely, a treatment of the *central* aspect of writers. I have chosen only the racial aspect, which is never the central fact in a writer. What I have said about Whitman, even, proves that; the important thing about him not being anything that concerns America but human beings as such." Aware that such partial argument could easily lead to tactlessness or distortion, Brooks fastidiously resisted temptations to stray beyond his self-imposed guidelines. In fact, his generalizations were, as they remain, deadly accurate, at least when applied to the narrow area of American life he had fenced off as his own. Moreover, his generally hyperbolic sense of the distinctions in American personality, as well as the heightened racial wisdom built into his point of view, lent to his prose a witty sense of incongruity, a dry, epigrammatic humor that he had not attempted in his earlier work.

Brooks used striking techniques from the beginning. He jumped immediately into the middle of his argument, opening *America's Coming-of-Age* with an anecdote about William Jennings Bryan which suddenly became the statement of his celebrated thesis. American life, he contended, was woefully polarized between antagonistic character-types—the "highbrow," "the superior person whose virtue is admitted but felt to be an inept unpalatable virtue," and the "lowbrow," "a good fellow one readily takes to, but with a certain scorn for him and all his works." "They are equally undesirable," he went on, "and they are incompatible; but they divide American life between them."

He did not invent his colorful juxtaposition of highbrow and low-brow—the terms had been in use at least ten years—but he did establish its cultural resonance and continuing popular currency. It was a nice touch to snatch a racy colloquialism from the rush of the language instead of imposing more elegant imagery from above, as he had imposed the terms of a similar dualism upon *The Wine of the Puritans*. His new metaphor was both native and organic. It assumed, without appearing to, that its premises concerning human nature were a matter of universal agreement. Thus authorized by popular mandate, Brooks could set to work with apparent innocuousness upon his bit of nonchalant folk wisdom, stretching it, redefining it, applying it in shocking new ways, extending it far beyond its original implications—until he had postulated an absolute opposition between theory and practice, refinement and utility, 'between university ethics and business ethics, between American culture and American humor, between Good Government and Tammany, between academic pedantry and pavement slang." The structure of *America's Coming-of-Age* (which is nothing more, really, than a series of variations on a theme) develops as a natural extension of the homely psychology which provides its ostensible occasion. By subjecting the living slang to the rigorous glosses and investigations of the trained intellect, the book becomes a solution to the problem it poses. Highbrow and lowbrow meet in a discussion conducted on the robust middle plane.

With his basic premises established, Brooks called up the sinister figure of the Puritan to answer for the flaw in the American character. The irresponsibility of these theocratic people, he argues, their abandonment of practical as well as divine affairs to the will of the deity, forestalled the development of a "centrality in thought" where social and eternal issues could be brought together and modify one another. During the eighteenth century their purely circumstantial unity ran itself out, and the rift became definitive in "the amazing purity of type and apparent incompatibility" of the philosophers Jonathan Edwards and Benjamin Franklin.

The highbrow strain, as Brooks sketched it, grew out of the divine errand of the colonizers of New England, "the current of Transcendentalism, originating in the piety of the Puritans, becoming a philosophy in Jonathan Edwards, passing through Emerson, producing the fastidious refinement and aloofness of the chief American writers, and, as the coherent ideals and beliefs of Transcendentalism gradually faded out,

103

resulting in the final unreality of most contemporary American culture." The lowbrow strain, "the current of catchpenny opportunism," had its origins in "the practical shifts of Puritan life, becoming a philosophy in Franklin, passing through the American humorists, and resulting in the atmosphere of contemporary business life." Brooks's symbolic usage of Franklin and Edwards is patently unfair to both, of course, but the categories suggested by isolating and contrasting them as types do explain subsequent cultural and economic history as well as any such huge generalizations can, and the exaggeration respects, intentionally or not, the popular debasement by which their ideas have influenced our society.

Whether or not Brooks was strictly just to his representative men is, in a sense, beside the point. He readily accepted responsibility for slighting the fullness of their achievements in order to concentrate on their "racial" aspects, and he applied his symbolism to good advantage in a subsequent discussion of American political and educational institutions. Moreover, he was clearly enjoying the iconoclastic fun of turning his analytic weapon to impertinent uses, and, gathering momentum, he swung into a famous attack upon the inadequacies of "Our Poets," those great men of nineteenth-century American letters, most of whom he had little trouble dismissing as unredeemable highbrows. It must have gladdened the artists and writers of the younger generation, whose own work had been too often denigrated by superficial comparisons to the traditional canon, to watch their champion have a go at Henry Wadsworth Longfellow—"Longfellow is to poetry what the barrel-organ is to music"—or at Edgar Allan Poe: "Orchids are as much a part of the vegetable kingdom as potatoes, but Poe is an orchid made out of chemicals." Or at the rest of the reverend grandfathers whose fading portraits still decorated the parlors of bourgeois America.

Despite the unmistakable pursuit of irreverence for its own sake in these critical portraits, the assessments Brooks drew from his study of the "racial" aspects of Our Poets stand up well. He seems to be of two minds about Emerson, but otherwise he describes his subjects in terms that would be unexceptionable to most critics now, and in several instances his discussion probably marks the point of origin of contemporary opinion. Most of these essays investigate literary failure, the mode of all of his early work, and by diversifying his approach he justifies and extends the implications of his formulaic contention that "those of our writers who have possessed a vivid personal genius have been paralyzed by the want of a social background, while those who have possessed a vivid social genius have been equally unable to develop their own personalities." That pivotal idea is expressed most aggressively in the discussion of the career of James Russell Lowell, who was, as Brooks contended, probably the most naturally talented writer of his time, potentially "the most complete, the most perfectly fused American literary personality." But, lacking the social issues a similarly qualified man would have found in Europe, Lowell's work degenerated and went "round and round in a large kind of way without involving the difficult intellectual act of clinching something." His portrait prefigures more clearly than the rest of Our Poets the presumptive method of analysis Brooks would apply to the problems of Mark Twain and Henry James.

The personal absolution Brooks granted Lowell was the rule, and not the exception. Generational animus aside, he did not damn any of Our Poets as individuals. They were themselves victims, he suggested; they were symptomatic of the larger social malady that divided America, and he was concerned less with lecturing the sufferers than with finding a cure. For healing he turned to Walt Whitman, the great transcendental artist who was also a man of action, and who, by fusing "the hitherto incompatible extremes of the American temperament," introduced "the sense of something organic in American life." Equally at home among the lofty reaches of the Oversoul and in a rude army hospital, "Whitman—how else can I express it?—precipitated the American character." The Whitman Brooks thus summoned up for his generation was only incidentally the poet considered for his poetry. His authority was rather that of the archetypal rebel, the liberated spirit who embarrassed the gatherings of the philistine and challenged the abnormal stuffiness of nineteenth-century letters. Above all, Whitman was the man whose personality was primordially whole, an announcement of the modern democratic ideal. He was to be the guide, as Brooks understood him, to a new world made harmonious at last.

That Brooks should single out Whitman as the moral hero of nineteenth-century America and the standard for democratic growth was a calculated insult to the older generation. In his *Literary History of America*, Brooks's old teacher, Barrett Wendell, had savagely attacked *Leaves of Grass*, which read, he suggested, "as if hexameters were trying to bubble through sewage." Such power to afflict the comfortable would probably have been enough to endear Whitman to the rebellious young even if his verse had not been courageous, sensuous, and free. By 1915 the poetic outlaw, dead only twenty-three years, had been enshrined as one of the spiritual fathers of the modern uprising. Brooks, however, distinguished his Whitman on the one hand from the Whitman of the "hot little prophets" who insisted on comparing their master to Christ and Buddha, and on the other hand from the Whitman of the conservatives, who asked the poet's blessing for selfish individualism. It was especially to such developments on the right, more sinister because they were agreeable to the logic of capitalism, that Brooks attended in *America's Coming-of-Age.* He took as his example of one-dimensional Whitmanian thought a defense of unlimited acquisitiveness called *Inspired Millionaires* and dismissed its argument for faith in the creative integrity of the financial wizard as "the apotheosis of the lowbrow." Brooks's vigorous attack gratified readers like Walter Lippmann but drew an outraged personal response from the author of *Inspired Millionaires,* Gerald Stanley Lee, a Congregationalist minister and amateur social theorist with a side interest in psychophysical therapy. Although Brooks probably did not take Lee's alternately wrathful and plaintive letter entirely seriously then, he was later, by one of the oddest chances in his life, to have much more to do with this good-hearted but altogether curious man.

Having presented his argument and its extensions, Brooks turned to his favorite nautical metaphor for a summarizing definition. "America," he suggested, "is like a vast Sargasso Sea—a prodigious welter of unconscious life, swept by ground-swells of half-conscious emotion." To discover the principle of harmony in that anarchy of impulse, he asserted, Americans must abandon both the anachronistic ideal of private wealth and the assumption of inflexibility in human nature that they inherit from the Puritans. Only socialism, only the economically just, the cooperative State, could induce the moral climate that will render obsolete the equally irrelevant types of highbrow and lowbrow, and sustain the dense "resisting background" of ideas from which a culture may be wrought. Curiously enough, Brooks's spirited appeal for a new communalism is tied to an apparently contradictory call for a hero—"one contagious personality, one clear shadowing forth of opposed issues"—for whom Carlyle and William Morris provide the analogous English theory and Whitman the American model. It is the Yankee voice asserting itself again. Socialism is less the process of reorganizing society from the ground up than the inevitable consequence of clearing the air. "A man arrives," Emerson wrote, "revolution follows," and Brooks's own ringing call for a leader and prophet may well have been for his contemporaries the most stirring element in his book.

What was finally to come of all this change and reformation? "Strange things," according to the "thorough-going Yankee" who momentarily borrowed Henry Thoreau's neighborly voice to muse about the future. "I have heard of seeds which, either planted too deep or covered with accretions of rubble, have kept themselves alive for generations until by chance they have been turned up once more to the friendly sun." Better, however, that we do not trust entirely to chance for our rejuvenation—that lesson is homely and clear. If we assiduously cultivate our garden, and our gardeners as well, "perhaps the dry old Yankee stalk will begin to stir and send forth shoots and burst into a storm of blossoms."

Whether or not *America's Coming-of-Age* had ever been written, the old literary New York of William Dean Howells would have passed into memory. The polite, industrious, substantial way of life, the nineteenth-century America for which it stood, was fated to change. But surely Brooks's lean book with the ambitious title hastened the demise of the Confident Years. It was not a prepossessing book—it was small and restrained and offered by a relatively obscure publisher. Neither was it a commercial success. Fewer than five hundred copies were sold during the first six months after publication. Yet *America's Coming-of-Age* quickly became one of the most influential American books of the twentieth century. It spread its message of hopeful defiance to far corners of the land and aroused a generation which was consciously seeking intellectual leadership.

Sherwood Anderson is an example. When Brooks's manifesto appeared he was still an unhappy businessman, emotionally committed to his writing but unpublished and frustrated. "I have always lived in such a barren place," he said of these early days, "felt myself so futile, because I have really always felt a lack of strength to continue struggling in a vacuum and looked forward hopelessly to the time when some quirk of the mind would lead me to adopt finally some grotesque sectional attitude and spend myself uselessly on that." Anderson's situation was, of course, potentially the cultural tragedy Brooks had described in *America's Coming-of-Age,* but Anderson escaped the pattern of American failure largely by recognizing Brooks's description. "It was in the guise of the most powerful outward bulwark of his mature life"—this is Paul Rosenfeld writing—"that the work of Van Wyck Brooks came to Sherwood Anderson. In it he encountered another conscious American who spoke his language. Here was a critic, a polished and erudite man, who brought him corroboration in his inmost feelings, and told him that nations had become great, and life burned high, because men had done what he was laboring to do; and that America had remained gray and terrible and oafish because men could not within her borders feel the truth. In that voice, Anderson recognized an America more real than the one that, outside and in, strove to deflect him and break his touch." Anderson himself swore to the justice of Rosenfeld's shrewd description, and, despite a certain touchiness in the relationship between the two men, he often praised Brooks extravagantly as the civilized, clear-headed man of his time. His Midwestern whoop of delight in the sophisticated Easterner's onslaughts against American torpidity—"Tell that man to keep his vision," he wrote Waldo Frank. "He is thundering along the right trail sure as hell"—expressed the sense of revival that excited the young artists who were everywhere arising to the call of *America's Coming-of-Age*.

That the time was ripe and the book excellent, the first mature text of a generation, cannot in itself account for the impact Brooks made upon his America. One dimension of his new stature was undoubtedly the unintentional gift of the old guard, who paid reluctant tribute by isolating him as the most dangerous spokesman of the youthful enemy. More important, perhaps, the confident authority with which he developed his critical personality evoked an imagery of embattled heroism. In Steubenville and Oshkosh, young intellectuals would have recognized, with a sort of startled awe, that they had a formidable champion. This learned, ironic Yankee, whoever he was, had taken up their cause. He had challenged the powerful elders on their own terms, asserting that he understood their treasured writers, their values, their mentalities, and, ultimately, their failure better than they could ever understand themselves. Brooks must have been astonished to discover that he was becoming in the eyes of his peers the very hero for whom he had called in his racy address to the Yankees.

VI

SLAYING ADOLESCENCE: *THE SEVEN ARTS*, 1916–1917

Van Wyck's new professional eminence left no immediate mark upon his personal life. *America's Coming-of-Age* did not sell enough to alleviate the Brookses' chronic financial difficulty, and even the first campaigns in a major critical war, touched off by such aggressive reviews as those of Walter Lippmann and Stuart Sherman, the one introducing a latter-day Isaiah to readers of *The New Republic,* the other staging a mock riot of cowboys and professors in *The Nation,* could not induce the reserved young author to accept the romantic role literary Manhattan would have awarded him. Determined to protect both his artist's discipline and his personal privacy, he chose to keep nearly the island's length away from the abundant good company and mad carryings-on of Greenwich Village. Life proceeded quietly and happily in the small apartment on West 118th Street. Eleanor gave birth to a second son, Oliver Kenyon, in January 1916.

The Brookses' domestic situation, however, continued uninterrupted only until the spring of 1917 when for financial reasons Eleanor and the boys returned to Carmel to live with Mrs. Stimson. Nothing in the surviving correspondence suggests that the marriage was in crisis. Both Eleanor and Van Wyck regretted the separation, worried about its influence on their relationship, and planned to be reunited as soon as possible. Yet, after the many frustrating years apart that had preceded their marriage, their decision to live separately, even temporarily, must have been painful and, for Van Wyck, humiliating. Not only did he thus acknowledge that he was then unable to support a family properly, he tacitly agreed that the standard assumed by Mrs. Stimson was, in fact, the proper way to support a family. Furthermore, Eleanor's move to California set an unfortunate precedent for the solution of domestic problems.

For the time being, however, life was uneventful. At the Century Company, Van Wyck continued to drudge for thirty dollars a week. Although both he and Eleanor were forced to supplement his salary by translating books from French, he preferred such intellectual day labor to the more remunerative employment he might easily have found with any number of newspapers or magazines. His various apprenticeships in London and New York had convinced him that profitable literary work was a moral trap. "I feared nothing so much as making money," he remembered later. "In offices, etc., my sole desire was not to be promoted, not to become entangled in the machine of business. I wished to be an underling, and in this I succeeded. I felt it was most important that my sense of responsibility should only be engaged in small routine tasks, in which I could honestly give my money's worth. Granting that I could pay my way, my major responsibilities always lay elsewhere." That unbending sense of fiscal integrity was scarcely a new development, of course—it simply adapted to married life an ideal of spiritual poverty—but Van Wyck's statement also expresses a curiously strong tendency to respect money in terms of its traditional significance. He implicitly accepts the Protestant work ethic by which money becomes a measure of service, and the relationship between work and pay is moralized.

Despite such complications of domestic economy, Van Wyck had lost none of his impulsiveness. He was still moral adventurer enough to sacrifice even the minimal security afforded by the Century Company as soon as he happened upon the right excuse. This time it came as a congratulatory letter from Waldo Frank, a young scholar-mystic a few years out of Yale, who invited him to join a new magazine. Frank was a passionately learned man, obsessed, or so it seems, with a conviction of destiny, both his country's and his own, and he was to become, for nearly fifteen years, one of the pioneers of what he was himself to call the rediscovery of America. Egotistical, at times offensively so, he had a fierce, genuinely compassionate social conscience that remained apparent beneath even the extremes of his stilted, declamatory prose.

Frank approached Brooks with all the good will of recognition. He saw in *America's Coming-of-Age* the inevitable statement of his generation, and in his letter he suggested to Van Wyck that the essay was in fact a spontaneous prolegomenon to the new periodical he and some friends were about to launch. *The Seven Arts* would harness art for the sake of community and attempt to create the sustaining culture for which Brooks had called in his epistle to the Yankees. Van Wyck must have nodded with some satisfaction upon seeing the program of the young socialists and Whitmanians behind *The Seven Arts:* the magazine extended and applied many of his own ideas. Although he at first involved himself only as a contributor of keynote articles and a nominal advisory editor, he soon quit the Century Company to join Frank, full time, as associate editor. Like Frank, he accepted *The Seven Arts* as a cause rather than a job, and both men were memorialized as "vicious workers." They appeared at odd hours of the morning and pushed themselves far into the night to coordinate the enormous artistic energy the magazine had suddenly awakened and gathered to itself.

The founder and chief editor of *The Seven Arts* was James Oppenheim, a veteran writer and social worker who occupied a celebrated apartment on Washington Square, the tangible reward for the sentimental fiction he sold to the popular magazines of the day. Oppenheim also had a certain reputation as a muckraking novelist, but he preferred to think of himself as a bardic poet. In 1914 he published his first collection of free verse, *Songs for the New Age*—largely in imitation of Walt Whitman. With Frank and Paul Rosenfeld, then a young, unpublished lover of music, he had dreamed aloud of revolutionizing American culture. The publication of *America's Coming-of-Age* helped persuade him, as it persuaded the excitable Frank, that it might indeed be possible to realize what he later remembered as their vision of "a magazine, *the* magazine which should evoke and mobilize all our native talent, both creative and critical, give it freedom of expression and so scatter broadcast the new Americanism which would naturally have the response of America." The only obstacle to that dream was the inevitable obstacle: money. Oppenheim had none. Frank had none. Rosenfeld had none. And the project would require an investment of some $50,000.

Oppenheim found the money. He had a sufficiently unpoetic head for business when the need was upon him, and he soon made the acquaintance of Mrs. Annette K. Rankine, a widow with a neurosis and a large collection of Whistlers, at which, as he explained, she was tired of looking. Mrs. Rankine's analyst agreed to a suggestion that a creative enterprise might be therapeutic, and this aristocratic, conservative woman sold her Whistlers to subsidize *The Seven Arts.* She took the business department for her own province, but under the remarkable condition that she would not interfere with either the magazine's content or its policies. Her patronage was more than generous. Oppenheim earned an annual salary of approximately $5,000, then and later an unheard-of sum for the editor of a fledgling little magazine, and *The Seven Arts* was for its year of existence probably the only organ of the new generation that could afford substantial payments to its contributors.

Encouraged by this extraordinary windfall, Oppenheim signed on Frank as a nominal assistant (although the younger man was, in effect, managing editor), and the two collaborated on a grandly immodest broadsheet, sent as a statement of both purpose and invitation to writers everywhere in the United States:

> It is our faith and the faith of many, that we are living in the first days of a renascent period, a time which means for America the coming of that national self-consciousness which is the beginning of greatness. In such epochs the arts cease to be private matters; they become not only the expression of the national life but a means to its enhancement.
>
> Our arts show signs of this change. It is the aim of *The Seven Arts* to become a channel for the flow of these new tendencies: an expression of our American arts which shall be fundamentally an expression of our American life. . . .
>
> In short, *The Seven Arts* is not a magazine for artists, but an expression of artists for the community.

The response to their manifesto was, as Oppenheim testifies, overwhelming, and he and Frank were forced to enlist the services of Paul Rosenfeld and Louis Untermeyer as well as a number of other sympathizers before they were able to put together a coherent expression of "renascent" America out of the abundance of manuscripts that poured into the pretentiously unpretentious editorial offices on Madison Avenue.

The first issue of *The Seven Arts* came out in November 1916, and a glance at its table of contents would have convinced Young America that Oppenheim and Frank had done yeoman work. There were critical articles by Louis Untermeyer, Floyd Dell, and Paul Rosenfeld, and poetry by Robert Frost, Amy Lowell, and the Lebanese mystic Kahlil Gibran, who, like Frost and Untermeyer, also appeared on the masthead as a member of the advisory board. Oppenheim reprinted in his editorial columns the invitation to the artistic community that had circulated earlier; Frank welcomed "Emerging Greatness"; "Peter Minuit" (Rosenfeld) paid tribute to the leadership of Alfred Stieglitz. Brooks's contribution was "Enterprise," a sharp attack upon America as a wasteland of both ideas and things, where, for want of a sustaining culture, all life was becoming "old without majesty, old without mellowness, old without pathos, just shabby and bloodless and worn out." Van Wyck's visions of "gaunt, silent farmers" and "heaps of ashes, burned-out frames, seared enclosures, abandoned machinery"—like his judgment of American culture itself—anticipated important developments of theme and imagery in the decade to come, but the tone of the first issue was set by Romain Rolland, the French romantic scholar, writer, and utopian theorist, who that year received the Nobel Prize and to whose significance Oppenheim gave over much of his introductory editorial.

In "America and the Arts," Rolland set upon America's younger generation a task equal to its aspirations. "I rejoice," he began," in the founding of a magazine in which the American Spirit may seek and achieve consciousness of its nature and its role." He reminded young Americans of their messianic heritage. Europeans are old and tired and defeated, he told them, but the New World was without a past, without traditions, without the moral weight of centuries of failure. Americans, he thought, "live at the center of the life of the world"; they need only study and express themselves in order to redeem that life. He spoke in the name of humanity, from a Europe where civilization was in danger of being extinguished forever:

We ask that you defend the cause of liberty; that you defend its conquests; and that you increase them. And by liberty I mean both political and intellectual liberty. I mean the incessant rebirth and replenishment of life that unfolds. . . .

Also, we ask that you so master your lives as to give to the world a new ideal for lack of which it bleeds—an ideal, not of section and tradition, but of Harmony. . . . You must make of your culture a symphony that shall in a true way express your brotherhood of individuals, of races, of cultures banded together.

Thus recalled, the old myth of national errand laid an embarrassing responsibility upon a generation of writers and artists that still looked to Europe for its model of culture, but the European spirit, as Rolland spoke for it, found cause for hope in an America already entered upon its destined struggle: "Behind you, alone, the elemental Voice of a great pioneer, in whose message you may well find an almost legendary omen of your task to come,—your Homer: Walt Whitman."

Rolland's faith in the utopian capacities of the artist captured the spirit that moved *The Seven Arts* through its entire twelve issues. Under Oppenheim, Frank, and Brooks the magazine was the lyrical fulfillment of the revolutionary program best expressed in political terms by *The Masses*. It was both truculent and idealistic, experimental and demanding, and despite its short life and relatively small audience (never much beyond five thousand) it became almost immediately one of the influential journals of its time, attracting to its pages many of the writers whose work established a new era. Sherwood Anderson's "Queer" appeared in the second issue, and Anderson continued to send in more or less regularly stories based on his life in Clyde, Ohio, the "Winesburg" of his famous book. The magazine also brought out short fiction by D. H. Lawrence, Eugene O'Neill, and Frank himself, as well as a number of lesser-known writers who attempted to raise "local color" to the level of naturalistic, or even mystical, art. A crotchety theoretician of such transformational Americanism, Horace Traubel, unbent to the "artistic crowd" enough to send in a chapter from his massive essay in hagiography, *With Walt Whitman in Camden.*

Theodore Dreiser contributed a dramatic fragment and a typically expansive article on "Life, Art and America," and he was seconded by his friend and apostle H. L. Mencken, who wrote on "The Dreiser Bugaboo." Like many other contributors, Mencken was fundamentally hostile to the magazine's liberal premises, but he was welcomed as an ally in the cooperative battle against everything fixed and old.

There were similarly controversial essays about the cultural scene from Harold Stearns, Joel Spingarn, Leo Stein, Max Eastman, Carl Van Vechten, and Lee Simonson. Once America entered the war the courageous openness of editorial policy also attracted John Reed, who dashed off an article, "This Unpopular War," that might have had the magazine suppressed. John Dewey contributed to the debate on war policy, as did Bertrand Russell, who asked, hopefully, if nationalism were not moribund. Such distinguished contributors might by themselves easily yield a history of much of the art and thought of their time, but they were only supplemental to the cultural barrage laid down by Brooks, Oppenheim, and Frank. Among others who appeared with some regularity, Marsden Hartley and John Butler Yeats discussed the new painting and Paul Rosenfeld modern music, while Louis Untermeyer kept *Seven Arts* readers abreast of important developments in the renascent art of poetry.

Untermeyer's monthly essay-reviews were a basic function of a rebellious magazine in a time when poetry was the most advanced expression of an emerging generation, and the respect with which the intellectual community regarded *The Seven Arts* was reflected in the quality of the verse that was attracted to its pages. Untermeyer himself appeared frequently as a poet, and Amy Lowell and Kahlil Gibran regularly claimed a few pages for their ambitious, exotic, but utterly dissimilar experiments in free verse. *The Seven Arts* stressed a self-consciously American poetry of statement, publishing such exemplary texts as Robert Frost's "The Bonfire," Carl Sandburg's "Grass," and Vachel Lindsay's mellifluous "The Broncho That Would Not Be Broken of Dancing," but the editorial policy was as open in regard to poetry as it was to opinion. The more esoteric poetry of technique, then one of the most dynamic forces of aesthetic modernism, was also well represented. *Seven Arts* poets ranged from Sandburg and Frost to such rarefied types as Arthur Davison Ficke, with his interest in the delicate art of Japan, and Alfred Kreymborg, widely regarded as the most demanding experimentalist of the new generation. Others who published verse in the magazine included Babette Deutsch, Robert Hillyer, Maxwell Bodenheim, Witter Bynner, the brothers Stephen Vincent and William Rose Benet, and Jean Starr Untermeyer. Although poetry was not, finally, the peculiar virtue of *The Seven Arts,* which was always most authoritative in its critical prose, these writers made the magazine an important vehicle for the theory and practice of new attitudes about verse, and from month to month an initiated reader could easily keep himself informed about current developments.

A few of the other writers who appeared in this remarkably comprehensive journal should also be noted. Mabel Dodge and S. N. Behrman, both better known for other things, contributed fiction; John Cournos, later a respected novelist, commented on the arts; and John Dos Passos, just out of college, sent in an article on "Young Spain," one of a series about the new world of youth as it found expression through particular nationalisms. Padraic Colum wrote another of these essays, "Youngest Ireland," and there were discussions of the movement in India and Japan, as well as Brooks's inevitable "Young America." This emphasis upon the generational revolution elsewhere enhanced the sense of utopian purpose that lay solidly beneath the magazine's policies, and it reflected an editorial compulsion to bring harmony out of apparent diversity. From the beginning the terms of that harmony were Brooks's. He was the cultural theorist, the spokesman for both the anger and the hope of the emerging young, and the polemical essays he scattered over the first eight issues made up the hard core of doctrine around which *The Seven Arts* cohered. These were tough, defiant articles, about culture rather than literature alone, and, with a brief preface and postscript added, Brooks later collected them under the characteristically heroic title *Letters and Leadership,* which came out in 1918. For book publication he made extensive verbal and structural revisions in his essays, but except for the more forceful statement growing out of a cumulative, unified structure he nowhere modified his assessment of the American scene. His book is quarrelsome and defensively bitter, a peculiarly sensitive apprehension of the moral disillusionment that overcame American intellectuals during the course of World War I.

Although it addresses itself directly to youth, *Letters and Leadership* is by and large a series of new forays along the analytic paths opened up by Brooks's own attack on cultural futility in *America's Coming-of-Age.* Like the earlier book, it takes its force from a theory of negative criticism. Brooks felt he must identify and destroy those barriers that American culture, or lack of it, raised against the development of an "organized higher life" into which native personalities and their self-expression could freely grow. Once personality was released from the social inhibitions developed to meet the wholly utilitarian needs of the Puritan and the pioneer, men could live the masterly life to which Rolland had called them. They could "cease," as Brooks concluded his book, "to be a blind, selfish, disorderly people," and instead "become a luminous people, dwelling in the light and sharing our light."

To the extent that destructive criticism was a favorite mode of his generation Brooks's approach was typical and appropriate, but even his allies pointed to his failure to balance his iconoclastic fury with a positive program. Randolph Bourne, for instance, agreed that "our sense of leadership would come from discontent, from the intolerable feeling that we are alien in a world that no one around us is trying with intelligent fervor to set right." He accepted cheerfully the "superb youthful arrogance" of Brooks's implication "that it is we and our friends who are to be the masters." But he felt that *Letters and Leadership* was only a preliminary volume, and he wondered why Brooks did not specify the form leadership must take. Bourne's disappointment was echoed by many of Brooks's fellow rebels, and their confusion, which was in a sense justified, must have distressed Brooks, who wanted, above all, to be clear. He sought to anticipate such objections by suggesting in a prefatory note that the astute reader might find a program "between the lines." The suggestion was not evasive. Brooks's concept of cultural leadership, as much as his evolutionist's view of socialism, was stubbornly organic, and it stressed potential rather than doctrine. Leadership would be what the leader, acting upon a profound understanding of specific cultural problems, did—the program for leadership could not exist before it was put into practice.

The fundamental subject of *Letters and Leadership* is established in the central third chapter, "Young America," a reworking of *The Seven Arts* article of December 1916. Young people, Brooks suggested, were trapped: they could no longer feel either economic or spiritual necessity for the acquisitive life of their fathers, but they were unprepared to meet the challenges of the creative life demanded by the new age. Frustrated, purposeless, morally disoriented, the more sensitive among them drifted into emotional anarchy, creating a "race of Hamlets" whose idealizing impulses were meaningless. Above all else Americans needed a native discipline through which their natural creativity could be put to the service of some great corporate enterprise. Men, Brooks points out, grow dull when they sense that they and their work are of no use to civilization.

Such was the demand; the promise of American life was otherwise. Brooks's opening chapter, "Old America," made up of "Enter-prise" (from *The Seven Arts* of November 1916) and the first two sections of "Toward a National Culture" (March 1917), and his second, "The Culture of Industrialism," adapted from parts of the essay of the same name (April 1917) and "The Splinter of Ice" (January 1917), defined and considered the cultural impotence which threatened to frustrate the progressive growth of generations. "Of all this," Brooks explains, returning to his socialistic critique of American values, "individualism is at once the cause and the result. For it has prevented the formation of a collective spiritual life in the absence of which the individual, having nothing greater than himself to subordinate himself to, is either driven into the blind alley of his appetites or rides some hobby of his own invention until it falls to pieces from sheer craziness."

Brooks was here approaching the familiar ground of his earlier studies. He was not, however, simply repeating his old argument. His ideas were now carried by a frighteningly intense imagery that alerted his reader to a cultural disease deadlier and more advanced than he had previously represented it. The Puritan of *Letters and Leadership* had created a physical and moral nightmare. Hot, dry winds whistled through the pages of this grim little book. Machines coughed and died. Burning sunlight threw into relief every deserted, ramshackle building and palsied old man, as American things moved relentlessly toward dust and silence. Surrounded by the corpses of their civilization, Brooks's solitary people shuddered with either physical rot or the sterile restlessness of insanity. The imagery of fragmentation and waste—shell-less oysters, alkali, weeds, "the splinter of ice," cracking buildings and cracked men—is, at least in its intensity, unusual to Brooks, who seems happiest writing about the abundance of nature, but it is an imagery with at least as much traditional authority as the edenic mode he had often employed. Instead of looking to Whitman or Emerson, Brooks this time turned for his native context to Poe and Hawthorne, both, with their blighted landscapes and crumbling buildings, imaginative chroniclers of a decadent Calvinism.

After propounding in the central "Young America" the problem from which the emotion of his book arose, Brooks went on in his last chapters to discuss the responses of two important groups—critics and philosophers—who had shirked, as he felt, their duty to a potentially healthy cultural and spiritual community. In "Our Critics" (May 1917) and "Our Awakeners" (June 1917), he returned to the slashing assault upon established authority that had impassioned the analytic discourse of *America's Coming-of-Age,* but once again he did so with a significant difference of emphasis. The earlier essay treated the patriarchs of American letters and their contemporary defenders alike as victims of a historically determined cultural schizophrenia, but now he accused Our Critics and Our Awakeners, as he had refrained from accusing Our Poets, of a real *"trahison des clercs."* Both contemporaneous critics and pragmatic philosophers had, in effect, sold out. By accepting the logic of materialism, he argued, or by accepting American "reality" as somehow normative, both groups succumbed to the authority of the Puritan-Pioneer and effectively worked to stifle all of the creative, imaginative impulses by which men and women sought a higher reality. Capping his argument against the pragmatists, Brooks returned to the image of the Sargasso Sea he had used in *America's Coming-of-Age.* The quality of life Our Awakeners promised, he suggested, already had us "becalmed . . . on a rolling sea, flapping and fluttering, hesitating and veering about, oppressed with a faint nausea." With that visceral explanation for the growing mutiny among his fellow crewmen and passengers, Brooks turned to a final call for a race of artists—the leadership that would draw the masses toward the majesty of which they were capable.

That call, brief and passionate, made up the epilogue, "Towards the Future," which was adapted from "War's Heritage to Youth," an essay Brooks published subsequent to his *Seven Arts* material, in *The Dial* of January 1918. Since it expressed the implicit hope behind his book's dominantly negative criticism, this little manifesto was sufficiently optimistic to draw a few hoots from H. L. Mencken, who reviewed *Letters and Leadership* in *The Smart Set.* But "Towards the Future" was purely a confession of faith. Judged according to his own relentless evidence, Brooks's final vision of triumph seemed pathetically forced. If the Whitmanian affirmation he demanded remained possible, the massive inertia he found in American institutions overwhelmed it, and, in general, the tone of his book is wistful, angry, pessimistic. The messianic vision that ran through *America's Coming-of-Age* had turned decidedly apocalyptic. Even the prose of *Letters and Leadership,* which still crackles with compressed energy, lacks something of the healthy risibility of the earlier study, and the narrative stance is no longer so comfortably homely. Almost against his will

Brooks seems to be drawing up the lists for the final battles of what he called "the secular conflict of darkness and light."

The *Seven Arts* essays Brooks collected in *Letters and Leadership* were hostile to the established order, but they were scarcely political documents. Although its editors and most of its contributors were socialists of one kind or another, *The Seven Arts* left political rhetoric to *The Masses* and during its first six months kept strictly to its own, perhaps more radical, utopianism of the arts. But in April 1917 the United States entered the war, and, coincidentally, *The Seven Arts* for that month ran the first of its articles by Randolph Bourne, who had just come over from *The New Republic*. Bourne was to contribute six major essays in the time left to *The Seven Arts,* and although his first, "The Puritan's Will to Power," had no reference to the war theme with which he was increasingly preoccupied, it is probably safe to suggest that his presence in this April issue touched off the magazine's dramatic change of emphasis during 1917. While Bourne published more, and more volatile, attacks upon the war and the society waging it, Brooks's own contributions dwindled, and after June he wrote no more for *The Seven Arts*. The disharmony suggested by this professional relationship was, however, only apparent.

Van Wyck had first met Bourne in 1915, a happy side benefit of his editorial work for the Century Company. Bourne had already begun to attract attention with the ironic essays he collected in *Youth and Life* (1913), and, in search of material for the house magazine, Brooks wrote to him suggesting an article on the impossibility of assigning things to absolute categories. Bourne never wrote the article, but he did respond cordially to Van Wyck's letter. Both men had emerged from essentially the same cultural background; both were known and admired in the same intellectual circles. Each of them, moreover, was rapidly becoming a "flying wedge" behind which the forces of Young America could advance (Oppenheim paid the tribute of that metaphor to Brooks, Brooks to Bourne). It was only natural that, since they were already allies, they would soon be friends.

Much nonsense has been written about Randolph Bourne. He survives as legend, his slight figure passing into mythical dimensions because of his stormy life and untimely death, and because of the moral shock with which people discovered the clean, shapely mind trapped in his gnome's body. Bourne had undergone, as he said, "a terribly messy birth," and disfigured further by an attack of spinal tuberculosis at the age of four, he came to manhood dwarfed, a hunchback with a disproportionately large head balanced awkwardly upon a spindly body. He had a long, heavy-featured, prognathous face, which lurched off to one side, a loud, rasping breath, yellowish skin, and an ear, twisted and useless, that flattened against the exaggerated curve of his skull. As if to emphasize that startling physical appearance he invariably appeared in the black student's cloak he had acquired in Paris. The garment softened the outline of his back, but it made him seem like some grim apparition of the Middle Ages, sprung up in the twentieth century to remind men of the ugliness of their moral failure.

Because of his twisted body, as well as his resistance to the war-madness of 1917–1918, Bourne has gradually come to be identified with the modern symbolism of the diseased spokesman. Like the characters of Dostoyevsky, Kafka, Mann, Hemingway, or Faulkner, he has been used to represent the nobly human spirit whose physical deformity renders him more sensitive than others to the spiritual deformities of the time. The symbolism figures most explicitly in John Dos Passos's celebrated portrait of the gallant, "sparrowlike" bit of flesh which embodies the American refusal to abandon idealism in *Nineteen Nineteen*. Here Bourne has become a cloaked, crippled ghost, haunting the streets of New York, and repeating, in a "shrill soundless giggle," his famous observation, "War is the health of the state."

Dos Passos's representation is metaphorically true to the novelist's imaginative history of those terrible years when the United States seemed about to degenerate into barbarism, and it is a moving tribute to Bourne. But it relies upon a literary, rather than a biographical, model. There was nothing spooky about Bourne himself, and he did not hop along the streets of Manhattan like a sparrow. His body was stooped and clumsy, but his legs were strong. And while the image summons up much of the moral hysteria of those days, Randolph Bourne simply was not one to giggle—shrilly, soundlessly, or in any other way. He was a rationalist, clear-headed and remarkably sane, certainly one of the finest minds of his time and place. He shared the usual ambitions of idealistic young men: good company, freedom, success, and love. Despite his appearance, he possessed an uncommon gift of friendship, and he inspired affectionate loyalty among both male and female companions. If Dos Passos's biographical sketch captures both the emotion of a historical moment and one of the "meanings" of Bourne's experience, it takes us far from the man himself.

Of his male friends Bourne felt closest to Van Wyck. In company they must have seemed creatures of two different worlds: the handsome, impeccably dressed young critic and his dwarfed, medievally cloaked counterpart: the one coming to represent the hope American writers felt in themselves, the other their despair. Allegory aside, they were as well fitted to each other as any brothers. Both were born in 1886 in solidly conventional suburbs of New York City (Bourne was from Bloomfield, New Jersey), and both grew up under a strong mother in the moral absence of the father. Bourne's background was not nearly so moneyed as Van Wyck's, but the traditions of family gentility were similar, and his father also deteriorated physically after the collapse of his business. In fact, the two men differed significantly in only two of the circumstances that helped prepare them for their rebellious life's work. Bourne's disfigurement had given him a feeling for the injustice hidden between the lines of the social contract that had no equivalent in Brooks's own, more fortunate, experience. Also the relative poverty of Bourne's background left him without money to attend Princeton, where he was first accepted, and he had been forced to work at odd jobs for some six years before he was able to begin his undergraduate work at Columbia. Along the way he acquired something of a laborer's resentment toward the inequities of capitalism.

As Bourne's titles, "Our Cultural Humility" and "The Puritan's Will to Power," might themselves suggest, he was also close to Van Wyck in belief and method, and for the year and a half of their warmest friendship the two men were, as Van Wyck remembered later, "more or less constantly together" in work and in recreation. During the summer of 1917 they made a walking tour of nearly the length of Cape Cod. "Bourne is a real companion . . . ," Van Wyck wrote to Eleanor from Providence, "and we have had fine times together. I admire him very much. He is a triumph of mind over matter if there ever was one. He enjoys everything—is an indefatigable walker, explores every cranny, sniffs the salt air, the honeysuckles, the baybushes, and is never depressed. . . ." Bourne also spent much of his next (and last) summer with the Brookses, visiting their rented house on Long Island, where for several days he relieved Eleanor in translating a French novel called *Jacquon the Rebel.* It was to this house that he had arranged to have delivered the famous trunk full of manuscripts that mysteriously went astray—at the hands of the Secret Service, everyone believed then—never to be recovered.

The quiet intimacy of these summer holidays by the sea says much about the quality of the friendship which memorably enriched Van Wyck's war years. These oddly matched men of letters cheered each other on by sympathy and example, and collaborated on a strategy for the cultural insurgence. Each man could discover in his counterpart an embodiment, a justification of his own ideas. Such cooperative stimulation probably marks the extent of any influence either way. Despite a widespread assumption that Bourne's idealistic fervor awakened Brooks to prophecy, there is no evidence that either man knew the work of the other before 1915, when their essential programs had already been formulated, and the prosaic truth of the matter seems to be that they arrived independently at their remarkably similar conclusions. Both were romantic theorists of a utopian community—agreeing about the basic nature of man and society. Both were exceptionally clear and forceful thinkers; both idealized the fierce emotions of youth; and both were convinced that it was possible to establish prosperity, justice, honor, beauty—civilization itself—through the reform and enhancement of culture.

But however nicely they responded to each other's moral sensibilities in regard to the situation at home, they could not agree about the war that was raging in Europe. Brooks felt, and said, that Bourne was wildly throwing all his energies into a peripheral cause. Bourne felt, and said, that his friend Brooks had no head for politics. Although the disagreement seems to have created surprisingly little tension in their personal relationship, it has continued to be resurrected as a key issue of those years. Especially in the shadow of the mythology that has grown up around Bourne, Brooks's stand has often been made to seem ignoble, as if he had abruptly joined forces with the Germanophobes or the superpatriots.

Bourne had come over to *The Seven Arts* in the spring of 1917. He was no longer welcome at *The New Republic,* where his attacks upon American foreign policy would not only contradict an editorial position but threaten the magazine's continued existence. He thought his old colleagues had betrayed their own cause, and although he continued to review books for *The New Republic,* as for *The Dial,* he had no outlet for his graceful, wickedly ironic essays against the war until "The War and the Intellectuals" appeared in the June issue of *The Seven Arts.* This period of American involvement in the first Great War has, of course, become proverbial for its intolerance: citizens with

123

Germanic surnames were suspect and physically harassed; the labor movement was branded treasonable; and Eugene Debs was only the most famous of dissenters to be jailed for the duration. By late 1917 *The Masses* had been effectively, if extralegally, suppressed, and early the next year its editors were tried for sedition. Although inconclusive, the proceedings did ensure the permanent silencing of this bright, inventive magazine, with its magnificent resistance to the war psychology. Among the respected periodicals of the time only *The Seven Arts* remained as a vehicle for the pacifist position, and Bourne quickly became the magazine's uneasy conscience, the single most important American representative of the spirit of youth rising against the madness that would destroy it.

He wrote about the war as a violation of the cumulatively progressive nature of history, as an outrage to the primal sanities and utopian visions of his generation. With the clean, biting style and thematic concentration of the born satirist, he seemed almost uncannily sensitive to the helpless fury that developed more slowly—behind him, as it were—among the larger body of young intellectuals. His subject was the fundamental breach of faith by which men violated their own ethical codes, and he wrote about it with unpretentious courage and dignity. So authoritative was his voice that it is startling now to be reminded that almost all of his battles against the war were conducted in the five compact essays he published in *The Seven Arts* during 1917.

Bourne's protest was aimed rather at the intellectual who collaborated in the "patriotic" excesses of the time than directly at politicians or munitions makers, and his tone, however angry, was rationalistic and always under control. There was nothing of the wild invective of *The Masses* in his painfully constructed investigations of the contradictions inherent in war logic. Only his anarchistic "The State" is even remotely "treasonable," and it was not published until after his death. If the moral climate of wartime America had been less brutalized, Bourne might have been tolerated as simply the most eloquent spokesman for a responsible opposition, but during hostilities the slightest hesitation to subscribe wholly to the current patriotism was taken as evidence that one was "pro-German." Moral neutrality was not recognized, and active protest was considered active treason.

Under such stringent political conditions Bourne stood in danger of going to jail and of taking much of the *Seven Arts* staff with him. Not only did his own essays invite prosecution after passage of the Sedition Act of June 1917, but he made a convert of Oppenheim, who began denouncing the war with a convert's zeal in the Whitmanian free verse he served up from month to month by way of editorials. Oppenheim also opened the magazine to such adventurous challenges to authority as John Reed's blazing "This Unpopular War." As Bourne and Oppenheim warmed to their theme and the magazine became increasingly visible as *the* vortex of American dissent, everyone involved waited nervously for the ax to fall. Robert Frost's much-quoted limerick was addressed to Louis Untermeyer:

> In the Dawn of Creation that morning
> I remember I gave you fair warning
> The Arts are but Six!
> You add Politics
> And the Seven will all die a-Bourneing.

Van Wyck himself strenuously opposed the new emphasis on politics and could not, as he wrote later, "see why a magazine of art should destroy itself by opposing the war." As an antimilitarist (rather than a pacifist), he felt that the growth of a belligerent Pan-Germanism must be checked. But more to the point: he was disinclined by temperament to the sort of legal dogfight that his friends were inviting. What use, he asked, to throw away one of the few tools available because it will not do a job for which it was not designed? For a while it looked as if he might succeed in returning the magazine to its old orientation. "I think *The Seven Arts'* anti-war policy is going to die a natural death," he wrote to Eleanor during his walking tour with Bourne. "Oppenheim is so volatile. He is already working in a half-different vein. If I am not mistaken, Waldo will cool off when he finds he is not drafted—and Bourne, on whom they still count for materials, tells me he has nothing more to say about the war and plans to write on other subjects. So, as Oppenheim has found it almost impossible to get war material anyway, I believe our pacifist propaganda is going to blow over."

The two issues that remained to *The Seven Arts* were doubtless already set by the time this was written, so that the accuracy of Van Wyck's prediction cannot be confirmed, and he soon came to feel that he could not in conscience go along with a situation he deplored in hopes that it would change. Eleanor was urging him to leave the magazine, and considerable friction was developing among its policy-makers, especially between Oppenheim and Frank. Early that fall Van Wyck followed the example of his good friend John Sloan, who had quit *The Masses* because of its increasing commitment to antiwar prop-aganda, and formally resigned his editorial position on *The Seven Arts*. He did not, however, break contact either with the magazine itself or with the circle of close friends he had made there; he figured promi-nently in the group's discussions and maintained an important voice in plans for the future.

It may well be that the government would not have acted against *The Seven Arts*. Several newspapers, the New York *Tribune* among them, editorialized against such literary "Enemies Within," but the magazine's circulation was small, and its political material aimed spe-cifically at the intellectual community. A prosecuting attorney would have been well advised to think twice before trying to demonstrate to a jury the treason in either Bourne's reasonable prose or Oppenheim's opaque jeremiads. But while there seems to have been no immediate plan to indict any of *The Seven Arts'* personnel, the deadlier censorship prevailed. Mrs. Rankine found herself increasingly embarrassed among her Republican friends by the "pro-German" policies of what they considered "her" magazine, and when she ordered the flag flown at half-mast for the conservative statesman Joseph H. Choate, Van Wyck saw only too clearly from what direction the wind was rising. The patroness of *The Seven Arts* may have been more offended person-ally, as Waldo Frank thought, by Oppenheim's sudden conversion to the rhetoric of pacifism, than morally, by Bourne's ideological lead-ership. She was close to the editor in chief, and, without experience in the conduct of public intellectual debate, she could easily have taken Oppenheim's indifference to her wishes as the betrayal of a trust. Whatever the precise object of her irritation, she wrote to Oppenheim in October, confirming formally a decision long since made in fact, and informed him that since she wished to publicize her opposition to the war policy of the magazine she could no longer honor her original agreement to refrain from interfering in editorial matters. In a post-script she added that she was terminating her financial support imme-diately. It must have been a harrowing choice: a few weeks later she took her own life.

Oppenheim was persuaded that backers to replace Mrs. Rankine could be found, and the October number contained an appeal to readers for enough money to tide the magazine over. There was a surprisingly good response, but it came too late. By October probably no amount of money could have saved *The Seven Arts.* During the summer of 1917 both Oppenheim and Frank had readily found men who were willing to put money into the magazine. Oppenheim's potential backer was probably Scofield Thayer, who became famous a few years later by making the venerable *Dial* over into the most important magazine of literature and the arts of the twenties. But Frank and Oppenheim were unable to cooperate in making use of what new funding was available. Both were egotistical, aggressive men, and they had been fighting almost since the beginning of their relationship. Frank wished to do away with Oppenheim's office and relegate final editorial authority to a board—the system developed by *The Masses.* Oppenheim stubbornly insisted that "good editing is a one-man job, just like good art," and he probably played the dictator with unnecessary tactlessness.

By the time of the crisis, Oppenheim and Frank were almost literally at each other's throats, and both demanding that their reluctant colleagues take sides. Van Wyck himself told Eleanor the story of those last days of *The Seven Arts* as clearly, perhaps, as it will ever be known. "The last week at the Seven Arts has been a series of sensations," he wrote to Carmel in October.

> . . . James & Waldo quarreled: and then, just as it was about to go under, each, separately, got enough money to continue it. But each insisted that it could only go on without the other, and only if I would stay. James & Waldo did not see one another, and I was the confidant on both sides. Bourne was quite willing to go on with it, but he refused to do so unless I did. So it ended with me as the strategic center! . . . It was very funny but rather trying, as you can imagine, and I should have preferred not to have the whole responsibility placed upon me. But really I had no confidence either in James or in Waldo, or at least in my capacity to work with them—or in the Seven Arts under their management, and so I thought it best to refuse all round. Consequently, the Seven Arts passed out of existence.

With the magazine on which he had wagered much of his idealism finally dead, Van Wyck looked around cheerlessly for some tolerable work in the publishing houses. Jobs were scarce, however, and the lit-

127

erary scene was no longer as attractive as it had been just two years before. The war was becoming more and more the single important fact of life in the United States, and radical intellectuals had lost much of the good humor of their revolution-in-the-making. For a while he planned with Randolph Bourne, who had also fallen on relatively lean days, "to start another magazine sometime, which really will be what the Seven Arts ought to have been," but, for the moment, these could be only dreams. It was no time to be starting a periodical with radical inclinations. On top of it all Van Wyck was sick of New York. He was separated from Eleanor once again, and he needed time to be alone with himself, away from the hyperactivity of the city. Like many progressive intellectuals Van Wyck had been thrown off his course by the war.

VII

REPRESENTATIVE MEN: 1918–1925

Van Wyck did not immediately leave New York, even after the full implications of the failure of *The Seven Arts* had settled in. It was time, he felt, that he and his friends put aside for the moment their radical dreams of community and settle down to write their books. Waldo Frank had established a base in Kansas, where he was putting together the long messianic essay that was to become *Our America* (1919). Randolph Bourne remained in New York, at work on his most revolutionary document, "The State." Van Wyck himself spent several months after the collapse of *The Seven Arts* trying to reestablish both a personal and a professional sense of direction.

For a while he continued to look for a job that would earn enough to bring Eleanor and the boys back from California, and he held onto the small apartment on West 118th Street until he was obliged to recognize that prosperity would certainly be delayed once again. His mother had been contributing regularly to his support—apparently out of the income from a paternal bequest which she refused to hand over even though he felt it was morally his—but she openly begrudged the expense. When she gave signs that she might be about to cut off assistance altogether, Van Wyck finally gave up the apartment and, with an "infinite repugnance," as he wrote Eleanor, he returned to his old position in the editorial rooms of the Century Company, where the pay would at least keep him going until other possibilities developed. During much of 1918 he was engaged in editing *America in the War,* a collection of militaristic cartoons by Louis Raemakers to which was added commentary by nearly every Eminent Living American, "the text comprising an anthology of patriotic opinion." The irony of the chance that dumped this particular bit of hackwork onto a colleague of Randolph Bourne could scarcely have been lost on Van Wyck.

During the spring of 1918 Van Wyck began his own new round of work when he wrote and published in *The Dial* "On Creating a Usable Past," an article which argued that American critics must discover or even invent a nourishing spiritual history. The title of this essay, one of his most influential, immediately became, and has remained, a sort of catchphrase for students of American life. He also began to write to friends about plans for a new book, one which would bring to bear upon a definitive representative all of the force of his long meditation upon the failure of American literary culture. The project was already arousing controversy. Late in 1918 John Butler Yeats wrote apologizing *"for my horrid words said of a book of which I had never read A LINE."* "It was," Yeats went on, "because you proclaimed an intention of pulling Mark Twain from his pedestal which made me think you had gone mad." Yeats's reservations, however, were only practical, and they found little support elsewhere in Van Wyck's circle. Randolph Bourne's encouraging letter of March 1918 was more typical: "Mr. [Stuart] Sherman on Mark Twain . . . made me chortle with joy at the thought of how much you were going to show him when you get started. You simply have no competition. . . . Mr. Sherman simply hasn't an idea in the world that Mark Twain was anything more than a hearty, healthy, vulgarian, expressing himself fully and with him the millions of common Americans. But you will change all that when you get started." Bourne's hurrahs were echoed by Sherwood Anderson and Waldo Frank.

Despite such encouragement Van Wyck was soon convinced that his new undertaking could not prosper in New York. He felt cramped by the city, beset by its social pressures, and, of course, troubled by its demands on his purse. His job at Century paid just enough to maintain his financial problem without offering any possibility of solving it, and most of the little salary he did receive was promptly sent off to Carmel. In the late summer or early fall of 1918, then, probably traveling on borrowed money with hopes that he and Eleanor could come by enough French books for translation to eke out their support, Van Wyck finally accepted Mrs. Stimson's long-standing, somewhat pointed suggestion that he rejoin his family in California. He went reluctantly, and, once arrived, he felt trapped by "the giddiest place I was ever in." The social life at Carmel was no less bothersome than New York's—"we spend most of our time dodging invitations," he wrote to his mother—and he revived his old fears about succumbing to the leisurely pace, both physical and intellectual, of California life.

To Waldo Frank, Van Wyck was even more emphatic about his hostility to California:

> As for me, I have been having a strange and very disturbing experience. I am too susceptible to atmospheres, shockingly susceptible,—that is my great weakness. And I begin to think that a battery which has lost its charge never gets recharged in California! I am full of an unreasoning disgust with this lovely village of Carmel and this crooning Pacific for seducing me into a void of somnolence I cannot seem to shake off. For three months I made magnificent progress with Mark Twain: then I encountered a very difficult problem concerning his humor which I wrestled with for several weeks, only to feel my strength ebbing away from me. It was extraordinary: I seemed to have no rebound and then I felt myself quite submerged. . . .
>
> People relapse here, they revert, they become extinct! . . . They are like simple peaceful domestic animals ruminating side by side in a field and occasionally blowing up in orgies of temperament that send them spinning worlds apart.—You see I watch it with a certain fascination, wondering if I am ever going to get back my valor and finish my book before I come to New York again.

The continuing rigidity of the cultural definition Van Wyck had learned at Harvard also revealed itself when he went on to point Frank a moral:

> One thing I have learned for life, and that is that all our will-to-live as writers comes to us, or rather stays with us, through our intercourse with Europe. Never believe people who talk to you about the West, Waldo; never forget that [it] is we New Yorkers

and New Englanders who have the monopoly of whatever oxygen there is in this American continent! Art is a property of Europe, just as religion is a property of Asia: we shall have it here some day but we shall never interpret America except through a conception of the literary life we can only gain by our contact with Europe.

Van Wyck also maintained a busy correspondence with Sherwood Anderson, who was profoundly excited, and occasionally quarrelsome, about the progressing study of Twain. Anderson's long, admiring, confessional letters supplied a few shrewd hints about Twain's personality and probably confirmed as well the sense of professional identity that Van Wyck sorely needed. The more volatile Frank, however, soon became something of an embarrassment. He urgently needed the intuitive grasp of both his personality and his work which, he was convinced, only Van Wyck could give him. His letters often ranged violently from aggressive self-assertion to demands for attention. "I must feel you beside me," he wrote to Van Wyck in 1919, "as my comrade, as my brother-in-arms, as one who believes in me as I in him. . . ." At other times, piqued by Van Wyck's failure to respond in kind, Frank composed long, desperate letters, a curious mixture of formality and intimacy, to ask whether he had given his faith to a "bad friend." One can imagine Van Wyck shaking his head over such effusions, but he was temperamentally incapable of speaking in the young enthusiast's cosmic tongue, and soon he was writing to Frank of the "certain obscurity" that had arisen between them.

During Van Wyck's residence in California, however, Frank was more an ally than a problem. He joined with Sherwood Anderson in the sympathetic applause and the assurances of common purpose that gave Van Wyck needed encouragement. His work on Twain seemed beset by endless interruptions; the saddest came just a few months after his arrival in Carmel. He was suddenly called upon to edit the literary remains of Randolph Bourne, who had died as ironically as ever he lived, struck down by the influenza epidemic of 1918, just a few days after the Armistice was signed. "This is a sad Christmas here with Randolph dead. We are all stricken," James Oppenheim wrote to Carmel in the letter informing Van Wyck that Bourne had wanted him as literary executor. In a subsequent letter Oppenheim added: "All of us unanimously, instinctively echo this. Only you can place Randolph in the American movement, and make him part of that past & present you are re-creating." In respect for the old difference of opinion between Brooks and Bourne, Oppenheim would arrange to take care of the political papers himself.

Van Wyck borrowed more time than he could easily spare from Twain and worked with the Bourne manuscripts through the first eight months of 1919. As it grew in his imagination, his editing came rather to sustain than to sadden him, and his introduction to the small volume, eventually published as *The History of a Literary Radical* (1920), was only incidentally the customary memorial tribute. The Randolph Bourne he rediscovered in a mass of papers and fragments could be memorialized only in a major statement to and about the radical generation he had served. Poring over the pungent expressions of self that survived Bourne's intense, truncated life, Brooks must have sensed that his friend, who had once asked of him a positive model on which Young America could build, was himself the answer to the demand. In his introduction, then, he tacitly contradicted the legends which were already beginning to grow out of the more sensational aspects of Bourne's career.

His Randolph Bourne was not the tragic victim of an oppressive America. He was not the jeering ironist; he was not the lonely agent of revolution. Illuminated by Van Wyck's inspired empathy, Bourne became instead the master of American life, who incarnated as well the cultural wisdom of "the contemporary European spirit." He was the integrated personality, both expressing and creating his nation, for whom Van Wyck had been calling since 1908: "Here was Emerson's 'American Scholar' at last, but radiating an infinitely warmer, profaner, more companionable influence than Emerson had ever dreamed of . . . ," the prophet of a "trans-national America, . . . a superculture, that might perhaps, by some happy chance, determine the future of civilization itself." Here was the leader who, in *Letters and Leadership,* could be identified only by the implications of his absence. Sensing that the primary function of the contemporaneous radical was to be intensely intellectual, Bourne avoided the confusions of purpose that had troubled earlier reformers. He concentrated on the problems of the literary and cultural life rather than on the reorganization of institutions. Bourne would have found no home in the world of economic power, Brooks was sure; he had already become his own first citizen, a native of "the Beloved Community on the far side of socialism."

That Van Wyck was, consciously or unconsciously, describing his own aspirations, plans, even his achievements, in his essay on Bourne—that he was "hanging a thesis" on him—does not, of course, invalidate either his method or his results. He could respond to Bourne with unusual sensitivity precisely because, with his remarkable feeling for contemporary movements, he discovered Bourne's logic developing in himself, and he could best respect his intuitive empathy for the other man by drawing his own conclusions about the natural growth of the consciousness they shared. If he told only one of the possible truths about Randolph Bourne, the truth he did tell is valuable, and his interpretations have held up well across the years.

Van Wyck wrapped up his work on the Bourne papers in September 1919 and was finally free to return his undivided attention to Twain. It may be that he owed some of the methodology by which he sought to define Twain's relationship to American life to his discovery of the exemplary symbolism inherent in Bourne. At least we find him complaining to Waldo Frank in February 1919, after he was well into the Bourne papers, that: "My work was swimming along—I had done 50,000 words on Mark Twain in two months. Then I found I should have to change my plan completely and go back to the original scheme of a biography." Just what reorientation he found necessary remains obscure; the manuscripts he abandoned have apparently not survived.

Whether or not Brooks's recognition of Randolph Bourne did influence indirectly his conception of *The Ordeal of Mark Twain,* these biographical inquiries were related in kind. As Bourne was the positive example held up to a restless, still incoherent generation, Twain was the negative—the protagonist of a cautionary tale. From the beginning of his career Brooks had been obsessed with the "something" that, having failed in our literary tradition, left our finest spirits unsure of their vocation and frustrated in their art. Earlier he had analyzed the problem in terms of national character, institutions, even cosmological law; now he wanted to get down to cases. *The Ordeal of Mark Twain* was his first sustained assault on the privacy of failure, and the first installment on what was to become, as he later recognized, the trilogy of biographical studies that attempted to anatomize the limits and possibilities of the creative life in the United States.

He had fixed upon his subject with deliberate iconoclasm. One of the most beloved of American writers, "the Lincoln of our literature," Mark Twain had been dead only eight years when Brooks began his study. Interest in both the man and his work had been kept alive by Albert Bigelow Paine's authorized biography (1912), his edition of the letters (1917), William Dean Howells's *My Mark Twain* (1910), and the continuing posthumous publication of Twain's own work. *The Curious Republic of Gondour,* for instance, did not appear until 1919. To both the professionally critical and the popular mind Twain had been the undisputed master of his times, and Brooks was keenly aware of the emotional impact he would create by urging Americans to see their hero as a failure. Here, as in his treatment of Jonathan Edwards, Benjamin Franklin, and the other hierarchs of *America's Coming-of-Age,* he was concerned less with a balanced critical appraisal of Twain's achievement than with isolating and defining the man in his "racial" aspect. The symbolic purpose, of course, informed Brooks's point of view and sharpened his tone. He playfully described himself as a sort of mischievous boy set loose among the treasured bric-a-brac in the literary parlor. "It came out rather well," he wrote to Alyse Gregory upon completing the book, "especially as I had to make up a special psychological brew of my own and write it out in such a way that every phrase must pass muster with a reader who has an antipathy to the long word & abstract notions. In short, I concealed all the snarls under masses of innocent verbiage—and the New York Times will have a merry time refuting a number of rather obnoxious ideas."

The book came painfully into being. Van Wyck never did write easily, and he was subject to fits of depression when his imagination flagged, but Twain seemed a knottier subject than any he had yet attacked. A letter he received from Sherwood Anderson in the spring of 1918 seems particularly revealing for its insightful appraisal of both Brooks and Twain:

> Something Waldo said gave me the notion that your digging into his [Twain's] work had made you a little ill—that you had seen, perhaps too clearly, his dreadful vulgarity and cheapness.
>
> Of course your book cannot be written in a cheerful spirit. In facing Twain's life you face a tragedy. How could the man mean what he does to us if it were not a tragedy? Had the man suc-

ceeded in breaking through, he would not have been a part of us. Can't you take it in that way? . . .

He was maimed, hurt, broken. In some way he got caught up by the dreadful cheap smartness, the shrillness that was a part of the life of the country, that still is its dominant note.

I don't want you to get off Twain. I want your mind on it. Please do not lose courage, do not be frightened away by the muck and ugliness of it.

For the Americans of the future there can be no escape. They have got to, in some way, face themselves. Your book about the man they love and in a dumb way understand will help mightily. I do want you to write that book.

Anderson was probably right to attribute much of his friend's distress to personal involvement with Twain. Van Wyck could never escape—nor did he think he should—the extraordinary empathy with his subjects that was at once his greatest power and the source of his most potentially damaging weakness. But there were other problems to be faced as well. The most immediate involved the very method of conceiving and describing a subject: the new emphasis on the private and the particular demanded a new conceptual vocabulary. Of course the analytic tools Brooks had long been shaping—the concepts of Puritanism, pioneer-logic, the iniquity of American materialism—remained pertinent, and he used them to good effect. Twain was a representative man of his times, and his time, his America, became one of the important presences characterized in the study. But what to do about the other presence—Twain himself? How was he to translate for a twentieth-century audience the secrets, the special expressions of that unique, but symbolic, nineteenth-century personality?

For his answer he turned to the literary Freudianism which was rapidly gaining currency in the United States. The new science would soon be so exhaustively worked and reworked that among literary people it would often become a parlor game or a subject for parody, but Brooks's borrowings from it mark the first time that psychoanalytic theory was used by an important writer in a major study. If only by its visibility, the *Ordeal* opened up exciting new vistas for many of the artists and critics who followed Brooks's leadership through the twenties. Postulating that the terrible pessimism of Twain's last years would provide the key to a contradictory personality, Brooks forced his way into the old writer's mind with a speculative curiosity unexceptionable to us but startlingly innovative then—so personal, so ready to discover pathology in apparently innocuous behavior, that it might have been morbid if it were not for the desperate earnestness behind it. Twain, Brooks argued, citing the humorist's obsession with twins, disguises, switched identities—even the involuntary dualism of the pen name—was a schizophrene whose disturbance stopped just this side of madness. The man who energetically damned the human race was the victim of stringently repressed guilt. Consciously, Twain mocked the basic tenets of his Calvinistic heritage, but he had internalized them so deeply that they dominated the subconscious mind which, in turn, frustrated his every attempt to rid himself of the compulsive moralism of his mother and his wife, as well as those other authoritarian agents of the prevailing orthodoxy to whom he was inevitably drawn. Whenever he indulged the instinctual artist in himself, then, he offended his conscience, which was conditioned to the values of propriety, conformity, and, above all, worldly success.

While Twain's social background made him emotionally a Puritan, the artist within him was tortured whenever he succumbed to his blandly conventional conscience. "That bitterness of [Twain's]," Brooks thought, "was the effect of a certain miscarriage in his creative life, a balked personality, an arrested development of which he was himself almost wholly unaware, but which for him destroyed the meaning of life." The two demands of identity existed side by side in his character, but they were suspended in what Brooks called "watertight compartments" of the mind, and could never be brought fully into consciousness, never purged, never mixed, never qualified by one another. Twain vacillated between them, unable to grow naturally into personality. He remained—emotionally, morally—a child, happiest when he was writing about Hannibal and his old times on the Mississippi when, as a river pilot, he had found a vocation which satisfied his needs for both creativity and material success. He struggled through a viciously competitive life, mistrusting his clownish, partial literary identity but driven to exploit it by his extrarational need for big money. Even as he boisterously enjoyed success, however, he drove himself to judge the magnate philosophy of the Gilded Age according to the very artistic, idealistic morality which offended his social orientation. Except for the cynical determinism Twain cultivated in self-defense, there could be no solution for such a problem.

In the six decades since the publication of the *Ordeal*, which remains one of Brooks's most celebrated and controversial works, much has been made of the system of psychoanalytic notation which informs it. On the one hand, the book had been applauded as the trailblazing study which established Freudian criticism in America—an attribution which perhaps claims too much for Brooks's psychological methodology, which was always eclectic and partial. (It also claims too much for his originality. Depth psychology had interested a few American intellectuals at least since 1915, although it had not yet found an important critical vehicle.) On the other hand, Brooks has been taken to task for his amateurism, his failure to respect the consistency of the system he borrowed, his impressionistic use of biographical evidence, his habit of skipping back and forth, as Bernard De Voto complained, between the methods of Freud, Jung, and Adler. Again, such criticism probably assigns greater priority than Brooks did to the psychoanalytic method as an end in itself.

Brooks always resisted attempts to rank him among the Freudians. He later told Robert E. Spiller—an exaggeration by way of dismissing the question, Spiller thought—that he had all he knew about the mind from a brief study he had read in 1918, Bernard Hart's *The Psychology of Insanity.* This excellent little handbook attempted to synthesize the various discoveries about human consciousness made by the new science and to restate them in language available to the layman. Although generally Freudian in orientation, Hart deemphasized the Freudian concept of the libido and included significant admixtures of Jung, Janet, and other psychologists in his essay. To a critic in need of a psychological vocabulary he offered working definitions of the unconscious, repression and its manifestations in the conscious mind, unconscious conflict, causal complex, projection, dissociation (the watertight compartments Brooks found so useful in explaining Twain), and "herd-instinct"—this last a rough approximation of the social origins of conscience which Hart borrowed from the sociologist William Trotter's *Instincts of the Herd in Peace and War.* Anyone acquainted with *The Psychology of Insanity* will immediately recognize the extensive uses to which Hart's system was put in *The Ordeal of Mark Twain.*

There is, however, other evidence to suggest that the indebtedness to Hart was neither wholesale nor inhibiting. Brooks remembered elsewhere that Randolph Bourne introduced him to the thought of Freud and Jung in 1918, the same year he discovered the *Psychology of In-*

sanity. Association with Waldo Frank and James Oppenheim would in itself have exposed him to the excitement as well as to the basic postulates of psychoanalytic theory, and it is useful to remember that even among writers the written word does not necessarily supersede other modes of communication. Hart permitted Brooks to work intelligibly with the complex body of material he had probably acquired from many diverse sources. Brooks was not concerned with bearing witness to the validity of psychoanalytic theory; he took depth psychology as a means, not an end; a tool, not a world view. It provided him with a system of analogy and metaphor that reinforced the truth about Twain he wished to divulge, but it was not the truth itself.

Brooks's interest in Twain was not, finally, psychological at all. He was concerned, as always, with culture and society, personality and literature, and not with pathology. To the critic of identity whose idea of the psyche always remained closer to the model of John Butler Yeats than that of Sigmund Freud, Mark Twain was less the contemporaneous neurotic than a character long familiar in Brooks's work, the homeless sufferer from the "malady of the ideal." Twain, to be sure, was a drastically advanced case, more inhibited by the social factor in the creative equation than the romantic souls whose careers Brooks had earlier chronicled. But in its essence, the problem of conflict between the idealism of art and the demands of (in its broadest sense) audience remained the same. However much his significance might be enhanced by the insights of the new age, it was the spiritual Twain, illuminated according to Brooks's nineteenth-century humanism, who stepped forward. Many of the other interests that seemed briskly up-to-date in 1920—the unconscious (or preconscious) instinctual life, dual personality, herd-logic, even dissociation—had figured prominently in Brooks's earlier studies of the dilemma of the American writer.

The Ordeal of Mark Twain was brought out in 1920 by Dutton, the publishing house with which Van Wyck would remain the rest of his life, and response to the book was both lively and gratifying. Although it was to touch off acrimonious debates among the champions of several critical schools, Brooks's reinterpretation of the popular hero whom Americans had for years unquestioningly adored drew surprisingly little fire from the general run of reviewers. Even *The New York Times* admitted that the *Ordeal* was the best book on its subject, and all over the United States and Great Britain Brooks's aggressive assertions about the nature of Twain's mind and art were greeted as revelation. Brooks had made of Twain at once a better and more troubled man than the good-natured savage who, according to the legends of the Gilded Age, had defended the sacrosanctities of taste, propriety, and economic individualism. Twain was now, as he has remained, a desperately complex figure—a confused, cynical Gulliver, entangled forever in the mores of a decadent Lilliput. That imagery of frustrated giantism has been often attacked, sometimes modified, but never entirely confounded.

Brooks's study survives as much as a creation of personality in its own right as for its seminal contribution to the scholarship of Mark Twain and his America. Much like a character in a major fiction, Brooks's Twain is at once a fully particularized individual and a daring, expansive symbol. So nicely are these elements of his portrait balanced that it becomes impossible to say, at any given moment, where particularization ends and symbolism begins. It is the symbolic Twain —more, perhaps, than the historical Samuel Clemens—who draws us back to Brooks's parable of the artistic life, but we should not ignore the danger Brooks runs in translating the details of a complex personality into moral exempla. He himself recognized later that the major weakness of his study lay in its radical tendency to overemphasize the typicality of its subject.

Other dangerous assumptions are at work in the *Ordeal.* David Starr Jordan, who applauded the critical insights of his former assistant, also expressed reservations about the book, suggesting that what Twain gave to his world was, in fact, all he had to give. Other readers have joined Jordan in balking at the could-have-been which necessarily underlies Brooks's contention that Twain had betrayed himself. Another weakness in the argument of the *Ordeal* was seized upon by Bernard De Voto a dozen years later: in a book which emphasizes the formative influence of cultural environment, Brooks prejudices his argument by conceiving of culture strictly in terms of Europe. He did acknowledge the importance of slave lore and piloting to Twain's developing imagination, but he was unable to see that the settlements along the Mississippi, however deficient according to the standards of London or Rome, possessed their own culture—embryonic, surely, but promising, and in some ways satisfying.

Such limitations left Brooks open to charges, not long in coming, that he imposed his theses as from above. While they force us to qualify somewhat his conclusions about Twain, they do not impeach his argument, which worked, as always, more by the play of the empathetic imagination than by the purposeful logic of scholarly inquiry. He made no bones about his subjectivism. The reiterated *I says*, which are scattered liberally through nearly every important discussion in the book, assure us that the critic prefers to develop his personal understanding rather than limit his case to factual evidence. The personal voice is salty; it is urbane; it has confidence; it is, above all, wonderfully compassionate. Brooks's ability to get "inside" his subject, as well as his keen feeling for the dignity of the artistic life, illuminated Twain with a kind of tragic splendor. The matter was not of historical interest merely, Brooks was insisting: here was an object lesson for all young artists. The cautionary tale built at last to a single question, as the critic wondered aloud if "the American writer of today [has] the same excuse for missing his vocation." Brooks did not wait for his generation to settle its own response. It was time, he concluded, that the creative American embrace his freedom, that he "put away childish things and walk the stage as poets do."

To the idealistic audience that Brooks addressed, *The Ordeal of Mark Twain* demonstrated that the dangers of the creative life were knowable and could be avoided. Once again, he had offered the new generation of literary radicals a usable past. Waldo Frank's is typical of the enthusiastic letters of recognition that poured in upon Van Wyck from allies and well-wishers all over the country: "Closing your book—which I raced through fascinated—I said aloud: 'We are off!' The race has begun. Our generation has already built a house of the fair and soaring timber of our land."

Almost before he finished with Mark Twain, Van Wyck was looking around for another subject. For a while he toyed with plans to extend the method of the *Ordeal* to a book on contemporary writers and the America that blighted their careers. It seemed to others as well as himself the inevitable sequel to his historical researches, but although he continued for several years to replan the study, he was never able to "see" the subject with sufficient clarity to begin serious work. As he searched unhappily through his mind and books, unable, it seemed, to break out of his terrible aridity, "living too much in the house, smoking and not working or being able to work," he hit for temporary respite upon a project in translation.

Most of the French books he and Eleanor had translated for the

American market involved nothing more than hackwork, but soon after completing the *Ordeal* Van Wyck decided to translate Léon Bazalgette's experiment in critical biography, *Henry Thoreau, Sauvage,* which, although six years old, was still unknown in the United States. He was not sure that the book could be published until 1924, and his translation, *Henry Thoreau, Bachelor of Nature,* did not come out until 1925, but he was privately at work, and carrying on a friendly correspondence with Bazalgette from 1920, when the French critic had written to thank him for a sympathetic review of his book on Whitman. During the four years it took to find a publisher, Van Wyck rediscovered Thoreau and became deeply impressed by Bazalgette's biographical method, which promised a distinctively more suggestive, more personal approach to the writing of lives than anything he had yet encountered. His leisurely work on this translation, which was relatively insignificant in itself, becomes in retrospect one of the important episodes in his life. Bazalgette's book was probably the only significant stylistic influence Brooks encountered after leaving Harvard, and his translation of it marks the methodological turning point of his career.

Bazalgette's *Thoreau* is a curious, passionate, inventive book. It abandons the thoughtful distance a biographer usually tries to keep from his subject and attempts instead to imitate the representation of character available to fiction. As a scholar Bazalgette was fastidious and thorough, but as an artist he invoked a more elusive truth, and he did his best to respect the integrity of his subject by removing from his narrative all traces of the means of inquiry. The biographer himself pretends to be gone from *Henry Thoreau, Sauvage.* The narrative mode is dramatic rather than expository, and the point of view always rests firmly in the subject. The book aspires to be an extension of Thoreau's personality.

At least as Brooks translates him, Bazalgette had a certain knack for this rather delicate business of persuading your subject to speak for you. His narrative voice moves fluently from the conventional third to the second, and, at times, even to the first person, when the essential Thoreau breaks in, as it were, to speak in his own Yankee twang. All of this shifting of authority goes on without quotation marks or other acknowledgment of external manipulation. Quotations and paraphrases from Thoreau's journals are woven into the narrative in a way indistinguishable from Bazalgette's own commentary, which itself imitates his subject's manner. The method is calculated to persuade the reader

142

that he enters a direct personal relationship with Henry Thoreau. At times Bazalgette's context is so precise, his lyric mood so evocative, that he does approximate that astringent Yankee consciousness. For the most part, however, his book is rather more charming than empathetic, more *tour de force* than self-effacement, and *Henry Thoreau, Sauvage* has dated badly. Van Wyck, who in old age reminded himself of his indebtedness to Bazalgette, responded more to the French biographer's inspiration than to his achievement.

Edmund Wilson later paraphrased the opinions of his contemporaries by naming it an "evil hour" when Van Wyck sat down with *Henry Thoreau, Sauvage,* but however one judges the influence of Bazalgette, it made itself immediately felt in Brooks's next major essay in reinterpretation. In fact, it may have helped to settle Brooks on his subject. Although he was rapidly acquiring a reputation as a social historian and a critic of the American past, as well as a man of letters, he had only reluctantly accepted his own conclusion that he would be wisest to press further his raids upon the nineteenth century. He was still tantalized by his visions of that book on the contemporary scene. Such a book must one day be written—that was clear—but Van Wyck also sensed that to write it now might be a self-indulgence he could ill afford.

He expressed some of his reservations about the subject in a letter of 1920 to Newton Arvin, the critic with whom he was just striking up a friendship. Responding to Arvin's request for personal advice, Van Wyck warned the younger man against his natural inclination to take on writers who were still active. Such undertakings were endless, he insisted—better to find a subject sufficiently removed from contemporary life so that a critic could be sure of getting all the available data. "Do I make myself clear?" Van Wyck went on. "One's undertakings ought to be beyond one's powers, but only a little beyond; if they are just far enough beyond one's powers, one's powers are educated by the task itself up to the adequate point. But if the task is too great one merely ends in despair with nothing done.... There is a logic in the fact that the critics who have most effectively met the problems of their own age have begun with subjects as remote as possible from it."

Van Wyck had positive reasons as well for settling, finally, on the elusive subject that was to occupy nearly four years. He had been fascinated at least since his high-school days by what seemed to him the enigma of Henry James, and the "strange, vain, fantastical" figure of the expatriate, a more troublesome character now that the Great War had exposed a generation of American intellectuals to the influence of European modernism, had lurked in the shadows of his critical imagination ever since *The Wine of the Puritans.* "The subject," as he wrote in 1922 to an old family friend, Dr. J. S. Zelie, "is Henry James and his pilgrimage, why he went to England and what happened to him after he got there, and I have a golden dream of what I want to say: it wouldn't interest me very much if I couldn't make it a typical, as well as an individual, story. Why do we all want to go to England and what is the self-protective interest, aside from necessity, that keeps us from doing so?" "Our romantic feeling for Europe," he continued in another letter to Zelie, "in itself precludes us, it seems to me, from coming to grips with it and renders it impossible sooner or later for us to keep in grips (so to speak) with ourselves. . . . It's the young man, or specifically the young writer, who goes to Europe to make his life that I have in mind." Such themes also demanded an exercise in self-criticism for a young writer who still looked almost instinctively eastward for his model of the good cultural life.

He was "keenly aware," he insisted, of his "tendency to impose a thesis on an individual," and he was determined that his Henry James should not suffer from it, but the symbolizing methodology Brooks brought from Mark Twain to his new exemplar showed few, if any, signs of adjustment. It was Henry James the representative man, the magnificent highbrow, the inevitable antithesis of Twain, he was after. Like Twain, Henry James promised a certain, useful *succès de scandale;* he was a writer of extraordinary reputation, who, recently dead, continued to dominate the imaginations of his American heirs. His position was so firmly entrenched, Brooks complained to Robert Herrick, the realistic novelist who had known James personally, that a "whole school of writers is growing up that begins where James left off, and regards the later James as its patron saint." He wanted to head off such a development, which must impoverish the dangerously small store of creative energy from which Young America drew.

"I am launched on a somewhat perilous voyage," Brooks admitted to Herrick. His most immediate problem was stylistic. Aware that he must anticipate attempts to discredit his empathetic analysis, he needed a critical language that would sustain the highly precarious balance between sympathy and judgment, and capture in narrative form "the precise nature and history of James's relations with English life." James demanded the nuance, the fine inflections of tone and point of view which alone could distinguish what was delicate from what was merely precious in his work. The remorseless hammering of the intellectual attack that had flushed the beast lurking in the jungle of Mark Twain would beat harmlessly past the chameleonic figure hidden in the Oriental carpet that was the life and work of Henry James. This was an altogether shyer creature. He could be trapped, Brooks was coming increasingly to believe, only in the labyrinth of his own cunning.

This series of technical problems, one breeding upon another, was partly of Brooks's own making. He was in possesion of a number of personal anecdotes about James which would, he felt, demonstrate the validity of his argument, but which he was reluctant to use. They were too raw, he complained to Robert Herrick, who had supplied some of the best: they unwrapped the bandages from the shrouded figure, but they were likely to remove the skin as well. His intrusions on James's privacy will scarcely seem criminal now, and Brooks himself, years later, finally did retell one of the sensitive anecdotes Herrick had given him—how Herrick went to visit James at Rye, and how James, visibly mortified at being forced to greet his guest at the railroad station without a servant in attendance, rebuked the young novelist for addressing him as "Mr. James." "Only butlers say that, my dear Herrick," the Master reportedly intoned. Another of Herrick's contributions to the research on Henry James—one Brooks never did repeat—was the strong suggestion that James was sexually impotent. The personally reticent Brooks felt that such raids upon a man's secrecy would betray both "the dignity and the pathos" of his subject.

Brooks was bothered further by the nagging intuition that he had missed something essential in James. The man stubbornly refused to come alive for him, and Eleanor began worriedly asking how long her husband must go on wrestling with the old novelist's "spook." Despite Eleanor's (and his own) anxieties about his state of mind, Van Wyck plugged away on his hated manuscript for nearly two years. It was an excruciatingly unhappy time; never before had he set himself a task before which, it seemed, he must ultimately admit defeat. Finally, early in 1923, Van Wyck put the whole project "on the shelf," fully determined to find something else to write about. However, the five months he spent away from Henry James apparently gave him the distance he needed to recognize his book, and by July he was excitedly writing to Sherwood Anderson that "Henry James really began to dawn on me about two months ago—came alive. I mean, inside of me, and since then the infant monster has been kicking and struggling so hard at the walls of my psyche that I am all out of breath." He spent another, happier, year finishing the book, and Dutton brought out *The Pilgrimage of Henry James* in February 1925.

It seems obvious that the frustrating questions of style and point of view, which for two years remained just beyond Brooks's grasp, were finally answered by the example of Léon Bazalgette's *Thoreau*. Like Bazalgette, Brooks adopted his subject's characteristic syntax, vocabulary, tone—contriving to let James speak for (and against) himself without overt interference from the critic behind the scenes. "The method is pretty much that of a novel," Brooks told Sherwood Anderson, "—that is, I am attempting to tell the whole story through his eyes—with, of course, my own running interpretation. But the difference is that every sentence I write must square with known facts. . . ." The reader of *The Pilgrimage of Henry James* was warned in a brief prefatory note that substantial excerpts from James's writings were often woven into the narrative without any indications of source, a plagiarism necessary because the author knew no better way "of conveying with strict accuracy at moments what he conceives to have been James's thoughts and feelings." The study read, as reviewers were quick to point out, like a psychological fiction in the ironic manner of James himself.

This nod to Bazalgette should not suggest discipleship. Brooks used the ventriloquistic mode more seriously and ambitiously than his teacher. He borrowed neither the French critic's gaudy shifts of narrative person nor his cinematic manipulations of point of view, and the "running interpretation" he picked up from time to time calls far less attention to itself than Bazalgette's acrobatic efforts to shun all open commentary. The *Pilgrimage* is really an exercise in the twentieth-century art of the pastiche, curiously paralleling the mosaics of quotation and allusion which in the hands of Eliot and Pound were becoming a major poetical form. Unlike the poets, however, who used their borrowings to refer to systems of meaning outside of their own work, Brooks attempts to create by implication the mysterious essence of identity, manifest only in the total experience of James's life and art.

One ventures a guess, finally, that Brooks's transcendence of his French source is a matter of character, that he identified more intimately with the personality of his subject than Bazalgette, across the boundaries of nation and language, could with his. But Brooks's adaptation of the method is also more dangerous than Bazalgette's. The French writer found most of his basic information and all of his quotations and paraphrases in Thoreau's journals—that is, in genuinely autobiographical documents—but Brooks did not distinguish between autobiography and fiction when he borrowed from James. He would have argued that imaginatively conceived experience was just as real a projection of personality as was cold biographical fact.

The Pilgrimage of Henry James was Brooks's first essay in the empathetic, paraphrasal style that was to characterize nearly all of his important work thereafter. A tribute to his continuing inventiveness in response to each new challenge, it is also a significant point of departure in his career. He was not so much concerned here with establishing a hierarchy of standards by which to judge his subject; he wanted instead to permit the judgment to develop naturally out of the subject itself. "[The poet] is judgment," Walt Whitman had written in the preface to his first *Leaves of Grass*. "He judges not as the judge judges but as the sun falling around a helpless thing." That is, truth is discovered not according to external, relative standards, which are merely institutional, but by casting light. I have no evidence that Brooks kept Whitman's organic ideal in mind as he put together his book on James, but his narrative is, nevertheless, a first step toward the literary monism his beloved poet had envisioned. It is also an evolutionary extension of Brooks's lifelong need for a critical voice uncompromised by an abstracted rhetorical machinery.

The Pilgrimage of Henry James depends for its success on its complex, allusive texture, but the intellectual argument at its core is straightforward and easily paraphrased. James was, for Brooks, the instinctual American who could not accept America. He grew up, Brooks contended, looking eastward to the enchanted kingdoms he discovered in the picture books and romanticized memoirs of aristocratic English life, feeling vaguely that his heritage and destiny alike were irrevocably European. Come into young manhood, this Anglophiliac artist of the beautiful was repulsed by the desolate surroundings and crude energy of American life. And thus the pilgrimage to the Europe that possessed a tradition of respect for the creative life, and a society in which a man's capacities might be brought into full play. In Italy, in France, and, eventually, in England, Henry James worked fervidly to make

147

himself over into a good European, but everywhere he found himself hopelessly American. Not only was he rejected by the arrogantly exclusive groups into which he tried to insinuate himself, but his instinctual life never followed his aspirations to a new citizenship. His attempts, however unsuccessful, to graft himself onto the life of the Old World unfitted him for life in the new, and when he later returned for an experimental tour of the United States he found himself more than ever appalled by its crassness.

Brooks's James was emotionally a man without a country. His inability to be either solidly European or solidly American expressed itself in the increasing rootlessness of his art, which had earlier represented one of the highest achievements of the American spirit. Deprived of his "racial" heritage, he was deprived of the point of view which, for a personalist critic, provided the only truly substantial basis for literature. "He had emerged," Brooks asserted in regard to James's later style, "as an impassioned geometer—or, shall we say, some vast arachnid of art, pouncing upon the tiny air-blown particle and wrapping it round and round." He had become all style, all method, all manner—and no matter.

The Pilgrimage of Henry James was anticipated by Brooks's audience, and it created as much stir as had the similarly truculent study of Mark Twain a few years earlier. By 1925 it had become a commonplace to refer to Brooks as an oracle of "the newness," and writers of the younger generation were prepared to rally round him once again. But this time there were murmurs to the effect that Brooks's preoccupations with culture and society had blinded him to the values of art, and a few of the more aesthetically oriented among his professional audience began to challenge the principles of his radical leadership. For many younger writers James was the incarnation of the artist; at the very least he remained a great favorite of the same cultural groups that Brooks had helped bring into being. His adherents resented Brooks's way of wrenching the novelist's phrases from context and turning them against him. Even more, they were appalled by the critical taste that preferred the work of James's early maturity to the dense, impressionistic novels of his last years. Their aesthetic argument has long since emerged triumphant.

Edmund Wilson, with his usual grace and good sense, managed to touch on most of the points raised then and since about both the *Pil-*

grimage and Brooks's later work in the essay-review he published shortly after the book came out. Suggesting that Brooks should be considered a social historian rather than truly a critic, he praised the *Pilgrimage* for its insight into American motives and its definition of James's social significance. But he balked at Brooks's use of documentary evidence, complained that the book submerged the creative spirit in the social symbol, and, most damning of all, he asserted that Brooks was unable to understand the nature and development of James's artistry.

In a sense Brooks does refuse aesthetic commentary, but in the same breath he pays his highest tribute to James as an artist: "Least of all can we penetrate to the heart of this genius, account for it, apprehend its secret. . . . can we draw out Leviathan with a hook, or his tongue with a cord which we let down? I will not conceal his parts, said the Lord to Job, nor his power, nor his comely proportion. But who can open the doors of his face? His scales are his pride, shut up together as with a close seal." Brooks is celebrating the work of the middle years, but the biblical splendor of his praise was both sincerely offered and necessary to the argument of his book, which dealt with a great writer come at the end to a tragic insubstantiality because of the cultural conditions that had impelled him to make an obvious, but unnatural, choice of life. He felt that once he amply acknowledged James's artistic supremacy, he would establish the sympathetic authority with which he could take note of a lack of center in the later career without appearing to belittle the man's general excellence.

He was wrong, as it turned out. His compassion has been ignored, and his discussion of James's culminative work remains largely incomprehensible or irrelevant to latter-day critics, for whom *The Pilgrimage of Henry James* survives only as a literary curiosity—at best an experiment that failed, at worst an aberration. Its argument, however, based upon premises about nationality and art that have failed to take hold in this country, at least offers a coherent explanation of the development of the later James, and Wilson thought that in terms of literary form the *Pilgrimage* was better than anything Brooks had previously written.

But the fact remains the Brooks's contemporaries did not much like it, and the *Pilgrimage* takes on a singular, rather unsettling importance in his life. For the first time Van Wyck had fallen out of phase with the dominant tendencies of the movement he had himself been instrumental in getting started. No one could have known it then, but it was a parting of the ways. Despite his efforts, his bemusement, his irritation, Brooks would never again be completely in harmony with his generation.

VIII

PRACTICAL LEADERSHIP: 1920–1924

By the time *The Pilgrimage of Henry James* was becoming an issue in the increasing factionalism among intellectuals, Van Wyck had been back in New York for nearly five years—had found a home and established himself as probably the most important critic of his generation. Almost as he was finishing *The Ordeal of Mark Twain* he had received a letter from Ben Huebsch, who was about to become the publisher of an ambitious new journal, *The Freeman,* and who invited Van Wyck to join the enterprise as literary editor. Van Wyck was asked for half of his time in return for forty dollars a week, and he was promised a free hand in setting the policies of his department. In February 1920, happy to break away from Carmel and the depressing household routine he had fallen into since the *Twain* was completed, he boarded the Overland Express for the long, familiar journey across the continent. He must have felt suddenly at home as he picked up his bags and joined the buzzing, restless crowd that spilled through the lobby of Grand Central Station into the streets of Manhattan.

Van Wyck was returning to a Manhattan self-consciously, hilariously, in reaction against the grim war shock of the city he had left two years earlier. Prohibition was law, and with the opening of Greenwich Village's first speakeasies the heady atmosphere of the twenties closed swiftly over a startled but grateful generation. A sort of reckless personal frivolity was, in fact, the only satisfying rebelliousness readily available in a decade that extended one aspect of the war years with a general stifling of economic and political dissent. In Greenwich Village there were new extremes of zaniness in expressions of personal freedom. Sexual mores were changing dramatically—Floyd Dell's Village was giving way to Maxwell Bodenheim's—and well-to-do "tourists" swarmed downtown for a peek at the hedonistic rituals of young Bohemia. Similar excursions to the romantically mysterious colony far uptown, where another artistic "renaissance" was in the making, expressed an equally self-indulgent interest in whatever seemed exotic or primitive. Moved by a frequently patronizing Negrophilia, modish people drifted up to Lenox Avenue, where they could sway to the erotic rhythms of Afro-American music, usually in clubs where black patrons were not welcome. Particularly under the patronage of Carl Van Vechten, the "Negro was in vogue," in Langston Hughes's phrase, from roughly 1920 until the onset of the Great Depression.

The uncritical enthusiasm that the awakened young showed for their new forms of play should not obscure the fact that theirs was truly an age of discovery. At its best, the nervous spirit of the twenties—its restless search for the new, its experimentalism, its uninhibited assault on life—found literary expression in the "little magazines" that proliferated during the decade: William Carlos Williams's *Contact,* for example, or Alfred Kreymborg's *Broom.* The comically cynical tone, the peculiar wisdom of the period, infected such serious journals of opinion as H. L. Mencken's *American Mercury,* which would begin publication in 1924.

Van Wyck himself had returned to join a more decorous magazine. *The Freeman* was founded by Francis Neilson, who had been an actor, playwright, and librettist, in both England and the United States. At one time a Liberal member of the British Parliament, Neilson was a follower of Henry George, and he planned to make of *The Freeman* an instrument of land and fiscal reform according to the doctrine of the single tax. Launching this latest program for the reorganization of the economy, Neilson found himself in the paradoxical position of having behind him the considerable, but indifferent, backing of one of the greatest capitalist families in the United States. He had married Helen Swift, heiress to a Chicago meat-packing fortune, and she purchased *The Freeman* apparently for no better reason than to give him something to do with his time. Even the title of the magazine was capitalist plunder; Mrs. Neilson bought it from the owners of a small Negro newspaper in Indiana.

Neilson had conceived his plans for the new magazine in collaboration with Albert Jay Nock, another Georgist, who had worked with Brand Whitlock, the Progressive mayor of Toledo. By any standards, Nock was uniquely, and, as it turned out, brilliantly prepared for his new role as radical editor. A direct descendant of Chief Justice John Jay, he had been at various times a classical scholar, an Episcopal clergyman, a professional baseball player, and an emissary for the State Department, but he deliberately kept his colorful past as obscure as the personal life that he stubbornly hid from even his closest associates. His mania for privacy was the subject of several standing jokes at the *Freeman* office: if you encountered Mr. Nock leaving the building and asked which way he was headed he would unhesitatingly and unvariably reply, "The other way"; if you were forced to communicate with Mr. Nock after office hours you must leave a coded note under a certain rock in Central Park. The mercurial, acidulous Nock cultivated his eccentricities as an artist cultivates his style. Even his compulsive reticence was part of his role as the "superfluous man." He was civilized, he seemed to imply, beyond the tolerance of modern civilization.

Nock's "radicalism" was exclusively a matter of economics, and he seems too readily to have conceived of his personal force in strictly negative or reactionary terms. He was, in fact, quick to defend almost any conservative attitude his generation attacked. His prejudices were as condescendingly antidemocratic as were his friend H. L. Mencken's, and, in fact, Nock was much as Mencken might have been if deprived of his uproarious humor. His biases were as complacently blatant; his tastes were as baronial; his prose itself has much of the bite and snap of Mencken's assaults on everything the farmer and the Christian held sacred. He modeled his style, or so he claimed, on the four "pillars" of Rabelais, Matthew Arnold, the Bible, and Artemus Ward—a characteristically eccentric combination—and he had little sympathy for the experimentalism that was becoming the important literary mode of his time. John Hall Wheelock remembered indignantly that he stopped submitting to *The Freeman* after Nock went through one of his poems, altering it so that each foot was a regular iamb.

Despite such regulations upon his sympathies, Nock made a surprisingly good editor, and the magazine quickly became his. Neilson, who usually remained in Chicago, was in time little more than an absentee landlord. Within its range, Nock's taste was impeccable, and he was shrewd enough to recognize both the value of an open forum and that his whimsical personality alone would not sustain *The Freeman*. He cheerfully tolerated nearly any opinion that was expressed with sufficient elegance. With the exception of a few writers (like Lewis Mumford) who used the vocabularies of modern disciplines that a superfluous man might consider vulgar (Mumford's was sociology), almost everyone concerned with *The Freeman* bore witness to the free atmosphere that attended Nock's eccentric pontificate. Even the composition of the editorial board attested to the magazine's defiant heterodoxy. Besides Brooks, who clung stubbornly to his Wellsian socialism, there were Suzanne LaFollette, a philosophical anarchist, Geroid Tanquary Robinson, whose radicalism was often overtly hostile to Nock's own, and Walter Fuller, a sardonic Englishman who seemed bitter about politics in general.

Whatever its disparities of political orientation, Nock's *Freeman* maintained for its four years of existence a consistently lofty tone. Not the least of the magazine's "eccentricities" was its commitment to a sort of Arnoldian high seriousness in what was too often a frivolous or flippantly cynical era. Nock insisted that the magazine respect the literary decorum of the nineteenth-century reformers with whom he was temperamentally allied, and his reactionary adherence to such proprieties as the use of British spelling caused one correspondent to wonder how in the devil the workingmen of Noah Webster's America could be expected to respond to even the most fervent appeal to "Labour."

Despite its subdued urbanity, *The Freeman* stood as an avowedly radical magazine in a politically repressive time. These were the days of the Palmer Raids, and the attorney general's crusade against the Red Scare was only the most spectacular expression of a national assault on heterodoxy. The Eighteenth Amendment and the Scopes Trial were equally significant manifestations of the intolerance that also fostered many quasipatriotic social groups, openly bigoted immigration laws, and the farcical Wobbly trial of 1918, presided over by Judge Kenesaw Mountain Landis, who after the "Black Sox" scandal would be hired to restore purity to baseball. In what remained morally Warren Harding's America, a nation abdicated its responsibility to the League of Nations, and a good shoemaker and a poor fish peddler were arrested in 1920 by the Commonwealth of Massachusetts, tried for murder, and eventually convicted of anarchism.

It was an awkward moment for Nock's impudent declaration that he alone was editing a truly radical magazine, but he relished his discovery of still another way to set himself apart from the general run of men and opinions. While Marxists and Socialists pointed to his claim as a supreme example of the state to which radicalism in the United States had fallen, Nock's liberal peers accepted his radicalism as a necessary complement to their own positions. He and his staff handled it with considerable grace and wit. *The Freeman's* tone yielded to the restraints of irony, and its arguments were based always on an appeal to intellectual decency rather than organizational or revolutionary rhetoric. The editors were provocative analysts of affairs and their work informed many of the "Middle Articles," the section that gave the magazine its heft and center. *The Freeman* also provided a forum for such other radical spokesmen as Lincoln Steffens, Bertrand Russell, Thorstein Veblen, and William Z. Foster. Complementing the Middle Articles was a regular section of "Current Comment," brief, ironic editorials noting the latest crimes of capitalism and its government.

So nicely did Nock's editorial practice assimilate and balance the various possibilities of radicalism that the most troublesome disagreement in the *Freeman* organization was probably the one between Nock and Brooks. From time to time their running debate about politics and art would flare into open quarrel, but Nock was content to endure the embarrassment of irreconcilable differences as long as he had the services of the man he considered the best literary editor in the country. It was Brooks's reputation and ability that from the beginning assured *The Freeman* a place in the front ranks of contemporary opinion. For his part, Van Wyck adjusted easily to Nock. He liked his eccentric editor, and he put up with Nock's frequently pigheaded sense of decorum for the sake of the excellence the man demanded of his motley group of editors, essayists, and reviewers.

His adaptation to the new professional life of *The Freeman* was only part of the major resettlement Van Wyck was making during 1920. In October he and Eleanor, who had followed him east that spring, moved into their first permanent home, the cottage they had purchased after much deliberation in Westport, Connecticut, about fifty miles from New York. Here Van Wyck could satisfy his need for a retreat from the city without cutting himself off from the stimulation of its intellectual life. After a day's work in Manhattan he could step off the commuter train and walk the pleasant mile home—past the small, white New England houses and the huge elms that shaded them, savoring the mild bite of the salt air that pierced even these residential solitudes. Home, when he finally entered the orderly garden paths and the arbor that led to his door, was set atop a hill overlooking town, in a "rocky, woodsy corner" of what is still a quiet neighborhood. Westport has since become a wealthy suburb of New York City, but in 1920 it was a New England coastal village. Van Wyck discovered that the cheapest serviceable furniture to be had in the area dated from the eighteenth century, and he thought that his neighbors preserved as faithfully the flavor and the economy of their traditionally thoughtful, efficient regional culture. For an American critic who cherished "racial" memories of Concord and had dared to appoint himself spokesman to and for the New England mind, that first autumn in the small community by the sea must have seemed like a return to his ancestral country.

Not only was Van Wyck finally putting down roots in the rocky soil of his favorite province; another of his emotional needs was satisfied by the host of friends, both old and new, who made the village an intellectual center in its own right. The southwestern Connecticut shore already supported several colonies of artists and writers who had left the city in their search for the congenial, inexpensive surroundings where they might live and work in peace. Paul Rosenfeld, an ally from *Seven Arts* days and one of Van Wyck's chief confidants during the twenties and thirties, lived in Westport, as did Karl and Ray Anderson and, for a while, their peripatetic brother Sherwood. Among other temporary residents who enlivened the living rooms and gardens of the village were Robert Frost, a thorny individual with whom Van Wyck kept up an uneasy relationship for many years, and F. Scott Fitzgerald, a great admirer of Brooks, whom he considered (reflecting a common misapprehension about Brooks's background) the foremost modern representative of intellectual New England. Fitzgerald was probably in his cups the evening he interrupted a formal dinner party by leaving his seat to walk carefully around the table, lift a leg of the startled Van Wyck's trousers, and return bemusedly to his place. When his fellow guests finally gave in to their curiosity, Fitzgerald told them that he had simply wanted to see for himself if Yankees always wore red union suits.

There were more subdued companions in Westport. The British author of the "Doctor Dolittle" stories, Hugh Lofting, was a neighbor, as were William McFee, the crotchety English sea novelist; the painter Everett Shinn; the critic Brooks Atkinson; and the gently eccentric brothers Charles and Maurice Prendergast, for whom Van Wyck always reserved a special affection. Another of Van Wyck's intimates was the Dutch historian, essayist, and painter Hendrik Willem Van Loon, a great, loud, boar of a man who managed to offend many of his Westport acquaintances but whose cosmopolitanism seemed attractive to a critic of American provincialism. Van Wyck was never able to take Van Loon's work with any seriousness, but he defended his friend as an heir of the traditions of European magnanimity.

Several other intellectual companions lived just outside Westport. Max Perkins had settled a few miles away in the village of New Canaan, where Bliss Carman, the Canadian poet, also made his home, and where Elinor Wylie, the legendarily beautiful poet and novelist, spent several years of her troubled life. Just down the street from Mrs. Wylie lived Padraic and Mary (or "Molly") Colum. Friends of Yeats and Joyce, the Colums had come of age during the Irish Renaissance, and by a lucky coincidence they had left Ireland just before the Trouble of 1916. Padraic was quiet and gentle, with his rich brogue and scholarly distraction a nice balance for the irrepressible Molly, who was fiery of tongue and hair, a fighter and lover of discord. Both were warm friends of all the Brookses, and Padraic was a particular favorite of the children.

Van Wyck quickly fell into a routine whereby he did most of his work in Westport, and rarely spent more than two days a week at the *Freeman* offices on Thirteenth Street in Manhattan. But whether he was at home or in New York, he made his presence unmistakably felt. "As the leader of the literary radicals," Susan J. Turner has said, "Brooks was the most distinguished addition to the staff made by the founding editors, and the most experienced writer. . . . [he] was a law unto himself." When he was in town, it seemed as if "all the young writers in New York tramped up and down the steps to his office all day long." He established reviewing policies and, especially during the first few months, wrote many reviews himself, but probably his most important contribution to the success of *The Freeman* was his weekly "A Reviewer's Notebook." Turner remarks that these columns were "regarded with the highest possible respect for the integrity of their composition by the editorial staff of the magazine and by Miss [Lucy] Taussig, who was in charge of composing the dummy for the paper. Because she felt that it was impossible to cut so much as a line, even a word, of the weekly 'Notebook,' the last item in the magazine, it was her habit to make the paper up backwards."

Despite the almost unqualified admiration of his contemporaries for these pieces, Brooks composed them resentfully, and he never wavered in his conviction that they were "half-baked and wholly inexpressive," as he described them in his autobiography. Almost upon his arrival in New York he was complaining to Eleanor about his inability to supply reviews and columns on demand. "But this *must* come," he told her, "I shall take it for granted." After a few months he gave up almost all of his reviewing of individual books, but the column itself continued to frustrate him. Three years later he was bitterly unhappy about "the spasms of difficulty which I have over my work. I have fallen to my lowest ebb in this (coming) week's 'notebook,' in spite of the fact that it involved 3 afternoons and 1 evening of reading (to get my subject, etc.) and thirteen virtually consecutive hours at my desk. The result is such as an amateur journalist could accomplish in a single evening." Once, when Nock was off on one of his infrequent vacations, he tried to talk Ben Huebsch into relieving him of "the vile *Notebook*—which I regard as a disgrace to the paper." Huebsch was soothing, but he stubbornly held Brooks to the original bargain.

Brooks's harsh assessment of his "Reviewer's Notebook" was, of course, unrealistic, an expression of his general sense of inadequacy, which was becoming increasingly disturbing as the twenties approached their middle years. It was a paradoxical symptom of his impending psychosis that his own persuasiveness could fill him with self-loathing, and it is important that we do not allow him to mislead us here. His *Freeman* essays were of surprisingly consistent excellence—highly polished, witty, influential statements of principle and purpose in the continuing development of an indigenous American culture. In their aggregate they comprised, as F. W. Dupee pointed out, a "prodigious anatomy of the creative life." Brooks wrote about the literary life in America, its thinness and its sterility, and he renewed his familiar call for the heroic artist who alone was capable of "calling to life the innumerable impulses that make a society rich and significant, of opening up new paths and directing floods of energy that refuse to flow in the old channels." That invocation culminated an early number of *The Freeman,* setting the tone for the long, calmly passionate series of lectures (as they might almost be called) to come.

During these, his last, most influential years as the orphic voice of Young America, Brooks's assessment of the cultural predicament in the United States grew more than ever to be almost unrelievedly pessimistic. He was soon to be widely, although unfairly, held accountable for the desperate nihilism that afflicted many writers and artists after World War I, and particularly in conservative literary circles his name became too easily synonymous with a sort of morbid anti-Americanism—a development that caused a self-consciously national critic great uneasiness. The increasingly gloomy tenor of his social prophesying was only one aspect of a mind that was still working toward a satisfying point of view. Defenders of traditional values and cynical Americophobes alike failed to notice that Brooks had developed, if not a new idea, a new emphasis in regard to his own generation. He insisted that the contemporary artist stop using the deficiencies of American culture as a rationalization for failure. "I say it with trepidation, lest the wrong people overhear me," he wrote in a "Reviewer's Notebook" of late 1920, "but there have been too many complaints lately about the fate of the American writer." The problem, he claimed, was less that America did not support the writer than that the American environment did not *nourish* him—an entirely different thing.

The sources of nourishment, as he developed other essays, were potentially there, awaiting only the vigorous hand that would cultivate them, and he urged young writers to turn to those nineteenth-century masters they had proved too quick to reject. Emphasizing the need for models, apprenticeship, and the extension of traditions, he returned again and again to the exemplary men of that part of the American past which had suddenly become usable—to Emerson, whom he had all but dismissed in *America's Coming-of-Age,* to Melville, the majestic fabulist who was just undergoing the curious process of rediscovery, and, of course, to Walt Whitman, who had also edited a paper called *The Freeman*—in Brooklyn during the late 1840s. Relying on his archetypal poet to bring out the indescribable flavor of the creative life, he liberally sprinkled Whitman's name like the necessary salt over the critical smorgasbord of "A Reviewer's Notebook" during his four years of editorship.

Those transcendental names reinforced one another, strengthening Brooks's assertion that Americans needed a "school"—especially a school of criticism. It was one of his oldest ideas, but he repeated it often, and he extended it by introducing, like a novelist's passing reference to what will become his major theme, the concept that would guide him through his later work. He pleaded with the American artist to demonstrate the selfless "guild-spirit" of all great collective enterprises, and he insisted that art must return to the utopian goals which had dignified the nineteenth century. As always, literature was for Brooks only a means. The end was the Beloved Community. Literature was to be judged not for its own sake, but according to how faithfully it served that end. Consequently, he attacked those contemporary movements that ignored the utopian mission of art, and this negative criticism immediately became the most visible and controversial expression of his leadership.

His favorite targets were the aesthetes, against whom he conducted a sort of guerrilla warfare, either openly, as with Gorham Munson, who debated Brooks through his columns in *Secession,* or more discreetly, as with Joel Spingarn, the Crocean whom Brooks had lumped with "Our Critics" in *Letters and Leadership* but who had since become a close friend and occasional ally. As much as he liked Spingarn, Brooks could not sympathize with the essential privacy of what the scholar prophetically called "The New Criticism." It was the war, Brooks thought, which had "made reality [so] hateful" that many of his contemporaries had sought to make a separate peace, addressing themselves not to the human community but to their own small, ingrown groups. Even the passionate dedication with which these writers pursued their experiments in form, he concluded, was essentially superficial: "in literature the subject, the content, dictates the form. The form is an inevitable consequence of the thing that is to be said and rises out of it as naturally as the flower rises out of the seed. And so to begin with the form, to seek the form, is to confess that one lacks the *thing.*"

The other groups Brooks attacked were closer to himself, their attitudes sometimes extensions or elaborations of his own, and the vigorous rebukes with which he concluded many issues of *The Freeman* must often have seemed, as indeed they were, essays in self-criticism. Despite his orientation toward Europe, he criticized the new generation of expatriates for succumbing to the American neurosis and leaving their countrymen "a headless and leaderless" people. Brooks could scarcely blame these pilgrims for respecting a truly artistic instinct of self-preservation, but he warned them that they were entitled to neither bitterness nor contemptuousness and reminded them that they could not abandon their responsibility for social leadership. The alternating praise and blame that characterized this essay on "The Wanderers," the hedging, the shifting back and forth between apparently irreconcilable poles of opinion, all reflect the renewed eruption of the debate Brooks had conducted within himself since he had gone to London in 1907. Some *Freeman* readers must have noticed the apparently inexplicable inconsistency in demonstrating that a serious artist could not possibly live in America while berating the serious artists who left it.

The other important group against which Brooks wrote was the newly orthodox company of Marxist revolutionists, represented best by Max Eastman and Upton Sinclair. During 1920 and 1921 he kept up a running debate with Eastman, who responded through his own columns in *The Liberator*. Eastman inspired Brooks to unusually pungent language, for this leader of New York's radical faction, despite his own influential literary career, insisted on thinking of writers as frivolous individuals who needed the supervision of men better grounded in reality. He cheerfully advised his readers to turn to books of science if they wanted substantial fare. In response, Brooks suggested that the radical celebration of science was simply another manifestation of a naïve bourgeois faith in material progress. In fact, he went on, the difference between the proletarian movement in the United States and the proletarian movement in Europe ("which differs from our own movement in having a backbone") was simply that Europeans had behind them a "really adequate literature."

The stubbornness of Brooks's position and his astringent wit quickly earned him a respectable number of literary enemies. For his first two years with *The Freeman* his posture as the leader whom the champion of each literary camp must challenge seems only to have added to his stature. Such authority continued until the spring of 1922, when he took a leave of absence from editorial duties, returning with his family to Carmel to work on *The Pilgrimage of Henry James*. Although he had planned to be away for no longer than six months, he was so relieved to be rid of the pressures of his office and his deadlines that he was still in California in late November and might never have rejoined *The Freeman* if he had not been needed back in New York. Nock was seriously overworked, partly because he had in Brooks's absence added the "Reviewer's Notebook" to his own regular duties. Ben Huebsch told Brooks that the other members of the *Freeman* staff were afraid that Nock would break down altogether if he could not get a prolonged vacation. After questioning Huebsch carefully about the urgency of the situation, Brooks reluctantly returned to New York and temporarily took over Nock's responsibilities in addition to resuming his own. He stayed in town, living at the Old Chelsea Hotel on Sixteenth Street until Eleanor and the boys rejoined him in the spring of 1923.

Perhaps it was only by coincidence that the literary climate changed while he was in California, or perhaps his absence from the editorial chair abetted an inevitable reorientation of taste that might have come more slowly if he had been at his post to ward it off. Whatever the explanation may finally be, by the beginning of 1923 Brooks was no longer firmly in charge of the literary situation. The debate he had conducted with the aesthetic modernists in particular was by no means settled, but he was becoming the object of increasingly serious criticism by writers and artists who were better attuned than he to the excitements of the new experimentalism. In an important article of 1924, Gorham Munson sought to resolve the issues of Van Wyck Brooks's "sphere" (which was social) and his "encroachments" (which were aesthetic). He concluded that however nobly Brooks had dedicated himself to the development of a society prepared for art he possessed no real understanding of the norms by which art itself was to be judged. Even Paul Rosenfeld thought in 1924 that his friend had become a "diminished figure," that he had grown old-fashioned, that he exhibited "the very want of sympathy for art and the artistic life of which he accuses society."

Rosenfeld's strictures were widely echoed. A new generation of modernists, discovering the possibilities of art as if for the first time, were puzzled by an apparent indifference to their accomplishments on the part of the critic who had cleared the way for them. Young writers honored their embattled Yankee for trouncing such representative enemies as Sherman, Eastman, and Hamilton Wright Mabie, and they willingly granted his premise that American civilization discouraged the arts. But they felt that the steadiness of the gaze he had turned on that negative truth had blinded him to the triumphs they had claimed despite it. In a wonderfully amusing imaginary dialogue called "The Delegate from Great Neck," Edmund Wilson portrayed F. Scott Fitzgerald, as a spokesman for his generation, complaining to Brooks that his leadership had become discouraging, that young writers, following his precepts, "have found you still brooding the wrongs of an earlier generation, the defeats of an older army. . . ."

Brooks's painfully conceived "Notebooks" were thus sometimes turned against their author, but they were helping to shape a collective artistic consciousness—and they were only one aspect, the most visible aspect, of the program for literary America that he attempted to realize during his years with *The Freeman*. Brooks expressed another aspect through his editorial duties, which might, he felt, make *The Freeman* a nucleus of a national "guild" or "school." He was forced to start almost at the very beginning—to create, as it were, the resources on which he might subsequently rely. "I found it all too easy," he pointed out in his autobiography, "to send a good many books to English reviewers, for they were so competent, as a rule, in contrast to our own that one could dispatch their copy straight off to the printer. But I soon saw that this would never do. We had to build up a staff of American reviewers, though this meant virtually double work for me." He encouraged writers of every background and interest to submit to the magazine. He read their work, commented upon it, rejected or accepted it, bullied them for more or better material, and spent many a dreary day "ironing out the gaucheries of eminent fellow-countrymen who were often professors." The method was slow and exhausting, but it worked: *The Freeman* could soon claim the most distinguished group of reviewers in the United States, and their authority was never seriously challenged during the magazine's short lifetime.

The tenacity of will necessary to hold together a heterogeneous collection of intellectuals must have strained a man who remained personally shy—whose shyness was, in fact, becoming proverbial. Malcolm Cowley, then just home from exciting days with the Dadaists in Europe and interested in reviewing for *The Freeman*, remembers his first meeting with Brooks: "Van Wyck, shy as he was, sat behind his desk, barricaded with books, and I, who was more shy than he would suspect, sat in front of him. I didn't say anything. Van Wyck didn't say anything. We sat there for about ten minutes, and finally Van Wyck shoved a pile of books at me and said, 'Here, take these.' So I reviewed some books for *The Freeman.*"

Among the other important reviewers whom Brooks, despite his shyness, managed to attract to the magazine were Daniel G. Mason and Walter Pach, the chief reviewers, respectively, of music and painting, Conrad Aiken, Robert Hillyer, John Gould Fletcher, Newton Arvin, Charles Beard, Isaac Goldberg, Howard Mumford Jones, Constance Rourke, Padraic and Mary Colum, Harold Stearns, Lewis Mumford, Llewellyn Powys, John Dos Passos, Henry Blake Fuller, Edwin Björkmann, John Macy, Ernest Boyd, Edwin Muir, and Louis Untermeyer. This is only a partial list, limited to reviewers whose names are still familiar and who wrote for the magazine regularly. Other important critics of the time—Edmund Wilson, Kenneth Burke, and Gorham Munson, for example—contributed occasional essays but never truly "joined" the *Freeman* "group." Although there were a few prominent foreign writers among Brooks's corps of reviewers, most of the regular contributors were Americans, and many of them, like Constance Rourke, were either discovered or developed by Brooks, as he cast his hospitable net over the teeming flood tide of the 1920s.

Two of the reviewers Brooks brought to *The Freeman,* Lewis Mumford and Newton Arvin, became lifelong friends and allies, and they can stand, in their separate careers and achievements, for the important results of his efforts to establish a community of American intellectuals. In 1921 Mumford was in England, editing the *Sociological Review,* and he often recalled later how through the "Reviewer's Notebook," "that quiet but vibrant voice of [Brooks's] called me home." Mumford had been born, raised, and educated in Manhattan. Under the influence of Sir Patrick Geddes, the Scottish biologist and city planner, he had developed a commitment to organic theories of art, society, and the mutual interdependence of the two. Now he declined an opportunity to accompany Geddes to Palestine, returning instead to the more immediate cultural challenges of New York, where he married Sophia Wittenburg, an editorial worker he met at *The Dial.* Although he had trouble breaking into the first eighteen pages of *The Freeman,* which the baleful eye of Mr. Nock protected against all intrusions of sociological "jargon," Mumford contributed reviews on a variety of subjects to Brooks's section of the magazine. Brooks encouraged the young utopian theorist to return to some of the interests he had first developed while a student at the City College of New York, with the result that his first book, *The Story of Utopias,* was published in 1922. It was also partly under Brooks's influence, Mumford remembers, that he made his important contributions to "reclaiming our American literary heritage" in *The Golden Day* (1926) and *Herman Melville* (1929). He also began his seminal work in the rediscovery of American architecture as an essayist for *The Freeman.*

As important as Brooks's influence and encouragement must have been to a writer ten years his junior, the relationship was not onesided. The two critics worked on totally independent projects, their "influence" upon each other limited to mutual understanding, shared assumptions, and a general sense of common purpose. Mumford was a strong man, remarkably learned, stubbornly idealistic, and Brooks quickly discovered in him a new avatar of that type of humanity which would always attract him most. Like Arthur Ryder, G. E. Marshall, and John Butler Yeats, Mumford became his model of the sage, content with bread and olives so long as the road stretched to new horizons. Brooks paid his friend supreme tribute when he described how his affirmative spirit assumed the emotional place beside him that had been left vacant by the death of Randolph Bourne. From the first, Mumford's clear, tough mind became a chief support of Brooks's own strength, and as he grew older Brooks often came, to Mumford's embarrassment, almost to idolize his companion as the principle of health and vitality itself.

The other important *Freeman* reviewer who became a lifelong friend was younger than Mumford and grew more closely to Brooks's hand than Mumford could. Newton Arvin was only twenty-one when he submitted his first awkward, self-consciously academic essays to the magazine. While Brooks promptly rejected them, he did acknowledge Arvin's potential ability—encouraging him to revise, to define his subject more precisely, to try a few reviews, above all to keep his work coming in. In subsequent months he carefully brought his talented apprentice through a course of practical instruction. He started Arvin off with brief review-notices, suggested new topics, demanded more work, demanded revisions, edited his manuscripts, and pushed him incessantly toward more ambitious projects. Before long Arvin was one of *The Freeman's* major reviewers, entrusted with the magazine's response to the chief critical documents of the period. He was also one of the few contributors whose work could be taken as it came from the mail and sent to the printer. More important, an inexperienced, confused young man had become a writer who would go on to a distinguished critical career.

At the same time that he trained Arvin professionally, Brooks responded generously to the younger man's personal problems. The drain on his time and energy must have been enormous, especially when one considers that this was only one of the many young reviewers to whom he gave similar attention, but Arvin was vexed by familiar demons, and Brooks thought that he might be able to help him. He tried to ease Arvin's financial plight by finding alternate publishers for his criticism. He commented sympathetically upon his reluctance but applauded his choice to accept a temporary post at Smith College (which, as it turned out, he held until his death). Perhaps his greatest contribution to Arvin's development was his willingness to share with the younger man his personal responses to the literary life, its frustrations, dangers, and satisfactions.

So the work went during those full days of the early twenties. The road that ran between Westport and lower Manhattan became an axis on which turned the literary movement that touched, in one way or another, every aspect of the creative life in the United States. One indication of the energy Brooks had unleashed was the increased personal contact, the proliferation of literary groups that characterized the decade. Whether in his *Freeman* offices or his study at Westport, Brooks stood at the center of equally satisfying circles of good company. A man who had gone hungry for talk in New Jersey, in California, even at times in New York, could now discuss the values of nationalism and its relation to literature with Padraic and Molly Colum, or argue painting with Walter Pach, who was so full of his subject that he had been known to deliver soliloquies on modern art to deaf men. Or he could talk music with Paul Rosenfeld, poetry with Jack Wheelock, and perhaps Catholicism with the novelist Henry Longan Stuart, for he had quietly renewed his interest in that forbidden subject. The literary atmosphere was dense and tempting, and many intellectuals had rejuvenated a venerable institution by holding, either in their homes or at some congenial restaurant, informal colloquia on topics of current literary or artistic interest. Brooks was enthusiastic about such occasions, and he was continually getting and sending invitations to meetings at someone's apartment for an evening's discussion of the question of "censorship," or "radicalism," or "experimentalism."

One of the most regular of these colloquia began meeting bi-weekly in 1921 at the home of Harold Stearns on Jones Street in Greenwich Village. Stearns himself was a colorful, provocative figure, a drifting "lost-generation" intellectual who fit as well, Brooks remarked, the older type of the literary bum. He was also among the most cynical of his generation, a great crier against America, and he eventually took his own advice and drifted on to Paris, to be memorialized as Harvey Stone in Hemingway's *The Sun Also Rises*. Under his aegis these meetings naturally attracted New York's most intensely critical artists and thinkers, and the discussions assumed a decidedly apocalyptic tone. According to Stearns, he and Brooks were the first to discuss seriously the possibility of developing from their informal gatherings a formal symposium, in "the spirit and temper of the French encyclopaedists of the 18th century," which would anatomize the condition of American civilization in their time. Their book, *Civilization in the United States: An Inquiry by Thirty Americans* (with the opinions of three foreign writers appended) appeared in 1922, and it quickly acquired the startling reputation that for a while made published symposia fashionable. So unrelievedly grim was the pessimism of the book that the simple fact of its existence explains one of the jokes Edmund Wilson inserted into his imaginary dialogue. "You probably think some of those people are lowbrow," Fitzgerald tells Brooks, inviting him to a party, "but Ring Lardner, for instance, is really a very interesting fellow—he's really not just a popular writer: he's pretty morose about things."

The public, as well as many intellectuals, would joke about *Civilization* for some time to come, but the book was a serious analysis of important aspects of American culture. For the most part the contributors were neither cynical nor modish. They were angry. And most of them brought impressive authority to the subjects they discussed. Lewis Mumford, for instance, wrote about "The City"; H. L. Mencken, "Politics"; Conrad Aiken, "Poetry"; and Ring Lardner, "Sport and Play." Other contributors were similarly qualified. Brooks, of course, was assigned the essay on "The Literary Life." It had developed from a *Freeman* article on the same subject, and it says, in effect, that the lit-

167

erary life in America is unlivable. Because of the notoriety accruing to the book, it soon became one of his most famous works, identifying him more closely with a general inclination to dire prophecy than he would have authorized. To Brooks, the value of *Civilization* rested less in its indictments of American institutions than in its expression of communal enterprise. The men and women who had gathered at Stearns's home represented for him the sort of group spirit that might take great projects forward. But the very gloominess of this particular symposium made its project a dead end, and the group itself had never been truly cohesive. Once Stearns departed for Europe the encyclopedic impulse found no new sponsors.

Another series of colloquia, at once smaller and more open-ended than those which resulted in *Civilization in the United States,* met regularly in Amenia, New York, about one hundred miles up the Hudson from New York City, where Joel Spingarn lived at Troutbeck, his lavish garden-farm. Lewis Mumford was soon to settle there, in the small old farmhouse he occupies today, and he claimed, with Brooks, a regular chair in these weekend discussions. Other neighbors who enjoyed Spingarn's hospitality included, from time to time, Walter Pach and his wife Magda, and Geroid Tanquary Robinson from *The Freeman.* The debates were informal but intense, the give-and-take over Spingarn's excellent Scotch of people who knew one another well. Lewis Mumford recorded one of the Troutbeck discussions, slightly fictionalized, in *The American Mercury* in 1924. The debate, which took place in 1921, involved Spingarn, Brooks, Mumford himself, and Ernest Boyd, an Irish critic who was both an aesthete and a follower of H. L. Mencken. All four men would contribute to *Civilization in the United States.*

Mumford gave his participants appropriate fictional names: Brooks became Charles Adams; Spingarn, Ernest De Fiori; Boyd, Edwin O'Malley; and himself, Percy Scott. In a discussion of aesthetics, of course, Spingarn, the American champion of Crocean aesthetic theory, would naturally oppose Brooks, and Mumford assigned them the important statements of position in the colloquium. The conversation is purely expository—it ends with the traditional agreement to disagree—but Mumford has a good ear, and a sampling from his transcription allows us to recapture something of the way in which dedicated intellectuals talked to one another then. Mumford also sets down here, almost by the way, one of the clearest available expositions of Brooks's critical theory. The debate begins with some good-natured banter about Adams's—that is, Brooks's—aesthetic position:

SCOTT: I have always wondered what Adams's aesthetic theories were. I have never been able to derive them, I confess, from your criticisms, Charles, although I enjoy your page perhaps more than anything else the *Ancient City* prints.

ADAMS: . . . I really have no conscious aesthetic theory: I recognize the aesthetic interest as only one of a number of interests that are served in literature; and it doesn't seem to me the supremely important one that so many of you now make it out. . . . I should like to use such a single canon as you, De Fiori, enjoy in your applications of Croce; but different kinds of literature seem to me to require different standards; and it is only in the realm of pure poetry that I find Croce's canon wholly justified. To dismiss the rest of literature because it is not pure poetry seems to me absurd.

O'MALLEY: It's all very well to keep your aesthetic from showing its bone through the flesh of your criticism: but my objection to your method, my dear Adams, is that you are not really interested in a piece of literature as such: you have always an ulterior interest in its background and you keep on asking yourself what sort of society this or that book will tend to produce. . . . you, God forgive us, refer to an ideal community which has not yet come into existence, and in a country ruled by the *booboisie* has no chance of ever being a reality.

ADAMS (*unruffled*): You object, do you not, O'Malley, to the fact that I believe that a community has a permanent self, made up of its best minds and embodied in its literature, as well as the shifting, temporary self which expresses itself in its daily actions and in the opinions of those who control it in the press and on the platform? I can't conceive what function you accord to literature, unless it is to embody that permanent self and make it visible.

DE FIORI: My dear Adams: you mustn't confuse an act in the practical world with an act in the spiritual world. The values of literature lie entirely in the spiritual realm: they are independent of the society that has produced a work of art or that may be affected by it. . . . A work of art is good or bad in terms of the author's own world. What was the writer's inner purpose, and how has he accomplished it?

ADAMS: Your rule of judgment is satisfactory enough, perhaps, when it applies to a poem or a novel whose position is already established. But I don't see how it enables you to distinguish between—let me take an extreme example—between the Nick Carter detective stories and the Divine Comedy. . . . The aesthetic value of literature is inseparable from its intellectual and moral value. . . .

And so the conversation burned far into the night, ending only with Scott's inevitable observation that "Discussion never gets anywhere; at most it shows more clearly where one stands."

Such groups of passionate men must have talked the sun up many a morning during the twenties, and among the best and most inspired of them Brooks more than held his own. He was a presence, as Paul Rosenfeld described him, with "his simple Harvard blandness, his smile like a pleased savage's, his cockscomb of hair, his abrupt pumping handshake and his watch-chain depending from the lapel of his miraculously precise and well-pressed coat." He had become for literary Americans the incarnation of integrity, of incorruptibility, of dedication to the life of the mind. His contemporaries recognized that he was a good man and responded to his goodness beyond all of their quarrels with his program.

Lewis Mumford speaks of his first attraction to Brooks, above all by the older man's "primal integrity." When I asked Malcolm Cowley about the basis of Brooks's personal force during the twenties, he told me that "Brooks very soon gathered about himself the prestige of a man who one feels is incorruptible and not self-seeking and has a devotion to literature." Paul Rosenfeld bears similar witness: "The man has in him a noblesse, a distinction, a largeness of spirit. . . . For many men there must ring a moment of faith in American life when first this spirit speaks to them." These are only a few sprigs and cuttings of the reputation that sprang from those "roots" Brooks had so diligently planted in America. From the books, magazines, newspapers, and letters of four decades one could easily gather great armloads like them, all redolent with moral admiration.

A similar admiration informed the language of the most important public acknowledgment of his stature that Brooks received during his early career. In January 1924 he was notified that he was to be presented with the third annual (for 1923) Dial Award. The first of these cherished prizes had gone to Sherwood Anderson, the second to T. S. Eliot, and later winners would include Marianne Moore (1924), E. E. Cummings (1925), William Carlos Williams (1926), and Ezra Pound (1927). Brooks's name seems almost misplaced in that company of modernists, and, coming from a magazine essentially hostile to his position, the award is a fine expression of the high seriousness with which his peers regarded him. The *Dial*'s announcement read in part:

> Our own award is for an American writer and goes this year to a critic whose chief interest it is that American writers should occur, should be able, in the American society, to exist and to create. One can recognize the supreme importance of such a figure even if one fails to accept the whole body of his doctrine. For there is in a critic as far removed as Mr. Brooks from the purely aesthetic attitude one assertion which underlies all others; it is that the creative life is the only life tolerable to intelligent men and women, that the life which is not creative, and more or less fully creative, is spoiled and stunted and unworthy. There have been eras in which the fine arts were only the highest type of creative activity, when politics and trade and everyday existence were blessed in some degree by the energy of creation. It happens that in our time the arts are the sole remaining medium for that spirit; if they go down, as in the Spenglerian hypothesis they must go down, there is nothing left which can be called creative, and the future belongs, as Thomas Mann ironically put it, not to such twaddle as art, but to mechanics, technology, economics, and politics. For us in America Mr. Brooks analysed the course of events before Spengler; and, as a good American, he refused to accept that course as inevitable. He holds to the claim of a creative society, against the acquisitive, against the merely constructive.

And it concluded with the observation that "every artist works in his interest and he in theirs."

In one sense the Dial Award was the high point of Brooks's long career. Even demurrals by such intellectuals as Malcolm Cowley, then with *Broom,* questioned only the ideological priorities of the award itself, and not the honor due its recipient. But in another sense—for Brooks's public and private experience had by now gone hopelessly out of phase—this culminative tribute was like the reminder of past glories that mocks a man fallen upon evil days.

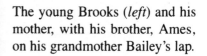
ABOVE: Van Wyck's mother and father, Sallie Bailey Brooks and Charles Edward Brooks.

The young Brooks (*left*) and his mother, with his brother, Ames, on his grandmother Bailey's lap.

Brooks at age three.

John Butler Yeats's 1909 portrait of Brooks.

Van Wyck in 1923 at the onset of his breakdown, with Eleanor and their two sons, Charles Van Wyck Brooks (*left*) and Oliver Kenyon Brooks (*right*).

Eleanor Kenyon Stimson, Brooks's first wife, before their marriage.

Brooks in 1931.

Brooks in his Con-
necticut study in the
early 1940s.

Brooks in 1952.

Left to right: Brooks, Lewis Mumford, George Biddle, and Mark Van Doren at a dinner at the American Academy in honor of Van Wyck's seventy-fifth birthday, in 1961.

Gladys Rice Brooks, Van Wyck's second wife, in 1967.

IX

HORRORS OF THE MIDDLE PASSAGE: 1925–1931

One day, not long before *The Freeman* stopped publishing, Isaac Goldberg, who often reviewed Spanish literature for the magazine, paid a visit to the busy editorial offices on Thirteenth Street. He was particularly struck, he remembered, by the austerity of Brooks's little room, with its "unpretentious desk" and stacks of recent books, and he was both impressed and disturbed by the modesty of the man he considered perhaps the finest literary editor in the country. Brooks, as Goldberg described him, "is somewhat under the average height; a rather stocky fellow who seems always to dwell in the middle distance of the picture. . . . About him, about his writings, is something crepuscular; there are all the noises of nature, all the colors, all the landscapes, but with a twilight hush that dims the hues and muffles the sounds. It is the crepuscular in other men that attracts his faculties of criticism and appreciation. He senses the hidden, the withdrawn." The uneasy reviewer then speculated that this eerie quality had something to do with Brooks's own "secret."

Paul Rosenfeld, who was particularly close to Brooks at this time, had similar intuitions. He perceived in his friend and ally a dualism, expressed in "two images, each trying to superimpose itself upon the other, and neither decisively succeeding." The first image was heroic—"a young man stepping out of a gaunt, dour house into a luminous dawn"—but the other was disturbingly gothic. The man of Rosenfeld's impressionistic portrait had grown older, and the spirit was gone from his flesh:

> There is a monumental, an almost uncontrollable wish to sit, in this body. In this picture, too, there is a house. The windows of this house are closed. Upon certain ones the shutters are shut; in others, the shades are drawn. It is a prim, pretty, but strangely introverted dwelling, turned in upon itself away from the street. And the young man is not coming out through the door. The door is shut; behind it, inside, he sits most of the time. Life drives up one morning in the shape of a lovely visitor and lifts the knocker and sends her merry summons. The young man seems to hear; and yet he does not rise to let the lovely caller in. Or, worse still, he does not hear the knock.

These imagistic responses to a puzzling change of character were unusually sensitive, but not unique. At times Van Wyck could no longer keep the funereal music that echoed in his skull from showing through his face, and his buried life was rapidly becoming an open "secret." Scofield Thayer of *The Dial,* a great admirer, had Brooks to dinner and afterward told Molly Colum how sick her neighbor was. On another occasion Van Wyck turned deathly pale at a casual reference to Walt Whitman's homosexuality, certainly no unexpected or forbidden subject, and abruptly abandoned his guests, John Brooks Wheelright and Malcolm Cowley, to finding their own way out of the Harvard Club. He began to talk to Jack Wheelock with frightening intensity about Poe and Hawthorne and his inability to understand them, and he had written about James, he also told his old friend, as no gentleman should. Such incidents recurred with startling regularity, and in fact, by the mid-twenties Van Wyck was seriously ill.

At least as early as 1920 Van Wyck had relaxed his precarious hold on the "double life" he had learned in Plainfield and succumbed to increasingly sinister expressions of the erratic behavior that had surfaced earlier in London and New York. Once again he swung helplessly back and forth between periods of exhilaration and despair, but now both moods were sharply exaggerated and the periods of depression longer and more tenacious. Like most writers Van Wyck found that once he had completed a sustained project he suffered an emotional letdown—a "spiritual malaise between books," as he described it to Newton Arvin, promising to cheer himself up with some new neckties. The gloom that set in when the *Twain* was finished, however, held on longer than usual, infecting his efforts to concentrate on either the *James* or his *Freeman* articles. He felt that he must take drastic steps to "shake off the dreamy, motiveless mood that crept over me during those latter months at Carmel." Once he had returned to New York he complained incessantly that he was depressed by the necessary visits to Plainfield, and he grew desperately lonely away from Eleanor and the boys. At other times, when he was cheerful and optimistic, these bleak moods seemed foreign to him, and he thought that the false self they expressed should simply be forgotten. "Burn up all the letters I've written since I left you, *please!* They are disgraceful," he wrote to Eleanor in the spring of 1920, and apparently Eleanor complied. Suspiciously little of Van Wyck's correspondence from this period survives.

It is significant that this new, more serious onset of an old malady followed closely upon the book about Twain. Van Wyck had kept no secret of his need to write about himself and his own problems in his biographical criticisms. Eleanor had long worried over his tendency to project himself into the psyches of troubled men, and Mary Colum reported that many of his friends and colleagues regarded his fifth chapter on Twain ("The Candidate for Gentility") as a veiled account of his own marital situation. Even Mrs. Stimson felt obliged to remark how very much Van Wyck had revealed about himself when she congratulated him on *The Ordeal of Mark Twain.*

Analyzing Twain's "double life," Van Wyck had for the first time acknowledged the seriousness of one of his own most persistent worries. He had faced, defined, and perhaps made logically unsolvable his lifelong problem about money and the divided loyalties it forced upon him. Like his representative candidate for gentility, Van Wyck devoted what seemed an unreasonable proportion of his energies to getting and spending the money he needed to support a respectable middle-class way of life. Neither he nor Eleanor could ever question his obligation to do so. Perversely, Van Wyck felt guilty for trying to live up to it. The romantic imagery of bohemian poverty and heroic otherworldliness remained strong as ever. Earlier it had sustained him; now it excited the problem. For the artist or the sage, Van Wyck was convinced, the world must be a place of pilgrimage. He relentlessly urged the strenuous life upon his contemporaries through the pages of *The Freeman,* but he must often have felt that he was mocking his own ignoble refusal to live it. "His idea of the good life," John Hall Wheelock told me, "was an heroic life—trying to do the impossible." He refused to comfort himself with anything less.

Van Wyck's anguish was not simply the familiar matter of the artist-rebel forced to come to terms with social demands. As guilty as he felt about trying to respect the standards of Plainfield, he was equally stricken by his apparent incapacity for the task. His job with *The Freeman* was the first to pay as much as forty dollars a week, and he and Eleanor were still obliged to devote long hours to the dreary French translations by which they supplemented his income. They kept up appearances, but since their marriage they had usually lived from hand to mouth—a condition well enough for an idealistic young man and woman but maddeningly precarious when the needs of two children were to be considered. Van Wyck gradually became nearly despondent about his relationship with his family. Much later he told Wheelock that a writer was cruel to bring children into the world.

Such misgivings about personal and financial nonfeasance were exacerbated by the disapproval of both Eleanor's mother and his own. Mrs. Hibbard and Ames, who joked contemptuously about "Wyckie's writing," let him know that they considered him an embarrassing failure. Mrs. Stimson had been abandoned by one bohemian and "lost" her daughter to another, and she could not at times keep from expressing her profound reservations about her son-in-law and his future. She pointedly suggested, for instance, that it would be unfortunate if Charles were to become a writer, unable to support *his* family.

The other dangerous contradiction in Van Wyck's "double life" emerged in the writing of *The Pilgrimage of Henry James.* Like his ambivalence toward money, his confused but powerful allegiances to both Europe and America were of long standing and had been relatively dormant since his marriage. When he put them into form and established the inevitability of their logic, they became absolutely exclusive and absolutely frustrating. He demonstrated to his own satisfaction that life in Europe must starve the American writer, but at the same time he argued with great authority that the life of the mind and spirit was impossible in the United States. Van Wyck approached his fortieth year, but in his heart he had not outgrown the boy who had discovered all that mattered of life in the galleries of Dresden, Florence, and

Paris. The passion with which he now returned to that dream of the Old World is nowhere better demonstrated than in his renewal (whenever Eleanor was absent) of his fearful, curiously Protestant flirtation with Roman Catholicism. Once again he began slipping into Catholic churches, seeking his lost Italy in the sensual liturgy, colors, and odors, and he fell back into another adolescent devotion when he hung a large white crucifix on the wall of his room at the Old Chelsea. His desperate gropings for Europe made Van Wyck feel a traitor to America, and he deliberately cut off access to expatriation by writing the *James*. The book thus seemed part of "a virulent disease," while his work for *The Freeman,* which methodically sealed the other exits from his emotional trap, soon became an object of his sheerest "revulsion."

These agonies of identity multiplied the serious problems Van Wyck had already encountered in his biographical study: the technical difficulties of style, the uneasy feeling that he was abusing James personally, the frustrating tendency of the book to become selfishly private—in one sense a cautionary tale written for himself. In 1923, when *The Dial* unexpectedly agreed to publish some of his early chapters, his problems of money, vocation, confused loyalties, and conflicting values became inseparable from the problems impeding the completion of the book itself. At first the chance to place his work seemed encouraging. *The Dial* was headquarters of the enemy camp, at least in regard to James, and, more practically, it was relatively well funded. "They will pay me about $400 for [the first three chapters]," Van Wyck reported to Eleanor in Carmel, "and that is the real reason why I am doing it. We might then be able to pay back Dutton in April without mortgaging the house. Of course, if & when I finish the whole manuscript, I shall be able to take Dutton's $600 & keep it, but I must pay them back this spring, for I cannot finish the ms. by April." This apparently businesslike letter reveals not only the Brookses' shaky financial condition, but also the extent to which Van Wyck created many of his own pressures. He never suggested that John Macrae of Dutton was being difficult about the advance on the *James,* and it is doubtful that he was under any real obligation to return it.

Although he was relieved by the money his chapters earned, Van Wyck almost immediately regretted the whole business. "It more or less commits me to go on with the book," he gloomily wrote Eleanor just a month later, "but when I think of the howling storm that is going to arise when it begins to come out I wonder if I was wise in acting so impulsively. . . . The difficulty is that these three chapters merely set the stage for an interpretation of James that I shall be, in a way, bound to develop. . . . and all this makes me feel that I should have been wiser if I had kept it all back until my own results were clear. I shall have to develop a strong head & not be rattled, for the situation presents certain alarming possibilities—as you can see."

Van Wyck's misgivings about selling his chapters to *The Dial* gradually subverted all of his confidence in himself and his work. He felt that he had sold his artistic integrity, his freedom, and his right to develop the complexity of his subject. He had, of course, simply published some excerpts from a work in progress; any refinements he might later bring to his original thesis would be applauded. But by this time Van Wyck's sense of identity had become so defensively rigid, so brittle, that any suggestion of error threatened to shatter it altogether. Significantly, he dated the beginnings of his breakdown to approximately this time, and by late 1923 his friends had started to notice his erratic behavior and worry about his health. His severe depressions began to infect Eleanor, and he was sufficiently alert to that danger to suggest to her that they both be psychoanalyzed.

When he was not being seriously depressed about his professional "failure," Van Wyck would, without apparent reason, suddenly shift to equally unrealistic bursts of optimism. "I have a mood in me," he wrote to Sherwood Anderson in September 1923, "a kind of harmonious, clear, happy mood which is, I think, my real mood and in which you and I would hit it off wonderfully well; and I have a sort of feeling that in two or three years I shall be able to get that mood on top for keeps. It depends upon my work coming out as I want it to and somewhat (I suppose) on material circumstances. But I expect things to be as I say, and then I shall really begin to live and really work (for everything I have done so far is the merest hint of what I feel I have to do). Then look out!" A similar exhilaration characterized his descriptions of the new book about Ralph Waldo Emerson he began in 1925. He wrote to Lewis Mumford that he was "living in a dream, writing a life of Emerson. It has been a sort of religious experience. . . ." The great transcendentalist, he believed, was leading him "right out into the midst of the sunny side" of things. He told J. S. Zelie that he had "never been so happy before in a book—or never so in love with a literary character," and he kept up his cheerful refrain in a letter to Joel Spingarn: "I have never before had such an *éclaircissement* & seem to be on the road to carrying out my long-cherished idea of writing the Paradiso of the American man of letters. . . ." It was the subject, Emerson himself, that sustained him—not any faith in his own powers. Van Wyck had always cheered himself with such periods of impractical hope. But now he was gambling on them. And he raised the stakes after each cycle of depression.

The other manifestations of this first breakdown were less obvious then, but critical, since they led Van Wyck directly into the psychosis that nearly claimed his life. He had worked himself into a position whereby he was no longer able to maintain his simultaneous hold on both aspects of his "double life." Neither could he abandon one in favor of the other. Unable to choose between impossible alternatives, Van Wyck simply gave up both of his troublesome identities. His "American" self, the breadwinner who had been born and shaped in Plainfield, barely survived the closing of *The Freeman* early in 1924 (Neilson and Nock were at odds, and Mrs. Neilson cut off her subsidy). Van Wyck caught on for a while as a half-time editor at Harcourt, Brace and Company, where he was instrumental in publishing important books on America by Vernon Parrington and Constance Rourke, but he found office duties as dreary as ever, behaved erratically at work, and the position was terminated (probably by mutual agreement) after a few months. From this point on, he seemed almost to be avoiding employment. In 1925 he declined Scofield Thayer's offer to make him editor of *The Dial*. He also turned down the literary editorship of at least two other papers—to say nothing of those he might have had for the asking—and he refused a number of relatively lucrative opportunities to write literary biographies. Finally he was forced to tell Joel Spingarn that he could not furnish the brief preface he had agreed to write for one of the *Troutbeck Pamphlets* of American critical documents. He did earn a few dollars with the interminable translations, an occasional review, a brief interval of "mechanical" work with the Yale University Press, and some articles for the *Dictionary of American Biography* (he refused to write the life of Henry James but did agree to submit biographies of Melville, Hawthorne, and Bronson Alcott). Except for the translations, none of this work was regular, and none of it brought any appreciable income. Van Wyck had, in fact, given up all but the appearance of making a living.

By 1926 Van Wyck had also despairingly let go of his creative identity. His refusal to Scofield Thayer, which amounted to a startling abdication of leadership, suggests how desperately ill he was. *The Dial* was the most influential literary publication in the United States, and one can only speculate about possible differences in the prevailing intellectual climate if Van Wyck Brooks, instead of Marianne Moore, had acceded to the editorial chair in 1925. Van Wyck later explained his general withdrawal from the literary scene with a sort of parable. In his autobiography he describes a visit in the mid-twenties to an old émigré writer, a famous but destitute man who for the joy of his own mind took no notice of his filthy surroundings. At another time Van Wyck would have seen here the transformational magic of the imagination, a fulfillment of his old dream of heroic poverty. Now he could see only "mere old men in sordid lodging-houses." "My own bubble burst," he went on, ". . . I was consumed with a sense of failure, a feeling that my work had all gone wrong and that I was mistaken in all I had said or thought. What had I been doing? I had only ploughed the sea . . . and I thought of my writing with 'rage and shame' . . . I saw myself as a capsized ship at night with the passengers drowned underneath and the keel in the air."

What he had in fact done was to identify literature and life so closely, and make both so strongly moral, that he became, according to his neurotic solipsisms, nothing more than a character in the fictions of writers he had criticized. Having committed, as he believed, literary crimes, he subjected himself to literary punishments. He began having nightmares in which he trembled before the "great luminous menacing" gaze of Henry James, and he enacted the gothic literary compulsions of Edgar Allan Poe. It was at this time that he began to develop those terrific fantasies of imprisonment, entombment, and live burial that were soon to become his most immediate reality. His own reputation, then at its fullest, inspired him with nothing but contempt, and he would turn away wearily when confronted with a favorable review or adulatory letter.

Even the *Emerson* failed him. He had started enthusiastically to work on his new book about the master to whom he had been ideologically close for many years. As he told Spingarn, this was the theme that made all of his struggles worthwhile, the *Paradiso* that gathered and redeemed "the *Inferno* of Mark Twain & the *Purgatorio* of Henry James." Like the *James* the *Emerson* was to be a lyrical biography, told from "inside," but this time Van Wyck's thesis involved the mastery of both letters and life, and the tone of his narrative was almost wholly celebratory. For a while it seemed that Emerson might prove a remarkable therapist. The calm old sage of Concord pulled his biographer out of his depressions for nearly a year and a half, but in early 1926 Van Wyck started to complain about the difficulty of his subject and the problems inherent in his method. His descriptions of Emerson's elusiveness began to sound suspiciously like his vilifications of the developing *James,* and before long it became clear that he was hedging. By June he had decided, as he told several of his closest friends, that his book was unwritable and must be "scrapped." He permitted much of what he had finished to be published in a collection of miscellaneous biographical pieces—most of them reissues—called *Emerson and Others,* which appeared in 1927. But from the moment he despaired of his American *Paradiso* the problem of finishing and publishing the study of Emerson became one of the keys to his emotional illness.

In one sense the problem was literary, a matter of technical and moral craftsmanship. "He couldn't finish it because he had a misconception of what the last chapter should be. You can't write a philosophical chapter about a man's ideas after doing a stream-of-consciousness interpretation of his life. You have to continue in that vein. As soon as Emerson dies, Brooks has to die. . . . Brooks would be an intruder if he tried to put an extra chapter at the end of such a book." Lewis Mumford's professional explanation helps to illuminate as well the other aspect of the problem, which involved Van Wyck's neurotic demands upon himself. He was determined, as a fellow patient from one of his sanitariums reminded him some years later, "to write the *perfect book,*" and when his inspiration faltered, he felt that he was "trying to shape a mass of air."

Thus Van Wyck convinced himself that he was utterly and hopelessly a failure. He needed money to rescue his spirit, but he was unable to earn money. He needed some literary triumph to reconcile him to himself, but he was unable to write. He proved to himself by the very fact of these disabilities the validity of the desperate mood which created them. Oppressed by guilt, he groped frantically for a way out, and, finding that he had sealed all of his exits, he simply retreated farther into morbid introspection. He managed, of course, to work himself into "a wretched state of nerves," all "disheveled and panicky," as he told Joel Spingarn, and he began to have moments when he instinctively knew that he could no longer control the animal terror that had slumbered at the roots of his identity since he had been a boy in Plainfield.

Like Paul Rosenfeld, I find myself responding to Van Wyck in pictures. At my own desk, thumbing through old photographs, the notes from a few interviews, the pile of despondent letters that tell the story of that time, I see a man in a darkened office, in Westport or Manhattan, at work among neat stacks of books and paper. He is still a relatively young man, briskly mustached and dressed with impeccable formality. His fine straight features and emphatic brows are handsome, but he looks preternaturally old. The haggard face, framed by a shock of short, unruly hair, is curiously inappropriate to the emerging stockiness of his body, and there is an occasional flutter at the corner of his eyes, as if he were wincing. He is struggling, I think, to concentrate on his work against the fear of madness that fulfills its own prophecies, so physically tangible in his chest that he breaks into cold sweats trying to choke it back. He does not, cannot, relax. When he leaves the study he will not be able to sleep. An unguarded moment, he senses, will expose him to the full power of that irrational thing which can suddenly overwhelm him forever. He gets through his days and nights on sheer strength of will.

In 1926 Van Wyck marked his fortieth birthday, what he himself called his *"crise de quarante ans,"* and, like any man, he paid his homage to frailty. He fell in love with Molly Colum, and the affair, brief but intense, seems to have been a last pathetic gesture toward life. It nearly became instead an accommodation to death. Van Wyck and Molly had long been friends and, perhaps more important, professional allies. Both were strong-minded critics who were committed to the priorities of the creative life, and Van Wyck could justly feel that Molly appreciated him as few other men or women could. To complement the announcement of Van Wyck's Dial Award, she had written a remarkably sympathetic assessment of his entire career. Especially as his literary identity became more and more elusive, he grew increasingly dependent on her support and assurances.

Particulars about their romance are skimpy and hard to come by—a matter of general information on the second or third hand, some cryptic remarks in letters, a few memories. People who were aware that Van Wyck and Molly were in love (apparently it was common knowledge) generally assume that their affair was adulterous, although some insist that the relationship was platonic. Both principals later asserted that "nothing very much" had passed between them. Their assurances might not satisfy the suspicious: Van Wyck described the affair when he was psychotic and probably genuinely confused as to what had taken place; Molly's statement was exceedingly defensive and evasive. Yet, Van Wyck's testimony is not easily dismissed. In advanced stages of his psychosis he was eager to confess to doctors all of the crimes that he hoped might justify a capital punishment. When he discussed his sexual misbehavior, however, he could claim only that he must be forever guilty because he had kissed Mrs. Colum.

The broad outlines of the story are clear enough. In January 1926 Eleanor left with the boys for Carmel. These separations had become so routine that probably neither she nor Van Wyck realized that this was a particularly bad time to be interrupting family life. Van Wyck was, as he had once told Eleanor, a carnal being, unsuited to the monastic life, and especially now, when he was suffering terrific attacks of anxiety, he could not bear to be alone with himself. He was made more anxious by the prospect that Eleanor would return with Mrs. Stimson, the disapproving mother-in-law who wished to settle again near her daughter. Gradually he took to spending more and more time with the Colums, often bicycling the few miles between Westport and New Canaan to pass the afternoon and sometimes the night there. This new attachment involved Van Wyck in another emotional conflict—between his love for Molly, with all of the freedom she represented, and his love for Eleanor, who still claimed his deepest sense of responsibility.

Molly had experienced frustrations similar to Van Wyck's. Unable to make a living with his serious work, her husband was forced to write children's books, and she either had to earn a few dollars teaching or stay home to cook and keep house—activities she detested. She was a type of the new liberated woman: outspoken, cosmopolitan, and contemptuous of the roles men and women were traditionally expected to play in society. She now convinced herself that Van Wyck was slipping into the routine of the American Philistia and urged him to break off completely. Better, she argued, that he abandon his wife and family than that he risk becoming another subordinate in the American corporation. Her suggestion was the last thing needed by a man who was only too eager to find hope in unrealistic schemes and desperate remedies, but Molly had not yet recognized how severely disturbed he was.

Eleanor may have caught wind of these developments. She returned to Westport after an unusually brief absence, thus putting an end to any wild plans Van Wyck might have been making with Molly. Probably Van Wyck was grateful for her return, which spared him the agony of making a decision, but Molly refused to be reconciled to the situation. Later that year she confronted Van Wyck in a hotel in Concord, where he had gone for further research on Emerson. Apparently there was an emotional scene. In one of the resentful letters she addressed to Van Wyck many years later, Molly remembered that the incident in Concord was her first real indication that he was seriously ill.

Her new knowledge did not deter her. From hints and allusions in the correspondence, it would appear that she decided to take over the management of Van Wyck's therapy; perhaps she did so at his request. According to her own testimony, she thus became involved in a bitter running quarrel with Eleanor, which exaggerated Van Wyck's neurotic sense of guilt. In May he entered his first hospital—Harrod's in Stockbridge, Massachusetts—for a few weeks of relaxation and gardening, the standard prescription of the sanitariums in which he spent most of the next five years. There was no urgency to his diagnosis as yet, and his stay was conceived purely as a rest cure. He made every effort to keep up with his normal life—continued his correspondence, took an occasional evening out, visited with dramatically mixed emotions the old Melville house at nearby Pittsfield, and tried to work on the *Emerson.* He remained, however, caught in an emotional and moral cross fire, for Molly refused to abandon him. She consulted psychiatrists on her own and wrote a series of stubbornly quarrelsome letters to Eleanor. To Van Wyck at Harrod's she sent advice, books, and sleeping pills—defying doctor's orders as well as Van Wyck's pathetic desire to be released.

She also wore out Eleanor's patience. Oliver Kenyon Brooks told me that about this time the Colums were the subject of a bitter family quarrel, which ended in Eleanor's demand, and Van Wyck's agreement, that he break off all contact with their old neighbors. Eleanor's unprecedented anger may have frightened Van Wyck into believing that he was about to lose not only his reputation, his career, his integrity, but also his wife and children. Now he felt that he *deserved* to be

abandoned, that some principle of justice would punish him remorse-
lessly for all of his wicked failures.

The doctors at Harrod's might have believed that they could ease
Van Wyck's conflicts by allowing him to succumb to one of his persistent temptations, and Eleanor agreed to send him to England for treatment. He was permitted to believe, unrealistically, that his family
would join him in a month or two. Whether deliberately or not, the
stratagem also took care of some of the complications raised by Molly.
By the time the patient returned to the United States the Colums had
left for one of their extended visits to France. Van Wyck, as he told
Joel Spingarn, undertook this new journey reluctantly. When he was
excitable any suggestion of change threw him into a fit of insecurity,
but he could no longer deny that something drastic must be done. The
fiction of normality by which he and Eleanor had been trying to live
had become untenable. Telling only a few close friends what was happening to him, Van Wyck withdrew from his usual literary and personal correspondence, formally abandoned the study of Emerson, and
occupied himself with the mechanical work of translation, which
Eleanor gradually took over alone. That August, accompanied by
Ames, he sailed for London aboard the Cunard Line's *Franconia*.

In England Van Wyck stayed in Bowden House at Harrow-on-
the-Hill, just outside of London. It was an elegant, leisurely sanitarium, offering little direct treatment. A patient's days consisted largely
of gardening and forestry, swimming, tennis, and lessons in driving an
automobile. Except for the presence of a few inmates with bizarre
symptoms and the restrictions imposed upon one's liberty, Bowden
House resembled a country club rather than an asylum. Yet his eight
months there and, experimentally, as a guest in a private residence in
London did Van Wyck more harm than good. A resident psychiatrist
tactlessly insisted that he snap out of his doldrums, assume financial
responsibility for his family, and earn a living by writing while in
England. Van Wyck knew from experience the frustrations an American would encounter in the British literary marketplace. That he was
held accountable for tasks he could not hope to perform inflamed his
already lively conviction of guilt, and, emotionally, he sentenced himself to death. Sleeping, he unconsciously crossed his arms upon his
chest, assuming the position of a corpse in a coffin. Awake, he became
desperately suicidal.

"It was a fixed idea," he wrote in his autobiography. "I saw every

185

knife as something with which to cut one's throat and every high building as something to jump from. A belt was a garrotte for me, a rope existed to hang oneself with, the top of a door was merely a bracket for the rope, ... even the winter snow fell in order to give one pneumonia if one spent a night lying on the ground." He shattered and swallowed the crystal of his watch, attempted to throw himself under moving vehicles, and persuaded himself that Parliament had passed a special law that would permit his keepers to bury him alive. Such compulsive fantasies of entombment soon became for him a cosmologically just reality in which he, the ultimate sinner, was punished for his murder of life. An observer of a year later described one of Van Wyck's hallucinations, "beginning with [Eleanor] and Westport being buried alive with him, God Himself getting into the grave last."

Van Wyck's sense of guilt was further exaggerated when he was required, for therapy, to review his relationship with Mary Colum. He drafted a detailed account of the affair for Eleanor, asking her forgiveness, and he wrote distractedly to Molly, announcing that he must abandon their friendship. Eleanor accepted her husband's expressions of contrition, but not gracefully. She responded in part by offering him a divorce, which he promptly declined. The gesture was doubtless intended to close the affair formally and to reassure Van Wyck by ostensibly allowing him to choose his future, but Eleanor later inclined to press her offers of "legal freedom" whenever Van Wyck showed signs of willfulness. Her willingness to forgive implied no willingness to forget, and she warned Molly to keep her distance.

Molly was both angered and alarmed by what she described as Van Wyck's "violent," "crazy," and "caddish" letter, which seemed to allude to a relationship she could not recognize, and for which she suspected that Eleanor was chiefly responsible. The accusations and counteraccusations that she and Eleanor continued to exchange for the next several years helped to keep Van Wyck's infidelity at issue, and eventually he became liable to seizures of panic at even the mention of either woman.

From this point on, the record of Van Wyck's illness becomes a tale of almost unrelieved horror. As soon as Eleanor realized how badly his condition was deteriorating at Harrow she went to England to bring him home. They returned to New York in May 1927 after a nightmarish passage, during which Van Wyck's suicidal impulses had become so evident that the ship's doctor wanted him locked in his stateroom for the entire voyage. Eleanor was forced to guard him, she told Lewis Mumford, until she could feel her hair turning gray. By the time they had arrived at Westport she was herself desperately nervous and confused, and, almost immediately, she made the mistake of bringing Van Wyck to Plainfield for a visit with his family. A relative who saw Van Wyck then remembers that he met all of her questions and advances with a blank stare. Later he told her that he had no recollection of their meetings during the years when he was ill.

Plainfield might have driven Van Wyck to the same ugly death that would claim his brother four years later if he had not had the good fortune to be "rescued" by Hans Zinsser, his old Stanford friend, now at Harvard, who became wonderfully generous to the Brookses as soon as he learned of their difficulties. Zinsser's "therapy" was simply to remove the patient physically from the contagious area. Once away from his mother Van Wyck showed immediate improvement, and while he remained severely melancholic, he was judged sufficiently fit to be taken to Cotuit on Cape Cod for a summer's vacation that is recapturable now only in a few photographs of depressed people doing their best to enjoy a picnic on the dunes. At first Eleanor and Zinsser hoped to keep Van Wyck in the Boston area, thinking that he had perhaps recovered enough to work, as for a while he did, on a local paper while seeing a doctor Zinsser knew and respected. Van Wyck, however, had become neurotically proficient at sabotaging every plan that would not return him immediately to Westport. Fighting for time, Eleanor brought him home that fall, hoping that she could keep him alive through the winter while she considered new strategies for his recovery. Henry Longan Stuart, both a professional and a personal friend, was persuaded to live with the Brookses, ostensibly as a house guest, but more practically as a companion and guardian to Van Wyck.

So things went: increasingly dangerous, but apparently interminable. Life in Westport permitted Van Wyck the secure feeling that his family could not escape him, but it reinforced his pathological conviction that he had betrayed his manhood. There were a few weeks of apparent improvement early and late in the year when Eleanor could almost be persuaded that her husband might be on an "up-curve," but, for the most part, his condition worsened steadily during 1928. He seized upon any word or action that he might interpret as a reprimand to justify killing himself and became utterly paranoiac at any hint of plans, however tentative, that involved the possibility of change.

Eleanor was forced twice to pull him "back before trains and any number of times from in front of automobiles." Because of his compulsive suspicions about punitive conspiracies, she was also obliged to consult doctors surreptitiously, routing almost all of her correspondence through her mother, who had moved into the small cottage that sat behind the Brookses' own house on the Westport property. Mrs. Stimson provided her daughter and son-in-law most of their living expenses during these years, while Mrs. Hibbard contributed smaller amounts to their support. Other members of the Stimson family occasionally helped Eleanor to pare away the huge medical debts the Brookses were incurring.

Beyond keeping Van Wyck alive the most urgent problem now confronting Eleanor was the choice of a doctor. After her husband's disastrous stay in England, she would not entrust him to anyone in whom she did not have absolute confidence, and Van Wyck compounded the problem by responding with panic to any suggestion that he visit Zinsser's friend in Boston. That city, he was convinced, was his appointed place of exile and imprisonment, and Eleanor was forced to continue her nervous search for the right man. One of the distinguished psychiatrists to whom she appealed, A. A. Brill, felt that there was no hope of even beginning therapy with a patient so depressed as Van Wyck. In desperation then, she discussed with Mumford, Spingarn, and Zinsser the possibility of sending Van Wyck to Carl Jung. The project eventually got as far as a letter to Jung, who responded pessimistically. Van Wyck was suffering , he said, from "chronic melancholia," and the cure would be difficult, perhaps impossible. Being overworked and understaffed, he could not take the case himself, but he suggested that a vacation in the West might possibly mitigate the condition to a point where it could be treated. Jung's diagnosis was disheartening, but his refusal to see Van Wyck was not a major disappointment. Since negotiations had begun Eleanor had realized that Van Wyck's tentative acquiescence was a matter of either panic or fatalism and that he would refuse to cooperate with any program involving psychoanalysis.

During the summer of 1928 Eleanor moved Van Wyck to Monhegan Island in Maine, the setting for one of the oddest coincidences of his life. One of the doctors she had consulted recommended a "school" run by the Reverend Gerald Stanley Lee, the apologist for inspired millionaires whom Van Wyck had attacked in *America's Coming-of-*

Age. The most naïve and altruistic of men, Lee was attempting on Monhegan Island to induce self-control (or "inhibition") in neurotic patients by training them with simple exercises in physical balance. He visited Westport in the spring of 1928 to persuade Van Wyck to accept the hospitality of his establishment for the summer.

The entire business was a disaster from the first. Eleanor could not afford to move herself and the boys to Maine during the vacation season, and it was, of course, unthinkable that Van Wyck be left on his own. At first she hoped to find some nonprofessional man, probably Stuart, who would accept a moderate salary simply to keep Van Wyck from killing himself. When that idea fell through she was forced to call upon Mrs. Hibbard—a "solution" that in itself shows how desperate she was. As Lee unhappily reported to her: Van Wyck's "lessons" were beneficial only until he had a chance to talk with his mother. Lee was personally able to brighten his student, but his course of instruction was ludicrously inadequate to Van Wyck's needs. For two hours a day this formal, self-conscious man did his best to balance balls on his head and the back of his hands, and such attempts to get him to inhibit seem to have left him only humiliated and hostile. His symptoms became increasingly severe during the summer.

From Monhegan Island Van Wyck returned to Westport. Still driven by his fear of losing his family and tormented by his visions of incarceration, Van Wyck insisted that he must live nowhere but in his own house. In this he was seconded by the psychiatrist, Dr. William White, upon whom Eleanor had settled for the moment. White felt that the discipline of living according to a fiction of normal family life might help restore Van Wyck to its reality and that institutionalization would depress him even more severely. Mrs. Hibbard and Ames, alarmed by the expense of private clinics, were willing enough to have Van Wyck stay at home temporarily, but they believed him incurable and wanted eventually to have him committed to the state asylum. Thus, an uneasy compromise of many motives rested upon Dr. White's decision—which may in itself, as Zinsser feared, have reflected less a commitment to his patient than a refusal to accept full medical responsibility even while making all of the important medical decisions. Everyone familiar with Van Wyck's condition noticed the unhealthful effects of the "family situation" upon him, Eleanor, and the boys. But for the moment Van Wyck's abject fear of separation and the various accidents of circumstance conspired to let him have his way.

189

Van Wyck's condition was described by Hans Zinsser in a letter of September 1928 to Henry A. Murray, Jr., the psychiatrist and literary scholar, also at Harvard, who had been one of the first to applaud *The Ordeal of Mark Twain* and was now taking an active personal interest in the Brookses' affairs. Zinsser felt that matters had deteriorated badly. The obsessiveness of Van Wyck's talk about guilt, incarceration, and suicide was more pronounced than ever, and Zinsser could no longer cheer him up with persistent expressions of optimism. In addition, Van Wyck's behavior had become increasingly purposeless and alarming. "He walked," Zinsser wrote, "or crawled around in the grass, continually pulling out weeds or fingering things—incessant motor activity of one kind or another accompanied by a stream of talk in which the fixed ideas that Mumford mentions were uppermost." But when joined by others, Van Wyck lapsed into silence, and his features would assume a "mask-like, melancholic expression." Zinsser also reported to Murray on the dangers of keeping Van Wyck at home and the problems raised by the choice of a doctor, especially since Mrs. Hibbard had, he thought, "badly messed up" relations with the congenial Dr. Charles Lambert. He proposed a joint action of Van Wyck's friends to support Eleanor both financially (although that was finally unnecessary) and psychologically.

Meanwhile, Dr. White did emphasize and help to set in motion one fundamental therapy. Like everyone who knew the history of Van Wyck's psychosis, he believed that if the writer could be persuaded to finish his book, or acknowledge that it was already finished by allowing it to be published, the act of authority would do much to bring him out of his depressed condition. Van Wyck, however, steadfastly resisted all suggestions that he return to the *Emerson*. He considered his book a contemptible failure, and he refused to allow portions of the study to be printed in *The American Caravan*, the literary annual Mumford was editing with Alfred Kreymborg and Paul Rosenfeld. Van Wyck's own name was carried on the masthead of this important periodical, but as a tribute and encouragement rather than a description of fact. Although Mumford kept him informed through Eleanor of developments in editorial policy, he was never able to take any part in putting the yearbook together.

Eleanor determined that the *Emerson* must be published, on her own authority if necessary. She was unsure how Van Wyck would react to her plan, and she was under pressure from John Macrae of

Dutton, who felt he had waited long enough for a manuscript on which he had paid a sizable advance. She worried the problem for several months before concluding that she must accept the risk to both her own and Van Wyck's peace of mind. Once she released the manuscript to Dutton, however, John Macrae reconsidered his position and spared her the possible consequences of her gesture. After a month of deliberation he returned the manuscript, telling Eleanor that he would like to have it immediately but had decided that it would be improper to bring it out without Van Wyck's personal authorization. Macrae's action was judicious, but it returned everyone involved to the stalemate from which they had started.

With Macrae's refusal in hand, Van Wyck's friends hit upon the idea of having the *Emerson* appear under the sponsorship of the new Literary Guild Book Club. Such publication, they argued, would testify to the appeal of the book and perhaps earn its author a sizable royalty. Although the Guild was hospitable to their proposal, the new plan quickly struck a snag. John Macrae hated book clubs and had stubbornly refused to permit them to distribute any of Dutton's titles. Max Perkins quietly went to work on the delicate negotiations necessary to placate Macrae and persuade him to transfer his rights on the *Emerson* to the Literary Guild.

Their manuevers took time, and as people shifted the *Emerson* back and forth, discussed doctors, and tried to agree on a strategy, Van Wyck's condition continued to deteriorate. The crisis came in early 1929, when he undertook to starve himself. Eleanor was forced to admit that she could no longer keep her husband safe, and her efforts to be both wife and psychiatric nurse were endangering her own health. Zinsser and Murray were worried also about the traumatic effect life with a psychotic parent might have on the boys. In April, then, Eleanor took Van Wyck to Bloomingdale, a large state asylum on Long Island, where Dr. Edwin Zabriskie would take charge of his treatment, and, more important, where a suicidal man would receive maximum protection. The move was purely defensive. No one pretended to believe that Van Wyck might improve in the prisonlike atmosphere of this impersonal facility, where patients had to be locked in their rooms at night. Eleanor was close to despair, and, recognizing how intimately her husband's psychosis was associated with his family, she expressed her willingness, even her desire, to remove herself from his life for as long as necessary.

"Van Wyck is surely no better and, I am inclined to think, probably worse than he was when we last discussed him," Zinsser wrote Mumford in June 1929, describing conditions at Bloomingdale. "His desire for death and his utter unwillingness to see any but the most tragic issues are uninfluenced by anything one can say." Almost any surroundings, Zinsser suggested, would be more therapeutic than the relentless monotony of the state hospital, where patients could do nothing but "play solitaire, croquet, walk about in a walled garden and converse with others in similar states." Van Wyck himself claimed that under the care of Dr. Lambert he might be able to work again, and Zinsser considered the problem of removing him to Lambert's sanitarium in Westchester County, near Katonah, New York. Although Lambert had been rebuffed earlier by Mrs. Hibbard, he both liked Van Wyck personally and appreciated the peculiar psychology of the artist. Turning a self-destructive patient over to him, however, would aggravate the critical problem of security, since his small hospital lacked Bloomingdale's elaborate facilities for preventing suicide. There was also the possibility that the state asylum would refuse to readmit Van Wyck if Lambert found him unmanageable.

Eleanor was thus forced to choose between risking Van Wyck's life and abandoning all hope that he might recover. Apparently she decided that for a man who lived in his mind no risk could be more deadly than the risk of incurable madness, for in July Van Wyck was taken from Bloomingdale to Katonah, "a charming place," as she described it to Joel Spingarn, "quite small—a lovely old private house set in delightful gardens—with two small outside cottages. There are only twenty or thirty [patients] there, many of them really delightful. . . ."

When Van Wyck arrived at this quiet retreat he was by any definition insane. He was aware that he had lost his mind and he was persuaded that his insanity was incurable. During his first few hours on the grounds, upset after a visit from Eleanor, he attempted to run away and resisted the two men who brought him back. He did not try to hurt them, but simply to escape into the woods and hide until he had died of starvation. He was, his doctors observed, an agitated, troublesome, suicidal patient, who frequently wept for hours at a time. His days were made eerie by voices that addressed him from a great distance and by anonymous presences who were about to lay hands upon him; his nights were haunted by bad dreams. He responded emotionally only to increasingly morbid variations upon the theme of guilt and punishment. For some period shortly after being admitted to the hospital he occupied himself with composing long, crazy letters to Eleanor, all of which compulsively beg her to kidnap him and abandon him in an old farmhouse, where he might starve to death unmolested. Otherwise, he thought, he must be either buried alive or returned to Bloomingdale, to be tied to a bed in the basement and kept alive for thirty years by intravenous feeding. When he tried to describe his condition to Eleanor he hit upon his most fearful nautical metaphor: *"Horrors of the Middle Passage!"* John Hall Wheelock, one of the few who were permitted to see Van Wyck then, remembered that he would find him either catatonic or maniacally talkative, or, even more distressingly, reduced to a pathetic childishness. Whatever his behavior, he seemed at all times inconsolably sad.

Wheelock's personal tenderness and stability made him perhaps the ideal companion for Van Wyck at this time, and he was apparently allowed more, and more intimate, contact with the patient than even Eleanor, whose visits, phone calls, or letters often broke Van Wyck down completely. Wheelock also was delegated to bring Van Wyck the first news that the Literary Guild wished to bring out the *Emerson.* Mumford and Perkins had done their intricate work in secret, but successfully at last, and Wheelock went out to Katonah that day "with very high hopes and treading on clouds, thinking this is going to make a big difference." His message did incite Van Wyck to one of his rare outbursts of speech, but it consisted simply of an emphatic "No!" To all of his friend's remonstrances and arguments—that the selection was a great honor, that the book was itself unusually distinguished, that it would earn him both money and a larger audience—Van Wyck would answer only "No! Bad! Bad! Very bad! Very bad!"

Somehow Lambert pulled Van Wyck through. Or, more accurately, under Lambert's direction and protection Van Wyck pulled himself through. In part, time worked its own cures, but the doctor seems to have handled his unusual patient with exemplary tact and wisdom. He told Eleanor that the *Emerson* should not be published without Van Wyck's consent, but that it would do him good to be pestered for it, and he was careful to isolate Van Wyck from people who might inadvertently touch off his hyperactive sense of guilt. Eleanor was permitted only monthly visits, and the handful of others who saw Van Wyck then were instructed precisely about conversation and behavior before they came to the sanitarium. But mostly Lambert treated his patient with the nonprofessional medicines of sympathy, under-standing, patience, and respect. By November Max Perkins was able to tell Mumford that their friend was improving, and in March 1930 Lambert sent the same news to Joel Spingarn, who had asked if he might visit. "He will put his most depressed foot forward," Lambert warned, "and will be full of lament to you regarding his condition, but dark as the cloud is the silver lining is beginning to show itself to us."

Van Wyck's emergence from his long dark night was a protracted, difficult process, but gradually he took hold of his mind and pulled himself back together. In time he resumed interest in the translations which Eleanor had continued, mainly to keep him aware of his literary orientation, and he showed some response to expressions of concern from his friends. He was also lifted from his melancholy by a dramatic gesture on the part of the large, wealthy Stimson family, many of whom contributed to the fund organized by Mrs. Landon K. Thorne that presented Eleanor with $100,000 in securities. The gift eased both his psychosis and the problems that had caused it. Van Wyck could now feel that he might devote himself to his writing without compro-mising his family. When he finally agreed that he had finished the *Emerson* after all and that the Literary Guild might bring it out, he had, in effect, met all of his own conditions for health. All he needed now was time.

After a difficult year at Katonah, he was eased back into the world by Lambert, who agreed that he might now spend his weekends in Westport. These were tense occasions—Wheelock remembered that Van Wyck was still ragingly excitable, and that the family had to de-vise rituals for calming him—but they were therapeutic as well, for he was learning by experience that he could live his old life in his old sur-roundings once again. Finally, in late April 1931, Van Wyck at last sailed, as he put it, from beyond "the shadow of the mountain" and came home to stay. He was still convalescent, and his return to West-port was kept private, but in October he more or less "officially" reap-peared in the world. He picked up his old point of view and resumed his extensive correspondence almost as if his five years' abdication had been nothing more than a bad dream.

He had experienced extremes of terror and humiliation, and he was left with a knowledge about himself which he could never thereaf-ter ignore. The photograph of Van Wyck that Dutton and the Literary Guild used in their publicity for *The Life of Emerson* presents the image of a calm, handsome, cosmopolitan author. But there is something evasive in the large, dark eyes—almost a cringing—which perhaps responds to the "hard ball of panic" at the pit of his stomach that he carried like shrapnel to the end of his days. When he came to confront and interpret his period of madness he turned almost instinctively to the imagery of theology, discovering in his descent into his hidden being an example of that dark night of the soul which in religious temperaments has traditionally signaled the destruction of an old, imbalanced identity and the birth of a man in harmony with himself. He thought he had lost his old ego, the ego so colossal that it called God into the grave to atone for a man's sins, and he hoped that he was entering upon a kind of inspired selflessness. "I was a great problem to my self during four very despondent years . . . ," Van Wyck told J. S. Zelie in 1933, "so much so that, after those years were over and I began to see how much work I had to do, I rather ceased to see my personal life as anything but an instrument, not worth bothering about in itself." In all of these things his psychology was strikingly like that of the mystics he had once emulated—or so, at least, he chose to view it.

But these are only metaphors and speculations. The fact was that Van Wyck was home and well again. Oliver Kenyon Brooks remembers that after the grim years of 1926–1931 these were wonderfully happy days in the little house on Kings Highway in Westport.

PART III

IN THE AMERICAN GRAIN
1932–1946

He was a very human man, full of prejudices in a way, and intensities, and he was a man who was hounded by the Furies.

—JOHN HALL WHEELOCK IN CONVERSATION,
October 23, 1970

I often think of you as the good physician who has helped to cure us—all of us—of a deeply seated American psychosis, a kind of mob inferiority complex out of which we gaze with hungry eyes toward Europe, towards the ruins of truncated statues and worn-out beliefs.

—HORACE GREGORY TO VAN WYCK BROOKS,
August 11, 1933

X

REENTRENCHMENT: 1932–1935

It is a comment upon the discontinuities of our literary history that we might be mildly surprised today by the enthusiasm with which Van Wyck Brooks was welcomed back to the literary campaigns when *The Life of Emerson* appeared in the spring of 1932. And it is sad to confess that research must supersede memory for our recognition of the esteem in which he was held. By 1932 he had been publishing for nearly a quarter century, and for seventeen years he had been the prophetic voice of an era. His public stature as the reliable veteran of the cultural offensive, more than his book itself, prompted an audience with a reawakening sense of socialistic priorities to the applause that greeted the *Emerson*. With the help of the Literary Guild's distribution and publicity, this curiously hagiographic study brought Brooks a more substantial sale and greater popular recognition than he had previously enjoyed, and it was accepted with almost unqualified enthusiasm by its first reviewers—even though critical admiration was to be short-lived.

The tributes must have pleased Brooks, who had as many private as public reasons for hoping that his book would do well. The *Emerson* he finally dared to publish was a monument to the tenacious courage of his wife and a few good friends. Beyond that, it was the first of a series of necessary excursions into his past by which he reestablished the continuity of his career and expressed a defiant faith in both himself and his old program. Despite the feelings of renewed clarity and energy with which he returned to life, Van Wyck's illness had left him susceptible. The residual panic that would forever trouble him challenged his self-possession almost beyond endurance when the shock of his brother's suicide exploded his own convalescence in December 1931 and he was forced to take up again his old, sad visits to Plainfield. Except for his lively expressions of homesickness for Westport, he left no record of his feelings during the three months after Ames's death when he was more or less constantly with his mother, and we can share them now only through a sort of informed sympathy. Eleanor reported in a letter to Dr. Lambert that Mrs. Hibbard had assigned her younger son to his brother's room and bed, so that Van Wyck tossed and turned in the night, imagining how Ames had lain awake there and planned his death.

There were more than psychological insecurities to be confronted. For five years the Brookses had subordinated their personal demands to the grim business of pulling a husband and a father through, but long-standing particular tensions remained after his recovery. Van Wyck had created a precarious family situation. Although he had deeply loved his wife and children for more than twenty years, he had distinguished sharply between the priorities of the domestic life and those of the literary life, and he had never yet committed himself to his home. Eleanor might justifiably worry that he would be unwilling or unable to take up family responsibilities, and she had cause to be uneasy as well about the personal implications that survived Van Wyck's attachment to Molly Colum, since that affair had been resolved more by circumstance than by decision. Charlie and Kenyon had also been generally ignored, shuttled about, and made unhappy during the ten years of their father's collapse. They had lost most just when they needed most, and if any family community were to survive Van Wyck must now become the parent he had never truly been.

These intimate claims inspired a domestic apprehension that was complicated by the old question of money. With his admiration for asceticism and his socialistic principles, Van Wyck felt guilty about accepting the bonds, securities, and other appurtenances of plutocracy which made up the Stimsons' $100,000. Guilt is at least suggested by the tactful remarks of George Russell (AE), who wrote him a long letter about spiritual poverty. "It does not mean," Russell argued, "that if somebody leaves them 100,000 dollars in a will that they refuse it. But that they stand ready at any time to desert prosperity if it conflicts with the spirit." Brooks maintained a long epistolary friendship with Russell, and the assurances of the visionary Irish poet probably helped him to settle some of his immediate reservations about the Stimson gift. But although he became accustomed to living with money, he never resolved his contradictory feelings about it, and his fluctuations of financial success would remain throughout the years a source of emotional unrest. Probably the income from the *Emerson* was already going almost exclusively toward paying off the large debt to hospitals and doctors he had incurred during his illness. He attacked this burden in his characteristically conscientious way, but it troubled him for years.

Moral problem or not, the Stimson money was of great practical help during this period of readjustment, since it released Van Wyck from the innumerable odd jobs of editing and translation that would keep him from his own work. It also assured the Brookses that there need be no more of the long separations that had weakened their early marriage. In fact, Van Wyck wholeheartedly gave himself over to the domestic identity he had resisted before his breakdown. "If," he wrote to Eleanor from Plainfield, shortly after Ames's death, "anything ensues [from the *Emerson*] in the way of publicity, invitations, etc., I am resolved to stick twice as close to my home & to have twice as much of your companionship—if you are really still there, and haven't blown away when I come back. *Deep obscurity,* and it cannot be too deep, is the only element I can breathe and write in, and any solicitation to the opposite will be met with a most uncharitable disregard." To Newton Arvin, who had just announced his own engagement, he wrote in a similar vein: "I am such a hopeless slave both to the fact and to the idea of marriage that I couldn't imagine life without it; and I have found it so much the happiest thing in the world—how can I help being happy on your account?"

From this point forward Van Wyck submitted gracefully to the rhythm of the quietly domestic life he shared with Eleanor in Westport. He also did his best to reclaim a natural intimacy with his sons, for whose troubled adolescence he felt particularly guilty. Charles, about to complete his studies at Harvard, was a little too old, his personality too set, to respond much to his father's dutiful letters, but Kenyon, at sixteen, showed a certain rebellious disinclination to study and came in for more than his share of paternal attention. Van Wyck made an uncomfortable parent, but his stiff attempts to call his family together probably healed some wounds by the sheer force of good intention.

Such efforts to buttress domestic life were complemented by the renewal and shiftings of old friendships, a process that was both joyful and anguishing. Van Wyck returned eagerly to his warm comradeships with Lewis Mumford, Newton Arvin, and Joel Spingarn—for whom he still felt deep intellectual as well as emotional affinities—and he strengthened the older, more sentimental ties that had endured since Harvard: with Jack Wheelock, of course, from whom he had never been completely separated; with Lee Simonson, now an important theatrical designer; with Max Perkins, still a neighbor in Canaan; and with Ned Sheldon, who lay blind and paralyzed in a New York apartment without losing either his good nature or his influence on the American theater.

At other times Van Wyck found that he was unable to resume an easy rapport with some of his closest companions of the twenties. Oliver Kenyon Brooks remembers, for instance, that Paul Rosenfeld became distinctly uncomfortable during a visit to Westport in the early thirties, and while there was no overt break with Rosenfeld, the relationship that went back to the stirring days of *The Seven Arts* soon lost all of its old character. The uneasiness may have been due to Rosenfeld's financial problems during the Depression, or it may have originated with Van Wyck, who had talked intimately with Rosenfeld just before breaking down completely and who might have involuntarily associated his old companion with the sickening fear of those days. Similar associations could have interrupted his friendships with Sherwood Anderson and Waldo Frank, but of course he had expressed reservations about both men long before his breakdown.

As he gradually drifted away from some of his idealistic companionships, he took quiet satisfaction from the more casual, more conventional associations his town afforded him—among cultured men and women, often not professionals, who reminded him anew of the intellectual traditions of New England. Curiously, few of Van Wyck's neighborhood acquaintances seem to have noticed the almost compulsive shyness that his closest friends insist he never lost. It is possible that his new acquiescence to the casual visits and light conversation he had never been able to abide was part of the tacit domestic bargain he had struck with Eleanor.

While he worked away at this slow process of personal reestablishment, Brooks also engaged his other important insecurity: the professional need to find his way back into the literary life he had abandoned in 1926. Trapped in his solipsistic catastrophe, he had, of course, missed the series of public shocks that had ushered in a new decade, and he had no way of knowing how much the intellectual world of the 1930s differed in its assumptions and temperament from the heady, experimental 1920s. "I am particularly anxious to talk to you about lots of matters of the last few years during which I have lived, unwillingly, more or less outside of things," he told Newton Arvin, admitting by the way that he was frightened by Arvin's new Marxist vehemence. He was learning that a literary radical could no longer be sure of either his identity or his function among an intellectual company that seemed to be lurching along a narrow tangent toward an Armageddon all its own.

Brooks responded to the challenge of the new order not by learning its rules and slogans but by carefully reasserting his old, now unfashionable, humanistic idealism in spite of it. One of his first letters upon returning from the hospital picks up this theme almost as if it had been written and left unmailed in 1924 or 1925. "You," he told Joel Spingarn in October 1931, "had laid some of the permanent stones in the foundation of our literary future—and . . . this will become more & more apparent as the fogs of 'pragmatism' and 'realism' (so-called) clear away, as they must, from the American landscape—as if the reality of the ideal world were less 'real' than the welter of mediocrity our eyes behold!"

The problem Brooks uncovered as he carried these attitudes further into a dreary decade extended one he had identified and attacked earlier: the economic aridity of the thirties encouraged a defeatism even more pronounced than the flippant pessimism with which a lost generation had responded to the cultural aridity of the twenties. "This is a very discouraging time, negative in almost all respects," he wrote to John Gould Fletcher in 1935, "and you must find it difficult to make headway. Hereabouts nothing new appears. Everyone is confused and troubled, and there is a sad absence of faith. The communists were active, but I agree with you that their way of looking at things is alien to our possibilities. . . . I shall never know a really happy moment until we see some revival of the human and hopeful spirit that was killed, temporarily, by the war."

The Life of Emerson served as a preliminary approach to many of the purposes Brooks would outline in that letter to Fletcher. This defiantly romantic biography opens with images of the puritanical morbidity to which the young Emerson was brought up ("Miss Mary Moody Emerson lived in her shroud. She had stitched it all herself . . ."), and sees its hero through a series of emblematic adventures: his discovery of an intellectual "circle" in Concord, his conquest of his desire for Europe, and his creation of an American audience—bringing him at last to an ultimately transcendental fulfillment. Brooks ends his study by moving it out of the world altogether. "And the strong gods pined for his abode"—so he interprets the obliviousness to surroundings that troubled Emerson's last years—"for the universe had become his house in which to live." The method, of course, was symbolic, pointedly appropriate to the problems of the writer, as Brooks understood them, in his own time. His book was to reassert his idealism, discover something of the peculiar virtue of the American past, and provide a model for contemporary American practice.

A fable or a morality rather than true biography, structurally a sort of crescendo, *The Life of Emerson* is at once one of the most ambitious and least successful of Brooks's works. His native sage remains too much the symbol, a character who is not allowed to develop naturally from the record of his experiences, but whose significance is imposed upon him from without. A similar impatience mars the exalted, celebratory tone of Brooks's episodic narrative. His generally heightened, lyrical atmosphere, all allusion and invocation, was potentially right for the theme of his American *Paradiso*—which involved the mastery of both letters and life—but he gives insufficient attention to either the process or the difficulty of mastery. *The Life of Emerson* is, finally, rather an imaginative paraphrase of, or apostrophe to, the Emersonian spirit than a study of Emerson himself. Without a sturdy representation of the man's fundamental toughness it betrays its own graceful lyricism, which sometimes goes embarrassingly flat. It soon came to seem little more than a charming anachronism to an intolerant generation of social analysts.

Whatever its defects of art or evidence, the *Emerson* is biographically important because it reaffirmed the possibility of American traditions and American models that Brooks had announced during his *Freeman* years. It also was the first of several republications through which he stubbornly continued to identify himself with his old position. In 1932 he brought out not only the *Emerson,* but *Sketches in Criticism,* a collection of his most important *Freeman* essays. Two years later he reissued *America's Coming-of-Age, Letters and Leadership,* and "The Literary Life in America" in a single volume entitled *Three Essays on America.* He edited these seminal statements vigorously, making innumerable verbal changes, pointing and polishing the style, but tampering with none of his earlier arguments or opinions. Most of his revisions were, in fact, calculated to strengthen the point of view he had defended since 1915.

The only substantial change he entered into this definitive volume was not professional but personal, the result of the kindness shown him in 1928 by Gerald Stanley Lee. "One part of [*Three Essays*]," he wrote to Lee in 1933, "is *America's Coming-of-Age,* over which I have bitten my tongue ever since I met you and which has caused me many a pang of regret. . . . When I took up the essay to revise it, I wished at first to omit the chapter dealing with your book, but I saw that this was impossible. It was woven with the structure of the book, and I found that I still believed in its *intellectual* content. It represents a difference of opinion. I also saw that by cutting it to the bone I could bring this out, and this alone, in such a way as to remove the personal matter which has caused me much pain. . . ." In the second edition of *America's Coming-of-Age,* then, the chapter originally called "The Apotheosis of the Lowbrow" lost its title and became a subdivision of the long chapter on Whitman. All direct reference to Lee was dropped. The revision (as Brooks may have had tactfully in the back of his mind) probably improved his strategy, which had been weakened by the important attention given to a relatively insignificant, now obscure, cultural theoretician. But it also robbed the essay of some of that sense of personal challenge that had delighted Young America in 1915.

The zest with which Brooks refinished these aggressive early works may have been sharpened by the heated controversy that had attended still another of his republications. By coincidence his revised edition of *The Ordeal of Mark Twain* (1933) appeared only a year after his thesis about Twain and his times had been savagely attacked by Bernard De Voto in *Mark Twain's America,* an ambitious study of frontier culture which De Voto himself called an "essay in the correction of ideas." This was by far the most powerful assault on his authority that Brooks had yet encountered. In effect De Voto accused him of being grossly ignorant about the America west of the Appalachians, of protecting that ignorance with a kind of sissified snobbishness, and of then using it to develop a false thesis about both Mark Twain and his culture. The indictment extended to other critics who had become associated with Brooks's ideas, particularly Waldo Frank and Lewis Mumford. Many of De Voto's strictures were just. He demonstrated the richness of life and possibility on the American frontier that Brooks, with his hungry glance toward Europe, had been too inclined to ignore, and he suggested many of the alternate approaches to the interpretation of American culture that have since become part of our collective knowledge about the West.

But De Voto allowed no degree of merit in the critical attitudes he opposed to his own, and he pursued his quarrel with unnecessary abusiveness. His remarks about Brooks were both personal and intemperate, and often couched in defensive, heavy-handed irony. As Edmund Wilson pointed out in his essay-review of *Mark Twain's America,* "Mr. Brooks is a kind of King Charles's head for Mr. De Voto: an obsession which is not altogether rational."

Despite such reservations, De Voto was widely admired, both for his refreshing faith in Western character and his great knowledge of the history of the region, and his study attracted more public attention than academic criticism usually does. These successes alarmed his opponents, not only because of the vindictiveness with which he attacked Brooks but because of his apparent desire, as Edmund Wilson put it, to argue only that Mark Twain was "a fine old boy." Progressives suspected that his critical truculence masked a conservative offensive against enlightenment and reform. The liberal counterattack, which quickly developed a vocabulary nearly as acrimonious as De Voto's own, was led by Mumford, Frank, and Wilson himself. De Voto, they argued, was too ready to throw out even Twain's testimony when it conflicted with his thesis, and he was guilty of rhetorical inflation. "At one point," Wilson noted dryly, "he seems to be wanting us to accept bear-and-badger-baiting as evidence that the life of the pioneer was not devoid of gaiety and charm."

The long debate that followed was frustrated by a singular rigidity on both sides. Probably the angry standoffs and refusals of truce that characterized both camps were more a matter of personalities than ideological position, for the theses advanced by the archrivals do not seem necessarily incompatible—nor have they proved so in practice. Both Brooks's psycho-economic theory of failure and De Voto's contention that Twain's environment gave him access to a peculiarly rewarding artfulness still provide students of this puzzling and contradictory writer with basic analytical tools.

Distressed as he was by De Voto's attack upon his integrity, Brooks took no active part in the fighting. He answered his tormentor only in his revised edition of *The Ordeal,* on which he was at work—had, in fact, already made some 1975 changes in the text—when *Mark Twain's America* appeared. The sheer weight of a historian's documentation prodded him to a few more corrections, but, as he told Lewis Mumford, who had asked for ammunition to use against De Voto, he could find little merit in the man's fundamental approach to literature and, while recognizing the limitations of his own study, he dismissed his challenger's claim to authority:

> all this seems to me of importance only because of a much more general point, the point where De Voto has scored in people's minds (as Canby's review showed): that De Voto "knows" about the West and we don't know about it. The question of what "knowledge" consists of, in the matter of criticism, is a very serious one. . . . And what in the world has "knowing" the West in De Voto's sense got to do with fully understanding the effect which the West had upon Mark Twain?

"As for my book," Brooks went on, "I am well sick of it, and am glad to think I shall never again have to psycho-analyze an author. The method is too clumsy and paralyzes one's intuitional sense, the one that really counts in criticism. . . . I had no chance to do him [i.e., Twain] justice, since my point of view was consistently psychological. I made about 2500 revisions, and the new version is better than the old—that's the best I can say." When the second edition of *The Ordeal of Mark Twain* came out in early 1933 careful readers found that Brooks had indeed acknowledged more generously the importance of a folk heritage to Mark Twain's art. Beyond that, he qualified his argument not an iota. De Voto continued to insist that Van Wyck Brooks had poisoned American life simply by contending that it already was poisoned.

These battles and alarums might have given Brooks some wry gratification that his work still retained power to offend, but controversy itself was irrelevant to the purpose that guided him through his recuperative years. In a sense, his reissues were a careful replanting of his roots, and they emphasize the fundamental continuity of his artistic development. The point is of some importance. Too many observers have found plausible the suggestion that Brooks's nervous breakdown marks the boundary between a pessimistic, reformist Brooks, overly inclined to reject all things American, who wrote before his break-down, and a celebratory Brooks, too inclined to indiscriminate af-firmation, who wrote afterward. The interpretation assumes that Brooks's early power depended on his neurosis, and that after being normalized by his doctors, he could no longer confront failure.

There are certainly dramatic changes in tone between, say, *Letters and Leadership* in 1918 and *The Flowering of New England* in 1936, but they are not radical changes. They develop along a continuum, ac-cording to the ambitious program for art and life in America that Brooks had announced as early as *The Wine of the Puritans.* His breakdown contributed to the change of tactics in his later work, per-haps accelerated it, but was not its cause. The "new" historiographical style, the montage of paraphrase and allusion, was first developed in *The Pilgrimage of Henry James* under the influence of Léon Bazalgette. The new emphasis on a collective American enterprise, with its cele-bration of American traditions, first surfaced in *America's Coming-of-Age,* was developed in the *Freeman* essays, and emerged full-blown in *The Life of Emerson,* which was all but finished before Brooks gave in to his psychosis. The indifference to personal identity which, as he told Dr. Zelie, he developed during his recovery may have contributed to the impersonal, empathic point of view that would characterize *Makers and Finders,* his series title for the five volumes of literary his-tory he would publish between 1936 and 1952, but that new reticence also fulfilled his resolve of 1908: "We must put aside anything that tends to make us self-conscious in this matter of American tradition and simply *be* American, teach our pulses to beat with American ideas and ideals, absorb American life, until we are able to see that in all its vulgarities and distractions and boastings there lie the elements of a gigantic art."

Brooks's other literary work during this period complemented his republications and, like them, was calculated to help him reestablish a productive routine. Once out of the hospital, he turned again to his youthful discipline of journal-keeping, that refuge of sufferers from the malady of the ideal, and he regularly set down his observations and reflections in the series of notebooks that would eventually provide the substance of *The Opinions of Oliver Allston*, his personal manifesto of the early 1940s. He filled at least eight thick volumes between 1932 and 1939, and destroyed all but one of them.

In collaboration with his son Charles, he also undertook his last translation from the French—working this time not for money but for the sake of a deeply loved book. Henri Amiel had been, of course, one of Brooks's spiritual masters, and when Brooks suggested to Macmillan that the house might bring out a new translation of the *Intimate Journal* he had in mind both the need for a sound text of this strange masterpiece and the possibility of creating a professional identity for Charles, who had literary aspirations of his own. With the ordinary tensions between collaborators exacerbated by the equally natural problems of authority between father and son, the translation progressed more painfully than Brooks had anticipated, and he was frustrated in his attempts to have Charles's name placed alone, or at least first, on the title page. The business management at Macmillan's firmly pointed out that his own name would sell books. Despite such worries and disappointments, the long, slow work with Amiel refreshed him with a return to one of the sources of his inspiration.

The other odd job to which he turned his hand in the early thirties had little significance of its own, but it pointed to the future. Gamaliel Bradford had been only a professional acquaintance, but when that historical biographer died early in 1932 Mrs. Bradford asked Brooks to be literary executor and to prepare her husband's papers for publication. The problem of selecting and introducing the *Journals* (published 1933) and *Letters* (1934) must have required some tact, for Brooks was no great admirer of Bradford's patrician interpretations of the past. "May I say in your private ear that I have not read the writings of Bradford which apparently justify your retort," Brooks wrote to Newton Arvin, who was disturbed by Bradford's sympathy with the reactionary South. He explained that he was "caught napping" because he had relied solely on Bradford's private correspondence, and the moral lesson he takes from his error is interesting. "I hope you will nail me in your review . . . ," he instructed Arvin; "I was wrong. And you have confirmed me in my feeling that I should never generalize, even for a moment, about any author, *all* of whose writings are not clearly in my mind. Therefore I shall profit by your comment, and I sincerely hope that you will repeat the comment publicly. It will do me no harm in the long run. Have no fear of that—in case you weaken for the moment, out of regard for our personal relations."

As it turned out, Bradford had been simply an excuse for repeated visits to a collection of useful papers in Boston. "As I was planning to give up a year to reading," Brooks had told Lewis Mumford upon receiving Mrs. Bradford's offer, "it is providential . . . I think I shall undertake it, for it will involve me in reading great masses of old New England diaries, etc., which are just in line with my plan for the *New England Literature.*" After years of false starts, he had found his subject at last. The seemingly endless series of reissues was to his mind little more than an exercise in recovery—to be placed on record and then forgotten. "These old things are not to be read. They are ancient history," he inscribed a copy of *Three Essays on America* for H. L. Mencken. Almost upon his return from Katonah he was writing to Lewis Mumford about the need for "the monumental, the classic thing such as the old fellows used to attempt and carry through: Prescott, Motley, the Carlyle of *Frederick the Great,* etc., who had their minds filled, as we have not in these last generations, with heroic and classic models."

In the same letter he announced to Mumford a plan "that I have cherished for years—twenty, I guess—and that Eleanor is always driving me to carry out—of a History of American Literature in two or three volumes which I can spend the rest of my life writing!" By the summer of 1932 he was telling his friend how, in connection with his work on the Bradford papers: "New England of 1812–1914 interests me more every minute as my reading advances and I have the sense— not illusory, I trust—of discovering now and then valuable secrets that have only to be given another life in our new terms."

As Brooks came to realize that he must settle his account with the great men of the New England Renaissance, he discovered the heroic project he had always sought. His new determination to read every work by every writer before assigning priorities or making judgments demanded a total immersion in the past, and he eventually went through a list of some 825 books for what was to be *The Flowering of New England.* Here was the "monumental thing" indeed. No literary history of similar depth and range had yet been attempted, and the task was possible only for a man who had the rare freedom of time, and the rarer dedication, to bring to it.

Gradually Brooks developed the routine that would carry him

through the twenty years' sustained labor on his history—which would, in fact, shape each day for the rest of his life. After rising at 5:30 A.M. and setting a pot of coffee to perk, he dressed himself formally—waistcoat and tie—out of respect for the work he was to do. As he liked to remind himself in his notebooks, he retained a mildly eccentric, a studied "fetishism" in matters of literary performance. Then, while he came fully awake, he would putter around his study, dreaming perhaps of Emerson in Concord or turning over the good anecdote about Oliver Wendell Holmes he could work into his story. At the same time he performed a little ritual of preparing his paper and pencils, holding the nibs of the day's pens between his lips so that they would take the ink properly. He was now a graying man, stouter and more florid of face, Edmund Wilson recalled, than the pale, ascetic type he had known during the twenties, quietly astir in a silent house in the cold, dark New England morning. Until midafternoon he wrote, painfully as always, scrawling his graceful, complicated narrative on white paper in the blackest ink to be had.

For the remainder of his day Brooks attacked the often tedious reading with pen in hand, jotting notes and quotations on three-by-five-inch slips of paper. He neither indexed these data nor put them in chronological order, but eventually arranged them according to the sequence the narrative was to take. The statement he affixed to the multitude of boxes holding these fragile, almost illegible slips, now on deposit at the University of Pennsylvania Library, reveals something of both the personal strengths and the methodological weaknesses of his practice. "Often," he writes, "on a page with heading of somebody's biography or study, I note this author's ideas and then (without warning) go on with my own. It will appear that I have stolen my ideas. (They are hasty jottings. I read them with secret understanding, knowing them by heart.) Why I hesitate to have them kept for students to see. Sometimes my own thoughts are placed on same page with those of the author. Only I can know which are which. Sometimes I knowingly copy erroneous statements to remind myself to reply to them." As a system of filing, this is a mess—as Brooks himself discovered when he wanted to look up some of his citations in order to reply to a scholarly critic. As a sort of prenarrative, however, it served his artistic purposes admirably.

None of this would ever come easily. Van Wyck had each day to brace himself for his encounter with the muse of history. John Hall

Wheelock recalled that he usually referred to his study as "the torture-chamber," and he expressed a similar bleakness of mood to many correspondents during his writing of *The Flowering of New England.* "It really is a hell of a business!—writing," he told Clarkson Crane. "I make no progress myself, or next to none; and have been in the depths of despair all winter, certain that I cannot finish my book." He used even stronger language to Dr. Zelie: "I almost always feel nervous and bothered, and almost desperate about my work, as if I hadn't begun yet and had never accomplished anything, and every morning, at my desk, I feel that I am on trial for my life." Much of this is no more than the vocational complaint of any writer who is forced to struggle for a language equal to his vision, but Brooks had come to feel that he wagered his being on the success of his art, and his illness had left him inclined to periods of extreme depression. Yet, he was not an unhappy man during most of these years. He had the intense satisfaction of finally submitting himself to America, and he looked for great results to dignify the sacrifice. His task was not so much to reclaim as to establish a fertile past. "I create," he would write somewhat grandly in a notebook of 1939, "an American memory."

Thus he might have sensed that he was discovering his country at last. It was an awakening attitude expressed in subtle ways, not least by his new interest in traveling at home—to Maine for summer vacations and particularly to the South for working journeys during the winter. His earlier shuttling back and forth between California and New York had been a matter of disagreeable necessity, but when he first visited St. Augustine in January 1933 he felt a tangible contact with the past he was trying to reawaken. Although appalled, as he told Lewis Mumford, by many of the survivals of slavery, he was delighted by the European flavor of the old Spanish town, and he thought "that for *writing conditions,* the South is beyond comparison."

He and Eleanor spent much of their next winter in Virginia, near Washington, and afterward Van Wyck tried to take an annual vacation in the South. Of course he was both enchanted and instructed by the writers he met on these journeys—Ellen Glasgow in Richmond, for instance, and DuBose Heyward in Charleston—but the Southern landscape itself inspired more deeply his imaginative grasp of the past. "We fled to this village, where we are living in the works of E. A. Poe," he wrote to Mumford from South Carolina early in 1936. "We found quarters here in a lovely, shabby old plantation house, which I call the

House of Usher just before it fell. Great dying oaks and pines surround it, dripping with trailing Spanish moss, and the alleys in the moonlight from our windows, all ashen and sober, save for the blossoming camelias, are for all the world like 'Ulalume.' You could never know Poe if you had not seen it."

It was essentially a quiet and peaceful life during those years when Brooks was laying anew the basis for his career. He had awakened in a strange world, the more puzzling because it seemed so familiar, and he needed to identify it to himself and himself to it before he could go on with his life's work. The world had changed more dramatically than he supposed, however, and he was baffled from time to time by the difficulty of rejoining old allies or making new ones. He had yet to realize that the confusion was not entirely his own, that the decade itself resisted any but the most doctrinaire assumptions of ideological stability.

XI

YANKEE SOCIALISM: THE INTELLECTUAL QUARRELS OF THE THIRTIES

"I have thought about you a good deal and wondered what you were doing . . . ," Brooks wrote to Newton Arvin, when he renewed their dialogue in January 1932, "for I always think of you as more or less of an ally as well as a friend and I have somewhat lost touch with the various battle-fronts." Then, almost as if it were still 1926, he went on with some of the professional advice that had helped bring Arvin along during his years with *The Freeman.* "Has it occurred to you," he asked, "that Stuart Sherman, treated biographically-critically, would be a capital subject? . . . A wonderful chance for a study of the academic view—the great problem of the 'English Department' in general and the relation of the life of letters to it, and of a strangely intense, half-awakened, intelligent, spiritual human being, torn between all sorts of deep half-temperamental, half-conventional preoccupations about Democracy & the West, with yearnings towards a sophisticated New York that was in part more enlightened than he and in larger part quite unworthy of him."

Looking at this letter, with its curious "racial" discussion of the problems inhibiting their old Humanist enemy, Arvin must have concluded that his friend had lost touch with battlefronts indeed. If he speculated further about the naïve document before him, he might have remembered that Van Wyck had awakened into financial security

214

just as the nation was realizing the full implications of its economic disaster. He might have reflected that a private nightmare had spared a sensitive man much of the trauma of public nightmares: the stock market crash of October 1929; the subsequent unemployment, with its harsh exaggeration of every social evil; the collapse of the Bank of the United States in New York City in 1930; the imprisonment of the Scottsboro Boys—like Sacco and Vanzetti the symbolic victims of a decade—which seemed all of a piece with new outbursts of lynching in the South. Civilized people might think with grim humor that all that remained of the "normalcy" of the 1920s was the heritage of Scarface Al Capone, for the gangsters continued their bloody raids unabated during these last Prohibition years—creating by the way a new popular genre in both fiction and motion pictures. There were even ominous suggestions abroad that American citizens were losing faith in the idea of democracy.

Whatever thoughts or reflections Van Wyck's letter might have inspired, Arvin replied with some care, for there was no faltering of mutual affection. "It at once pleases me and troubles me," he wrote, "that you still speak of me as a kind of ally: in the deepest sense, I hope that is true; but superficially I am not sure how you would now feel. The last two years have simply ripped out the foundations for me, and now nothing seems to me really important except the onslaught upon capitalism on every front—on the 'cultural' front as well as on others; and for this, I now see, our only intellectual weapons are the body of theory in Marx, Lenin, and such writers. Middle-class culture, it seems to me, is stinking with corruption; and everything must be done to discredit it." His letter touched off a private debate that would last nearly eight years and help both men to find their way through the ethical minefields of the thirties.

Van Wyck immediately resisted Arvin's implicit challenge, falling back almost instinctively upon the old-fashioned socialism that since college had provided him all the political and economic theory he needed. "I always looked forward to the Socialist state," he responded, justifying his ideas to himself as he explained them to Arvin, "as one in which each of us who had proved his capacity could do his work in uninterrupted security. . . . All the conditions for spiritual success of every kind were better, as I find in my daily reading, in the 'narrow' world of our New England forebears."

He developed the implications of these attitudes on several occasions. That first January he reminded his friend that

> my adherence to Karl Marx (in a sense that would need to be defined) is of long standing. I don't quite know what you imply by "middle-class culture." I merely make a clear distinction between the ends of life and the means. Love, grief, nonsense, humor, tragedy, poetry, are subjects on which Marx & Lenin have nothing to say, except in so far as they are philosophers, not economists, and culture is concerned with these things. In so far as culture is "middle-class," it is decadent, and in that aspect ought rather, I think, to be ignored than discussed at all. I always liked AE's phrase, "democratic in economics, aristocratic in thought," as more or less expressing what I feel.

A few months later he was doggedly returning to his fundamental distinction between culture and economics: "There surely is a spiritual sphere as well as a social sphere, the one concerned with values, the other with applications. Nobody now seems to me to represent the sphere of values—to my mind, the proper sphere for critical minds." His letters grew long and sometimes heated—partly because he was questioning his beliefs and hoped to learn from, as much as refute, Arvin's position, and partly because he refused to take refuge in the traditional agreement to disagree. To Arvin's tactful suggestion that they were simply judging the literary life from fundamentally different perspectives, he replied: "I don't believe very much in *points of view*, even in my own personal right to a point of view, believing as I do that there exists a truth in regard to every question upon which we should all agree if we were sufficiently informed and enlightened."

No matter how much Brooks insisted that his duties as a writer were more complex than his duties as a citizen or propagandist, Arvin stuck to his Marxist credo. "I don't agree," he wrote in June, "that middle class culture, decadent as it is, can be ignored, or allowed simply to decay from within. It still has a kind of vitality, as many spiritually dead things do, and the first task of American criticism seems to me to be to destroy it with every weapon at one's command. It will *take* destroying, for it is the possession of a class that is not going to surrender its privileges—or its culture—without a struggle. This is why I be-

216

lieve Marx and Lenin do have, by implication, much to say about culture...."

After several months of similar pronouncements and standoffs, Brooks and Arvin tacitly agreed to leave ideological dialogue out of their correspondence, but they continued their intense discussions during many visits at each other's homes, now that their automobiles had eased the distance between Northhampton and Westport. At first the thoughtful give-and-take of these debates seemed to be all on the older man's part. In the early thirties Arvin was a true convert, untroubled by complexities, but Brooks had no orthodox base for his humanitarian socialism. Not being philosophically minded, he had perhaps been too content to accept rather than verify his assumptions about man and society, and he could not claim the certainty as to his position that he admired in Lewis Mumford, who firmly declared himself "post-Marxian." Thus he often repeated to Arvin his ready acknowledgment that he found himself "confused a little about what a writer's attitude should be toward these economic problems—and how he can make himself useful as a writer in regard to others."

During the early thirties Brooks was also subjected to serious attacks from both extremes of the literary community. On the right, an energetic revival of Humanism complemented the boisterous Americanism of De Voto, calling into question once again the premises and arguments by which Brooks had become the spokesman for the Literary Radicals. Seward Collins, in an ambitious essay for *The Bookman,* and Norman Foerster in *Toward Standards,* both published in 1930, accused Brooks of either rabid antitraditionalism or the abuse of tradition. They mocked his Romanticism and his "gospel of humanitarianism" and grouped him with those determinists who unwittingly trapped themselves and their values in historical process.

This Humanist counteroffensive was of little immediate consequence. Ideological differences with the Literary Radicals apart, both Collins and Foerster exhibited serious misunderstandings of their enemy—Foerster, for instance, insisted that Brooks was a "disciple" of Randolph Bourne, and Lewis Mumford a "disciple" of Brooks—and the revival of Humanism flared only momentarily before it was lost among more timely outcries. But many Humanist attitudes—orthodox traditionalism, classicism, and the stubborn distinction between artistic and social values—were being subsumed by a group of intellectuals who would soon call themselves "New Critics," and Brooks privately kept up an angry muttering against their influence in both his notebooks and his correspondence of the thirties.

The outburst of hostile criticism from the left was more immediately disturbing, since Brooks had always associated himself with radical causes, even while he had rejected the strictly Marxist point of view in some of his most biting *Freeman* columns. During the twenties he had been able to turn aside with relative ease the challenges of a Max Eastman or an Upton Sinclair, but with the emergence of Communism as a major intellectual force, leftist demands that a writer submit substance and method to party discipline gained considerable authority. That an old-fashioned socialist could not in conscience become an overt propagandist or relate all of his analyses to the priorities of class warfare left these doctrinaire intellectuals unimpressed, for they seemed to become only harsher and more demanding the nearer another writer approached their position without embracing it unreservedly. The case of Communists and their fellow travelers against a reluctant cousin can best be represented by one of their most restrained sympathizers, Bernard Smith, who took the occasion of Brooks's fiftieth birthday to "reevaluate" his career in the pages of *The New Republic.*

After praising *America's Coming-of-Age* for its sharp analytic demonstration of the necessity for collectivism, Smith noted a hint of softness in *Letters and Leadership* and the biographical studies that followed. That was, he thought, the inevitable "consequence of introspection upon [Brooks's] esthetic judgments as well as his social interests." For, as Smith explained his own position, "to look inward in the search for either origins or solutions of social and cultural phenomena is apparently fatal.... It was Mr. Brooks's error that he pondered overmuch on the brute strength of men as compared with the frailties of man.... This in turn led him to an acutely sorrowful pity for the artist in his tragic dilemma. We are now, I believe, discussing an attitude that is downright unhealthy for a social critic." From this failure, Smith went on, Brooks succumbed increasingly to an elegiac melancholy that left his later work without significance, a matter of "scholarly story-telling." The article ended with regrets for the passing of his leadership and the suggestion that for serious intellectuals Mr. Brooks was in effect dead. Such assertions became critical commonplaces dur-

218

ing the early thirties, but they were serious charges, and they stung Brooks sharply.

He was morally and by party affiliation a Socialist. "I caught it from my wife," he told Malcolm Cowley, "who caught it from her father, an old New York artist who caught it in France, when he was a student there in the 1870's, and who formed a school in New York to teach art and socialism, so that we are both socialists in the grain." To him socialism meant that one trusted the fundamental decency and intelligence of human beings, favored an end to economic competition, and fought for social justice, but he was suspiciously inclined to define it by metaphor. On one occasion he equated socialism with Jeffersonian democracy, on another with "pure Christianity," and he was fond of quoting a Spanish proverb to the effect that "the Left is on the side of the heart; the Right is on the side of the liver."

These sentiments would have had little effect on Brooks's Communist critics, who demanded that writers first take sides and then take action. Probably Brooks agreed, at least tentatively, with that general principle, for he set to work forming a "Socialist local" in Westport. Eleanor ran for the Connecticut legislature in the elections of 1934 and "raised," her husband proudly told Arvin, "the Westport socialist vote from 18 to 139." Van Wyck himself was the Socialist candidate in 1936. But even such encouraging signs of the times as the election of Jasper McLevy, the Socialist mayor of Bridgeport, could not keep him from observing that his efforts to introduce any form of collectivism into the capitalistic world of Westport were at best quixotic. He characterized the whole affair to Lewis Mumford as "mainly a sop to my conscience for not doing anything else with or for the Children of Light—who load the mail heavily these days!"

Brooks's political campaigns provide a clue to his state of mind during the middle thirties. That he would violate both his personal shyness and his professional aversion to active politics suggests that he was experimenting with his confusions. Here, as often, Brooks's experience epitomizes the intellectual and cultural history of his time, and he can guide us through one of the important developments in American life during what has come to be called the "Red Decade." He cooperated with Marxists out of moral conviction, but with deep misgivings about their purposes and tactics; he resisted their attempts to direct a general enthusiasm for social justice to their own ends; and, finally, he broke off sharply when their leadership failed to meet the challenge of a series of European crises.

His involvement with the Communism of the Great Depression came almost exclusively through the League of American Writers. This group developed as a successor to the John Reed Clubs, which were ordered disbanded in 1935 when the Party turned its attention to the establishment of its myriad "fronts." The new tactic was calculated to unite even heterodox sympathizers against the common capitalist and fascist enemies, while dignifying orthodox causes with the names of respected non-Marxist intellectuals. More immediately, the League grew out of the first American Writers' Congress, an impressive gathering of "revolutionary" artists held in New York City in April 1935. The call for a congress went out in leftist journals in January. It included the following points:

> Fight against imperialist war, defend the Soviet Union against Capitalist aggression;
> against Fascism, whether open or concealed;
> for the development and strengthening of the revolutionary labor movement;
> against white chauvinism (against all forms of Negro discrimination or persecution) and against the persecution of minority groups and of the foreign-born; solidarity with colonial people in their struggles for freedom;
> against the influence of bourgeois ideas in American literature; against the imprisonment of revolutionary writers and artists, as well as other class-war prisoners throughout the world.

The Congress promised to be an exciting affair. Brooks, who loved the company of other writers and had always championed cooperative efforts, must have been hard put to resist the urgings of Waldo Frank and Malcolm Cowley that he join the proceedings. But resist he did. He still responded to this newly orthodox Marxism with an alternate attraction and panic that resembled his ambivalent feelings toward his adolescent Catholicism. Communism was, as he had once reminded Newton Arvin, a sort of a church after all. Moreover, he was offended by parts of the call to congress. "Now about the paper you enclosed, concerning the Writers' Congress," he wrote to Frank:

I dislike to be always saying no and I feel that by doing so I place myself in an equivocal position. But you know, Waldo, from many things I have said, that there are certain things in this programme which I simply cannot accept. . . . I do not believe in a "workers' government" [a phrase from the prologue to the call] if this means, as I assume it means, the "dictatorship of the proletariat." Every fibre of my being revolts against dictatorship of every kind, and I shall have to see more signs than I do of an imminent *Fascist* dictatorship before I could align myself with the other kind. And I should violate my whole nature if I subscribed to item 5. "Fight against the influence of bourgeois ideas in American literature." I know this is a matter of definition, but I know that, in many respects, what is "felt" to be *bourgeois* to most of the writers in this list is to me sacred and real; and to say anything else would be for me to deny my conception of the ends of life.

As it turned out, his misgivings did not affect his colleagues. He was one of the forty writers who during that first session were elected to the League's National Council. Although he did not immediately respond to this new pressure, he apparently did begin to reconsider some of his objections to the League, and to wonder if he might not be wrong to judge it according to his distrust of a minority—albeit the most vocal minority—of its membership. He was, after all, involved in other politically oriented causes over whose policies he had no control, freely giving his name, and sometimes his money, to many of the committees and associations that flourished in that era. Although the first Congress displayed unmistakable political overtones it had not become merely a political creature. The intellectual business of the proceedings had been taken seriously and presented well, and several key offices in the new organization were filled by his friends. Waldo Frank was elected chairman of the League; Malcolm Cowley, Kenneth Burke, and Alfred Kreymborg were on its seventeen-member Executive Committee. Finally, Brooks was drawn toward the League by its fundamental appeal to his sympathies. It stood for the leftist idealism that was now the romance of America, and as one of the most impressive gatherings of writers in common cause the country had yet witnessed it seemed to him an incorporation of his "guild-spirit."

Meanwhile, as the decade rolled toward its bloody climax, Brooks could well believe that the fascist dictatorship he had mentioned to

Waldo Frank was more nearly imminent than he had supposed. Franklin Delano Roosevelt's famous "Hundred Days" of relief legislation were already history, and economic conditions were gradually improving, but the destructive forces unleashed by the collapse of old-fashioned capitalism continued to batter both personal and community life. Proto-fascist groups of small but determined membership sprang up everywhere and claimed an amount of public attention all out of proportion to their essential weakness. Racial hatred directed at blacks and Jews was more openly expressed and more respectable than it had been at any time during the century. The brutal suppression of strikes in Michigan or Kentucky, where Waldo Frank had been beaten by goons, might have reminded Brooks of the open warfare management had waged against labor in the bloody mining camps of the West when he was young. One did not have to be a Communist to wonder if republican forms themselves were not helpless before the challenges of totalitarian mentality. An uneasy intellectual might well have decided to join the Front after a disquieting conversation with friends about the implications of the life and death of "Kingfish" Huey Long, or after an evening spent listening to Father Coughlin on the radio.

Events in Europe cast more doubt upon the ability of democratic governments to survive. Intellectuals had been disturbed by the accession to power of Adolf Hitler in 1933, as by his ideological alliance with Benito Mussolini, who until that time had been widely regarded as a sort of vulgar joke, but it was not until the advent of Francisco Franco and the Spanish Civil War that the situation came to seem critical. El Caudillo, as he modishly titled himself, was less demonic than his German and Italian counterparts, but in some ways he seemed the truer embodiment of the fascist spirit. He ignored the lip service those dictators paid to progress and social justice, and insisted simply that Spain become again the rigid, exclusively Catholic nation that had dominated continental Europe in the sixteenth and seventeenth centuries. Once Italy and Germany had openly sided with Franco and the Soviet Union began supporting the Republic, the civil conflict in Spain became for many intellectuals on the left the supremely romantic war of this century—a true Armageddon, in which good squared off against evil, progressivism and the future against the barbarism of the past.

The Spanish War was a vicious war. Both sides were guilty of exceptionally ugly atrocities. But the full news from Spain filtered through newly sophisticated techniques of propaganda only slowly, and for leftists of the time both vice and ugliness were definitively symbolized by the shock of Guernica, the open city indiscriminately bombed by the German Condor Legion. Gradually, the Spanish conflict came also to seem a literary war, full of lore and poetry and music, the war of the Lincoln Battalion and the International Brigade, of the German Communists who sang that they had not lost their fatherland but discovered it "just outside Madrid." Among other writers, André Malraux of France was in Spain with a squadron of fighter pilots; W. H. Auden of England was there, working in Republican hospitals; Ernest Hemingway of the United States, ostensibly a war correspondent, was training Republican volunteers in the use of small arms. The names of intellectuals who abandoned the study for the trenches helped lend to the Civil War the flavor of leftist romance which it sometimes retains even today, for it was the cause of Spain, rather than the conduct of hostilities there, by which its agony has passed into the rebellious imagination. Later, such witnesses as Hemingway and George Orwell would report to a chastened generation how disorganized and irrational the workings of the loyalist "front" had been, and the crusade in Spain would often come to seem an example of the great fraud of politics, the more disillusioning in proportion to the idealism it had originally inspired. But at first one knew simply that young men from all over the Western world, whose blood became Spanish only as it soaked into Spanish earth, were dying in mountain villages or defending Madrid against the superior forces of *los cuatros generales,* for the sake of a democratic cause. There could be no ambiguity about *that* stirring conflict. Like almost all of his colleagues Brooks publicly "took sides" against leader Franco and his poisonous chums.

It was this fundamentally anti-Fascist rather than pro-Marxist impulse that moved Brooks closer to the League during 1936 and 1937, as the time for a second Congress approached. This time he joined his friends Arvin, Cowley, Mumford, and Frank, in addition to such writers as Erskine Caldwell, Langston Hughes, James Weldon Johnson, Archibald MacLeish, Claude McKay, Clifford Odets, Upton Sinclair, and Carl Van Doren, in signing the call to Congress, a document which, reflecting the Communist Party's increasing emphasis on sympathy rather than allegiance, was oriented predominantly to cultural issues. "Today in America," it began, "there are signs of a literary revival that may resemble or surpass that of the period from 1912 to 1916—the period of the 'poetry renaissance' and the 'revolt against the genteel tradition.' Those of us who remember the hopeful activity of those years can also remember how it was cut short by the War. And we can see that the promise of the 1930's is threatened in a still more definite fashion."

The American Writers' Congress in New York in June 1937 was much less overtly political than its predecessor. Several of the papers read referred directly to the value of Brooks's early leadership, and the Congress commended as the best work of nonfiction for 1936 *The Flowering of New England,* which had already won the National Book Award and would be given the Pulitzer Prize for History that November. Brooks was elected chairman of the Connecticut writers, one of the seven vice-presidencies of the League, and he was also named an honorary vice-president of a "permanent national organization to support the Spanish Popular Front," along with Malcolm Cowley, Ernest Hemingway, Erskine Caldwell, Upton Sinclair, Langston Hughes, Archibald MacLeish, Donald Ogden Stewart, and Meridel Le Sueur. He accepted these offices gladly, feeling now that League members "were irresistibly drawn by the idea of a guild that would bring them together." Later, when he better understood how Communists had done their best "to kill democratic socialism," he insisted: "I would have been ashamed to say I had not known communists or shared the great hopes of the Russian revolution."

That same June Brooks was awarded an honorary degree by Tufts College, one of the many tributes following upon the critical and popular success of *The Flowering of New England.* Addressing the graduating class, he took occasion to denounce the literature of reaction, which he defined primarily as an art and criticism preoccupied with technique at the expense of substance and with despair at the expense of health:

> It seems [he complained] as if our writers passively wallowed in misery, calling it fate; as if the most powerful writers, from James Joyce to Hemingway, from Eliot of *The Waste Land* to Eugene O'Neill and Theodore Dreiser, were bent on proving that life is a dark little pocket. . . .

Such tendencies, he suggested, were suicidal:

It seems to me it represents the "death-drive," . . . the will to die that is said to exist side by side in our minds with the will to live. Defeat and unhappiness can reach a point where we accept them and embrace them and rejoice in our enervation and disintegration.

What's more, they were childish:

You know this is infantile; and in fact it seems to me that most of our recent literature has been written by adolescent minds. Mencken is a boy. Cabell is a rather silly boy. Hemingway's brag and bluster are as boyish as Sherwood Anderson's gropings, and if T. S. Eliot exalts the minor poets over the major poets is it not because he does not feel the major emotional problems?

This was a political speech. Brooks made clear that he was not associating the writers he named in his address with the "literary Hitlers and Mussolinis," and (while he sometimes faltered in private) he was always careful to avoid the unfortunate public habit of the time that associated literary enemies with Fascism. But he did believe that Fascism and the literature of despair were complementary symptoms of a prevalent modern disease. An attack upon one was in effect an attack upon the other. The speech was not published and seems to have caused no controversy in 1937.

While he launched this personal critical offensive and prepared in his notebooks to press it further, Brooks also went ahead with the complementary work of the League. He attended meetings and conferences, gave lectures, did his best to enlist sympathy for anti-Fascist causes, and donated the manuscript of *The Flowering of New England* for the relief of Republican Spain. It brought $800 at an auction for the benefit of the Medical Bureau to Aid Spanish Democracy in 1938. At the same time he remained uneasy about Communist tactics, about the "political sitters-in" who were not writers but were determined to direct writers to their own partisan ends. With all the good will in the world, he could not force himself to put up with the inflexibilities of Marxist literary criticism.

Even Newton Arvin felt the bite of Brooks's critical whip when he brought out his Marxist interpretation of Walt Whitman in 1938. His old friend and teacher, who had helped him with suggestions about strategy and access to manuscript materials, praised the insight and earnestness of the study but balked at what he considered irrelevant Marxist demands upon Whitman:

> I think that you schematize him too much in the light of a range of ideas that seems to me too narrow & doctrinaire. . . . You know how I feel about the communist classifications,—bourgeois moral-ity, etc. The *American character eludes them,* they do not hit off the American character, the history of which inevitably repels them as alien; and I think that to say this is quite "scientific," though I do not share your reverence for science—which seems to me instru-mental purely and altogether irrelevant to the question of ends.

"All this, to my mind," Brooks concluded, "speaks to me, in regard to you, of a very inadequate notion of personal ethics, . . . an inadequate notion of what the *individual* means, in your preoccupation with social ethics."

The friendship between Brooks and Arvin survived this scolding, and Arvin's many countercharges as well, and it speaks for the quality of both men that it did, but the confused mixture of personal loyalty and professional outrage typifies all of Brooks's dealings with the or-thodox left during this morally trying period. His discomfort with Communism and its tactics became the basis of an important address, which he delivered to a mass meeting of the League in New Haven in November 1938 and which was subsequently printed in the League magazine, *Direction.* He had taken great pains with this "Personal Statement," and it is worth considering here because it is the most comprehensive expression of the position at which he finally arrived—in regard to both his conception of what the League should be and his stance as an American writer toward radical politics. It also defines the social and moral traditionalism which informed all of his later work. In keeping with his theory of evolutionary models, Brooks did not de-scribe in this quiet manifesto the League he knew, but rather at-tempted to create the spiritual League that must be.

He opened his talk anecdotally, quoting a "Yankee poet" who had been disappointed in his early attraction to Communism and was now troubled because the League seemed to him compromised by its Communist element:

... this Connecticut poet ... is not a Communist now—no more am I—but why was this fellow-Yankee a Communist once? Because he saw in Soviet Russia something his country did not give him and something he is not sure that it gives him at present—else why should he speak of *reviving* the Yankee tradition? I, too, believe in reviving the Yankee tradition, although I am not so sure that it needs to be revived. It seems to me that it only needs to be stated.

Brooks devoted most of his further remarks to the contention that "we do not have to go to Russia" for our collectivist models, but could find them amply demonstrated in the Declaration of Independence, or in such patriotic writers as John Quincy Adams, Benjamin Franklin, Edward Everett Hale, and Elihu Burritt—a gathering of exemplars chosen less for their invitation of mutual consent than because they would seem downright unlikely to a group of radical intellectuals in 1938. He suggested that Communism was a side issue, that writers were "flocking to the League" not for the sake of Marx or Lenin or Stalin but for a share in the traditions of their national guild.

It must have been personally satisfying to get his feelings about the League on record, but Brooks soon discovered that his appeal made no impression on the League's politics. The same issue of *Direction* that carried his text also printed a rejoinder by Granville Hicks, speaking as a writer and a member of the Communist Party, who praised the veteran "soldier in the struggle for civilization" but suggested, with all politeness, that when it came to Communism Mr. Brooks simply did not know what he was talking about. In spite of such continuing frustrations, Brooks still held that institutions were to be changed or refined, not abandoned.

From this point forward his relations with the League—again, like those of many intellectuals on the American left—were largely determined by increasingly swift, increasingly unsettling developments in international affairs. In March 1938 Hitler annexed Austria to his new Empire, and in September he occupied the progressive republic of Czechoslovakia. The hasty trip of Neville Chamberlain to Germany that September, and his acquiescence to Hitler's demands, confirmed many intellectuals in their suspicion that democracy had lost its will to resist. Even the supposedly comic-opera Mussolini was behaving like a conqueror. Emboldened by his success in Ethiopia, he moved Italian troops into Albania early in 1939. In Spain, meanwhile, Franco's columns pressed ever closer to Madrid. Desperate people who felt they were watching the overthrow of civilization itself might well grope for the elusive spirit of the Soviet Union as a lonely hope for resistance in an increasingly brutalized world.

The new consolidations and obvious insatiability of the Axis powers lent the League and its Communist leadership considerable ethical authority, but Brooks no longer could persuade himself that Fascism could be effectively opposed by supporting its political antithesis. If he had been disturbed by the Party ruthlessness he had observed at League meetings, he was appalled by the implications of the Moscow "purge" trials of 1936–1938. And when reports began filtering back from Spain after the fall of Madrid in March, he must have been utterly disillusioned by the cynicism that had characterized Soviet involvement there. This was no Popular Front, but the most inflexible sort of totalitarianism. As Brooks tried to work off the bad taste left by the betrayal of Spanish democracy he was shaken by a series of even more opportunistic developments in Soviet foreign policy: the treaty of nonaggression Stalin signed with Hitler that August, giving the Führer virtual permission to invade Poland; the secret protocol, observable if not officially acknowledged, which promised the Soviet Union what was left of the Baltic states after the *Wehrmacht* was finished with its butchery; and finally the Soviet invasion in November of an unprotected Finland.

When Party members defended the Hitler-Stalin pact as a tactic necessary for the preservation of the Soviet Union, Brooks perhaps shrugged and continued the debate. There was much justice in the allegation that England and France had shown little stomach for alliances against Fascism until Hitler had threatened them directly. But when the Communists, and after them the League, sloughed over the Soviet adventure in Eastern Europe, he balked. His first gesture toward resignation followed shortly upon the Russian invasion of Poland. "I do not want to break with [the League]," he told Newton Arvin, "but I agree that it should stand unequivocally against nationalist aggression and pacts with Fascist & Nazi powers." He proposed that he and Arvin draft a statement to that effect as a final attempt at reform: "I hate the idea of breaking up the League over some point of policy of some foreign nation. But then I have always believed that the League should

228

never depend on policies of foreign nations. Our only chance lies in refusing to do so. And if the N. Y. commissariat refuses to stand by this principle, I can see nothing for me to do but withdraw." Two weeks later the first Soviet incursions upon Finland provoked a similar, but more pessimistic, outburst to Malcolm Cowley. "The Finnish affair has settled Stalin for me," he noted grimly. "There is nothing in all this that I can recognize as Socialism, and I am as much a socialist as you are an American. . . . [The League] has certainly made a fatal mistake in assuming a doctrinaire position, even when this was only negatively assumed. Nothing that happens in any other country should ever be a bone of contention to split it asunder. And I think you will agree that it is an American instinct to be revolted by what is happening in Finland."

Both Cowley and Arvin responded sympathetically, for they were themselves troubled about the overt Communist takeover of the League, especially at a time when they were reexamining their own commitments to Marxism and arguing for essentially Brooks's position at League meetings. But they tried to dissuade him from resigning, arguing that, whatever its faults, the League represented their best chance for solidarity against a vicious and insidious enemy. He received a similar rejoinder when he entered an official protest to the League secretary, Franklin Folsom, who assured him that his objections had stirred up new policy debates but admitted that they had been unfruitful. "If we were to take a stand critical of the Soviet Union at this juncture," Folsom explained, "we might precipitate an inner League controversy which could easily end the League's existence. Some of the hardest workers in the League approve the Soviet Union. . . ."

Brooks resigned immediately. "You suggest," he wrote to Folsom,

that our "foreign policy" cannot be aired and must therefore remain under cover. But our members, who know Freud, know what this means. What cannot be aired breeds poison, and this will surely be true in the case of the League. Meanwhile, if it is not aired, it becomes a veiled defence of Stalin, whose methods are now openly undemocratic. And even if Stalin's ends were known, and these ends were democratic, it would be Jesuitical to defend his means. . . . This Jesuitism is a worm at the core of the League that will eat away its fabric, and the League can have no health until it is killed. There is only one way to deal with worms and poison, and this is not the way of caution,—which may serve politicians but is ruinous for writers.

May I add that it seems to me degrading for an American League to hinge its policy, even incidentally, on another country.

He concluded somewhat snappishly, "When the League finds its head and decides to be an American League, I shall be one of the first new members."

That last statement expressed as much hope as resignation. Brooks told Lewis Mumford, who was planning to make his own withdrawal public and urging his friend to do the same, "My apparent tenderness is owing to the fact that I want to *save the League.*" The duplicities of Soviet policy were at this time prompting many liberal members to follow Brooks's course, and he feared that public controversy about League ideologies would tempt professional demagogues, particularly Martin Dies and his House Committee, to "iron out the subtleties that prevail among writers." His closest approach to public statement came in a letter to Malcolm Cowley, who had urged him to reconsider his decision. He asked Cowley to regard it as a letter to the League, and he himself sent copies to many of his colleagues:

Now here is the basis of my quarrel with the League. It simply is not *in the American grain.* For there is an American grain, and I wish to live with it, and I will not live against it knowingly. I believe in a socialized world and a socialized country; and so, for a wonder, do most American writers. But we know that this country can only be socialized *in the American grain. . . .* And therefore I say that I cannot rejoin until the League accepts this fact and throws itself in line with the American grain. It is not sufficient to say now that the League is opposed to Fascism. In so far as its aim is negative it must oppose *Fascism and Dictatorship together. . . . And we must have no members who are not writers, in the substantial sense of this tortured word. We must have no mere political sitters-in.*

That for Brooks was the end of the League of American Writers, and, in fact, the organization was all but dead after its failure to meet the crises of 1939. Lewis Mumford withdrew from the League within a few weeks of his friend's resignation. Malcolm Cowley continued a while to fight for saner policies but resigned early in 1940. Newton Arvin argued for several months with Brooks for the value of a "united front" but finally came to his own anti-Soviet conclusions. By November he was speaking as an "American socialist" in his letters to Westport, and he withdrew from the League in December. I am not suggesting that Brooks personally led a general exodus from the organization—the hard Stalinist line discouraged most of the membership during this period—but only that his experience, as that of his friends, is typical of one important development in the intellectual history of an era.

The 1930s had been among the hardest times Americans had known. Van Wyck might personally have looked back upon them as years of both public and private failure, begun in insanity and ending in war. His guild spirit had been flouted by men who were interested only in power, and even the great triumph of *The Flowering of New England* could earn him neither the professional nor the economic security he emotionally needed. In another sense the thirties was one of Brooks's most fruitful decades. By struggling through those years he learned better the laws of his own mind and arrived at a position from which he could continue his fight into the forties. Perhaps the best appreciation of his stature at this moment comes in a letter of praise from a chastened Newton Arvin, who attributed to Brooks the moral authority of the man who first discovers his belief and then lives by it. "All of us who took that great bumpy detour of Marxism," Arvin wrote, "at any rate can very justly be accused of making smooth the way for the college of cardinals [i.e., the "New," or formalist, critics, their idols, and their allies] that came after us . . . That is one reason, a minor one, why you in particular (not having taken the detour) can so cogently give them a dressing-down at the hour that is."

231

XII

IN WARTIME: 1939–1945

In 1939 Van Wyck was ill prepared for either the outbreak of hostilities in Europe or his own crisis with the League of American Writers. Despite his commercial and critical successes of the late thirties, he had once again failed to meet his own standards and was falling back into his old sick depression. The symptoms were familiar: he felt guilty about Charles, recently married, and Kenyon, just out of Harvard, whose difficulties in life were exacerbated by his own public stature; he was depressed about his work on *New England: Indian Summer,* which went more slowly than he had anticipated and bogged down seriously when he had once again to consider Henry James; and he was nagged almost to distraction by money problems. The Stimson bequest that had helped bring Van Wyck back from psychosis was largely in the form of securities, which yielded a relatively small income, usually around $400 per month. To people whose emotional response to money had been conditioned by Plainfield, an erosion of one's principal was all but unthinkable. Eleanor had sold some of her securities and stood ready to sell more, but this was only a temporary and somewhat desperate expedient. It shrank the regular income and eventually threw Van Wyck into another spasm of neurotic guilt. Even the royalties from *The Flowering of New England,* which must have earned around $50,000 in 1936–1937, could apparently do no better than hold him even in his struggle for security. Most of the earnings from his most popular book went either to the Internal Revenue Service or toward paying off his old hospitals and doctors. As late as 1937 he told Waldo Frank that he hoped someday to see the end of these haunting debts, and he insisted on sending unrealistically large payments to his former benefactors.

These were emotional, not practical, problems, but they threatened Van Wyck's sanity all the same. By late 1938 Eleanor had again begun surreptitiously consulting Dr. Lambert, and early the next year she wrote to Lewis Mumford in desperation, hoping that he could help her borrow $3,000 from the Carnegie Foundation in order to stave off the dangerous psychological attack she anticipated. "I see us heading straight for the rapids and another 1931, unless a way out can be found by about June 1st," she told Mumford, and went on to explain Van Wyck's responses to his financial situation: "You see, it is not in Van Wyck's nature to think or plan about money matters. He places the bills, unopened, on my desk. He refuses to even consider them or to talk about ways and means until the very last moment, for the anxiety and excitement it always arouses makes it impossible for him to go on writing. He just shuts his eyes and goes ahead, hoping for a miracle, until circumstances bring him to an abrupt halt. Then, if there is no way out, he goes into break [sic]. Consequently, I have not told him that I am writing you!"

Mumford found the director of the Carnegie Foundation sympathetic and managed to give Eleanor better than she asked by quietly arranging a grant. So tactfully did he handle these affairs that Van Wyck believed his unexpected gift to be the work of Lee Simonson. The good spirits he caught from his April windfall helped him through a trying summer. However, Van Wyck's depression was as much caused by his fears for *New England: Indian Summer* as by money, and he was forced to struggle with his demon at least through 1940. The seriousness of the relapse that beset him these two years is indicated by his return to his nautical metaphor. "I seem stranded on a reef," he complained to Mark Howe, "and I feel not only shipwrecked but actually drowning. I always feel, this is the last time, as I see the evening lights go out on the shore, extinguishing any possible hope for a lifeboat."

Van Wyck's depression gradually, painfully passed, and while he was never to be entirely free of his nightmare, his sanity would not be seriously threatened again. His recovery was probably due in part to his satisfaction in meeting anew the challenge of "that silly old man," as to Newton Arvin he dismissed the Henry James of the later manner. More important, he apparently discovered by experience that his financial difficulties, although they continued for several more years, had lost much of their sting. He would never escape his ambivalence about money, but he managed to isolate his contradictory impulses in something suspiciously like the "watertight compartments" he had once ascribed to the psyche of Mark Twain. The young Brooks would have balked at the duplicity by which an older self lived like a Plainfield burgher while thinking like a Wellsian socialist, and truly he was compromising cherished ideals. It is a part of the "contraction" those close to him noticed about his later life.

While the paradoxes of money, fear of sickness, and arguments about the League wound down, another crisis was building up. A bitter quarrel between Brooks and the champions of what we may loosely call "literary modernism" had been simmering for many years, but it took war and the inflexibilities of war emotion to bring things to a boil. The intellectual temper at home grew strained as in dizzying succession Denmark fell before German forces, the Netherlands fell, Belgium fell, France fell—as Nazi troops goose-stepped through the streets of Paris and Adolf Hitler danced his maniacal little jig in Compiègne Forest. Appalled and frightened by these triumphs of barbarism, American writers once again hurried to "take sides"—but this time often against one another—and public debate became too often hypersensitive, partisan, and denunciatory. One might argue that in several instances the war years bore witness to a virtual collapse of intellectual integrity, and that the historical significance of Fascist-baiting would reveal itself only in the ideological excesses, both political and literary, that debased the Cold War era of the 1950s. If there is a single point in our cultural history at which the great traditional debate between Classicist and Romanticist went all out of balance, these years are it.

Brooks sided almost reflexively with Waldo Frank, Lewis Mumford, and other writers who argued that they must commit themselves publicly to a national charge against Fascism and its culture. Mumford's confident assumption of world values inspired much of Brooks's participation in the truculent dialogues to come, although almost until Pearl Harbor Brooks remained cool to Mumford's urgent argument that the United States should enter the war on Britain's behalf. He did not side with the isolationists in the great political division of those prewar years, nor did he oppose Roosevelt's all but belligerent programs to aid Britain. He had, however, caught an antipathy to British values and British politics both from his political experiences of the 1930s and, as an admirer of Gandhi, from accounts of British colonial rule in India. At times, he thought, the conduct of the old British Empire, its sense of responsibility to human values, seemed distressingly like the conduct and values of the new German Reich. He and Mumford had a brief moment of antagonism, which was caused by his careless description of himself as an isolationist when he fended off Mumford's interventionist argument for England. Mumford took the occasion to deliver a stinging epistolary sermon on the duties of brotherhood. Brooks responded with a curt note to the effect that he shared Mumford's goals but was holding firm to his reservations about the British Empire. Nevertheless, in September 1941 he announced himself in favor of a declaration of war.

Their disagreement on the most sensitive issue of the day never strained Brooks's and Mumford's friendship to any serious degree. The dialogue lapsed into several months' uneasy silence, which apparently restored each man to his affectionate alliance with the other. They shared common ends and, for the most part, they agreed to adopt similar means: as internationalists they felt that Germany must be stopped; as patriots they believed it their duty to combat moral lethargy at home. Their position allied them with the majority of American intellectuals, but it also occasioned a surprisingly intense response among other contemporaries, including many who still clung to some form of Marxist or neo-Marxist ideology, and who felt they had been badly used by politics. After the disappointments of the Red Decade, small but vocal movements, often including some of the most influential writers and critics of the time, returned to the priorities of craftsmanship and aesthetics, contending that their creative work must remain nonpartisan and essentially amoral, that truth was served best by permitting art its own ends and letting governments and causes go their own way.

A preliminary brouhaha was touched off through the somewhat unlikely agency of *The Irresponsibles*, a "declaration" by the poet Archibald MacLeish that first appeared in *The Nation* (May 1940) and was subsequently brought out in pamphlet form. MacLeish's stately but ironic denunciation of the intellectuals of the ivory tower contended that, despite unmistakable warnings about its nature, the Fascist onslaught against the traditions of Western civilization had gone unchallenged by writers and thinkers whose privilege and responsibility it was to guard those traditions. Although MacLeish did not in *The Irresponsibles,* as he did in a similar declaration of a month later, name the writers he blamed for the collapse of traditional values, his contemporaries responded to this first essay as to a personal message. Much of its force *was* personal, for MacLeish, whose early antitraditionalism (as Brooks was fond of reminding himself) once led him to walk out of a concert at which the music of a dead composer was played, admitted his own guilt in this new *trahison des clercs.* At first his recantation inspired a chorus of *mea culpas,* but both the aestheticians and the political left reacted violently to it. It was not long before several literary quarterlies charged that MacLeish wanted to turn art over to state censorship, that he was himself the great "Irresponsible"—and several varieties of a Fascist to boot. The disagreement renewed one of the oldest of literary debates—whether art exists for its own sake or for the sake of society—but in the explosive mixture of literature and politics that were the heritage of the thirties the debate became unusually emotional, unusually intemperate—at times downright nasty.

Brooks was an important belligerent from the beginning. MacLeish's reaffirmation of the moral imperatives of art seemed to him to point all of the issues he had himself championed these thirty years, and he went so far as to provide a covering letter of praise to the group that sent copies of *The Irresponsibles* to nearly every American intellectual of note. Then he took the occasion of the inauguration of George N. Shuster as president of Hunter College in June 1940 to deliver a speech, "On Literature Today," which created a furor as the latest attack on the integrity of modern writing. In fact it was substantially the same speech that he had delivered at Tufts College in 1937. This time, however, his remarks were published, and, since he more sweepingly than MacLeish named names and specified particulars, he deepened old resentments and touched off new ones.

As the opposition shortened its temper and prepared its counterattack, Brooks continued to develop his ideas publicly in connection with his "guild" of the 1940s, the Conference on Science, Philosophy and Religion in Their Relation to the Democratic Way of Life. The Jewish theologian Louis Finkelstein, along with several other scholars, called in 1939 for an interdisciplinary conference that would fight compartmentalization in American thought and thus resist the intellectual menace of totalitarian systems. Franz Boaz, Enrico Fermi, Moses Hadas, Alain Locke, Jacques Maritain, Paul Tillich, Margaret Mead, and Albert Einstein were among the scholars who participated in the conferences of the first few years. Despite its academic character, Brooks was excited by the group's promise of both high earnestness and unyielding discipline, and he immediately became one of its working chairmen.

The first meeting convened in New York in September 1940, largely for purposes of organization and planning. Brooks prepared an official report on these opening proceedings. He also chaired several sessions of papers and discussion, opened a meeting on "Religion and the Philosophy of Education" with a short statement about the relevance of literature to the purposes of the convention, and reread "On Literature Today," which was becoming a sort of personal manifesto.

By the time the Conference held its second symposium in September 1941, the list of participants had grown dramatically, and it would continue to do so throughout the forties. Brooks remained active in Conference affairs for many years (he was still an officer in 1950), but he offered his fellow members no important statements after this second meeting, at which he read a paper on the distinction between what he called "primary" and "coterie" literature. Primary literature, he argued, was regenerative and progressive. It was not artifice or form, but "the great man writing," the flowering of racial ideals through their representative, and its themes were "those by which the race has risen, courage, justice, mercy, honour, love." He named as his primary writers Whitman, Tolstoy, Goethe—all of his old favorites—and he asserted that their primacy was characterized by affirmation and health.

There was nothing startling in this. Brooks had championed these values and named these names for many years. He characterized "coterie," or secondary, literature, however, almost exclusively in terms of the admired writing of the twentieth century. While he sympathized with the modernist reaction to the disillusionments of World War I, he argued that modernists had abandoned their responsibility to challenge the accidents of history. He listed these writers also. The most important were Proust, Joyce, Pound, James, Stein, and especially T. S. Eliot. But he also named a great many others, and his address created a stir. Although he had insisted that his speech was not yet ready for publication, it was released by the Conference to the press, earned a somewhat uncomfortable statement of praise from Thomas Mann, and generally excited more attention than he could have anticipated.

The hubbub about "Primary Literature and Coterie Literature" had little to do with the distinctions and definitions Brooks had advanced. The speech was newsworthy only because of its dramatic impact. Brooks was associated in the public mind with the modern revolution in literature. Now it seemed that he had broken ranks and challenged all of the great men and women that revolution had brought to power. In a deliberately regicidal mood he had singled out for special abuse T. S. Eliot and made him his symbol for whatever was inverted or diseased in modern civilization. Eliot was selfish and solipsistic, a failure, a reactionary, a destroyer of tradition. He was a "dog in the manger," and a "bat that flew in the twilight between the wars." His influence had contaminated the work of better writers and encumbered the younger generation with a model of literary decadence.

It was a curious quarrel Brooks picked with Eliot. He pursued it until he died with a dogged ill humor that was all out of keeping with his usual tolerance and amiability. Ordinarily, he was capable of striking up friendships with literary enemies. He could write favorably about Ezra Pound, as he had in *The Freeman* and would in *The Confident Years;* and once he went so far as to make overtures (brusquely declined) to Bernard De Voto. "Brooks could forgive a writer almost anything as long as he didn't steal the spoons," Malcolm Cowley remembers: "That devotion to writers was something quite rare and special . . . he couldn't bring himself to believe that any good writer was a complete son of a bitch. . . . In other words . . . he would forgive a lot of divergencies of opinion—unless they were T. S. Eliot's."

The abnormal bitterness with which Brooks attacked Eliot may be explained in part by the suggestion that Eliot was his symbol of something "wrong" almost from the beginning of both men's careers. Probably the two never met while they were in college but they knew of each other at least by 1908 when Eliot praised *The Wine of the Puritans* in a *Monthly* review. A gossipy, allusive letter of a few years later suggests that Brooks was already familiar enough with Eliot's personal legend to appreciate stories about his peculiarities. His Harvard friend Tommy Thomas wrote from Europe in 1912 or 1913 with much news about old schoolmates. "[Tom Eliot] was here in Paris a whole year," he mentioned; "I knew him at first, at the end he had become an abstraction. He combines (and confuses) a critical and utterly detached attitude toward life with a cynical state of mind, so that he does not allow himself a single emotion—friendship, or pleasure, or even contentment."

Brooks had surprisingly little to say about Eliot during the postwar years and the twenties, when Eliot was establishing his literary dictatorship. He made a few casual references to him in print and in his private correspondence sometimes described him as a sort of literary curiosity, but for the most part he scarcely seemed aware of the poet of *The Waste Land* or the new authority he wielded—even when he was most vigorously denouncing expatriation and aestheticism in *The Freeman.* That puzzling reticence about a writer who after 1922 should have been his obvious target, as he became the enemy of such nativists as Hart Crane and William Carlos Williams, suggests that Brooks was somehow confused about Eliot and that the confusion was personal rather than critical. Despite their radical differences of personality and temperament, Brooks and Eliot were in many ways remarkably alike. In 1908 one might have been hard put to distinguish sharply between their ideas or their taste, and they had begun their careers according to similar patterns: the voyage to England, the aesthetic Catholicism, the superrefinement of sensibility. They held similar opinions about the nature and value of tradition and they frequently used similar images and modes in their early writing.

As this curious relationship developed, each man became a sort of negative mirror for the other. As Brooks choked back his juvenile Anglophilia, Eliot became a British subject. As Brooks steeled himself to resist his hunger for Europe, Eliot became the most celebrated of expatriates. As Brooks wrenched himself away from Catholicism, Eliot announced his Anglo-Catholic orthodoxy. Brooks, of course, finally purged himself of these "foreign" allegiances only in the fires of his breakdown, and it was not until he had returned from his hospitals that he began to express overt hostility toward Eliot and what he called the "Elioteers." When he did break his long silence, it was no simple matter of professional or ideological disagreement, but a deeply personal outburst of raw hatred. His public statements about Eliot are unusually strong, but they were nothing to what he permitted himself in private. "T. S. Eliot and his vulpine face, the face of a bird of prey," he wrote in a notebook of 1939: "I call him 'a traitor to human hope' . . . and therefore by definition a traitor to America." And once, when told by John Hall Wheelock that Eliot was ill, Brooks blurted out, "I hope he dies in agony!" Edmund Wilson reported the incident.

As a critic Brooks was obliged to oppose Eliot. His attacks, however violent, on Eliot's reactionary position, inflated reputation, and overwhelming influence were not only inevitable; they were healthy. If only for the sake of a traditional dialectic, we may be grateful that he made himself an agent of resistance at the time of Eliot's greatest sway. Yet, Brooks's personal rancor remains distressing. To his credit, he tried to keep personalities out of public debate and, particularly in later years, did his best to give Eliot his due, but his hatred of the man was forever breaking through his usual reserve, and it was, finally, unworthy of him. Probably it was also beyond conscious control. Nothing is easier or more dangerous than amateur psychoanalysis, but it seems plausible to suggest that Brooks made Eliot a projection of secret fears and deadly sins. In this laconic British gentleman—Anglican, Classicist, Royalist—he may have sensed a demonic shadow self, an embodiment of every disease he had been forced to expunge violently from his own personality. Brooks had made creative use of similar projections in his work of the twenties, and later in life he admitted to himself that he had used Eliot as a foil. "I owe him much," he noted, "for defining my point of view in reverse."

At another time Brooks's attack on Eliot might have passed without much reaction, as it had in 1937. By 1940, however, the nation was morally if unofficially at war, and in a wartime atmosphere of mutual recrimination the speech on primary and coterie literature touched off a series of counterattacks. Many intellectuals were touchy and defensive; many were looking to pick a fight. The Communists, for instance, blamed the war and its confusions of American society on the "Fascists" (everyone to their ideological right), while the Trotskyites blamed both the Fascists and the "Stalinists" (everyone to the left of the "Fascists" who was not a Trotskyite. According to James T. Farrell, Brooks was morally a Stalinist). At the other extreme, "classicists" and New Critics, many of whom were politically conservative, often blamed either literary nationalism or a "romantic" contempt for reason. The intellectual community was thus beleaguered by a number of mutually exclusive and hostile groups. It is only a slight exaggeration to suggest that these isolated factions could agree among themselves only about the iniquity of Van Wyck Brooks, Archibald MacLeish,

Lewis Mumford, and the other writers who shared their position. In turn, Brooks, MacLeish, and particularly Mumford leveled volleys of their own against all comers.

The bad temper of these years was in many ways unfortunate, but it was also understandable. There were no academic issues in wartime. The issues had to do with survival: with the isolationism that might leave a complacent nation surrounded by villains and the interventionism that might "plow every fourth American boy under." They had to do with the implications for democracy of the military draft; with questions among a mixed population of commitment to Britain, Germany, Finland, or the Soviet Union; with the lesson that was to be learned from the experience of World War I. In a period of ideological disappointment, as men and women prepared to fight a war for which there was as yet little enthusiasm, everyone was under pressure, and the widely different ideas of what must be done disturbed many close friendships—to say nothing of the uneasy alliances that had survived the thirties.

In that charged emotional climate Brooks became a center of attention when, after substantial serialization in *The New Republic* and *The Yale Review, The Opinions of Oliver Allston* was published in September 1941. This old-fashioned wisdom-book, bursting with all the eccentricities and prejudices of its eighteenth-century models, reprinted bodily the lectures "On Literature Today" and "Primary and Coterie Literature," and added to them belligerent material advancing similar arguments. It also rallied the various factions opposed to Brooks's romantic traditionalism.

Although Brooks had courted antagonism, the harsh reaction to his chapters on modern writing obscured the general sense of what is surely one of his most attractive works. The weight of the book is not so much in the opinions as in the character of an American critic, recently dead, whose literary remains were examined by an anonymous narrator. Oliver Allston was the last of those personal avatars—Graeling, Storrington, Henry Wickford of *The Freeman*—who by "dying" completed one spiral of Brooks's development and released him, as it were, to rise into another. Named according to his nature, after both Washington Allston, the American painter memorialized in *The Flowering of New England,* and Oliver Wendell Holmes, the jovial autocrat for whom Brooks had also named his second son, the high-spirited

241

Allston represented the enlightened wit and shrewdness of that cosmopolitan Yankee who was Brooks's ideal American type.

By abstracting the most treasured aspect of his personality and using it as a persona, Brooks could view himself with enough detachment to discuss calmly such sensitive material as incidental memories of his breakdown. With distance came the genial self-irony that saved an indulgent book from egotism. The Allston of particularly the first chapters of the *Opinions* emerges as a tolerant, witty, and urbane gentleman, a true son of the Enlightenment, but dignified, finally, and tough-minded. He is established in the mass of little details, the whims and foibles, that shape a writer's consciousness as keenly as do the great issues. Since this is both an essay in self-creation and a record of the literary life, Brooks uses his representative Yankee to establish images of a symbolic self at symbolic times: the brash "puppy" at Harvard, the self-indulgent young ascetic in London, the cosmopolitan intellectual in his New England village, the fattening, middle-aged critic doing his best to avoid exercise. The *Opinions* are, finally, a mildly comic portrait of an old-fashioned man of letters finding his way through a strange and sometimes dangerous world. Their great antecedent in our national literature is *The Autobiography of Benjamin Franklin.*

Like Franklin, Brooks used comic images of himself primarily for moral definition. His Allston is an enemy of all imposture and humbug; he likes "bleak" not "cozy" thinking. His opinions are full of terse, provocative wisdom. To the degree that these things become humorous they comment upon both the human frailty that cannot sustain them and the indifference of a society that is preoccupied with material advantage. By thus juxtaposing his idealistic Yankee to his unrealized America Brooks was able to give resonance to the wide range of notes and essays on American culture that he lifted almost without modification from his notebooks, letters, and speeches of the 1930s.

The controversial chapters—"Literature Today," "What Is Primary Literature?" "Coterie-Literature," and "What a Set!"—came later in the book and were different in both tone and genre from the genial character-sketch with which it opened. Allston's initial opinions fell naturally into the mode of the eighteenth-century familiar essay, but his later statements, thunderous and unrestrained, were in the tradition of Old Testament prophecy—a flaring up of the wrath that had once laid waste the camps of another generation of highbrows.

One might argue that such mixing of genres marked a flaw in the art, if not the opinions, of *Oliver Allston,* but Brooks was careful to sustain his mediating fiction, having his narrator comment from time to time on the state of Allston's temper or the justice of his observations. Structurally the book was, like the *Emerson,* an emotional crescendo, beginning in puzzled tolerance and ending in outrage, a development that might in itself be a valid imitation of the responses of good people to the deterioration of Western culture and the coming of war.

After the book was fully published, however, the chapters on literary values were almost exclusively attended. Only a few reviewers bothered to notice the presence of the good-natured Allston, and even critics who were determined to be just were forced to acknowledge their reservations about Brooks's discussion of modern writing. In his two-issue review of the *Opinions* for *The New Republic,* Malcolm Cowley welcomed the healthy energy of "Mr. Brooks Dissenting," but wondered if his colleague hadn't "carried the reaction dangerously far; and whether he always takes the time to distinguish the human and valuable from what is anti-human." Waldo Frank expressed similar doubts in the *Saturday Review.* He defended Brooks against the more outrageous charges of his critics, but complained himself about "the incapacity of Mr. Brooks to recognize among contemporaries those very writers whose affirmative, adult vision diverges from the conventional forms of an exploded world in exact proportion with their receptivity and command of the fresh elements and substances of a world-in-the-making." Many other commentators were inclined to discover no virtues whatsoever in the book. Brooks was accused of reducing literary values to the demands of patriotism and wholesomeness, of wishing to institute both a "Cultural Protective Tariff" and an official censorship. He was also accused of being, at various times, a Communist Social Realist, a Victorian, a Fascist, an ally of Bernard De Voto, and, after all these turntable years, a Puritan.

The most serious of these attacks came in late 1941 when Dwight Macdonald announced to the readers of the New Critical, anti-Stalinist, but still Marxist *Partisan Review,* "Kulturbolschewismus Is Here." He saw in Brooks's papers the most significant expression of an ominous "tendency to rally to the concepts of Hitler's (and Stalin's) 'new order.'" Guilty of "impudent condescension" and "historical illiteracy," this "incredibly venomous and silly" Brooks, Macdonald thought, had become "our leading mouthpiece for totalitarian cultural values." Much of this unqualified judgment and extraordinary invective is explained by Macdonald's Marxist point of view, and his diatribe might not by itself have carried much authority. But when the editors of the *Partisan Review* invited comment on "the Brooks-MacLeish Thesis," they rallied an impressive array of writers to Macdonald's support. Allen Tate, William Carlos Williams, John Crowe Ransom, Henry Miller, Louise Bogan, James T. Farrell, and Lionel Trilling all responded to Macdonald in the magazine's next (February 1942) number. T. S. Eliot, who rarely deigned to consider attacks on his own authority, contributed a few dour comments to a subsequent issue. By an accident of history, Macdonald's statement was separated from the response by three traumatic months. The attack on Pearl Harbor, the first frightening reverses and the subsequent firming of national belligerence could not have much affected the substance of what writers had to say about Brooks, but these developments might have put an edge to their voices.

The *Partisan Review*'s improbable alliance brought together a wide range of ideologies, from the reactionary (Eliot, Ransom) to the anarchistic (Miller), and the writers involved were not usually much inclined to agree among themselves. This was probably the only time in either man's career that Williams or Miller found himself on the same side of a question with Eliot, and there is evidence to support Brooks's contention that at least several of his antagonists were responding not to his essay but to Macdonald's angry description of it. Whether they were as ignorant about Brooks's position as Miller or Ransom, who did not pretend to have read the essay on primary and coterie literature, or as informed as Eliot, the only respondent to comment directly upon its text, they unanimously condemned Brooks. With its range of loyalties and list of influential names, the symposium could not help but suggest that any serious person must find something sinister in Brooks's recent work.

It is necessary to discuss some of the specific questions that arose in regard to *The Opinions of Oliver Allston* because that controversy marks the end of an important man's reputation for seriousness among the majority of leading writers and critics of his day. Brooks had long since encountered substantial opposition to his ideas, but until Macdonald's attack he had been respected as the chief spokesman for an intellectual position of which thoughtful people were obliged to take account. Now he was simply dismissed, and picked up, almost as carelessly, as a champion of the popular culture he had always viewed with amused contempt. Not the least of his misfortunes during these years was his emergence as the hero of the Sunday supplements and the book clubs, the avuncular old literary master, whose wholesomeness and traditionalism shamed the excesses of the avant-garde. That position, to which he was indifferent, gave new ammunition to his enemies, who never tired of repeating Louise Bogan's contention that he was "an official critic functioning on the behalf of an official literature." Caught between indiscriminate judgments, Brooks became defensive, unable to profit from even sympathetic criticism of his work. He was cheated as well of many of the alliances or mentorships he might naturally have established with younger writers during his culminative years. More than unfair, the situation was wasteful.

The argument against Brooks as it surfaced in *The Partisan Review* and as it has substantially endured was twofold: first, that he was aesthetically illiterate, and second, that he was morally subversive. In a world at war the moral accusation was the most immediately damaging, and it was pressed hard. Brooks's enemies possessed the potentially damaging argument that his appeal to national traditions and character, and his emphasis on bringing a people forward, however well intentioned and genuinely different from Fascist emphases, were similar to the appeal by which the dictators had worked their way to power. Once such emotional questions of value were introduced into art, his critics thought, there was no way to ensure that even genuine idealism and morality would not be perverted. But this argument was never really made; the monologue remained too much on the level of simple abuse. Even Eliot stooped to the Fascist-calling of the period when he suggested that Brooks's opinions were "depressingly reminiscent of a certain political version of biology."

This was an ugly business. Brooks had fought the literary totalitarianism of both left and right for many years, and however one may question his judgments, there is nothing in his papers on modern writing to suggest that he had abandoned his belief in tolerant humanitarianism. To suggest that he had suddenly become an advocate of censorship, a spokesman for the orthodox state, or a theoretician of racial superiority was a shabby tactic. Unfortunately, it was also effective.

A similar unresponsiveness marred the aesthetic argument against Brooks. His detractors refused to notice his sympathetic discussion of the cultural origins of negativism, his concession that modern writers "could only have written as they had." Neither would they acknowledge his open admiration for the intensity, power, and beauty of much contemporary work. (He would repeat in all the sincerity of private correspondence his praise for James T. Farrell's *Studs Lonigan,* even after Farrell had attacked him savagely.) Brooks was not attempting to tell his enemies either what to say or how to say it. Rather he was calling a generation to account for what he considered its failure to meet the challenge of the times with all of the resources of the human spirit. One would scarcely expect important writers to be pleased by the suggestion that they were defeated by life, but one would expect them to respond to that charge and not to imagined scoldings.

One of the most amusing (and frustrating) distortions of Brooks's position was the widely repeated accusation that he was in the vanguard of a "back-to-Whittier" movement. Macdonald seems to have first raised the subject in his contemptuous assertion that "this apostle of the positive, the 'life-drive,' recommends to the contemporary American writer that he nourish his art on ... Whittier." Allen Tate developed that line of attack by speculating in his contribution to the "Kulturbolschewismus" symposium that Brooks preferred Whittier to Henry James because "though tame and pious and limited Whittier is safe." By April 1942, Conrad Aiken, writing in the *Atlantic,* could be appalled that "Mr. Brooks makes the really startling admission that he prefers *Snow-Bound* to *The Waste Land.*" Brooks, of course, had admitted no such thing. His sole comment upon the author of *Snow-Bound* came in a footnote that referred to neither Eliot nor James and suggested only that Whittier, as a folk poet and an Abolitionist, possessed a special interest for Americans, although he was not otherwise an important writer. But his outraged attempts to certify the modesty of that remark went ignored, and by early 1942 Brooks was angrily telling Waldo Frank that he had seen the allegation that he "had praised *Whittier* as a 'primary writer' " repeated in at least a dozen papers. The episode itself was little more than a curious example of the way a hypothesis can control evidence, but the collective sneer about Whittier represented a general disparagement of Brooks's taste that was, again, wastefully unfair.

Despite the crude tactics by which it was forwarded, the aesthetic complaint remains the most damaging mark against a major reputation. Brooks did not try to censor Joyce, Proust, Eliot, Faulkner, and the other writers who inspired his wrath. He was not judging them according to some orthodoxy. He simply did not understand all that they were saying. Temperamentally intolerant of experimentalism, indifferent to the implicit "statement" of technique, he was unable to respond to several of the most important devices of modern fiction: the intrusion of unreliable or limited narrators, the manipulation of point of view, and the use of defensive irony to protect both author and reader from the pain of tragic experience. Because he read for an explicit statement of values he could not have felt with what complexity Joyce, say, viewed his Stephen Dedalus. Like most of the important moderns, the cranky Irishman was writing in a special language, more difficult but more expressive than traditional literary English, and Brooks too often read it like the impatient schoolboy who wants to translate Virgil by finding each word in a glossary, not understanding that Latin is an inflected tongue. If he had been willing to crack the private, often gratuitous, literary and personal code in which Joyce presented himself to the world, he might have discovered an ally in the fight for a "primary" view of life.

That same deafness to technique kept Brooks from nearly all of the poetry of his time, and, in fact, poetry of any period was the one art to which he remained surprisingly indifferent. He read even Whitman's verse as prose, for the sake of its statement, and early in his career he gave up any attempt to keep abreast of the hypersophisticated genre of the twentieth century. Again, he could not, or would not, translate the hints in a formally eccentric sonnet, an apparently formless stanza of free verse, or an ironic monologue. By thus ignoring the most severely disciplined art of the new age, he in effect cast away the Rosetta Stone that held the key to all of its literary languages. That indifference not only cost him an effective voice in the literary give-and-take of particularly the forties and fifties, it also kept him from recognizing his natural affinities with such self-consciously American poets as Hart Crane and William Carlos Williams. It was only later in life that he acknowledged the importance of Crane's attempt at an American synthesis in *The Bridge* and recognized in the prose of *The Farmer's Daughters* and *In The American Grain* the alliance he might have had with Williams. Such abdications of critical presence suggest that Brooks should either have said less or learned more about modernist writing.

As the war went on, the attacks upon Brooks's position increased in both number and volume. *New England: Indian Summer,* which was published in 1940, was the last of his books to be greeted with general applause. After that, he took so much satisfaction in the research and writing of *The World of Washington Irving* that the work compensated in part for his disappointment over the reception of *The Opinions of Oliver Allston* and even helped him to forget his anxiety about the progress of the war, which was particularly agonizing now that Kenyon was on duty as a naval officer. He would always consider *The World of Washington Irving* his finest single accomplishment, but upon its appearance in 1944 it met a chilly reception in many critical quarters. In his front-page review for *The New York Times* book supplement, F. O. Matthiessen found it bland, impressionistic, and indiscriminate. "Brooks is not really a critic," he wrote, "but a lyric poet *manqué,* who endows selected aspects of our history with the overtones of his own sensibility." His criticism complemented and extended the reservations about Brooks's adequacy to tragic literature that he had earlier expressed in his influential *American Renaissance* (1941), and his judgments are representative. The critical response to *The World of Washington Irving* established most of the negative attitudes to Brooks's entire series of histories and formed a durable body of opinion that has since influenced readers of all the work he published after 1932.

Two other documents of 1944 culminated the attack upon Brooks's literary and personal integrity. The first came in April when Bernard De Voto returned to his obsessive quarrel by publishing *The Literary Fallacy,* which he had delivered as a series of lectures at Indiana University in 1943—a vicious performance which made his comments on *The Ordeal of Mark Twain* seem genial. The "fallacy," which De Voto attributed specifically to the writers of the 1920s, consisted in the belief that the truth and values of a culture could be adequately known and best expressed in its literature. He argued further that in our time that fallacy was incarnated chiefly in Van Wyck Brooks, who had exploited bookishness at the expense of truth. The "movement" Brooks established and the "disciples" he made, De Voto asserted, introduced a pervasive negativism into American life, influenced a generation of talented novelists, and led the nation into its present "catastrophe." I am making no effort, in my paraphrase, to imitate De Voto's violent abusiveness.

De Voto was a strong performer, and in happier times his colorful wrath might have produced a funny regional scenario: the effete Easterner, his head all muddled with books, being called short by a burly Westerner, the friend of the engineer and the cowpoke, who was not ashamed to tell the world that a novelist would have been better off if he "had studied English at high school under the basketball coach instead of the generic middle-aged woman who admired the poems of Thomas Bailey Aldrich in the *Atlantic Monthly.*" The bluster stopped being funny, however, when De Voto in effect accused Brooks of making the mistakes that threw the United States not only into confusion but perhaps into war—and this before an audience of young people who might be forced, as De Voto carefully reminded them, to pay for those mistakes with their lives. He went so far as to suggest (but not so far as to assert) that Hitler had been encouraged to invite war with the United States by the portraits of a decadent culture to be found in those American books of the 1920s whose content Brooks had determined. He described Ezra Pound's treasonable broadcasts from Italy and asserted that Pound merely repeated the official clichés of the movement Brooks had started. Moreover, he suspected that Pound had been the one intellectual indicted for treason only because he had had the "guts" to go on saying what his fellows had since decided to keep to themselves.

Naming writers whose negativism Brooks had conditioned, De Voto had mentioned, albeit with some kindness, James T. Farrell. It was not a particularly fortunate example. By the time *The Literary Fallacy* appeared Farrell was mounting his own charge from the left against Brooks's position, and he dismissed as "farce" the suggestion that serious writers had been "ruined by an unpatriotic New Englander named V. W. Brooks." Farrell's bitter enmity against Brooks went back at least to 1940, when he had been mentioned by name in the Hunter speech, and he seems to have felt that he was fighting a rear-guard Trotskyite action against "the economic and police power" of American society as it had rallied behind Brooks and other "ideological policemen." His diatribe against "The Frightened Philistines," which appeared in *The New Republic,* added little to the Marxist-aesthetic criticism of "Kulturbolschewismus" days, except for a strong tinge of self-pity, a sense of battles lost and dreams betrayed. This was perhaps another of the inevitable moods of wartime, when the mobilization of American society had put an end to many radical hopes for

249

an immediate future, and one may even sense in Farrell's nervous prose a foreboding of the hysterical anti-"communism" and demands for bland conformity the postwar years would bring.

To Brooks, Farrell's attack was simply the latest in a succession of new lows. Accustomed as he had become to serving as the favorite target for an abusive generation, he remained, as he told Lewis Mumford, "as curious [about other writers] as a puppy is about other dogs and . . . always astonished when they bite." Farrell's utter hostility upset him badly, particularly because the attack had appeared in *The New Republic,* to which he had been a contributing editor since 1941, with a note to the effect that the editors were "inclined to agree with Mr. Farrell's main position." Not only was this both unfair and impolite, Brooks thought, it was also a snide indication that his services were of no account to the magazine. He resigned his editorship.

Thus, as he returned to work on the fourth volume of his history, Brooks had become persona non grata in most of the serious intellectual circles of the day. To the intense modernists who had overwhelmed nearly all opposition, he was now a quaint old gentleman, a sort of reincarnation of Edmund Clarence Stedman, determined to reorient literature to the pieties of the Genteel Tradition. His position was not so much resisted as it was ignored. This reduction of both his public stature and professional influence was largely a political accident, a typical expression of an atypical period, but it was nevertheless a crushing defeat.

XIII

LAST
DAYS IN
WESTPORT

While World War II became the time, and at least in part the subject, of Brooks's most bitter public battles, it also developed more quietly into a period of private enterprise, with its own satisfactions and frustrations. The Brookses had moved out of their cottage on Kings Highway in 1941, when Van Wyck, in a fit of impracticality, built a lavish new house atop an isolated hill a few miles away, in the Weston area of Westport. The Weston house was architecturally impressive, filled with light and space, and situated in a wooded area where an occasional deer might still come to feed on windfallen apples. On a clear day one could look out across the rolling landscape of coastal Connecticut to Long Island Sound, some twenty miles in the distance. But despite the beauty of the house and its setting neither Van Wyck nor Eleanor ever truly settled into it.

Some of their disorientation and uneasiness during these years was due to such wartime tensions as coping with rationing or looking apprehensively through lists of casualties. Like any citizen Van Wyck tuned his radio to the news each evening, both eager and afraid to know the progress of battles on strange islands in the Pacific or across the continents of Africa and Europe. Even family sympathies were complicated or redirected by the times. Eleanor's uncle, Henry L. Stimson, was Roosevelt's Secretary of War, and Kenyon, of course, was continually in physical danger. Van Wyck and Eleanor endured long weeks without word when his ship was out on coastal patrol or on convoy duty with the Atlantic and, later, the Pacific fleets. But such anguish was, as Brooks himself noted, the "common lot" of those days, and in a sense the war lifted one responsibility from his shoulders. However worrisome Kenyon's silences became they remained part of the menace of the larger world and did not excite an uneasy father's inclination to spasms of personal guilt. Furthermore, Kenyon showed every sign of thriving on his naval responsibilities, becoming more self-confident with each letter home. At last Brooks seemed able to enjoy an easy relationship with his younger son. His letters to relatives from these years glow with pride for Kenyon's achievements. In them he sounds for the first time precisely like a parent.

Relations with the older son were more difficult, in part because Charles was aggressively distinguishing his values and purposes from those of his father. Especially after the birth of his son Peter in 1940, Charles inclined to prepare himself for his parental role by reviewing his own childhood with some anger. Brooks was forced to admit the justice of many accusations and often found himself on the defensive. Probably he committed more emotional energy than he could easily spare to a vicarious undertaking of Charles's struggles to support his family and to his crisis of vocation. He developed an irrational sense of despair at both Charles's and Kenyon's decisions, at different times, to abandon the intellectual life.

When he first moved with his wife to California and took a defense job in the San Francisco shipyards, Charles still thought of himself as a writer. For some time he attempted to define both his point of view and his artistic integrity in long, often acrimonious, epistolary debates with his father. He was willing to accept, or at least pass by in silence, the older man's ideas about the nature and value of tradition, but like other commentators he balked at what he considered a too sweeping rejection of the modern. He passionately defended James Joyce, for instance, and pointed out that his father only dimly understood the importance of Joyce's authority among younger writers. The truculence of such letters was clearly the result of a young man's determination to resist what might easily have become intellectual domination, an attitude that in itself would probably have gratified Brooks. But the personal and critical dialogues contaminated one another, and the letters that passed between California and New York probably seemed to both men more hostile and defensive than they were meant to be. To Brooks their tone became almost frightening as it grew increasingly apparent that Charles was taking more satisfaction from his work in sheet metal and carpentry than in writing. For a man who throughout his life held firm to a simple faith in the superiority of the writer's life Charles's abdication must have seemed a wild bohemian prank. But as Charles became a craftsman and a maker of fine furniture, Brooks was forced to acquiesce to this latest reorganization of an already baffling world.

After the war, Kenyon went through a similar experiment in vocation, with similar results. For a time he worked in New York as an editor, but he eventually abandoned the literary life to become an unusually skillful machinist. Brooks took these acts of independence as rejections of himself and his values—which, of course, they both were and were not. Certainly Charles and Kenyon were establishing their own terms of life, but if Brooks had been less defensive he might have seen in their decisions extensions of his own principles. Both men examined themselves honestly, worked creatively at their trades, and maintained an admirable material simplicity. Ironically, both eventually came to live more freely than ever their father could, and they adhered more closely to the heroic model of the unfettered spirit on the open road that Van Wyck had held up to himself since he had met Arthur Ryder in Venice in 1899.

Such disagreements and changes were neither startling nor traumatic. Most families have similar stories to tell. I make these altogether natural developments a part of my own story because Brooks had become hypersensitive. At least when he was in his depressed moods, he searched the external world for accusations he could turn against himself. While his relationship with Charles and Kenyon would ultimately become more comfortable, during the war years his worries for them seriously drained his emotional energy.

That drain was quickened by other empathies of these years, particularly with Newton Arvin, whose marriage was ending explosively in the serious breakdowns of his wife and himself. In February 1941, persuaded that he could no longer cope with life, Arvin entered the gloomy state sanitarium in New York where Van Wyck had himself spent his most suicidal months. Alert to the susceptibility from which his friend had not yet completely recovered, he insisted that his hospitalization was not sufficiently alarming to warrant any attention on the

Brookses' part. However, it soon became clear that this was a serious illness indeed, and despite Arvin's uneasy demands that he keep his distance, as well as his own sense of danger, Van Wyck forced himself to analyze for a friend's sake his personal experience of psychosis. He also paid several difficult visits to the haunted wards of Bloomingdale.

In addition to such emotional burdens—perhaps at times an extension of them—both Eleanor and Van Wyck suffered physical disabilities during the early 1940s, and the first confirmations that bodies decay disturbed people who were accustomed to taking their energy for granted. "I have had the scare of my life," Van Wyck told Mumford in January 1943; "I sat down to work here the first morning and suddenly felt my left side paralyzed—arm, hand, leg and foot useless." "It was what they call a 'spasm' in a blood vessel in the brain," he went on cheerfully, "and just a sort of pleasant warning." But when he learned the next year that his arteries were hardening and realized that he could walk only a short distance without uncomfortable sensations in his chest, he could not so convincingly shrug off the minor coronary attack of that summer. At the same time he was beset with an unprecedented bout of asthma, which made him, as he told friends, "bark all day like a mad yellow dog," and early in 1945 he was badly frightened by a hemorrhage in his right eye. At his doctor's insistence he gave up smoking ("for which I thank and curse God"), and he grumpily made gestures toward reforming his diet, which, if he had been left to his own devices, would have consisted almost exclusively of scrambled eggs and spaghetti. More gracefully, he abandoned gardening, which since 1926 had lost all of its charm, and he was quietly pleased with his new excuse to avoid tasks he had resisted for years. His exemplary behavior made him proud, and perhaps a little boastful, but it was temporary. After a while he eased himself back into his characteristic disdain for the needs of the animal. He would raid the refrigerator whenever Eleanor relaxed her vigilance, and he insisted on taking long walks even after his angina had become chronic. "I really don't think he knew," John Hall Wheelock reflected, "which side of his body his heart was on. And he didn't care. It bored him."

The threats to Eleanor's health during these years were even more serious. She had developed an alarming susceptibility to pneumonia and seemed unable to get through a winter without at least one prolonged convalescence. Her doctors thought she might have developed a permanent "pocket" of the disease in her lungs. By the late autumn of 1944 Van Wyck was distractedly reporting her eleventh attack. Eleanor herself was no less scornful of physical disability than was her husband, but as, year after year, winter brought upon her a familiar and increasingly debilitating torture, she must have grown more uneasy than she would let even those closest to her know. She had always been an active person, and months of enforced idleness seemed to her wasteful and somehow foolish. As she turned sixty in 1944, and Van Wyck in 1946, both of them were frustrated, and more than a little humiliated, by the incapacities of the flesh.

As physical restrictions increasingly set the pace of domestic life, Westport itself began to seem restrictive. Especially in winter, and especially in wartime, when gasoline was scarce and his automobile often out of service, Van Wyck sometimes felt exiled from the intellectual society in which he thrived. Long winter nights at home became unbearably tedious, and the doctors were insisting that Eleanor must be moved to a better climate—to the Southwest, perhaps—if she were to rid herself of pneumonia. Furthermore, she needed relief from household work, for she had never acquiesced to her husband's residual bohemianism in regard to domestic order. Unable to find help in wartime, she devoted a good part of her day simply to keeping things clean. "Eleanor, don't do that!"—as Wheelock paraphrased Van Wyck's reaction to his wife's stubborn tidiness—"Be gay. Have a good time. Don't spend your time worrying about cleaning the house. . . . Let the house get dirty." If Eleanor heard these outbursts of irresponsibility, she paid them no heed, but simply smiled again at her husband's persistent boyishness and turned back to her floors. All of this had been well enough in the small rooms of their old home, but Eleanor soon found that the demands of the new house were too much for her.

The Weston establishment continued to be a burden for both of the Brookses. A friend called it "a rich man's house"—a phrase to touch Van Wyck's persnickety economic moralism, especially since Westport itself had increasingly become an enclave of wealthy businessmen from New York. His sensitivity to such concerns is in part betrayed by his renewed restlessness. Between 1939 and 1946, even as a war economy severely restricted private transportation, the Brookses were only once in Westport for as long as eighteen months at a stretch—from June 1941 to January 1943, while Van Wyck was finishing *The World of Washington Irving*. Otherwise, life at home was only a breathing space between summer vacations in Maine and winter expeditions to Virginia, the Carolinas, and Florida. Van Wyck often complained about the folly that had led him to acquire his "white elephant" in Weston, and he felt that it had somehow trapped him in a routine of superficial hospitalities. No doubt it was his own uneasy conscience at work, but he soon came to associate the place with sordid visitors and suspicious telephone calls. He reached the end of his patience with such portents when, during one of Eleanor's convalescences in 1945, he managed to hire a German-American cook, only to learn that she was a "virulent Nazi" with a psychopathic son who "thinks he is going to be the next German führer. He has epileptic fits, raves about Nazi wolf-hounds, and threatens to murder the children at the Weston school." These unfortunate people were known to the police, who quickly put an end to the "movie-melodrama" in Weston, but to Van Wyck the incident seemed all of a piece with his experience of that place, and he found himself wanting to get away. That same year he told the novelist Hamilton Basso that he had "never been able to make my mind up on this question of local attachments. . . . After 25 years my own ties with Westport are almost invisible, they are so light. We have so few deep connections there, yet I somehow want to belong to some spot on earth and sometimes feel lost not having one."

Significantly, the letter to Basso was written from Carmel, California, the alternate home of Brooks's early manhood, during the second of two prolonged visits to California, in 1944 and 1945. The trips west were primarily visits to Charles and a first grandson, but, at least for Van Wyck, there was the ulterior purpose of finding a few months' refuge in Carmel again. He thought that except for the swarms of soldiers and sailors the place had not much changed in twenty years, and in his letters he described it with none of the intellectual hostility it had aroused in 1923.

When they were back east, Van Wyck and Eleanor continued to shun Westport, spending several months at a time in New York, the city where he once feared he "should die of stimulus," but which now seemed more hospitable with each visit. In fact, by 1946 he had about decided to abandon his village life altogether, and during that spring he and Eleanor made plans to sell their mansion and buy an apartment in Manhattan.

These were serious disharmonies of life, but to list them makes them seem more unsettling and saddening than they were. Van Wyck had learned more elasticity than he had shown as a young man, had learned that there is a principle of resistance in human affairs, and that he need not abstract some "logic" from unfavorable developments and then resign himself to it. Although he suffered cruelly, for instance, from attacks upon both him and his work, he took great satisfaction in his personal sense of achievement. With the publication of *The World of Washington Irving* and the slow but exciting growth after 1944 of the manuscript which would be *The Times of Melville and Whitman,* he believed that he had become a mature writer at last. "[I am] wishing now when I am on the very verge of 60," he wrote to Mumford in late 1945, "that I had got a real start with my work thirty years before. For I only began at 45 or 50 and I feel as if life were just opening for me now." In Melville's poetry, which he had always read with some distaste, he might have found an expression of the mature wisdom that encouraged him to assert his sense of life against a deteriorating situation. "I know a wind in purpose strong," Melville had written in "The Conflict of Convictions," "It spins *against* the way it drives."

In addition to the consolations of work, Brooks took refuge in his old gift of friendship, for, despite his complaints about the distractions of Westport society, he continued as always to be a happy visitor and a generous host. His chapter on the Weston house in his autobiography lists among the acquaintances of that time Victor von Hagen, William Allan Neilson, C. C. Burlingham, Edith Hamilton, Mark Howe, Henry Dwight Sedgwick, W. E. B. Du Bois, S. K. Ratcliffe, Frank Jewett Mather, Mahonri Young, Samuel Eliot Morison, George Biddle, and Bruce Rogers. Other significant acquaintances of the early 1940s included Thomas Sergeant Perry, John Steinbeck, Lillian Hellman, Maxwell Geismar, Louis Untermeyer, Glenway Wescott, Thornton Wilder, Hamilton Basso, and Lin Yutang. Brooks seemed to know everyone—or at least to want to know everyone. For a theoretician of literary communalism that was a duty as well as a pleasure. "Sinclair Lewis asked me once," he noted in his autobiography, "what sort of man Steinbeck was, for Lewis had never seen him and knew little about him, and it struck me then that we had no community of literature, such as we had had in the nineteenth century and even later." He did his level best to remedy that situation. He either invited writers to

257

him or stubbornly sought them out, seeking to establish personal relationships and interconnections as much in his social life of the twentieth century as in his literary re-creations of the nineteenth.

One important new friend of these years moved into Westport in 1944. Helen Keller was already an old woman when Jo Davidson introduced her to Van Wyck, but she was still bright and enthusiastic as any child, an incarnation of the yea-saying spirit that Brooks was forever seeking in the hidden corners of the modern waste land. She soon made Van Wyck a favorite, the companion whose proximity she sought during social gatherings, and to whom she addressed an extensive correspondence, full of warm praise for his humanitarian enterprise. An old-fashioned socialist who had dreamed utopian dreams out of Ruskin and Wells, voted for Eugene Debs, and known the brief flight of the spirit of Randolph Bourne could not but be moved by her unembarrassed affirmation.

As he struck up this friendship with Helen Keller, Van Wyck was also gratefully renewing acquaintance with the ebullient sculptor Jo Davidson, whom he had not seen since 1915, when they had together made part of the bohemian company at Dan Rider's bookstore in London. It was about this time that Davidson made the bust of Brooks that is now in the public library in Bridgewater. "I had a wonderful time working on Van Wyck's head," Davidson remembered, "trying to put into his bust the sensitive beauty of his spirit."

Another friendship which was renewed during the early forties was with Lee Simonson, who since Harvard had become an important theatrical designer. While Brooks admired his commitment to art, he was attracted primarily to the largeness, energy, and lack of inhibition of Simonson's presence. It was like having a "brass band playing in the house," Brooks thought—at least when Simonson was in the right frame of mind, for he was manic-depressive, and his moods were unpredictable. People who were either less familiar with his erratic behavior or less tolerant of it might justifiably remember him as rude, surly, or despondent.

Oliver Kenyon Brooks believes that Simonson was his father's most intimate friend during the forties. However he came by his authority, Simonson seemed able to say things that his defensive colleague would have accepted from no one else. "That was evidently the day," reads a letter from Simonson of 1943, "when you wanted to kick the cat; or rather have a cat to kick. . . . How can you seriously think that I . . . take a crack at you and your work? Or send you what you so elegantly call a turd? . . . Because certain literary circles take pot-shots at you these days, is no reason for you to be so morbidly sensitive. Foutez-vous en!" "Lee is a great entertainer, and he always puts on a show," Van Wyck noted to himself. "Wherever he sits, he is the end-man of the minstrel show, and he desires to be given all the rope. He is like Hendrick [Van Loon], of whom he said last year, when the two dined here together: 'It is always the same show. But it is a great show.' "

The deepening of the undergraduate comradeship with Simonson is perhaps typical of the peculiar happiness of the war years, when Van Wyck seemed to come into full possession of his gregariousness. In fact, for all of the real problems and dangers of those days, he often caught himself feeling, as he told Lewis Mumford, as if he had "never had such a sinfully good time, for, when I stop to think, it seems positively wicked to enjoy life in war-time as I am doing." "The cause of this enjoyment," he went on, "is nothing more than innocent talk with a great number of good people, old friends and new *young folks* who have delighted me with their spirit and with whom I feel ten miles more congenial than I felt with the post-war generation. . . ."

The approaching end of a decade of warfare also contributed to the relatively relaxed atmosphere that Brooks so guiltily enjoyed. Kenyon would at last come home—and with him the countless other young men whose dangerous absences had sobered every community in the country. More selfishly perhaps, Van Wyck might hope that with peace at hand he would be spared some of the political cross fire in which he had been caught since he had emerged from his hospitals in 1932. To be sure, a new menace had reordered human affairs in a moment over Hiroshima, and the great powers were brandishing their weapons like belligerent children, but one could at least take comfort in the restoration of a personal normalcy. One could buy gasoline again, butter and tobacco, perhaps even a new automobile. One could pick up the strands of life war had broken and weave them back into the old, familiar patterns.

That sense of familiarity was not long sustained. During the first year of peace Van Wyck was disturbed by the deaths of several of his closest friends and relatives. Eleanor's mother, who had continued to occupy the little cottage behind the old house in Westport, died late in 1945. His own mother died in the early spring of 1946. Neither death could have been particularly traumatic. Mrs. Stimson had been weakening for some time, and Van Wyck's mother had been gently senile since her husband had died in 1942. "My mother's death had been long expected and it had been three years since she had even recognized me," Van Wyck told Mumford, and he went on to explain that he felt "unhinged" and "bedevilled" largely because her death "was followed by the death of my very dear Edward Sheldon, with whom I had dined just three days before."

Sheldon was a loss indeed. Despite the arthritis which had paralyzed and blinded him for some twenty years, he had deepened his gaiety of spirit, and maintained in his apartment on East Eighty-fourth St. a sort of salon by which he kept himself at the center of theatrical life in Manhattan. His courage, resourcefulness, and sensitivity, the accuracy of his judgments and the inspiration of his presence, had for years made him far more celebrated than had the romantic melodramas by which he had first become famous.

Van Wyck and Eleanor were as close as anyone to Ned Sheldon. Like Jack Wheelock and Max Perkins, they often visited his apartment for dinner and an evening of talk. Van Wyck once described such occasions. "Most people are shocked & troubled when they first enter the room," he told Kenyon, who had not previously visited Sheldon, "but all within two or three minutes feel at ease, and in half an hour they eventually feel that they have never had such a happy time. But you must know that he lies motionless on a couch with a black bandage over his eyes. He is totally blind as well as immobile; and the table for your dinner is drawn up beside his bed, and you dine alone. He will do all the rest[;] he will sing out at once, and within a minute you will feel that he & you are friends."

He was still missing Sheldon in July, when Paul Rosenfeld died abruptly after suffering a heart attack while watching a motion picture. The intense friendship Brooks and Rosenfeld had shared during the days of *The Seven Arts* and the literary battles of the twenties had become most intimate during Van Wyck's illness and cooled visibly in the years after he returned from Katonah, but just recently the two men had resumed a close companionship. "Last week," Van Wyck happily reported in March 1945, "we snared Paul into having dinner with us. I say snared because for the last three years he seemed to take flight at the mere sight of us, but when we finally caught him he was as friendly as ever and it seemed that we had a very happy evening together. When I saw him the next day, at the Public Library, he was as cordial as of old. . . ." Almost Rosenfeld's last act, as Van Wyck remembered it in his autobiography, was to appear at Eleanor's room in the hospital, bearing a gift of flowers. His heart attack, two days later, confounded his promise to return and read aloud to her from *Tom Jones*.

Eleanor was having a worrisome year. She had been hospitalized by her twelfth case of pneumonia in March, and after an unusually long and difficult period of recuperation, her right knee had become oddly swollen and painful. Three doctors, Van Wyck reported, diagnosed the condition inaccurately, and it was not until June that the growth on her knee was recognized as a serious malignancy and she was returned to the hospital. Although her surgeons felt that they could do little for her, her condition was too far advanced to allow for any gradual therapies, and in mid-June her right leg was amputated above the knee.

Through all of this, Van Wyck expressed no fear that Eleanor might not survive her ordeal. He assured friends that she stood well out of danger, and he finally carried through his plan to sell his "rich man's house" in Weston, speaking confidently of moving Eleanor into the more comfortable quarters of their new apartment in Manhattan by the first of October. One may wonder about the almost willful blindness with which he refused to confront the implications of his wife's condition, but it is probably true that Van Wyck literally could not conceive of life without her. She had been at his side, both morally and physically, since they were children together, and she had supplied a principle of strength to a life he had often lived susceptibly—too recklessly, too stubbornly, too intensely.

His uncritical emotional dependency was one cause of his blindness; Eleanor's personality was another. She suffered the pain and uncertainty of her last days with a cheerful stoicism that was, by all accounts, nearly inhuman. "Let it rain!" she wrote to Marion Wescott a month after her operation, "My horizon is radiant." She came home in late July with a merry self-irony about locomotion. Mrs. Wescott, who visited Weston during that last month of Eleanor's life, remembers her hopping about on her crutches, full of schemes for the future, talking happily about the one-legged man she had once seen riding a bicycle.

How was Van Wyck to acknowledge her situation when she herself would not?

Van Wyck was almost childishly happy to have Eleanor in the house again. He ran about fussily, probably inefficiently, trying to make her comfortable and—a more challenging matter—quiet. Only gradually, hostilely, did he come to recognize that his wife must die. "Since I wrote you," he reported to Lewis Mumford on August 26, "Eleanor has taken a turn for the worse and cannot live through September. . . . I don't know what lies ahead or whether I can work without a home, infantile as I am in so many ways emotionally. At present I am paralyzed mentally and see no break in the blank wall ahead. I go about methodically packing up the house, while Eleanor lies upstairs heroically cheerful, thinking only for me and the boys. . . . Few words I have ever read would do justice to her spirit. . . ." Four days later, on a quiet August afternoon, Eleanor was dead.

Van Wyck's state of mind at this time may be illustrated by the reports of Eleanor's death he addressed to friends and relatives. On the sixteenth of September he inaccurately told S. K. Ratcliffe that Eleanor had died on August 27; a few days later, in a letter to his stepsister, the date, still confused, had become August 29. In his autobiography he remembered that Eleanor had died when they "had just come back from California"—which is rather the time when his mother and Edward Sheldon had gone down. "I had no reason to suppose she was not going to be well again," he wrote in a poignant letter to his stepsister, "but apparently everyone else knew it was bound to be fatal from the start. . . . I was reading letters to her four hours before she died. I don't need to tell you how lovely and touching and tragic she was, so young with her hair quite untouched by all these years, smiling and anxious *only for me."*

There were times when he felt strengthened by the goodness of a death which had kept faith with a goodness of life—"It was beautiful," he told S. K. Ratcliffe, ". . . and I realized for the first time that if you are made in a certain way there is nothing really to fear in death." Yet, if it had not been for the presence of Kenyon and the "momentum," as he called it, of his nearly completed *Times of Melville and Whitman,* he might have given way altogether. "It is a strange feeling," he wrote to Ratcliffe, "after having in a way made my life, to have it taken out of my hands,—to be cast adrift without a rudder." And when he remembered those days for his autobiography, he reflexively fell back upon that same fundamental metaphor: "I felt like a man who is drowning and who does not know which way to turn. . . . I seemed to me, after thirty-five years with her, that life had been taken out of my hands and that I was cast adrift on a desperate sea."

PART IV

INDIAN SUMMER
1947–1963

I think Van Wyck is a true Confucian scholar—I mean by Confucius' own definition of a true gentleman. He takes the right as his material to work upon and ritual as his guide in putting what is right into practice; he is modest in setting out his plan and sincere in carrying it to a successful conclusion. Indeed he is both a preserver and promoter of tradition showing a sense of honour in his personal conduct holding the torch to lead American writers in the path of the long and flourishing tradition of Western civilization.

—CHIANG YEE
ca. 1961

XIV

A NEW LIFE: 1947–1959

One evening in November 1946 John Hall Wheelock crossed the quiet hallway from his apartment in the brownstone house on East Fifty-seventh Street to knock on Van Wyck's door and extend an invitation. His friend Gladys Rice Billings was holding a small dinner party that evening, and she had welcomed his suggestion that she invite Van Wyck, whom she had met briefly on a similar occasion at the Wheelocks' two years earlier. Van Wyck remembered Mrs. Billings agreeably and seemed well disposed to Wheelock's inducements until his friend innocently sought to strengthen them by mentioning that Allen Tate would also be present. "I can't go then," Van Wyck blurted out; "Allen Tate is my enemy. He hates my point of view. I," he went on, warming to his obsessive subject, "hate *his* point of view."

"Oh, don't be foolish," responded Wheelock, whose patience and good will had never been more valuable than in these first months after Eleanor's death. Probably Van Wyck was convinced despite himself when Wheelock tactfully suggested that his inclination to explosions of literary partisanship was generalized and might, in particular cases, deprive him of the pleasure he customarily found in the company of writers. Allen Tate was a charming person, Wheelock told his scowling companion; Allen Tate was a true man of letters and an admirable friend. As was becoming more common in these autumnal years than

267

when they were young together, the poet's courteous good sense prevailed.

Van Wyck enjoyed himself at dinner and during the spontaneous musical entertainment that accompanied it. He may have disconcerted Tate when he mischievously announced, upon introduction, "You are a literary enemy," but he had clearly decided, as his hostess remembered, that he would not indulge himself in professional dialogue. For the most part, he remained on the periphery of the small group and its conversation, subdued without being aloof, claiming his turn to speak only when he saw an opening for an anecdote about Jo Davidson. Later, as he and Wheelock walked home through the chilly November streets, he pestered his friend for information about Mrs. Billings, by whom he had obviously been much impressed.

Although there still were, and would be, many spasms of pain and confusion when he realized afresh that his wife was gone, Van Wyck was recovering with remarkable elasticity from the sense of purposelessness that had overwhelmed him only three months earlier. In October he, Kenyon, and Margaret Cobb, the widow of an old friend who had come down from Westport to keep house for them, had moved into the comfortable but unostentatious building on New York's east side where Jack and Phyllis Wheelock had already owned an apartment for many years. His work on the nearly completed *Times of Melville and Whitman,* Van Wyck often said, kept him from falling apart during those first few months as a widower, for he had accepted the corollary to his old conviction that if he could not write he could not live and he sensed now that he was destined to go on living by the simple fact that he had continued to write.

Van Wyck was also renewing himself socially and personally with a purposefulness that might have alarmed him a few months before. In particular, he reestablished with surprising alacrity one interrupted pattern in his life when he resumed his acquaintance with Padraic and Molly Colum, probably at Molly's invitation, either in late 1946 or, as seems more likely, in February 1947, when Molly sent him a cordial message for his sixty-first birthday. Molly did not date her correspondence from this period, and it can be only occasionally and tentatively dated by her reference to events. All but a handful of the letters Van Wyck wrote to her after 1946 have been either lost or destroyed.

At first it seemed that the renewed relationship might avoid the issues that had been left unresolved in 1925. Van Wyck felt guilty about Molly and apprehensive of her passionate bluntness, but her first letter of invitation was good-natured. "Please don't," she wrote, "ask the large rotund lady who opens the door for you if you can see Mrs. Colum as another long absent friend did recently, for that large dame will be I." Once he was inside the apartment on Central Park West, however, the atmosphere must have turned uncomfortable. Van Wyck spoke "a lot of rubbish," or at least apologized for doing so, and even after twenty-two years Molly appears to have lost little of her indignation about his defection. In a letter which apparently continues some of the interchange of that meeting she writes of her intention to avoid any further "misunderstandings" and implicitly criticizes his long silence. "Until you actually appeared," she reported, "I was not sure you would come, because I had been told that since your illness, we were among the people you never wanted to see again.... You looked very well," she went on in a more dispassionate tone, "but naturally enough somewhat sad. However, you have your work always."

The relative restraint of this letter did not last long. Mary Colum was not a restrained woman. A letter of that summer (apparently June, since its occasion is the death of Maxwell Perkins) becomes openly angry and abusive in regard to both Van Wyck and Eleanor. Molly accused Van Wyck of hypocrisy and concluded her letter with some aggressive professional advice: "Stop starting another book so soon, and give yourself a little time to rub one thought against another . . and indulge in a little meditation . . meditation is what your recent works lack . . I know that to your mind any criticism of you is like criticism of God and the Universe . . and the people who indulge in it just don't know nothing." (Colum's punctuation)

Molly continued at odd intervals for at least another half-dozen years to write in much the same vein. Particularly, it seems, when she was made unhappy by other losses and conflicts, she tended to pour out her bitterness upon Van Wyck: accusing him of complacency, money-grubbing, and personal treachery; suggesting that he had selfishly abdicated his literary authority; and defending her own behavior at the time of his illness. Van Wyck's surviving letters to her are conciliatory in tone and rather distantly formal in their expressions of regard. Since the correspondence does not survive in its entirety, it would be dangerous to read too closely between the lines of what remains, but it does seem fair to suggest that Molly still cared greatly for Van

Wyck and that she was turning all of her ideologue's passion to reclaiming, as she understood them, the values of the literary warrior whom she had memorialized on the occasion of the Dial Award for 1924. As *Life and the Dream,* the autobiography she published in 1947, amply demonstrates, Molly loved to play the role of iconoclast and gadfly, born to trouble as the sparks fly upward, and her shrew's letters to Van Wyck had more than a bit of self-conscious gamesmanship behind them.

Van Wyck seems to have felt the good will and fundamental decency that underlay her bad manners, and he continued to see Molly and Padraic whenever he had the opportunity. He never failed to admire the "saintliness" he ascribed to Padraic, and he betrayed nothing but pleasure and satisfaction in the company of the fearsome Molly. Their abrasive friendship continued until Molly's death in 1957.

While this awkward but important reengagement of sympathies was being marked out in 1947, Van Wyck was also establishing a new domestic life without Eleanor. Although Mrs. Billings, who was herself adjusting to a divorce, felt that after her dinner and the brief, rather formal visit a courteous man made to acknowledge it she would not see her guest again, Van Wyck had apparently already conceived other ideas. Their courtship was decorous but not prolonged. By March 1947 Van Wyck had told his sons and closest friends about his engagement, and on June 2 he and Gladys were married in a civil ceremony at New York's City Hall. It may seem ungallant to Gladys to say so, but this hasty courtship and marriage, begun not three months after a disorganizing loss, was Van Wyck's final, involuntary, and most moving tribute to Eleanor Stimson Brooks.

Gladys and Van Wyck began married life in what must have seemed an emotional welter. Their wedding reception was held uptown at the home of the psychiatrist Carl Binger, but it was on that pleasant afternoon that Van Wyck greeted for the last time his oldest friend and last personal tie to Plainfield, Max Perkins. Perkins's death two weeks later, and the unhappy letter from Molly it inspired, may have exacerbated Van Wyck's own illness of that time. As he and Gladys were about to pack for a summer honeymoon, he developed an alarming fever. The doctor Gladys anxiously summoned, despite her husband's protests, at first suspected leukemia but finally diagnosed mononucleosis, and he spared his troublesome client hospitalization by entrusting him to Gladys's nursing. He made only an indifferent patient, Gladys remembers, but by the end of June he was allowed to accompany her to the Silo, her summer home near Chilmark on the western arm of Martha's Vineyard.

Once arrived, Gladys was bemused to learn that her husband's idea of a vacation was to establish a study, keep his habitually heroic working hours, and avoid sun, sand, and water. He would never succumb to either the lure or the rituals of the out-of-doors. Gladys could not persuade him to shed his jacket when he accompanied her on walks along the beach, and the sacrifice of his necktie was a rare and magnanimous concession. What he took from his vacations on Martha's Vineyard, then, was less the recreation the area offered than its solitude and the sense he found there of contact with the elemental. During his first two summers at the Silo, he prepared for publication his *Chilmark Miscellany,* a collection of favorite pieces from his books of the decade past.

Back at East Fifty-seventh Street that autumn, Van Wyck and Gladys agreed almost at once that they would bide their time in the city until they could find a suitable house in one of the villages of western Connecticut, where Van Wyck still felt "racially" at home. Not only was Manhattan expensive, but city life exposed a busy writer to the round of invitations and hospitalities which he much enjoyed but which threatened his work. Shortly after their return from Martha's Vineyard in the autumn of 1948, they put their apartment up for sale, rented a comfortable old house with an ample study in Cornwall, Connecticut, and began hunting in earnest for their permanent home. Eventually they settled upon the formidable dwelling that stood atop a gentle rise in the center of the village of Bridgewater, just a short drive from Danbury, close enough to New York so that the cultural and social life of the city was readily accessible, but not so close that it became routine. They had examined the house off and on for nearly a year, but they had first seen it deserted, unrenovated, with its handsome gardens overgrown and seedy—a noble building in its way, but somehow melancholy. It reminded Van Wyck of President Taft, Plainfield, and the early life that had cost him so much pain, and he remained for some time disinclined to it. Gladys, however, was sure that renovation and refurbishment would open the old house to the light and make it, if not handsome, gracious and hospitable. After long months of fruitless searching Van Wyck was finally persuaded. They took possession of their new premises in March 1949.

The Brookses' residence was situated on the village green, facing the community's two churches, the grocery, and the post office, a convenience essential to Van Wyck, who out of a combination of necessity and conscience maintained a staggering correspondence. It was a substantial three-story dwelling with a wide piazza, and its dignity was enhanced by the great trees, maples, magnolias, birches, and a fine copper beech, which contained its bulkiness and shaded its lawns and gardens. Too big for two persons and soon furnished with many of the cumbersome possessions Van Wyck had inherited from Plainfield, the house became an extension of a more leisurely era, and it often seemed to its increasingly pleased owner to "bring back the peace of fifty years ago." That suspiciously idealized memory of a lost time indicates that once again Brooks had become self-conscious about his roots, feeling, even after he had lived in Bridgewater for eight years and in Connecticut for thirty-seven, that he was still a foreigner among the Yankees. It does not seem farfetched to suggest that his imperturbably patrician house represented both an alliance with the local traditions he coveted and a truce with the personal past which still claimed the power alternately to repel and attract him. In any case, he was finally and irrevocably home.

Houses, of course, are symbolic—just as, Van Wyck never tired of noting, clothing is symbolic. The correspondence between the man and the garb, whether sartorial or architectural, is immediate and inescapable. If we may better understand a writer by reminding ourselves from time to time that his inclination to formal dress helped keep him alert to the traditional dignity of his calling, we may also, with due caution, respond to the hints about himself that he let drop by his selection of lodgings. His was a comfortable, decorous house, a little self-indulgent, greatly hospitable, amply suited to the way of life of the gentleman who has earned his stature in the world. It was not much in keeping with the character of American life in the late 1940s. In it Van Wyck's life became charged with ritual, social as well as professional. He discovered himself more eager now to enjoy the pleasures of a dinner party in his high, oak-paneled dining room, with its dark old furniture and the huge ancestral portraits upon the walls, or, when the weather was fine, an afternoon's gathering upon the lawn. Soft-spoken in his still faintly British way, but affable as always, mildly extravagant in his gestures of hospitality, he lived the unselfconsciously magnanimous life in the style he had learned from a supremely self-conscious era. It was, generally speaking, a quiet, satisfying old age.

For if we must posit some turning point in the life of Van Wyck Brooks, some prolonged moment when the terms in which he thought and felt were redefined, it is less to be found in the traumatic breakdown of 1926 than in the peaceful days of his marriage to Gladys. A man who had always depended on his relationships with women, Van Wyck could not have chosen a companion better able to enhance his culminative years. Gladys Rice was attractive and sophisticated, with a quick, sharp smile, a roguish wit, and a happy aptitude for the good-natured bullying that was necessary to keep Van Wyck from succumbing to his willful disinclination to care for himself—especially when he seemed about to sink into his old depression. Her worldly wisdom was far greater and more subtle than Van Wyck's own, and she took the trouble to anticipate a writer's problems and to master the tactics that might help resolve them. She shared and defended his values without exciting him to the sense of utter responsibility that had so often weighed upon him. Even her family connections were appropriate to her new marriage. As Van Wyck announced to one and all, her father had been Mark Twain's doctor and she herself had been the last adoptive "niece" of Henry Adams, who had read aloud to her from the manuscript of *Mont St. Michel and Chartres*—heady stuff for a young girl, and probably better relished in the memory than in the experience. A talented violinist, she knew her way in the world of music and musicians, and from her first two marriages was familiar with the social life of Boston, Washington, and New York.

In many of her traits, then, Gladys stood in marked contrast to Eleanor, and at least part of the differences between the Van Wyck Brooks of, say, 1936 and the Van Wyck Brooks of 1955 may be attributed to the differing qualities of the women who influenced, more than he knew, his day-to-day life. Gladys was better attuned to society, its demands and its pleasures, and could draw upon a far wider range of experience than Eleanor, whose interests and purposes, although always intense, had remained narrow. She laughed more easily than Eleanor, and brooded less, and had little of the dogmatic conscience that Eleanor had perhaps developed too closely along the lines of Van Wyck's own. Eleanor had always challenged her husband, directed him toward the olympian tasks of his desire, kept him at the cutting edge of his aggressive moralism; Gladys enabled him, at last, to relax with himself and his wages. At sixty-one Van Wyck Brooks made peace with his private ghosts and stopped changing in response to experience. Although he would still occasionally drop, less dangerously than of old, into his depressed mood, the tensions that had so long threatened to tear his life apart were greatly eased, and his compromises of identity accepted. For the sixteen years that remained to him he simply went on being the Van Wyck Brooks he had become in 1947.

That was no mean thing to be. More than most men he had established his models for identity, grown deliberately into them, and come into his own at last. The Confucian tribute by Chiang Yee which I have borrowed as the motto for my record of these latter days was neither empty praise nor an exercise in transcultural ingenuity. The "silent traveller" of an excellent series of illustrated books was responding to a deeply cultivated strain in Van Wyck, who had refreshed himself with the wisdom of the Analects since he was a high-school boy in Plainfield. His lifelong insistence on personality as the expression of the man in harmony with himself and his world, although it had diverse sources, is radically similar to the Confucian concept of the gentleman, which assumes that the decorum of the outer man exists in mutual interaction and sustenance with the decorum of the inner man, that by learning and practicing the public proprieties of relationship and behavior one refines the spiritual self. Indifferent to metaphysics, it applies a utopian philosophy that seeks to harmonize the subjective and objective, the social and the personal, the spiritual and the practical. Its ultimate goal is a rich and dynamic way of life in this world, and it might be well described by the remark of Samuel Taylor Coleridge that Van Wyck quoted to himself in his meditative notes: "I live in another world indeed but not to come."

"Come out strongly for secularism," Van Wyck urged himself in a working note of this time. "There is only one world, and we had better make the best of it. Our only chance. Anything else is evasion, mythology or self-deception.—*get all spirituality into it.*" He often elaborated to himself what a robust secularism should mean to an American: "I have been bewildered and shocked by the current misrepresentation of the word 'secularism.' To me a devotion to spiritual ends is the great thing in life, and I cannot see how secularism is at odds with this or with what I understand as essential religion. How can a fellow countryman of Emerson, Thoreau and Whitman feel otherwise? All three were completely devoted to spiritual ends and all within what I should call a secular perspective." One further passage from the memoranda should complete his unpublished credo of these years: "I believe in humanism—believing that good is *in* man and has never been anywhere else. Don't repudiate the adjective *secular,* but do repudiate the adjective worldly—for I emphasize the god that is in man over the mundane in him. (I notice how ready those who repudiate the *secular* are to swallow the *worldly*)."

It would be worse than farfetched to suggest that Brooks was in any precise sense Confucian; he was a child of the Age of Reason and the American Revolution. But it should not be surprising to discover that a man who always turned to the Chinese for ethics and courtesy, associated the traditons of Chinese humanism with those of the Western Enlightenment, and esteemed Confucius as a great teacher and the Confucian concept of "Superior Man" as an illumination would grow according to temperament and belief into something very like the "gentleman" who informs the discipline set forth in the Analects. The Confucian analogy can thus help us to understand at least one important aspect of a life that in later years might otherwise seem both stodgy and complacent. During the years after World War II many modernists were convinced that they found in the old Van Wyck Brooks anachronism, stuffiness, and bland conformity. Without discarding their judgments out of hand, we might do better by translating their accusations into Confucian terms—reading for "anachronism" *tradition,* for "stuffiness" *propriety,* for "conformity" *ritual.*

The ritual of a successful man's old age perhaps bothered Brooks's detractors most. The annual round of honorary degrees, tributes, and keynote speeches at literary and historical gatherings seemed tedious and egotistical, all of a piece with the succession of gold medals and the front-page review in *The New York Times* book supplement that invariably greeted a new publication by "America's Foremost Literary Historian." Brooks, to be sure, was more interested than many of his colleagues in ceremonial occasions, but he received his accolades with a certain distance and understood that he would call more attention to his honors if he were to refuse them. Each commencement address and tributory banquet was suffered in defiance of the shyness he never mastered. His exercise of the proprieties was not priggish, but rather an expression of the profound decency that had always distinguished his character. There was, for instance, the occasion of the tribute to

W. E. B. Du Bois in May 1957, when William Zorach's bust of the black leader was dedicated in the Schomburg Gallery of the New York Public Library. Du Bois's color, of course, had long excluded him from the consideration of most Americans, while his Marxism had made him both suspect and feared during the McCarthy years. There were unofficial attempts within the Library administration to suppress the ceremony, and although a great crowd spilled out of the small Schomburg building, only a handful of the writers and other intellectuals who had been invited put in an appearance. Among them was Brooks, who delivered an address praising Du Bois as "one of the great renovators, and one of the great builders of the future world," the kind of spokesman who "becomes, like Gandhi in India and Unamuno in Spain, the personification and soul of a great human group." On the other side of both the political and the personal spectrum, Van Wyck was among those writers whose petitions helped to effect the release of Ezra Pound from St. Elizabeth's Hospital, where he had been held in lieu of a trial for treason.

His dedication to writers and their work was as much in evidence in private life at Bridgewater as it was in the avuncular figure who seemed to be perpetually on hand for public display. Like any prominent writer, Brooks was inundated with correspondence—not only from friends and colleagues but from aspirants to literary success, quarrelsome people who wanted more information about minor figures in his books, admirers, fund raisers, collectors of bookplates and autographs, disciples and bravos, crackpots of every description. If you were saddled with an Eminent Foreign Visitor who wished to be introduced to literary Americans: a letter to Bridgewater. If you were upset because Leslie Fiedler had called Walt Whitman a homosexual: a letter to Bridgewater. If you were determined to outlaw bullfighting in Spain or Catholicism in New Jersey: a letter to Bridgewater. If you had been incarcerated in a mental hospital and needed money in order to write a book about your experience: a letter to Bridgewater. The mail was so heavy that Van Wyck simply dropped it to the floor once he had done with it and every two months or so Gladys took a day to file it away. But each letter, except for the obscene or utterly zany, was answered; the manuscripts were read; the bookplates were autographed; the money, more often than not, was sent. Van Wyck was a sucker for anyone who was a writer, claimed to be a writer, or thought he might like to be a writer. No talent was so small that he refused to respect it.

He never lost his altogether innocent delight in the company of literary people, nor did he hesitate to open his house as well as his pocket to the younger men and women who requested his attention. To their cause he dedicated much of his time and energy, although their literary postures were, for the most part, antithetical to his own. Much of his quixotic magnanimity was inevitably lost upon the weak or the fraudulent, but among the younger writers who profited, whether morally or practically, by Brooks's good offices were such diverse talents as Charles Olson, Karl Shapiro, and Seymour Krim.

Despite such distractions Van Wyck continued to maintain the old schedule that had him up and fully dressed before dawn each morning. During the years from 1947 to 1959 he produced eleven books, a multitude of introductions and prefaces, most of which remain uncollected, and a wide variety of speeches, lectures, and ceremonial tributes—everything from a talk on the historiographical art of Theodore Roosevelt to memories of childhood for the Plainfield Public Library to reminiscences of John Butler Yeats for Irish radio. While he was proud of such achievements, he was also aware that he seemed quaint to the younger generation of the fifties, whose cultural heroes— so the contemporary formulation had it—were Dylan Thomas, Charlie Parker, and James Dean. "I was 50 years old," he noted resignedly, "before I had learned how to write a good book, and by that time the bright young people had ceased to read me." But although he deplored the developments in taste that had made him seem "a common scold" he went right ahead with the literary and personal conservatism that never became political, deploring the avant-garde and resisting the moral implications of the Kinsey Report. His willingness to enact proprieties and represent established wisdoms can make his old age seem ironically "puritanical," but he never lost his peculiar spiciness. "I thought you were a stuffy old man," exclaimed Henry Miller upon meeting Brooks in 1955, "but you're neither one nor the other. And you remind me of Nietzsche as well as my grandfather." Gladys recorded Miller's words in her memoirs.

Van Wyck's respect for the ceremonial also characterized his dedication to his most important "group" of these years, the National Institute of Arts and Letters and its inner circle, the American Academy, which he had served more or less continuously as an officer from the time of his election in the late thirties. Besides working tirelessly at the routine activities of the organization, he sought to encourage a lively new membership and to resist the influence of certain mossbacks. His distaste for the "trimmers and spongers and dull dogs" of the Academy was sometimes expressed to his closest friends, and he infrequently allowed himself an uncharacteristic cynicism about the possibilities of reform. But on official occasions he stifled such feelings and worked with his usual idealism for a revitalization of institutional life that even most of his allies considered hopeless.

The so-called Beard affair of 1947–1948 may illustrate both the priority he assigned to the demands of the institution and, perhaps, the weakness or confusion of personal will that attended a man who continued to insist that he had died as an ego in 1932. When, under Brooks's chairmanship, the awards committee nominated Charles Beard for the Institute's annual Medal of Distinction, it wished to honor the historian who had helped to restructure American attitudes with *The Economic Interpretation of the Constitution* and *The Rise of American Civilization* and who, in a famous moment of intellectual integrity, had resigned his professorship at Columbia University after two young instructors had been dismissed because of their opposition to World War I. As it turned out, that heroic figure of thirty years past was not the Charles Beard of 1947. Brooks caught his first hint of trouble when Lewis Mumford announced that he would resign from the Institute if the award were made. To Brooks's confused protest about his attitude, Mumford explained that Beard had in his recent work demonstrated himself an isolationist and an "intellectual Quisling," whose polemic against democratic systems and in favor of totalitarian values had led to the suppression or distortion of fact in his scholarship. Any award made to such a man would outrage both moral and professional standards.

Mumford was at white heat, but, as Brooks soon learned, his position was not idiosyncratic. During the spring of 1948, as the occasion for the official presentation of the medal approached, Brooks was addressed privately by Samuel Eliot Morison, who protested an old classmate's personal association with what he considered a disgrace to American scholarship, and several members of the Institute threatened to follow Mumford's lead in resigning. At almost the last moment, Henry Seidel Canby, who had been scheduled to deliver the award, decided he could not do so, and Brooks was left with the unwelcome responsibility of presiding over the occasion. In what seems to have been a confused gesture of compromise, he resigned as secretary of the

Academy, and in his remarks upon presenting the medal he emphasized the general climate of disagreement with Beard's later work and implied the nature of his own, insisting that the award had been made for the achievement of a lifetime. Needless to say he satisfied no belligerent party.

As Mumford resigned from the Academy, he put the quarrel between himself and Brooks into personal terms by suggesting that the "gentleman" in Brooks had overwhelmed the moral agent, and that the incident was characteristic of a general "withdrawal" from the intellectual's responsibility to confront evil. Brooks, who privately left no doubt that he had come to agree about the "poisonous" quality of Beard's representations of recent history, fell back defensively on the lame, but doubtless straightforward, excuse that he had not read Beard's later works and had no idea of the nature of the moral and political argument he was rewarding until it was too late. He had last been forced to plead ignorance when Newton Arvin had caught him tacitly condoning some of the racial and political conservatism of Gamaliel Bradford in 1932.

The moral tightrope Brooks obliged himself to walk during the dispute over Charles Beard may remind us that our theoretician of the unified life remained, like any man, to some degree an accumulation of illogical impulses and could, like any man, be contradictory, cantankerous, or whimsical. There are also a number of minor incidents that catch some of the more elusive flavors of his life, with all of its little paradoxes and pratfalls. One of Van Wyck's favorites (he told it on himself in *From a Writer's Notebook*) involved the fly that had gotten itself trapped between the windowpane and storm window in his study. Invoking the sentimentally good-hearted Uncle Toby of *Tristram Shandy,* he sympathized with this pilgrim in a "desert of glass," and finally he "walked over to the inner window and raised it so that this fellow-creature might be delivered from so sad a fate." Once free, however, the fellow-creature became simply a fly buzzing in one's study. "All my tender feelings suddenly turned cold . . . ," Van Wyck reports, "and before I knew what I was doing I had crushed that fly." The man who wouldn't hurt a fly but did, and then felt mildly chastened by his failure to respect the whimsical altruism of Laurence Sterne, compromised his literary models in a similar way when he became a tacit accomplice in effecting the transmigration of a woodchuck who had been dining upon Gladys's flowers. In each case, one thought wistfully of the examples of Schweitzer and Gandhi only after the nuisance had been dispatched.

Despite their sad endings, the narratives of the fly and the woodchuck are interesting chiefly as examples of Van Wyck's tenderheartedness. The mild-mannered old gentleman had not forgotten the lesson of the young firebrand who wrote *The Soul:* that it is the responsibility of an evolving species to caress life with its little fragile offerings of light. Yet the tenderhearted, the amiable, the decorous old fellow with his "Polish aviator" haircut and quaint mustache was also subject to unrealistic and apparently unmotivated outbursts of temper, which "flared at a touch, a tone of voice, a fancied affront, someone's lapse in loyalty toward a friend." Particularly when his sensitivity to injustice was provoked, Van Wyck could still summon to hand all of the extraordinary vehemence of thought and feeling that had startled John Hall Wheelock in 1904.

The old rage survived, perhaps, as the necessary salt in a blandly genteel old age, but when friends talk affectionately about the elder Van Wyck, their anecdotes inevitably turn to the spasms of compulsive shyness which forever characterized him. Muriel Cowley reported that Van Wyck once accompanied her to a large rally for Adlai Stevenson, whose candidacy he had already publicly and enthusiastically supported. When at five o'clock Mrs. Cowley announced that she must leave the meeting, her companion, she reports, broke into a cold sweat at the prospect of being left alone in a crowd of unfamiliar people. Malcolm Cowley tells an even more revealing story about Van Wyck's sixty-fifth birthday, which Gladys had arranged to celebrate at home in Bridgewater with the family and a few close friends—the Cowleys, the Hamilton Bassos, and Walter Pach. When the cake was brought in and the guests began singing "Happy Birthday," Van Wyck, "in a show of embarrassment, which was a real embarrassment," crawled under the table.

In April 1951 the Brookses sailed for Ireland. Van Wyck's head may still have been ringing from his latest cuffing by Molly Colum, for she had chosen the occasion to compose one of her most stingingly personal epistles, but she had also, as had Padraic, provided letters of introduction which would be put to good use once ashore. After landing at Cobh, the Brookses made their way to Dublin where they set up headquarters at the Shelbourne Hotel. Their first excursion reunited Van Wyck with his stepsister, Dorothy Whyte, who lived now in

County Down, and whom Van Wyck cherished as a companion and an ally in his long, quiet struggle with his mother and Ames.

The Brookses spent most of their remaining weeks in Ireland becoming acquainted with the cultural and literary life of Dublin. Van Wyck, as always, was on a kind of pilgrimage, and one of his necessary devotions was completed when he delivered his brief radio talk on John Butler Yeats. Although Van Wyck nowhere says so, one motive for visiting Ireland may have been his desire to make contact, however ghostly, with the spirit of his teacher once again. He spent an evening at a nursing home swapping anecdotes with Mr. Yeats's son, the painter Jack Butler, and he saw again the familiar, unfinished self-portrait that he had once described to Eleanor as an example of Mr. Yeats's compulsive perfectionism. The painting hung now in the home of William Butler Yeats, and the memories it evoked of grand days at Petitpas' must have relieved for Van Wyck an otherwise gloomy visit to the poet's widow. Another of the women in William Butler's life, Maud Gonne, provided the Brookses with a more pleasant evening when she shared with them some of her memories of the fight for Irish independence. At other times, Van Wyck and Gladys passed hours with the literary, theatrical, and scholarly people of Dublin, to whom they were introduced by either the Colums' invaluable letters or their new acquaintance, the poet Monk Gibbon.

In June Gladys and Van Wyck left Ireland for England, where they visited some of Gladys's relatives at Buckinghamshire, then traveled to London for a brief stay before crossing to Paris in July. The chief event of their month in France was a visit to Jo Davidson in his home at Saché, near Tours—Rabelais's country, where the burly sculptor, with his explosive beard and fiercely high spirits, surely belonged. Van Wyck found Davidson's company tonic as always during his stay at the great stone manor house, but as he and Gladys prepared for their return to the United States aboard the *Mauretania* in August, he was enjoying its refreshment for the final time. His friend died of pneumonia that winter.

Van Wyck and Gladys made two other trips abroad during the 1950s: to Italy in 1956, when they spent the winter in residence at the American Academy in Rome, and to England and Scotland in 1959. Van Wyck's return to Italy after fifty years, like his visit to the Ireland of John Butler Yeats, took on something of the character of a pilgrimage. Officially in Rome to finish writing *Days of the Phoenix,* his memoir of the 1920s, and to prepare for *The Dream of Arcadia,* the study of American expatriates in Italy he would publish in 1958, Van Wyck maintained his usual working schedule and managed as well the full social round that had by now become as much a part of his day as the hours at the desk. He was introduced to such major Italian literary figures as Mario Praz, Alberto Moravia, and Ignazio Silone. His good friend Alexander Calder was in Rome that winter, as was Thornton Wilder, and he made the acquaintance as well of the younger writers Ralph Ellison and Theodore Roethke.

In late March Van Wyck and Gladys left Rome for Florence and the eighteenth-century villa, I Tatti, where Bernard Berenson, now in his ninety-second year, continued to work on his catalog of Italian Renaissance painting. Berenson had, of course, been among Van Wyck's undergraduate enthusiasms, and Van Wyck had been in correspondence with him at least since 1951. In 1952 he had written Berenson that since "far long before I entered Harvard . . . your name has been for me *sheer magic."* Just prior to leaving Rome for Florence, he had written to Berenson of his enthusiasm for the coming visit, telling him, "more than any other writer you have confirmed my own belief that liberalism and humanism are permanent realities. (Instead of the 'Victorian' realities or, rather, illusions that so many call them in our sick time.)" Berenson did not turn out to be as liberal as anticipated, but Brooks was inclined to explain away the illiberal aspects of people he otherwise admired, and he was persuaded that he shared with Berenson fundamental concepts of human nature.

When the Brookses were not traveling abroad during the 1950s, they were often traveling at home. Their most ambitious trip in the United States came in 1955 when they drove to California to take up residence for a quarter at the Huntington Hartford Foundation, just outside Los Angeles, where Van Wyck worked on his sketch of Helen Keller, and Gladys on her biographical study, *Three Wise Virgins.* Leaving the Foundation in March, they traveled north to Berkeley to renew both acquaintances and memories before turning toward New Mexico to begin the long drive home. Van Wyck went out of his way to see, among others, Upton Sinclair, Henry Miller, and Robinson Jeffers—all literary enemies of long standing—and he was pleased that he could at last exchange pleasantries with men who had reputations for prickliness. At other times, he and Gladys traveled to upstate New York and Washington, D.C.; several times to Philadelphia and Cape

Cod; to Boothbay, Maine; Cambridge; Savannah; and even to Missoula, Montana, for a summer seminar. Most of these journeys were made to accept awards, attend colloquia, or respect the other social demands upon a famous writer. A few were simply for the pleasures of tourism.

But whether on the road, at sea, or in the study in Bridgewater, Van Wyck remained purely and aggressively a writer. It was his fixed and intense literary identity that invoked his sense of satisfaction during these years. Naturally enough, that same literary identity provoked his most worrisome irritations. He had always been professionally quarrelsome—that was one of the responsibilities of the critic—but during early 1952 he became involved in two personal literary disagreements. It says something of the strategic isolation in which an invoker of community now found himself that these dialogues were conducted almost exclusively in private. They had no exemplary value in the literary forum.

The least deeply personal and thus least serious of these arguments was with Alfred Kazin, who reviewed *The Confident Years* for the *New Yorker* in January 1952. Brooks and Kazin had not been close friends, nor could they consider themselves in any real sense allies, but there had been a professional friendship and mutual respect between them at least since 1942, when Kazin had included a sensitive, although not wholly positive, discussion of Brooks's career in *On Native Grounds*. As the review was about to appear, Kazin wrote to Brooks, apologizing that he had felt forced to be harsh with *The Confident Years* and hoping that their personal relationship would not be affected. The complaints he voiced were familiar: that Brooks either could not or would not distinguish between major and minor talent, so that his pages were crowded with names which deserved to remain forgotten; that his principle of selection seemed to be nationalistic and messianic rather than literary; that he did not understand and could not be just to the important writers of the twentieth century.

Brooks must have known how much pain it cost Kazin to write negatively of a man he liked and admired. The conflict between personal feeling and professional duty must test and either confirm or defeat the integrity of any critic. But he also felt, as he brooded over those pages in the *New Yorker*, that Kazin had almost willfully misrepresented him by repeating clichés about his "method" that should have been laid to rest years before. Beyond any question of justice or understanding, Brooks was deeply and irretrievably hurt by bad reviews. Even Lewis Mumford had felt compelled to be circumspect and apologetic about a negative sentence in his laudatory review of *The Times of Melville and Whitman,* and Gladys had recognized early in her marriage how badly upset Van Wyck became by what he perceived as the stubborn insensitivity of his enemies. She attempted to spare his sometimes alarmingly vehement feelings by the discreet use of scissors on periodicals he had not yet seen, but he angrily told her, "You mustn't do this. I mean to keep every one of these reviews and some day, when the moment comes, I shall answer my critics together at one time." He responded, then, not to Kazin's personal appeal but to a professional attack. The brusque note he returned to Kazin suggested that he was above worrying about his judgments, but that the review was careless and inferior work.

Kazin responded in turn with a long letter in which he particularized the difficulties that he felt with Brooks's literary stance. There is nothing in Kazin's defense of his position that is not implicit in the review itself or familiar from the myriad criticisms of Brooks's later "phase" and the letter is of interest here chiefly because it was heavily, angrily annotated by Brooks. He seems to have gone through it in a rage, and at times his comments press deeply into the paper. His comments attain a sort of crescendo of outrage and dismissal. "That is a LIE," he scrawled beside Kazin's suggestion that he had not read the moderns as "makers" in the fullest sense, and to Kazin's remark that intellectuals must resist literary nationalism, he responded, "HELL!!!"—an unusual exclamation from Brooks, who remained forever reticent about his written vocabulary. Such implacable vehemence is scarcely to be found elsewhere in the private papers, and that it was provoked by the relatively congenial Kazin, rather than by Eliot or De Voto, suggests just how susceptible Brooks was to the barbs of the "bright young people."

A more prolonged and probably more unsettling quarrel broke out at about the same time, when Waldo Frank read *The Confident Years* and dashed off a characteristically tactless and inflammatory letter to Bridgewater. Like most of the reviewers who found the history unsatisfactory, Frank was particularly disturbed by the concluding chapter in which Brooks had shot a somewhat jaundiced "forward glance" toward the development of American literature after 1915, but he came at Brooks's rejection of the modern pessimism and aestheticism from a different angle entirely. He was not concerned that Eliot and Hemingway had been denied their due, but that Waldo Frank had not received his. He suggested that Brooks had egotistically suppressed the contributions of Lewis Mumford and himself to the "counter-action to Eliot and Mencken," and he implicitly accused him of plagiarizing from his own *Universe of T. S. Eliot.* He concluded his letter with the alternate pleading and bullying with which he had always assaulted his old friend's sensibilities: "My hurt is personal, but it is far more. For in ignoring me . . . in your 'history and prospect,' you have done a grave injury to the cause you profess. . . . In 1919, in the pages I wrote on you (*Our America*) as one of the captains of a little army, I called you 'the creator of the consciousness of America.' Have I failed in my life work so completely that this 'consciousness' cannot know me—or, possibly, is it you who have failed?"

Brooks understood that Frank was bothered less by possible lapses in *The Confident Years* than by what he considered a personal disloyalty at a time when all the world seemed to conspire against him. Since the late thirties Frank had felt that he was continually losing his position of eminence among American intellectuals, and he feared, accurately as it turned out, that his reputation was about to be submerged utterly. Brooks did not worry himself that he should have rewritten the end of *The Confident Years* in Frank's favor, nor did he have any difficulty resisting demands that he maintain a role he had in fact abandoned in 1920—or, more accurately, played only in an excitably messianic imagination. He was long used to Frank's wheedlings and scoldings, and he never had been able to abide the earnestly metaphysical novels his friend turned out. His letters in response to Frank are apparently lost, but since Frank paraphrased parts of them in his own letters, we can at least catch the flavor of the dialogue. Brooks, characteristically, tried to be conciliatory; Frank, characteristically, was having none of it. A few months later he was again accusing Brooks of betraying "the cause of literature" in that last chapter of *The Confident Years,* and when Brooks apparently tried to persuade him that he was being oversensitive, that it was the lot of them all to be ignored these days, he shot back: "I don't see how you can feel you are 'ignored.' You're a compulsory and most conspicuous target. . . . I am simply ignored and overlooked, consistently not mentioned."

Frank gradually cooled off, but the uneasy silence that subsequently characterized the relationship between him and Brooks hid a

kind of lingering resentment on the one hand and a fearful cautious-
ness on the other. Van Wyck's sense of danger surfaced again in 1955
when he was faced with the problem of portraying Frank in his autobiographical *Days of the Phoenix.* "What am I to say about Waldo?"
he asked George Biddle. "I'm keeping him till the last, not even re-
reading him yet, hoping that when I do I'll find him alive and exciting. He scares me, as you know; so don't tell him that I'm writing
to you."

What Brooks finally did write about Frank in *Days of the Phoenix*
represents no discernible compromise with his private assessment of
his friend's work. He praised Frank's leadership in the "Young
America" movement, his personal courage, and, in particular, his special affinity for the Spanish cultures of Latin America—that aspect of
an uneven career he had always admired most. He also acknowledged
Frank's eminence when he described the intellectual New York he had
known during World War I—which was appropriate, in fact critical, to
his story of his own life in the days of *The Seven Arts.* But he also announced his distaste for most of Frank's novels, which he thought "be-
fogged" by their mystical atmosphere. His tribute was paid to the character, energy, and integrity of the man; his reservations touched, by
and large, on the quality of the artist and the intellectual. It was a conscientious performance of which he had every right to feel proud.

Happily, the pages in *Days of the Phoenix* passed muster. Or, at
least, Frank responded to them more graciously than Van Wyck had to
Alfred Kazin. No doubt Van Wyck was relieved, but he soon learned
that Frank was determined to keep up his moralistic sniping. It was not
until the fall of 1959 that he could write triumphantly to George Biddle: "I have become very fond of Waldo, and, now that he knows I
don't like his work, I'm not *afraid of him any longer.*" It was one of a
number of happy endings near the end.

If even this record of disagreement seems essentially tame, that is
because it was so, at least when one compares it to the rough-and-tumble cultural brawls that punctuated Van Wyck's career between 1915
and 1945. According to most of the admired writers and intellectuals of
the new generation, Brooks was no longer a literary principal; the editors of little magazines no longer awaited the publication of his next
book in anticipation of a major scrap. Probably Brooks never resigned
himself to the loss of his old platform, for he conceived of his access to
audience in terms of a cause, as much as a matter of personal recogni-

tion. Nevertheless, his adventures of these twilight years are all interior, and the record of them is to be found in his books. After completing *Makers and Finders* with the publication of *The Times of Melville and Whitman* and *The Confident Years,* he wrote, instead of the sixth volume on the history of American writers in the twentieth century he had tentatively planned, *The Writer in America* (1953), a small book of essays which constituted a defense of *Makers and Finders* as well as a personal credo. For the rest of his life he published annually, turning out a series of studies and memoirs which have been described as essentially footnotes to *Makers and Finders,* although they are, of course, often more than that.

The most ambitious project he undertook once his history was finished was the record of his own life in three volumes: *Scenes and Portraits* (1954), which takes his story to 1914; *Days of the Phoenix* (1957), the account of the years which culminated in his breakdown; and *From the Shadow of the Mountain* (1961), concerning the period after 1932. In 1965 the three books were collected in a single volume called *An Autobiography,* but while they are autobiographical in nature, Brooks's reflections on his past are not generically autobiography—or else they are autobiography with the necessary egotism gone. He displays remarkably little of the autobiographer's interest in understanding the forces, motives, and processes that shaped the man he became and he acknowledges only intellectual influences—and not many of them—in what development he records.

A curious entry in his notes from the period in which he began work on the autobiographical writings hints at the peculiar quality that informs them. "I see the past largely in pictures," he tells himself, "—as a dream comes back to me in pictures—and as more and more life seems to me a dream." On another slip he has noted, with a later mark of approval, "Freud's teaching that man is primarily a sleeper—must go down into his dreams to discover his treasure." Brooks's creative imagination was always distinguished by a strong visual dimension, and the phrase by which he identified his first volume describes all of the autobiographical books aptly. They are not really his story at all, but rather the "scenes and portraits" among which he moved and, by memory, gathered in defiance of time. The visually evocative power that captures Plainfield, Harvard, California, and England, Uncle Nick and Mr. Yeats, in the glow of a dream of youth makes *Scenes and Portraits* one of Brooks's most attractive books.

287

Brooks treated himself as a subject in these writings in much the way he had treated many of the subjects of *Makers and Finders.* He read through his youthful diaries, notebooks, and correspondence, circling key phrases and abstracting significant moments as if he were analyzing a nineteenth-century text. When it came time for writing, he transferred this material, often verbatim, into the very fabric of the narrative, so that the quotations, perceptions, and orientation of the young self retained at least as much control over its literary representation as did the reflections of the mature author. Thus we find in the autobiographical writings, not what the old Brooks from the vantage of the years understood about the young Van Wyck so much as the way the Brooks of any moment conceived of a contemporaneous self—or, more frequently, the environment and neighbors by which that self found reference.

His autobiographical method seems to have been successful in inverse proportion to his distance in time from the Van Wyck Brooks he described. *Scenes and Portraits* is not only charged with the flavor of the past and the high spirits of youth, it has a continuous narrative and at least some sense of the causality that might have moved an apprentice writer back and forth between the settings of those years. *Days of the Phoenix* is more impressionistic than *Scenes and Portraits,* and more likely to replace the record of events with symbolic portraits and landscapes. One learns relatively little about what Van Wyck was doing during the years after World War I, but one does learn much about his acquaintances and their work. Narrative continuity is established with suspicious frequency by such phrases as "then came a time," "one day," and "it was during." *From The Shadow of the Mountain* is the least cohesive of the three books. Except for the first and final chapters, it suggests almost nothing of the passage of time, and occasionally the text becomes little more than compilations of jottings and fragments. Its sporadic and uneven quality is, of course, not simply a result of literary method. It was written by a man whose capacities were drained by the serious illnesses of his last few years.

A corollary impulse to autobiographical self-examination was expressed in the slender bedside volume *From a Writer's Notebook,* a selection of meditations, memories, and aphorisms that Brooks culled from his journals and published in 1958. This agreeable, unambitious little book, shot through with both good humor and unpretentious wisdom, may simply represent the attitudes and episodes for which

Brooks could not find room in his more ambitious works, for he was the most economical of writers and, excluding correspondence, scarcely a paragraph he wrote after 1908 escaped publication in one form or another.

Brooks also returned to "the shores I knew" (his original title for *Scenes and Portraits*) in his study of his old friend of Petitpas' days, the painter John Sloan, which appeared in 1955. His biography of the American artist who had resisted the temptations of the European idiom and discovered the peculiar richness of the American scene gave him a parallel for his own story of the coming-of-age of American writing. With Sloan as his subject he could write again about New York in the days of the Armory Show, about intellectual socialism and the circles of writers and artists it inspired, about the American leagues and guilds through which Sloan had moved, about Petitpas' and the good company there, and, above all, about Mr. Yeats. He told Sloan's story affectionately, with an attention to sensual detail and the bawdy high spirits of Bohemia that does not always characterize his other work.

Brooks's other writings of this period adhere closely to the method and purposes of *Makers and Finders. Howells: His Life and World* (1959) was the only study of a single literary figure Brooks turned out after his trilogy of the twenties. It amplifies the story of Howells and his great circle of literary contacts that Brooks told in two of the volumes of *Makers and Finders* in much the way that *The Dream of Arcadia: American Writers and Artists in Italy 1760–1915* (1958) extends and amplifies the method and scope of the larger history to account for a particular foreign influence. *Helen Keller: Sketch for a Portrait* (1956) was "hagiography." Brooks considered it a gesture in honor of an admired friend rather than a seriously conceived project. It is the slightest of his books.

By 1960, then, a stocky writer might well thrust his hands in his pockets, cock his head, and regard the very heft and number of his books, which now required nearly a "five-foot shelf" of their own, with the feeling that he had earned the deep satisfaction of his Indian Summer years. Although the old scars burned at times, these were characteristically days of work and honor, fulfillment and security. He had climbed over rocks to shake the hands of Robinson Jeffers and Henry Miller, adjusted his eyes in the gloom to be reconciled with Upton Sinclair, and endured hours without wincing in a parlor with Allen

Tate. There had even been a truce with James T. Farrell, who had eaten Van Wyck's bread among the ancestral portraits in Bridgewater. Perhaps now Brooks could divest himself of another literary hostility—at least long enough to exclaim, with D. H. Lawrence, "Look! We have come through!"

XV

MAKERS AND FINDERS

In the spring of 1951 Brooks completed the massive history that since his breakdown had shaped and directed his life. His enterprise had absorbed nearly two decades of his energy and dedication and, by his own count, had required the careful reading of some five thousand books. Malcolm Cowley has called the history "our greatest sustained work of literary scholarship," and it seems unlikely that the grandeur of Brooks's conception or the scope and density of his portraiture will be approximated in any future we can easily envision. The method by which he considered every American writer of even relative importance between 1800 and 1915, with all of the groupings, influences, movements, intellectual contacts, and wanderings of the literary life, had by 1932 already become, in the best sense, old-fashioned. *Makers and Finders* (the title is borrowed from Walt Whitman's "Mediums") is related to the encyclopedic scholarly undertakings of the eighteenth and nineteenth centuries rather than to the characteristically more specialized work of the twentieth. A scholar of similar ambition would not only have to share Brooks's financial and personal circumstances, he would have to be willing to forgo some of the advantages of modern scholarship. Nothing in Brooks's methodology was more anachronistic than his insistence that he must do all of his own research. Only thus, he thought, could he get the genuine feel of his material and infuse it with that distinctness of personality by which art is nourished.

The history excited much controversy while it was being published, and it remains controversial. From the frequently passionate debates and arguments of four decades two chief criticisms have emerged: first, that Brooks was essentially uninterested in the art of literature and was not writing true literary history or criticism at all; second, that morally and critically he had shifted, in Claire Sprague's words, from "analysis and judgment [before 1936] to description and celebration [after 1936]." These assertions have been so often repeated that over the years many of their proponents have come to assume that they are matters of fact and have felt no need to justify them. Since they are in part valid and in part misleading, they can perhaps be best addressed by some preliminary definitions of Brooks's conception and method, which will in turn lead naturally to a reading of the narrative itself. We owe it to Brooks to look hard at these issues. If he was at all justified in his claims for the work he did between 1932 and 1951 he invites the rigorous scrutiny that can be sustained only by art and scholarship of major significance.

Makers and Finders is a romantic history shaped according to the familiar liberal analysis that divides American society between the progressive, democratic values best represented by Thomas Jefferson and the aristocratic reaction represented by Alexander Hamilton and the Federalists. That interpretation has been influential during much of this century, and Brooks might have had it most directly from Vernon L. Parrington's *Main Currents in American Thought* (1927–1930), among any number of other sources. As the patriarchal symbolism suggests, the history is not concerned exclusively with literature, but rather with broad developments in all aspects of the nineteenth-century American culture that grew from and extended the values of the American Revolution. Literature, for Brooks, was the most sensitive and powerful expression of that culture.

Although their jeers have been unwarranted, Brooks's detractors have thus generally been right to question the genre of *Makers and Finders*. Brooks was not really a critic or historian of literature, at least not in the terms understood by most recent critics and scholars. He was not interested in full analyses of individual works, only incidentally offered aesthetic judgments of any kind, and in particular was unresponsive to the lively contemporaneous interest in literary forms and structures. "A literary history confined to 'forms,' " he asserted in *The Writer in America,* "would perpetuate the fallacy that books breed books by a sort of immaculate conception. In reality books are bred by men, men by life, and life by books through a constant interrelation and cross-fertilization, so that an element of social history can scarcely be dispensed with in any account of literary phenomena and forces." He eventually abandoned the potentially misleading term "literary history" and described *Makers and Finders* instead as "a history of the writer in America." His emphases were biographical, regional, political, and economic.

The continuing disagreements about the value of Brooks's history as a record and an interpretation have often obscured the important consideration that it is itself a work of visionary art in the tradition of Jefferson, Emerson, and Whitman that it champions. Much of the hospitality to minor figures, assumption of moral values, and method of judgment of *Makers and Finders* is attributable to the influence of particularly Whitman, and it might almost have been written to fulfill his prophecy of 1855, "As soon as histories are properly told there is no more need of romances." Brooks was less concerned with recording or analyzing the past than with recognizing or even establishing it. As always, he believed that tradition is not inherited; it is made and it is earned. Here he attempted to create tradition by envisioning tradition. *Makers and Finders* is a vision of an America growing during the first half of the nineteenth century (with a subsequent falling away) to a sort of collective consciousness of linkage and continuity.

We are but a chapter into the opening volume when we encounter the anonymous farmer from New Jersey "who invented the modern wagon-wheel, of which he had found an exact description in Homer. This was the wheel with a circumference made from a single piece of wood. American farmers, Jefferson added, when the invention was claimed for an Englishman, were the only farmers who could read Homer." This learned husbandman is not sufficiently important in himself even to be named. Nor is he important as an exemplar of some regional virtue, for Brooks notes that Jerseymen of his era "seemed to have little concern for enlarging their minds," although they did buy books from Parson Weems. He is, rather, a first tentative example of an awakening, an example of native ingenuity put to the services of a cause. Minor writers often appear in that same light, becoming important beyond their own achievement for the sake of their function in a larger pattern—as models, influencers, agitators. The rural inventor in

New Jersey, the neoclassic painter in Philadelphia, and the literary amateur turning out sentimental verses in old Charleston were contributing their services to an American community, of which they had not yet themselves fully conceived. The tradition thus becomes a larger "self" which dignifies the minor achievements of those who share its sustenance. John Greenleaf Whittier, for instance, can be an important character in *The Flowering of New England,* praised for his courage, generosity, and sweetness of spirit, even while it is clear that Brooks thinks his poetry is wretched.

"I had in my reading discovered," Brooks explained in *The Writer in America,* "traits that many of our writers possessed in common, which gave them a general character that was properly their own, and it struck me that they contributed to a sort of common fund, a fund of similar experiences, desires and hopes. It seemed to me that, collectively speaking, our writers formed a guild, that they had even worked for a common end,—an elevating end and deeply human—and that living writers, aware of this, could never feel as they had felt before, that they were working alone and working in the dark."

Brooks's critics would call this a fiction—as indeed they did, when they were not calling it "an enchanted dream," "scholarly storytelling," or something equally disagreeable. Sympathizers, however, compared *Makers and Finders* to a Tolstoyan novel, a "historical romance," and a "fable." Brooks himself feared that his history might seem so fictive that readers would forget that it was factual. That *Makers and Finders* "reads like a novel" became a critical cliché, and each year a few letters to Bridgewater urged Brooks to try his hand at genuine fiction. Sometimes he was offered plots, settings, or other aids to composition.

Of course *Makers and Finders* is fictive. All history in a sense is fiction. So is all philosophy, theology, anthropology, and most physics. Man might be called the fictionmaking animal. Humanity makes fictions as biosis begets plasma or gods create light. The process by which the imagination observes raw, apparently random, data, the sparks and flashes that attest to the existence of some generative source, and creates for them a context in which they assume proportion and meaning is among the oldest ways of knowledge. Call *Makers and Finders* a sort of "novel," if you will, or a "romance." Either term might be useful, although neither is strictly accurate. Whatever its genre may be, Brooks invented it, and we define it only by hints and indirection. It is related to romance, however, in its "plot" or "story line," which is shaped by the interaction of two hostile forces, both regularly embodied in symbolic characters who earn more or less sympathy to the degree that they share the common purpose that first arises in, and then flows from, the spirit of Thomas Jefferson. The conflict in Brooks's narrative is not quite the opposition of goodness to evil of generic romance, but it is a related conflict, and at times it approaches moral absolutism.

The specific detail by which the narrative is advanced is related more closely to the traditions of the realistic novel than to formal romance. Setting is of major importance. Many commentators have noticed, with Malcolm Cowley, Brooks's peculiar ability to evoke, "as a landscape painter might do, the special atmosphere of cities or sections where literary movements started or flourished or declined." Against backgrounds drawn in rich detail, as Lewis Mumford points out—"the houses they lived in, the places they ate and drank in, the countryside where they farmed or rambled . . . the family connections and who invited whom to dinner when Thackeray was in town"—Brooks develops his artisans chiefly as social characters, recording with particular relish the contacts they make with one another. He delights in the accidental meeting of men of talent on the frontier, in sketches of inns and clubs where writers gathered, and in details of conversation and correspondence. As a happy side effect of this interest in literary society, *Makers and Finders* provides our only approximation to a history of American talk as itself a minor art form.

The authorial point of view in the history has also been developed according to techniques borrowed from fictional genres. At times it is detached and judgmental, but more often it is absorbed by the point of view of the writers discussed. Brooks's avowed purpose was to "sympathize with their state of mind, . . . [and] accept them, in part, on their own terms." He did so chiefly through his use of paraphrase, which attempts to re-create the perceptions of a past age and restore to forgotten artists the importance they once possessed. However, the submergence of the critical voice into its subject has repeatedly led to serious charges that Brooks refused to discriminate between writers of unequal merits, that he refused, in fact, to make judgments at all.

Malcolm Cowley noted that "Brooks's critical comments on his authors are often expressed as comparisons with other American authors of the same period," and we might extend his observation to suggest that, in perhaps the strictest sense, each of Brooks's subjects is judged simply as he or she exists in a context. Whitman's idea of an ethical literature for which the "expression . . . is to be transcendent and new . . . indirect and not direct or descriptive or epic," in which the vision itself contains its own inescapable standard, is deeply part of the organic method of *Makers and Finders*. Given the thematic development and innumerable points of reference of the history, Brooks no more needed to make explicit his judgment of a Rufus Griswold or Eugene Field than Whitman needed to stop "Song of Myself" to deliver an opinion on slavery.

Edmund Wilson inadvertently noticed one virtue of this method in his review for *The New Yorker* of *The World of Washington Irving,* when he considered Brooks's treatment of the antarctic seascapes in James Fenimore Cooper's *The Sea Lions.* "If there is something in Cooper as good as Mr. Brooks seems here to suggest," Wilson wrote, "then you feel that you ought to know about it. But when you look up the icebergs in *The Sea Lions,* you find that Van Wyck Brooks has not merely been reflecting the glory of something that is much better in the original: he has put together his very pretty passage out of more or less undistinguished bits scattered through a great number of pages. . . . The creation is not Cooper's but Brooks's: he has sifted out the images from *The Sea Lions* and made out of them something quite new." One might suggest in amendment that Brooks had not made something new so much as he had renewed something that was old and in danger of wearing out. He passes implicit judgment on Cooper by rescuing passages of living description from a rhetoric whose peculiar woodenness is partly a function of its time, so that Cooper's imagery comes to seem as fresh and powerful to us as it must have seemed to his first readers, who would have accepted the rhetoric as convention and not stumbled over it as intrusion.

For those who would resist Whitman's authority, Brooks also offers plenty of judgment, most of it to some degree negative, according to extrinsic norms. The way in which judgment works and the problems it creates in *Makers and Finders* might be illustrated by the examples of Henry Wadsworth Longfellow, whom Brooks had trounced in *America's Coming-of-Age,* but for whose representation in *The Flowering of New England* he was often criticized, and Nathaniel Hawthorne, who challenged the range of his sympathies. Brooks says harsh things about Longfellow in *The Flowering of New England:* that his poems lacked "finality or distinction, whether in thought or phrase"; that his poems on slavery were childish; that his mind was all "music and pictures," "poor and thin" except when draped in the lush moods of his verse. Longfellow, Brooks thought, was a minor figure because of his inadequacy to extremes of feeling and particularly to the challenge of tragic emotion. His "flaccidity" sets him among the "popular" poets. Further, Brooks treats Longfellow severely by the adjustments of tone and imagery that accompany his appearances in the narrative. The young professor arrives in Cambridge in a shower of petals, flowers, aromas; he takes up residence in a "garden of memories, songs and tears, softly bright as a spring bouquet, tinted with rose and apple-green, pale canary-yellow and the palest blue." He remains the large sweet spirit of a world where "the flowers melodiously kissed one another, keeping time with the music of the moonbeams." This sentimentalism is not Brooks's; it belongs to Longfellow and the moony romanticism in which he flourished. The function of such syrupy language would be apparent if encountered in a serious novel.

In general, however, Brooks is less concerned with demolishing or even defining Longfellow's reputation than with understanding why this blandly mellifluous poet excited such extraordinary affection and admiration during the nineteenth century. Approximately thirty-five pages in *The Flowering of New England* are given to more or less sustained discussion of that question. Brooks emphasizes Longfellow's emergence as the representative of the spirit of youth, his importance as a scholar and translator of European poetry, and his influence as a teacher of modern foreign languages at Harvard. Longfellow is also significant for his propagandistic and exemplary work in the service of a national literature. He is admired for his technical facility and for his part in establishing a community of literary minds in New England. Evocations of his personal generosity, sweetness, and simplicity explain much of the affection with which he was regarded. Further, Brooks considers these things not from the point of view of a twentieth-century critic, but as much as possible according to the perceptions of Longfellow and his contemporaries. He wants the Longfellow of his narrative to correspond to the Longfellow of the nineteenth century, and in a sense he enacts his subject as he writes about him. The explicit judgments he occasionally makes, then, remain a function of the twentieth-century point of view and are effectively suspended. Brooks thus creates a balanced vision that permits his reader both to experience and to evaluate a condition of life and mind that is accessible now only to the imagination.

Hawthorne is less successfully developed. F. O. Matthiessen suggested in his *American Renaissance* that Brooks's "graceful dismissal of the entire problem of evil" had led him to a reductive reading of Hawthorne in *The Flowering of New England* and "deprived one of our few tragic writers of his chief significance." That Brooks was unresponsive to writers who wrestled with the problem of evil is the consideration that seems most likely permanently to qualify the reputation of *Makers and Finders.* In extenuation of Brooks it should be noted that the quarrel with his insensitivity to evil was often part of a larger quarrel with a familiar American philosophy. Brooks shares with Emerson and other American prophetic figures a vision of life in which evil is essentially a negative quality only, man is noble in nature, and tragedy in the classic sense by definition cannot exist. He recognized evil, but like Emerson he inclined to think of it as a temporary and local imbalance, and felt that one met its challenge best by creating models for positive action through which human potential might be realized.

Brooks is interested in Hawthorne as a personality, a representative of an intellectual and emotional climate in New England, and a writer who is inspired by regional history and folklore. He emphasizes Hawthorne's preoccupation with compulsiveness, failure, and sin sufficiently to give his Calvinistic sensibility its proper weight among the more genial biographical sketches of the transcendentalists. On the other hand, Brooks treats Hawthorne's concern with evil almost exclusively as a biographical problem—there was something morbid and crepuscular about Hawthorne—and not as a vital issue in American art. In *The World of Washington Irving* he recognized in the obsessive hallucinations of Edgar Allan Poe, although he thought Poe stood outside the mainstream of American letters, a major talent that opened an "intenser, profounder" age of literature. In fact, Brooks's Poe is one of the triumphs of *Makers and Finders.* But he could not direct the same insight to Hawthorne. His portrait of a reclusive, introverted, melancholic figure set Hawthorne apart as a personality, but little in *The Flowering of New England* suggests how distant he was from his optimistic contemporaries in the integrity of his thought and art, in his vision of human nature and the possibility of life in a democratic society.

Brooks had a similar problem when it came time to consider Herman Melville, the only American writer of the nineteenth century who simply baffled him, and there is justice in the many complaints that his history did not represent the tensions and abrasiveness that accompany the dissemination of important ideas. The partisanship that attended great debates in American life is fully and accurately described, but Brooks's characters rarely seem to become angry or nurse a grudge. The "acts of the anti-slavery apostles" are rendered fierily, but the Civil War is not. Other divisive quarrels, even the seminal debate between Jeffersonians and Federalists, often seem indistinguishable in tone from one of Margaret Fuller's "Conversations."

Such evidence too often justifies the criticism that Brooks slighted the intense, introverted, "darker" side of both our literary tradition and our national character. On this point he has found few to defend him. Whether this general weakness results from a philosophical disinclination to confront evil, a personal disinclination to consider unpleasantness, or partiality of interpretation, it too is inseparably part of the history. In fact, in important ways it is less a detraction from, than an integral part of, the very substance and power of Brooks's vision of the American past. The serious flaws in *Makers and Finders* must modify its authority, but they do not disqualify it. As with any writer of power and conviction, Brooks's limitations sometimes sharpen his focus, and he is important, finally, not for his defects, which are inevitable, but for his virtues, which are rare.

The World of Washington Irving opens the narrative of *Makers and Finders* in 1800, as the irrepressible, somewhat raffish Parson Mason Weems scurries up and down the Atlantic seaboard, getting books into the hands of the people and collecting anecdotes for his life of Washington. He is an agent of learning in the dawn of American consciousness, and as a democrat who has freed his slaves and rejoiced in the election of Jefferson to the presidency, he also prefigures the great debate with the Federalists. That conflict of ideologies informs not only *The World of Washington Irving* but each of the subsequent volumes. Through it Brooks defines his tradition and its complex of values. He anticipates his statement by a series of simple comparisons—Federalists were the body of the state, democrats the soul; Federalists preferred European forms, democrats the native—before making it explicit in his portrait of Jefferson, whom he calls "the earliest crystallization of what might be called the American prophetic tradition." Jefferson is the central figure of *The World of Washington Irving* and the point of departure for the books that follow.

As Brooks invoked it, Jefferson's was a liberal, progressive, utopian tradition. It affirmed life and maintained that man was by nature good and trustworthy. It encouraged the organic development of native expression without abandoning what was of value in the culture of the Old World. After Jefferson himself, its major representatives are Emerson, Whitman, Lincoln, and to a lesser extent the early Melville, the early Twain, and William Dean Howells. Against it, Brooks set what was less an alternate tradition than a sort of antitradition. This complex of belief and practice was aristocratic and conservative, pessimistic, preoccupied with man's inclination to sin, and oriented to the Old World. In other years he would have called this composite figure the "traitor to human hope," the "puritan." Now he identifies his life-denier as the spiritual descendant of Alexander Hamilton, the Tory, the expatriate, who hates "the rabble," admires Napoleon, and hopes to reestablish a republican court. Among Hamilton's successors are Poe, Hawthorne, Henry James, Henry Adams, H. L. Mencken, and, inevitably, T. S. Eliot.

The Tory and the democrat are locked in moral combat almost from the first page of *The World of Washington Irving*. As he establishes his context in this opening volume Brooks is inclined to introduce his characters according to their political allegiance. Joseph Dennie was a Federalist; Philip Freneau was a radical democrat. Timothy Dwight and John Trumbull were Federalists, but Joel Barlow was a democrat and a comrade of Tom Paine, and so forth. The narrative often discovers its logic in just this ideological and ethical question, since even the best writers of Irving's period were only of relative merit. Gouverneur Morris, for instance, moves in and out of *The World of Washington Irving* with a frequency disproportionate to his creative contribution. His *Diary of the French Revolution* and work on the American coinage are mentioned in passing, but he is more important as a symbol of the arch-Federalist, the Frenchified dandy and enemy of the masses. He also becomes the first expatriate. Finally Brooks associates him with that intellectual attitude that would later be drawn to the philosophies of Franco and Mussolini. Brooks's minor characters are often thus able to represent the full implications of

300

trends in thought or taste, which would be distortive if attributed to the more complex, more balanced major figures.

The World of Washington Irving celebrates the ascendancy of Jeffersonian and Jacksonian democracy and the confusion of the Federalists. The narrative draws to a close with a vision of a bright republic of arts and letters, crackling with creative energy and moral purpose. With the possible exception of Poe, who exists almost despite the impulsions of the "American wager," the literary achievement of American writers remains slight. Brooks does not allow even James Fenimore Cooper the place of honor to which he has been raised by many students of American culture. But the "guild" that these makers, still unconsciously, are forming has established the basis for flowerings to come. The potential developed by Irving's age is suggested by the anticipatory discussions of two New Yorkers of mingled Dutch and English stock, Walt Whitman and Herman Melville, who are coming of age as the volume closes.

The power and influence of the Jeffersonian ideology of *The World of Washington Irving* are developed further in *The Flowering of New England,* which considers the literary history of its region from approximately 1815 to the onset of the Civil War. Although it is the second volume in the history, *The Flowering of New England* was, of course, the first one to be written, before Brooks had clearly envisioned his full scope and method. While it remains the most popular and critically admired book in the series, it is not composed in the mature style that distinguishes *The World of Washington Irving* and *New England: Indian Summer.* Brooks himself thought his first effort was "too idyllic," and its sometimes annoying fulsomeness suggests that he had not always got full control of the writers he considered.

The Flowering of New England also does not point Brooks's central argument as emphatically as do the other volumes. There is, for instance, little of the need to align writers with the camps of Jefferson or Hamilton that had informed *The World of Washington Irving,* and Jefferson himself is a minor figure. The political metaphor for the spirit of the region is not American, but classic. Boston is at times the Athens or the Sparta of the New World; at other times her great citizens are compared to the famous men of the Roman republic. The figure suggests both the earnest self-importance of the New England mind and its respect for scholarship.

301

The theme of *The Flowering of New England* complements the theme of *The World of Washington Irving*. The first volume of *Makers and Finders* records the political and ethical extension of the Revolution by which the American spirit overthrew its European masters; the second considers that same emancipation in theological terms. New England flowers to the degree that it maintains the intellectual fastidiousness, moral rigor, and capacity for awe of its ancestral Calvinism, while casting off that religion's preoccupation with human depravity. "The Boston of Gilbert Stuart," with which the narrative opens, glistens with all the fresh light of morning, largely because it has abandoned the "revolting forms" of the Pilgrim Fathers in favor of a mild, humane, and tolerant Unitarianism, weak in dogma but intellectually as tough as the discipline of Jonathan Edwards and the Mathers. A negative example of the relationship between theological climate and artistic inspiration is afforded early by John Quincy Adams, who aspired to some "enduring work of literature" but whose "instinct had been blighted by the long winter of Puritanism."

This thematic reliance on the moral disfranchisement of Calvinism helps to explain the undue respect paid Oliver Wendell Holmes. The gregarious Holmes is, of course, more important to a chronicle of literary community than he would be in a history of literature, and Brooks is simply and unabashedly fond of the genial old autocrat, with his bright wit and charming eccentricities. But the judgment implied in the two chapters awarded to Holmes (when Hawthorne, for instance, claims only one) rests upon the symbolic importance of the civilized man of the Enlightenment, the reformer who by ridicule "slew in a thousand households the pestilent lion that masked itself in a Geneva gown."

Despite the lively affection with which he is portrayed, Oliver Wendell Holmes is not close to the moral center of *The Flowering of New England*. He lacks any feeling for the spiritual, which is the essence of New England genius. Instead, the quickening force of the region is invested in Ralph Waldo Emerson, who focuses and informs *The Flowering of New England* as Jefferson had *The World of Washington Irving*: he integrates in his person the random characteristics of his time and heroically puts them in action, thus revolutionizing his culture. In him a welter of regional traits and generational interests is brought under verb and noun, made harmonious, transformed into major philosophy and art. By Brooks's symbolism, Emerson emerges as the Yankee democrat, attending always to the familiar and the low but casting an occasional glance to the metaphysical West and the state that is to be, where his faith in humanity would be justified. He controls by juxtaposition or implicit comparison nearly every characterization that follows his own first extended appearance, and he dominates the tone of the narrative. It is he as much as Brooks who is responsible for the exhilarated, sometimes breathless prose of *The Flowering of New England.*

Emerson brings the history of the native tradition to a high point of integrity, expression, and influence. A similar peaking of the Jeffersonian synthesis, with a subsequent falling away during the years following the Civil War, was to have been recorded in *The Times of Melville and Whitman,* which considers developments in American letters in areas exclusive of New England from approximately 1840 to 1880. Here Brooks uncovered his most potentially rewarding theme. This volume opens in an excited flurry of utopianism, and the towering figures of Melville and Whitman, with the almost equally powerful presences of Abraham Lincoln and Mark Twain, gave the era an unparalleled grandeur. Because of both methodological and interpretative problems, however, *The Times of Melville and Whitman* remains the least fully realized volume of *Makers and Finders,* the only volume that exhibits serious structural weaknesses.

The fault of *The Times of Melville and Whitman* followed Brooks's generally inadequate response to the importance of evil as a literary theme, particularly when he considered the late work of Herman Melville. The Melville he recognizes is almost exclusively the author of the early *Typee* and *White-Jacket*—glorious books surely, but scarcely representative of Melville's range and power. Brooks's Melville, at least his essential Melville, does not say "No!" in thunder but is a life-affirmer, brimming with the self-reliant high spirits of republican youth. In fact, his Melville is ironically like the Melville of nineteenth-century opinion, whose late excursions into invisible spheres, formed in fright, sent his reputation into the long decline from which he was rescued in part by Brooks and his allies.

Brooks's argument is essentially this: Melville was not by birth, but by profound conviction, a radical democrat. He turned instinctively to the celebration of such "kingly commons" as Jack Chase and Queequeg, whose "austere dignity" he had recognized during his years aboard ship and roaming South Sea islands, but once he had achieved that miracle of democratic art, *Moby-Dick,* Melville began to turn out fiction that cannot be taken seriously. *Pierre* was "quite unreal," *The Confidence-Man* a "laborious satire," "Benito Cereno" spoiled by the legalese annexed to it by way of a conclusion. Melville, Brooks thought, was a writer of natural gifts; when he felt himself forced to turn to "theorizing" in lieu of autobiographical description, he fell apart.

Brooks's sense of the early work is accurate, vigorous, and important, and he may remind us that our Melville, that geographer of unseen spheres, is too often claimed at the expense of the invigorating, good-natured Melville who stood up for democracy in *White-Jacket.* But the Melville of the half-known life simply eludes him. Even *Moby-Dick,* praised as a masterpiece, is only partially recognized in *The Times of Melville and Whitman.* Brooks sees it as a triumph of the democratic theme, an epic vision of industrial community, and a yarn of men who go down to the sea in ships. The evocations of *Moby-Dick* he scatters through some half-dozen pages contain no hint of the terrors of the Grand Armada or the coral insects of raving Pip. Old crazy Ahab himself is invoked only twice: once as a poet of the sea, once to testify to the truth of a sailor lad's "mild, mild wind and the air that smelled as if it blew from a far-away meadow."

In Brooks's vision of mid-nineteenth-century America Melville was to have been Whitman's equal, the planetary writer of darkness who sustains and balances the radiant light of *Leaves of Grass.* One easily finds implicit in *The Times of Melville and Whitman* the interpretative power that might be derived from these complementary giants. They should align themselves naturally with the other major characters—Whitman with Lincoln, Melville with particularly the later Twain—to create axes on which might turn the stories of two important artistic ideologies in the United States. They might also carry the history across the Civil War, from the ideology and method represented by Whitman and Lincoln to that represented by the older Melville and the older Twain. Under Brooks's pen, however, Melville is a local phenomenon and at best a minor artist. In his absence the structure disintegrates, and instead of pattern we find a number of important figures spinning in their own orbits, with only Whitman exerting significant gravitational influence upon others.

The unconcerted but genuine excellence of *The Times of Melville and Whitman,* then, is finally sustained chiefly by Walt Whitman, long

Brooks's favorite writer, who emerges as perhaps the most fully developed character in all of the history. Even outside of the roughly seventy pages of which he is the primary subject, Whitman is everywhere present, commenting on new departures in writing, denouncing money-grubbing, supporting such minor figures as Sidney Lanier by expressing boldly what they perceived dimly. True, there is a Whitman who eludes Brooks as Melville eluded him, of whom we catch a hint only when we look for a moment through the eyes of John Burroughs. One searches elsewhere in vain for the fitful author who wrote "As I Ebb'd with the Ocean of Life" or the poems of defeat in wartime. There is no sense in Brooks of Whitman sweating over his "perturbations," nor any of the hallucinatory poet of "The Sleepers," who captured the essential tragedy in his "beautiful gigantic swimmer." Brooks's Whitman is the utopian and the personalist, less important to the history as a poet than as the radical democrat who drew sustenance from every healthy strain of American life and, by incarnating it most fully, elevated it to the "orbic" plane. He is invoked most happily among the crowds he loved: in New Orleans and Manhattan in the 1840s, in Washington during the war, later in Philadelphia and Camden.

In *The Times of Melville and Whitman* Brooks also developed a powerful evocation of cultural bleakness—a theme he had left untapped since the twenties. This new emphasis is particularly apparent in his chapter on the antebellum South, when the defense of slavery stifled democratic creative energy, in his discussion of the Confederacy in the first days of Reconstruction, and as the volume draws to a close. By the end of *The Times of Melville and Whitman* the America of Jefferson, Jackson, and Lincoln has passed, and its optimistic spirit is in decline. The "Transition" that concludes the volume bristles with a new vocabulary of industrialism, urbanism, and economics. Whitman, of course, is summoned in the last moments to have a final say about the spread of poverty he encountered in 1879—"in a country where Thomas Jefferson had never seen a pauper, where few had ever thought of a pauper existing. . . ." This grimly uneasy chapter, however, seeks a central figure in the reformer Henry George.

The theme of the decline of the Jeffersonian synthesis before the advance of a disenchanted realism is repeated and amplified in *New England: Indian Summer,* which carries the narrative of its region forward to 1915. This volume has no hero of the stature of Jefferson,

Emerson, or Whitman. Democracy's prophetic mantle is here invested on the figure of William Dean Howells, "mild in manner and modest in appearance," who "quietly slipped" into Boston in the symbolically muted opening scene to receive from Holmes and Lowell the laying on of hands. He symbolizes further the energy of the West come to reinvigorate, if it can, the thinning blood of New England. The early pages of *New England: Indian Summer* are crowded with images of diminution: Longfellow in his twilight years, at work on his translation of Dante; Whittier among his flowers at Amesbury, reliving in memory the adventures of Abolitionism; and in Concord, Thoreau dead, Hawthorne gone, "Emerson's voice . . . lost in a babel of other voices." Howells must resume the democrat's role in the battle with the Tory which Brooks had been permitted almost to ignore since *The World of Washington Irving*.

Brooks admires Howells for his sharp eye, democratic credentials, and dedication to the literary life. He is as personally fond of his earnest, ambitious Midwesterner as he was of Oliver Wendell Holmes, but he does not confuse affection with judgment. His Howells is conventional to a fault, a prude, and too inclined to superficial optimism. His good nature and good sense pale before the challenge of the new Toryism, which is symbolized chiefly by the ironists Henry James and Henry Adams, artists larger and more intense than Howells, and more sensitive to the demands of their age.

Howells confronts a New England changed by more than the passing of years, just as Brooks is forced in this volume to rely heavily upon more, and more complex, economic and social analysis than he had previously found necessary. The region had lost its agrarian and mercantile identity to the triumph of industrialism. Beneath his wealth of particularization Brooks discovered a pattern by which Anglophilia waxed fat as Jefferson's America was forced into retreat. In Brooks's latter New England, republican virtue came increasingly to seem quaint when compared to the sophistications of European culture, and the most spirited and capable young people involuntarily resumed a Toryism that had lain dormant in the region since the age of the Connecticut Wits. A subsequent insinuation of European models in place of the American resulted in expatriation, whether physical or moral. A new generation of pilgrims looked hungrily to the lands across the water. Just as farmers and mechanics packed up to seek their fortunes out West, intellectuals, artists, people of breeding, and people of wealth turned themselves particularly to England, where they sometimes felt they had recovered the "perfection of human society" in "our old home." The rootless Henry James and the perhaps too deeply rooted Henry Adams were only the most talented and authoritative of those citizens who cut their ties to the promise of their revolutionary homeland and joined the party of the past.

Against this blight of spiritual, economic, and intellectual Toryism, made more sinister by the hints of decadence with which it is rendered, Brooks sets his brave, dogged, but severely limited Howells, whose function in *New England: Indian Summer* is not so much to harvest the dry Yankee stalk as to keep its frostbitten seed somehow alive. Although he is temperamentally incapable of the heroism of Emerson's cultural "berserkers" or Whitman's "cannoneers of song and thought," he has the weapons of good will, a passion for justice that considerations of propriety could never silence, and the influence he wields as editor of *The Atlantic*. Thus equipped, he fights almost alone, for, significantly, the creative forces that support his campaign are essentially unknown to one another—or, at least they are not in collaboration. His important allies are the architects H. H. Richardson and Louis Sullivan, whose native ingenuity and organicism were equal to "the conditions of a democratic world," and William James, the democratic philosopher who "kept the buoyant faith of Emerson and the old Brook Farmers." Later, perhaps, Howells's camp might claim the Emersonian vision, ranged against bleakness, of Edwin Arlington Robinson.

Brooks acknowledges Howells's stewardship when he records a reawakening Yankee voice in his concluding chapter, "Second March." But the tradition has only endured; it has not prevailed. Despite their artistic vigor, most of the young writers considered here— E. A. Robinson, Robert Frost, Eugene O'Neill, E. E. Cummings, and Wallace Stevens, among others—are to some degree cynical; many are hostile to the traditions of their region; some threaten to pitch their tents in the enemy camp. The volume closes uneasily. March is neither a comfortable nor a fertile month in the land of the Yankees.

Brooks resumes the story of the writer in areas outside of New England in 1885 and carries it to 1915 in *The Confident Years*. This volume is the most nearly a conventional history of literary trends and fashions, for Brooks can discover here no positive unifying figure of even the stature of the Howells of *New England: Indian Summer*. The theme of *The Confident Years* is the perplexity and incompleteness of artists, however talented and dedicated, who lack the sustenance of a strong tradition. Its method is often as much analytical as evocative, for most of its characters are symptomatic of a pervasive cultural malady. Especially as the late nineteenth century achieves its firm entrenchment of laissez-faire capitalism and its values, writers become aimless, joyless, and pessimistic.

The Jeffersonian spirit illuminates *The Confident Years* only in wan flashes. Tradition has become incoherent and diffuse. A number of writers display one or another aspect of the old American character, but no writer coordinates them all. Among the important representatives of democracy are Theodore Roosevelt, as a writer and frontiersman as well as a politician, Carl Sandburg, Theodore Dreiser, Sinclair Lewis, the popular writer O. Henry, W. E. B. Du Bois, and Randolph Bourne, but these figures are invoked less to embody an organic way of life and art than implicitly to comment upon the inaccessibility of a wholly informing vision. Roosevelt is essentially an amateur; Sandburg slight, a children's author really; Lewis unimaginative. Of course Brooks is also inhibited by his obligation to ignore his own contribution to the emergence of the younger generation of 1915.

Brooks's vision in *The Confident Years* might be considered in the examples of Theodore Dreiser and O. Henry, who stands in relation to Dreiser as the cowboy writers Andy Adams and Will James might stand to Roosevelt, or Claude McKay to Du Bois. O. Henry and Dreiser are related as urban realists who delight in the lives of common men and women and faithfully record the democratic scene. For Brooks the development of an important realistic fiction is the redeeming principle of honesty and health in a century that is running down. O. Henry, however, expresses the manner of democractic art without the matter. He churns out stories of indistinguishable quality in great numbers, thus becoming an example of literary mass production, more closely related to industrial than intellectual developments. Only "occasionally an artist," he symbolizes the superficial, even the decadent application of the democratic idea in a machine age. The presence of Dreiser in his world identifies both his saving graces and his essential mediocrity. Dreiser himself is among the most fully and sympathetically drawn characters in *The Confident Years*, "unique in his time" because of his depth of compassionate insight. However, he remains "incomplete" as an artist, frustrated finally by the conflicts of temperament and aspiration he derived from his culture as well as by his "elephantine" craftsmanship.

Dreiser is a qualified success. More typical of Brooks's tone are the various degrees of failure among writers who root about aimlessly, seeking a cause, a home, an identity, to which they can direct their energies. Without tradition, there is no direction, no assurance that a writer's work is valuable to a community. The consequence of the inability to feel oneself in the service of larger than personal ends is symbolized most dramatically in the despondent cynicism of Ambrose Bierce and the suicide of Jack London, but it infects stronger personalities as well. Edith Wharton's inherited Toryism shamed her American identity, a personal insecurity reflected by problems of characterization and sympathy in her novels. H. L. Mencken's wholesale rejection of democratic values found expression in a childish Germanophilia.

To these individual examples Brooks adds the regional example of the turn-of-the-century South, which, having fallen victim to its own destruction of democratic intellectual traditions during the defense of slavery, has become impoverished and decadent in culture. Living now in an idyllic historical fiction based on a racial myth, the South has lost its capacity to know or represent reality. Its characteristic form is the chivalric romance, the solipsistic genre of James Branch Cabell, whose taste might have been developed in the years of "the Walter Scott disease" before the war. Surveying the South in the first decade of the twentieth century, Brooks takes heart only in the realists Kate Chopin in Louisiana and Ellen Glasgow in Virginia.

The torpor of the America that lies south of the James is a cautionary example of what befalls a community when it lacks traditions to put the imagination to work. The region does not represent the nation, for Brooks finds great vigor in the North and West during this period, particularly in the cities, but it does represent a logic of entropy that must be arrested. Despite the restorative powers of realism, the course of *The Confident Years* is downward, toward the First World War, which ends this second, essentially negative cycle of *Makers and Finders* as the Civil War ended the first, and which numbs the moral sensibilities of an extraordinarily talented younger generation. Nihilism begets a preoccupation with technique; writers defeated in a secular world turn to "the religion of art." In Brooks's romantic vision, this latter-day Toryism, more intellectually powerful and thus more dangerous than the old, threatens to defeat the American Revolution at the last and sabotage the planetary "Rights of Man."

Against it Brooks sets essentially himself and his allies from the days of *The Seven Arts.* He cannot describe himself in the narrative, but he can assume his place there by authorial prerogative. He considers the thought and work of Randolph Bourne with sufficient emphasis to make explicit the cultural program of Young America, but, more than that, he abandons the point of view by which he enacted his characters and enters his history as a distinct prophetic voice, most aggressively in his final chapter, "A Forward Glance." There he reviews the past he has invoked and reasserts the primacy of the Jeffersonian tradition against the ways of the life-deniers. It is fitting that by his art he can defeat the necessary professional modesty and enlist himself at last among the ranks of his own makers and finders, assuming about the same authority and using the same analytic and hortatory method that might characterize him in another historian's narrative of the literary life in 1915.

The final two chapters of *The Confident Years,* then, are different in stance and genre from the narrative that preceded them, but Brooks has prepared his emergence by those shifts from the empathic to the judgmental point of view that characterize his method throughout *Makers and Finders,* and his voice has been heard increasingly as the narrative approached him in time. His passage from historian to participant is part of a long, slowly developing pattern, the completion of which he announces with his invocation of Jefferson and the world view he bequeathed to his countrymen. That reengagement of the opening volume brings the history full cycle, formally closing the narrative that began in the busy republican morning of Parson Weems in 1800. *Makers and Finders* thus ends with a vision of its democratic tradition embattled, almost overwhelmed, but alive, awaiting the great personality who will engage it anew, revitalize it, and again transform both the culture of the United States and the future of humanity.

XVI

DEATH'S OUTLET SONG OF LIFE

Van Wyck had always had an eye for springtime. He noticed the opening of the magnolia outside his study window, could tell you at what time the migratory birds began nesting or when the first young rabbits would timidly raid Gladys's garden for new shoots. Although he lacked all taste for being out-of-doors, he observed the colors and the rhythms of the year with gratitude and delight, and he enriched his prose with botanical metaphors and descriptions of landscape. He was pleased when he could work a list of birds or flowers into a paragraph on some old writer, and he invoked apples and pumpkins as heartily as he invoked the lilies of the valley. One might even hazard a guess that his partiality to residence in Connecticut had something to do with the distinctness of the seasons there, the continual change and renewal of natural patterns that keeps life on its toes.

But in this spring of 1963 Van Wyck recognized few signs of the reawakening year, for his world had grown small, the size of a room, and his senses no longer distinguished clearly among variations of heat, light, and sound. When he had first come home from the hospital that January he was allowed to sit an hour or two each day in his study, but as time wore on he was forced increasingly to lie in bed. Now he was scarcely able to get to his feet. Gladys read to him, passing the hours and sustaining his tenuous hold on the life that he lived through

311

his books. He did not speak of ultimate things, nor did he make any overt preparation for them, but he must have known, as he groped futilely for his old authority, that he had come home to die.

The latest medical ordeal had bought time, not hope. The doctors at New Milford had discovered and removed a malignant colonic tumor, the second in three years, but Van Wyck was not responding to the surgery, and he seemed to fail perceptibly each day. He was approaching the end of a gradual straying from health. Although for nearly twenty years he had been required to take nitroglycerin for his angina, he had remained remarkably hale until the onset of this terminal illness, which had struck in 1960, when he and Gladys were in Georgia for a winter vacation. At first the doctors thought that he had simply been exposed to a virus, but as various remedies failed, they came to suspect cancer. Van Wyck was inclined to have his exploratory surgery done in Savannah, but he finally agreed with Gladys that everyone would feel better at home. They returned north by ship, and Van Wyck entered Grace Hospital in New Haven for preliminary tests and surgery. The malignancy was removed from his colon in March.

Van Wyck recovered quickly from that operation, as he did from the removal of a benign tumor the next spring. His animal health was in fact remarkable for a man who so determinedly refused to care for himself. But during the summer of 1962 he suffered a slight stroke, and although he required only a brief confinement, he seems from that time to have lost his recuperative powers. He returned from his autumn vacation that year to enter Grace Hospital for a new series of tests, and the doctors were sufficiently alarmed by his condition to open his carotid artery in order to prevent another stroke. The surgery was minor, but it was performed under local anesthetic, and it drained Van Wyck both physically and mentally. Only a few weeks later his cancer attacked him again, and he was rushed to New Milford for his last operation. This time, Gladys could find no comfort in the prognosis.

For three years, then, Van Wyck was dying, but so long as he remained able to carry himself to his desk he continued to write. For his final project he considered studies of Edmund Wilson and Lewis Mumford, settling in mid-1962 on ambitious plans for a biography of Mumford, whom he had celebrated in *The Writer in America* as an American prophet of the line of Jefferson and Whitman. Mumford tactfully did his best to discourage the whole business, protesting that the materials for such work were not available, but Van Wyck was stubborn as always. He worked courageously on this latest expression of his great theme, but the chapters he produced are symptomatic of his physical decline after the stroke of 1962. The biography is thinly written, often inaccurate, and it survives in only the twenty-two pages of nearly indecipherable manuscript Van Wyck managed before he was forced to abandon it in December.

His last published book bears similar witness to his declining power. *Fenollosa and His Circle: With Other Essays in Biography* was begun in 1959, before he had completed *From the Shadow of the Mountain,* and it demonstrates even more starkly than the final volume of memoirs a pronounced incoherence of style. It is a happily conceived book, valuable for its contributions to the scholarship of a number of obscure or exotic episodes in our literary life, but it is written in nothing that resembles the prose of the Van Wyck Brooks of *Makers and Finders.* Brooks's sentences are now often syntactically spineless. They remain essentially declarative, statements of information merely, rather than the dynamic units of his earlier work, which both advanced and interpreted information. Brooks is now suspiciously prone to quote extended passages from other writers rather than integrate them to his own voice. Two sections of the title essay are nothing but unaltered quotation from notes, journals, and memoirs. All the ingredients of the mature style are present but remain distinct, uncoordinated. The prose of *Fenollosa* is a literary mulligan stew, potentially delicious, but only a collection of vaguely identifiable flavors so long as it lacks heat.

Such stylistic lapses reveal how badly Brooks had been damaged by his illness. "The man is only half himself," Emerson thought; "the other half is his expression," but his latter-day colleague would surely have insisted on giving expression a better count. At its full, Brooks's prose is lean, rhythmic, and highly figurative, continually being transformed and redirected by the power of metaphor and allusion. Consider, for instance, a tasty passage from *Scenes and Portraits,* describing an occasional visitor at Petitpas':

Blaikie Murdoch followed his own personal notions of style, sprinkling commas over his writing as a Parsee sprinkles red pepper over meat so that the substance is invisible under the coating. His writing was packed so tight with commas that it could neither move nor breathe, and I once had to spend half a day removing from one of his articles enough at least to let in light and air. Bald as a tonsured monk, with a mind as ripe as an old Roquefort cheese, Blaikie Murdoch was living in a basement somewhere, cooking his meals on a gas-jet, not far away; and, as he talked, he would stealthily manoeuvre stray crusts of bread on the table into the yawning pockets of his old brown jacket. How similarly helpless in the brazen world were many friends of mine who were only at home in the golden world of art.

We know Murdoch's character and world more fully as we are able to feel the suffocation of his writing, see the yawning pockets and the sprinkling of the pepper, smell that Roquefort, taste the pungent meat. The entire description both justifies and is interpreted by the final sentence, which shifts our reference from the local figure to a complex of values and a condition of life. As it identifies and enhances the emotional force of the passage, the sentence might almost be broken into lines of irregular iambic and anapestic verse. As if by the way, it brushes off a venerable truism.

One further example of the peculiar skill with which Brooks works the basic units of prose describes the heroic spinsters who are celebrated for their part in keeping culture alive in one of the "Country Pictures" of *New England: Indian Summer:* "As they could not alter conditions, they lived within them; and, living within the conditions, they mastered the conditions and kept a margin for their souls to grow in." The sentence develops according to repetition, particularly of "conditions," so that the reference to that fact before which the characters are at first helpless, but according to the discipline of which they attain mastery, is kept emphatically in mind. Like the genius of a certain spinster of merit, the sentence unfolds "New Englandly." It is syntactically straightforward, but ingrown, self-referential, almost knotty, until its racy final clause opens it out, winning its meaning, so to speak, room to grow in. The connotations of "alter" that suggest tailoring remind us of the housewifery of the women and are picked up and extended by that final clause. People who need a margin to grow in are, of course, children—one alters children's clothing so—and the muted association of children with these barren women brings into play the logic not only of their anguish but of their motives, their routine, and finally their triumph. The sentence epitomizes and interprets

314

psychologically the entire narrative interlude in which it appears, and it represents well the sympathetic power by which Brooks transforms the familiar comic stereotype of the unmarried woman into a character of flesh and years, desire and sorrows. One feels hovering gently above it the spirit of the Walt Whitman who wrote the eleventh section of "Song of Myself."

That was the prose of Van Wyck Brooks when he took hold, but by 1962 his richness of idiom and compactness of syntax had quit him. If *Fenollosa and His Circle* is disappointing for this reason, however, it is still a delightful book, full of adventure and discovery, a final exploration of exotic worlds, past and to come. Each of the essays in *Fenollosa* follows some literary wanderer as he or she attains a reality inconceivable to those businesslike countrymen who remain behind. Ernest Fenollosa and Lafcadio Hearn discover a land of perfect courtesy, perfect honesty, and extraordinary beauty in nineteenth-century Japan. John Lloyd Stephens unearths the antiquities of the Mayan civilization in the jungles of Central America. The odyssey of George Wilkes establishes the existence of an Antarctic continent. George Catlin records the passing culture of the Indians of the American West, just as Charles Godfrey Leland finds wisdom in the tents of the Gypsies. Finally, Randolph Bourne, embarked on the adventure of youth, discovers access to the future. Like all of the "makers and finders" in *Fenollosa*, Bourne extends horizons, creates possibility, and announces a world at once more unexpected and more hospitable than the world he left behind. Despite the crippled body that denied him the physical movement of other explorers, he is perhaps the most compelling representative of Brooks's theme: the happiness of travel in search of the new and the strange.

In the ambitious title essay Brooks hit upon a particularly congenial subject. He had long held an amateur's interest in Oriental thought and culture, and he may have been encouraged to develop it professionally by his friendship with Chiang Yee. In any case, he devoted himself to the study of Chinese and Japanese history, Buddhist thought, and Noh theater, becoming particularly familiar with the various periods and styles of Japanese art. His preparation for writing about Fenollosa occupied him, although not exclusively, for more than two years, and in the pioneering Orientalist himself he seems to have found a character through whom he could express some of his own sense of mission, as well as his disappointment at what he considered the indifferent uses to which his literary cartography had been put. His Fenollosa, a prophet of "one world," had recognized a great national art among the dustheaps and damp storerooms to which neglect had consigned it, and he had fought for it, collected it, in his own person kept alive a number of traditional crafts and rituals. By returning Japanese traditions to the Japanese, Fenollosa not only renewed a national continuity, he awarded new possibilities for expression to artists in every corner of the world. "He was," as Brooks quotes Ezra Pound at the conclusion of the essay, "a forerunner, without knowing it and without being known as such."

Van Wyck nearly followed Fenollosa to Japan, using an ostensible need for further research as an excuse. He was making excited although tentative plans for the trip in 1959, and in one corner of his heart he remained as much the wanderer and vagabond as any of the Ishmaels he celebrated in his book. Whether he finally concluded that he was being romantic and impractical, or whether his failing health discouraged him, that voyage to the East never got beyond the talking phase, and he and Gladys settled cheerfully enough for the roads of home. Their vacation in Savannah during the early months of 1960 was interrupted by Van Wyck's medical crisis, and his convalescence from his major surgery of that March kept him quietly at Bridgewater for the balance of the year, but only a few weeks after his less serious operation of 1961 he and Gladys departed for a month's working vacation by the sea at Stonington, Maine. In January 1962 they undertook the long, difficult winter drive from Connecticut to the Southwest, where they remained in Tucson, working and touring until March, when they returned to Bridgewater by a circuitous route through the Southern states. No sooner were they arrived than they departed again for Washington to attend a dinner for Nobel Prize winners at the White House.

Van Wyck made his final journey, to New Hampshire, in September 1962. Although he refused to appear less than jaunty, he must have taken to the road in something of a spirit of defiance. Everyone was deceived by the alacrity with which he regrouped himself after his stroke of late summer, but he really had not sufficient time to recover fully, and his doctors had not fully released him. They had ordered him to return to the hospital for extensive testing, which might, as he and Gladys unhappily considered, confirm their own deep fears. The brief trip by automobile, while tiring, turned out to be uneventful, but it is less important as an episode in his medical history than as it becomes, in its small way, an emblem of his spirit. With all of his chronic disdain for the logic of the flesh, Van Wyck remained to the last the restless wanderer whose ethos he had always admired, not knowing himself how well he incarnated it. Throughout his life he had, in one way or another, forever been starting in search of that bright landscape just over the hill.

But now he was home again, in a warmth of light and air, where the world seemed composed of curious half-perceptions, and one could not keep one's mind to the task of recognizing the shapes and sounds that fluttered about the bed. Life had come down to a series of sensations, which would not always apply themselves one to another, but they were familiar sensations, and heartening: the rustle of Gladys's skirts as she moved about the quiet room, the silhouette of her figure against the window, the flow of her voice as she read, often from the favorite final chapter of *Scenes and Portraits*, about "turning homeward" from the Old World to the New. Sometimes visitors came, and floated over the bed, but their features were not always clear, and often their voices came indistinctly from a distance. One day Jack Wheelock had come, stooped now, and frail with age, but leonine and handsome as ever. And Jack had said in his grave, courtly way, "Now Van Wyck, I want you to tell me when you are tired and want me to leave," and Van Wyck had whispered, "Oh Jack, I *never* want you to leave."

Then came simply the flutter and murmur of nights and days when no visitors arrived, and time was the inflection of Gladys's voice. The rhythms of sunlight grew longer, but probably he did not know it. There was little suffering, just drifting banks of pain at the edges of sensation, and the perpetual, gentle flickering of things in the room. On an afternoon in early May he quietly bade Gladys pause in her reading, whispered, "You must have rest," and died.

As Van Wyck Brooks joined the past he had so loved and had in such large part created, he abandoned all advocacy and gave his legacy to time, to let time make of it what time will. To his wife and sons he left a house, some goods, some money. To the University of Pennsylvania he left his papers, great cabinets and boxfuls of manuscripts, letters, journals, scrapbooks: all of the triumphs, false starts, speculations, and marginalia of a writer's lifetime. To his countrymen, and through them to the world, he left a few good books and the model of a robust prose. He left a national tradition enriched and redirected, and a fiery enactment of integrity. His marks and his scars he carried with him.

LIST OF WORKS QUOTED

This list includes all material, exclusive of correspondence, anonymous journalism, and familiar passages by classic authors, from which I have quoted more than a few words. Wherever access to materials might pose a practical difficulty, I have listed the most accessible (and not necessarily the original) source. Asterisks identify unpublished manuscript material by Van Wyck Brooks, which is housed in the Charles Patterson Van Pelt Library of the University of Pennsylvania.

BIDDLE, FRANCIS. *A Casual Past.* Garden City: Doubleday and Company, 1961.

BROOKS [CHARLES] AMES. *Mauna Roa and Other Poems.* Princeton: Princeton University Press, 1922.

BROOKS, GLADYS. *If Strangers Meet: A Memory.* New York: Harcourt, Brace, & World, 1967.

BROOKS, VAN WYCK. "Address at Tufts College"*

―――. *America's Coming-of-Age.* New York: B. W. Huebsch, 1915.

―――. *An Autobiography.* New York: E. P. Dutton, 1965. Includes *Scenes and Portraits, Days of the Phoenix,* and *From the Shadow of the Mountain.*

―――. "A Book of Limitations"*

―――. *The Confident Years: 1885–1915.* New York: E. P. Dutton, 1952.

―――. "Diary" 1903*

―――. "Diary" 1939*

―――. *Emerson and Others.* New York: E. P. Dutton, 1927.

————. *Fenollosa and His Circle: With Other Essays in Biography.* New York: E. P. Dutton, 1962.

————. *The Flowering of New England.* New York: E. P. Dutton, 1936.

————. *From a Writer's Notebook.* New York: E. P. Dutton, 1958.

————. "Imaginary Letters"*

————. Introduction to Randolph Bourne, *The History of a Literary Radical.* New York: B. W. Huebsch, 1920.

————. *John Addington Symonds: A Biographical Study.* New York: Mitchell Kennerley, 1914.

————. *Letters and Leadership.* New York: B. W. Huebsch, 1918.

————. *The Life of Emerson.* New York: E. P. Dutton, 1932.

————. *The Malady of the Ideal.* Philadelphia: University of Pennsylvania Press, 1947.

————. "Miscellanies" 1904*

————. *New England: Indian Summer.* New York: E. P. Dutton, 1940.

————. "The New Testament of Taste"*

————. *The Opinions of Oliver Allston.* New York: E. P. Dutton, 1941.

————. *The Ordeal of Mark Twain.* New York: E. P. Dutton, 1920.

————. "A Personal Statement," *Direction* 2 (May–June, 1939), 6–9, 40–44.

————. *The Pilgrimage of Henry James.* New York: E. P. Dutton, 1925.

————. *Sketches in Criticism.* New York: E. P. Dutton, 1932. Includes many of the *Freeman* essays.

————. *The Soul: An Essay Towards a Point of View.* San Francisco: Privately printed, 1910.

————. *The Times of Melville and Whitman.* New York: E. P. Dutton, 1947.

————. "The Twilight of the Arts," *Poet Lore* 24 (1913), 322–332.

————; with John Hall Wheelock. *Verses by Two Undergraduates.* Cambridge: Privately printed, 1905.

————. "W. E. Burghardt Du Bois"*

————. "What Is America?"*

————. *The Wine of the Puritans.* In Claire Sprague, ed., *Van Wyck Brooks: The Early Years.* New York: Harper & Row, 1968, pp. 1–59.

————. *The World of Washington Irving.* New York: E. P. Dutton, 1944.

————. *The Writer in America.* New York: E. P. Dutton, 1953.

CABLE, GEORGE WASHINGTON. "New Orleans Before the Capture," *The Century Illustrated Monthly Magazine* 29 (1885), 918–922.

COWLEY, MALCOLM. Interview with author, August 9, 1970.

————. Introduction to Van Wyck Brooks, *An Autobiography.* New York: E. P. Dutton, 1965.

————. "Mr. Brooks Dissenting," *New Republic* 105 (November 24, 1941), 705–706; 105 (December 1, 1941), 738–739.

COWLEY, MALCOLM, and CANBY, HENRY SEIDEL. "Creating an Audience." In Robert E. Spiller, ed., *Literary History of the United States.* New York: Macmillan, 1963, pp. 1119–1134.

DAVIDSON, JO. *Between Sittings: An Informal Autobiography.* New York: Dial Press, 1951.

DELL, FLOYD. "Review of Waldo Frank, *Our America*," *The Liberator* 2 (January, 1920), 44.

DE VOTO, BERNARD. *The Literary Fallacy.* Boston: Little, Brown and Company, 1944.

———. *Mark Twain's America.* Boston: Little Brown and Company, 1932.

DUPEE, F. W. "The Americanism of Van Wyck Brooks," *Partisan Review* 6 (1939), 69–85.

ELIOT, T. S. "A Letter to the Editor," *Partisan Review* 9 (1942), 115–116.

ELLMANN, RICHARD. *Yeats: The Man and the Masks.* New York: Macmillan, 1948.

FARRELL, JAMES T. "The Frightened Philistines," *New Republic* 111 (December 4, 1944), 764–769.

FRANK, WALDO. "Sermons for Criticism," *Saturday Review* 25 (February 28, 1942), 3–4, 17. Review of *The Opinions of Oliver Allston.*

GOLDBERG, ISAAC. "Review of *The Pilgrimage of Henry James*," *Haldemann-Julius Monthly,* June 27, 1925.

MACDONALD, DWIGHT. "Kulturbolschewismus Is Here," *Partisan Review* 8 (1941), 442–451. The response to Macdonald was published as "On the Brooks-Macleish Thesis," *Partisan Review* 9 (1942), 38–47.

MADISON, CHARLES A. *Book Publishing in America.* New York: McGraw-Hill, 1966.

MATTHIESSEN, F. O. *American Renaissance.* New York: Oxford University Press, 1941.

———. "Pilgrimage to the Distant Past," *New York Times Book Review,* October 1, 1944, pp. 1, 20. Review of *The World of Washington Irving.*

MORISON, SAMUEL ELIOT. *The Oxford History of the American People.* New York: Oxford University Press, 1965.

MUMFORD, LEWIS. "Esthetics: A Troutbeck Dialogue." In *My Works and Days.* New York: Harcourt, Brace and Jovanovich, 1979, pp. 260–268.

———. Interview with author, August 7, 1970.

———. "Our Rich Vein of Literary Ore," *Saturday Review* 30 (November 8, 1947), 11–13. Review of *The Times of Melville and Whitman.*

OPPENHEIM, JAMES. "The Story of The Seven Arts," *The American Mercury* 20 (1930), 156–164.

ROLLAND, ROMAIN. "America and the Arts." Translated by Waldo Frank. *The Seven Arts* 1 (1916), 47–51.

ROSENFELD, PAUL. *Port of New York: Essays on Fourteen American Moderns.* New York: Harcourt Brace and Company, 1924.

SMITH, BERNARD. "Van Wyck Brooks," *New Republic* 88 (August 26, 1936), 69–72.

SPRAGUE, CLAIRE. Introduction to *Van Wyck Brooks: The Early Years.* New York: Harper & Row, 1968.

STEARNS, HAROLD E., ed. *Civilization in the United States: An Inquiry by Thirty Americans.* New York: Harcourt Brace and Company, 1922.

WENDELL, BARRETT. *A Literary History of America.* New York: Charles Scribner's Sons, 1907.

WHEELOCK, JOHN HALL. Foreword to Van Wyck Brooks, *An Autobiography.* New York: E. P. Dutton, 1965.

———. Interview with author, October 23, 1970.

WILSON, EDMUND. "Bernard De Voto." In *The Shores of Light*. New York: Farrar, Straus and Giroux, 1952, pp. 650–661.

———. "The Delegate from Great Neck." In *The Shores of Light*. New York: Farrar, Straus and Giroux, 1952, pp. 141–155.

———. "A Picture to Hang in the Library: Brooks's Age of Irving." In *Classics and Commercials*. New York: Farrar, Straus and Giroux, 1950, pp. 224–230.

———. *Upstate*. New York: Farrar, Straus and Giroux, 1971.

INDEX

Stimson, Eleanor M. (ESB's mother), 75, 76–77, 78, 79, 109–10, 131, 175, 176, 183, 188, 259–60
Stimson, Frank (ESB's brother), 64, 76
Stimson, John Ward (ESB's father), 75, 219
Stimson, Henry L. (ESB's uncle), 251
Stuart, Henry Longan, 166, 187, 189
Stylus, The (Harvard), 30, 39
Sullivan, Louis, 307
Swinburne, Algernon Charles, 32, 70
Symonds, John Addington, 85

Taft, William Howard, 64
Tate, Allen, 244, 246, 267–68, 289
Taussig, Lucy, 158
Thayer, Scofield, 127, 174, 179
Thomas, Augustus, 64
Thomas, Dylan, 277
Thomas, Thomas, 59, 61, 238–39
Thoreau, Henry David, 32, 35, 107, 142–43, 306
Thorne, Mrs. Landon K., 194
Tillich, Paul, 237
Tolstoy, Leo, 67–68
Traubel, Horace, 66, 114
    With Walt Whitman in Camden, 114
Tresca, Carlo, 93
Trilling, Lionel, 244
Trotter, William:
    The Instincts of the Herd in Peace and War, 138
Troutbeck Pamphlets, The, 179
Trumbell, John, 300
Tufts College, 224, 236
Turner, Susan J., 157–58
Twain, Mark, 15, 32, 105, 130, 131, 134–41, 144, 145, 300, 303, 304
    The Curious Republic of Gondour, 135
    VWB on, 134–41, 145, 300

Uccello, Paolo, 24
Unamuno, Miguel de, 276
Untermeyer, Jean Starr, 115
Untermeyer, Louis, 112, 113, 115, 125, 164, 257

Van Doren, Carl, 223
Van Loon, Hendrik Willem, 157, 259
Van Vechten, Carl, 96, 115, 152
Van Wyck, Cornelius Barente, 7
Van Wyck, Theodorus, 6
Veblen, Thorstein, 95, 155

Viking Company, 99
Vitelli, James, 102
Von Hagen, Victor, 257

Warner, Charles Dudley, 97
Weber, Max, 94
Weems, Mason, 293, 299, 310
Wells, H. G., 87–88, 258
Wendell, Barrett, 31, 32, 105
    Literary History of America, 105
Wescott, Glenway, 257
Wescott, Marion, 261
Wescott, Ralph, 76
Wharton, Edith, 309
Wheelock, John Hall, 27–28, 29, 30, 33, 35, 39, 43–44, 51, 52, 58, 64–65, 66, 76, 98, 153, 166, 174, 176, 193, 194, 202, 212, 240, 254, 255, 260, 267–68, 280, 317
Wheelock, Phyllis, 268
Wheelright, John Brooks, 174
Whistler, James McNeill, 55
White, William, 189, 190
Whitlock, Brand, 153
Whitman, Walt, 32, 34–35, 85, 86, 92, 102, 105–6, 111, 114, 145, 147, 159, 174, 247, 291, 293, 296, 300, 301, 303, 304–5, 307, 315
    "As I Ebb'd with the Ocean of Life," 305
    Leaves of Grass, 105, 145
    "Mediums," 291
    "The Sleepers," 305
    "Song of Myself," 296, 315
    VWB on, 102, 105–6, 159, 300, 304–5
Whittier, John G., 98, 246, 294, 306
    VWB on, 246, 294
Whyte, Dorothy, 280
Wilde, Oscar, 32
Wilder, Thornton, 257, 282
Wilkes, George, 315
Williams, William Carlos, 94, 152, 171, 239, 244, 247
    The Farmer's Daughters, 247
    In the American Grain, 247
Wilson, Edmund, 143, 148–49, 163, 164, 167, 206, 211, 240, 296, 312
    "The Delegate from Great Neck," 163
Wilson, Woodrow, 80
Wittenburg, Sophia, 164
Workers' Educational Association (W.E.A.), 82, 83, 85, 88, 91